FOREIGN
CLIENTELAE

FOREIGN CLIENTELAE

(264–70 B.C.)

BY

E. BADIAN

OXFORD
AT THE CLARENDON PRESS

Oxford University Press, Ely House, London W. 1

GLASGOW NEW YORK TORONTO MELBOURNE WELLINGTON
CAPE TOWN IBADAN NAIROBI DAR ES SALAAM LUSAKA ADDIS ABABA
DELHI BOMBAY CALCUTTA MADRAS KARACHI LAHORE DACCA
KUALA LUMPUR SINGAPORE HONG KONG TOKYO

FIRST PUBLISHED 1958

REPRINTED IN GREAT BRITAIN
AT THE UNIVERSITY PRESS, OXFORD
FROM CORRECTED SHEETS OF THE FIRST EDITION
BY VIVIAN RIDLER
PRINTER TO THE UNIVERSITY
1967, 1972

PREFACE

THIS study was begun in the autumn of 1950 and submitted for the degree of Doctor of Philosophy in 1956. Much new work relevant to the subject appeared during these years, and I constantly tried—sometimes by extensive rewriting—to consider the more important publications. During the last few months the work has been carefully revised; but no attempt could be made to give due weight to work appearing during that time, so that the study must be taken as virtually concluded in the summer of 1956. As it is founded mainly on the sources, and as paper and printer's ink would not suffice to deal adequately with all—or even all noteworthy—modern work, citations of even the greatest of the moderns have deliberately been kept down to a minimum. Nor could the Bibliography usefully aim at being exhaustive: it is, in fact, merely a list of the works cited more than once or twice in the notes, giving those full details, the repetition of which would have been wasteful and distracting. It should therefore not be assumed that what is not cited (either *ad locum* or in the Bibliography) has not been read—or even that it has not been profitable.

While refutation has been confined to views that seemed widely held but erroneous, or characteristic in their error, debts have been acknowledged wherever I was conscious of them. Needless to say, there will be many cases where I ought to have been, but was not. Yet some debts call for special acknowledgement in this place. First, there is that to Professor Syme, who suggested the subject and the bipartite treatment, and to whose constant advice and encouragement I owe more than *pietas* can hope to repay. I also owe a great deal to the patience and kindness of my examiners, Mr. Balsdon and Mr. Lepper, and to Mr. Sherwin-White, whose book, *The Roman Citizenship*, is the work most frequently cited in the notes. Without that masterpiece of scholarship, and the Oxford lectures in which he introduced so many of us to the possibilities of the difficult period from 146 to 70 B.C., this study would never even have been thought of. Among foreign scholars, Gelzer and Münzer, who revolutionized the approach to the study of this period, claim pre-eminence; and among younger scholars I have learnt most from those of the school of Professor Fraccaro. I hope that occasional disagreement in detail will not be allowed to obscure my consciousness of these debts.

I also hope that there is still something new in this study—an approach that will perhaps fit many details into a more intelligible pattern. Much detailed study has been necessary to establish its validity; and though some of it has been published—where it belongs—in the scholarly periodicals, and some (directly and inescapably relevant) banished to appendixes, a great deal still remains in the notes and even in the text. That there is not more, and that this book is not longer still, will add to my gratitude—and the reader's—to the Oxford University Press and to Professor Syme.

Many friends have helped me by their kindness and interest: I should particularly like to mention Mr. G. L. Cawkwell, of University College (Oxford), and Mr. J. Janiurek, of Thornton's bookshop. And many patrons of scholarship have generously supported this work: it was begun under the auspices of the Craven Committee and the British School at Rome, and continued with the assistance of the University of Sheffield and later the Durham Colleges. I am happy to acknowledge that help and interest. Such as it is, however, this book is above all an Oxford work: almost every idea in it was formed in Oxford and almost every word in it written there; and, as far as I am concerned, it could not have been anywhere else. I therefore regard it as the chief reward of my labours that the book is being published by the Clarendon Press.

E. B.

January, 1957

CONTENTS

CONTENTS

Part II. INTERNAL POLITICS

ABBREVIATIONS

For periodicals, the system of abbreviations of *L'Année Philologique* is generally followed, with some slight modifications (e.g. *AJP* for *AJPh*) that should not cause any difficulty. The following journals, frequently cited, have been specially abbreviated:

Ath.	= *Athenaeum*
Cl. et Med.	= *Classica et Mediaevalia*
H	= *Hermes*
Hist.	= *Historia*

For standard works of reference the usual practice of abbreviation by initials has been followed (e.g. *CAH* = *Cambridge Ancient History*; *RE* = *Real-Encyclopädie*); similarly in the various standard collections of inscriptions (e.g. *ILS* = Dessau, *Inscriptiones Latinae Selectae*; *SEG* = *Supplementum Epigraphicum Graecum*). 'Ditt. *Syll.*' has been preferred for Dittenberger, *Sylloge Inscriptionum Graecarum*, to differentiate it at a glance from *SEG*; for similar reasons of clearness, *Eph. Ep.* = *Ephemeris Epigraphica*; *I. v. Perg.* = *Inschriften von Pergamon*; *Insc. It.* = *Inscriptiones Italiae*.

The following should be specially noted:

    FIRA = *Fontes Iuris Romani Anteiustiniani*² (ed. Riccobono)

    MRR = Broughton, *Magistrates* (see Bibliography)

    RC   = Sherwin-White, *The Roman Citizenship*

For expanded titles of other works, see Bibliography.

INTRODUCTION

Clientela

THE relation of patron and client[1] is one of the most characteristic features of Roman life lasting, in some form, from the origins to the downfall of the city and beyond: Romulus created it[2] and Justinian provides for it.[3] To the historian, its origins are obscure—shrouded in the darkness of primitive Rome, and re-created by each modern theorist in the light of his own views on the latter. When the light of history becomes more certain, the institution appears in a highly developed form, though still (like many Roman institutions) in that penumbra of religion and inescapable custom that is not quite law—or is more than law. Fortunately, it is only at this point that we need take it up and briefly recall some well-known facts about it, before proceeding to our main theme.

The client may be described as an inferior entrusted, by custom or by himself, to the protection of a stranger more powerful than he, and rendering certain services and observances in return for this protection. This state the Romans called 'in fide alicuius esse'.[4] The meaning of the phrase has been much discussed. Polybius tells us that the Aetolians misunderstood it;[5] and modern historians, lawyers and philologists are still arguing about it. That 'fides' originally meant 'protection' and nothing more,[6] is unlikely on many grounds.[7] At least as early—and as late—as

[1] The standard article is still that on 'clientes' in *RE* (Premerstein), based largely on Mommsen (especially 'Das röm. Gastrecht u. die röm. Clientel', in *Röm. Forsch.* i. 319 f.). The article on 'patronus' has not yet appeared. The fundamental treatment of the political importance of *clientela* is Gelzer, *Nobilität*, a large part of which deals with this question. Cf. also Premerstein, *Werden*, 13 f., and Syme, *Rom. Rev.*, *passim* (for the late Republic).

[2] Cic. *rep.* ii. 16.   [3] *cod.* vi. 4, 4, a. 531 (and *passim*).

[4] See *TLL*, s.v. 'fides'; also the articles on *fides* by E. Fraenkel (*RM*, 1916) and R. Heinze (*H*, 1929), to which reference is made below.

[5] xx. 9, 10 f.   [6] Fraenkel, op. cit.

[7] Not least its etymology; but the fact that it appears, as early as we can trace it, in the penumbra of religion and tradition is enough to warn us against positing any over-simplified 'root meaning'—a procedure that in any case runs counter, in most instances, to the natural development of language.

we find it, it implies trust, and therefore trustworthiness: it is a term of moral obligation and of moral judgement,[1] with the religious implications such terms often have.

There are many ways of forming this relation of trust,[2] some resting on status and some on contract (in the widest sense of these terms). We shall discuss those which are certainly the most interesting to the lawyer; they are: manumission; inheritance; *deditio*; *applicatio*. The first two rest on status; the last two are voluntary. In the course of our discussion we shall examine the common view that the relation established was in all cases identical.

(i) *Manumission*. This was the most common and historically the most persistent way of forming the link. The latter arose, of course, out of the mere act, and was independent of the words or the intentions of either party. This is so obvious that it seems surprising to find Premerstein denying it and assuming a 'Gelöbnis oder was ihm gleichstand'[3] by the patron—a fiction which goes back to Mommsen's view that manumission was originally only morally and not legally binding,[4] but which is not entailed even by acceptance of this view.

The power of the patron over the man whom he had given freedom was at all times wide and originally almost unlimited.[5] What was the legal foundation of this power—or whether indeed there was any such foundation—remains obscure, despite investigation and debate.[6] Its content, however, is known with some precision:[7] the patron had certain rights of inheritance and *tutela*, as well as to '*operae munera dona*'. These rights, more and more closely defined—and circumscribed—by law, remain fundamentally intact until Justinian and after. Apart from this, the patron had a right to *obsequium* and *reuerentia*—vague extra-legal terms, tending to crystallize into defined rights and immunities.[8] These rights were protected by the patron's *potestas*: a

[1] Heinze, op. cit.

[2] Premerstein (*RE*, l.c.) and Mommsen (op. cit.) mention only the most common ones (cf. also the latter's *Str.* iii. 55 f.). Though where the outline is so vague, it is difficult to say whether Mommsen gives too little or too much.

[3] Op. cit., col. 30.   [4] *Str.* iii. 58 *et al.*

[5] Though never perhaps entirely so, like true *patria potestas*. On the whole subject cf. M. Kaser, *ZRG*, 1938, 88 f.

[6] See below for a more detailed discussion of a few points of some relevance to us.   [7] See Kaser, op. cit., or any handbook on Roman Law.

[8] See *Note A*, p. 291.

coercive power of the same nature as *patria potestas*—and probably one aspect of it—and originally equally independent of the State.[1] It included the *ius uitae ac necis*, as we see from two Republican examples;[2] and this entitles us to conclude that minor punishments were allowed. Relegation was permitted in some form, it seems;[3] if this, as Mommsen believes,[4] was enacted under Augustus, it does not follow that it was prohibited before—Mommsen rightly stresses the probability of its being the limitation of a wider power rather than the expansion of a narrower. Lesser *coercitio* was always permissible: the jurists thought it inconceivable that a freedman should be granted an action for it.[5] It is more doubtful whether the freedman could be re-enslaved: the first example of this that we find mentioned is under Claudius;[6] when the possibility is suggested under Nero,[7] *mos maiorum* is cited as decisively against it; but Nero's final decision seems to contemplate it as a possibility in individual cases—and Tacitus, who did not necessarily have a good source for this discussion, is not at his best on early history.[8] It is only under Commodus that this penalty is generalized. But De Francisci believes that it was not legally enacted till very much later.[9] This would seem to do away with the view of Premerstein[10] that this later *reuocatio in seruitutem* is evidence for an originally 'precarious' freedom.[11] But we must not forget that all that can

---

[1] Cf. Kaser, op. cit. (also 'Der Inhalt der patria potestas', ibid. 62 f.) and Wenger 'Hausgewalt u. Staatsgewalt' (*Misc. Ehrle*, ii).

[2] Suet. *Caes.* 48; Val. Max. vi. 1, 4.

[3] Tac. *ann.* xiii. 26—though the relation of this to Gai. i. 27 is doubtful.

[4] *Röm. Forsch.* i. 369.

[5] Kaser, op. cit. 98 f., discusses this. Like many others, this power tended to be restricted in later times.

[6] *dig.* xxxvii. 14, 5; Suet. *Cl.* 25 (probably wrongly generalized).

[7] Tac., l.c.

[8] It was pointed out to me by Professor Syme that the scene of the discussion is not the Senate (whose *acta* might have been available), but the Emperor's *consilium*. For Tacitus on early history, *ann.* xi. 22 is a favourite reference; in this case, moreover, he certainly made the mistake of ignoring the precedent set by Claudius—perhaps because the whole passage is intended to be rhetorical rather than historical.

[9] *Mél. Cornil*, i. 297 f.

[10] Op. cit., coll. 31 and 42.

[11] On precarious freedom after *deditio* we shall have more to say. The 'seruus qui in libertate moratur', chosen by Mommsen as the picture of the original freedman, is admittedly a late Republican phenomenon and of no value as evidence for true manumission. There is, in fact, no valid evidence for Mommsen's and

be proved is that there was, in earlier times, no legal provision for such re-enslavement and that under the early Empire it was not customary. Whether, originally, re-enslavement was—like execution—one of the penalties permitted by unquestioned custom, is simply unknown.[1]

However, it should be stressed that the patron's *potestas*, though extra-legal and without defined limits, was not arbitrary in another sense. *Hausgewalt* implied *cognitio*, at least in serious cases,[2] for freedmen as well as for sons. Cruelty towards slaves was noted by the censors,[3] for it was unworthy of Romans and against *mos maiorum*. There is no doubt (despite our lack of direct evidence) that the same customary sanction protected the freedman.

(ii) *Inheritance.* The freedman's son (normally) was born into his father's obligations, and conversely the patron's son normally inherited his father's position as regards his freedmen. Details do not concern us here. But it is worth mentioning that, although the taint of unfree birth normally faded with the generations, and the freedman's grandson (or even his son) was for most purposes an *ingenuus*,[4] *clientela* continued, in theory, until the patron's or the freedman's family had died out. The famous lawsuit between the Patrician Claudii and the Plebeian Claudii Marcelli[5] shows how far some families were prepared to go in their insistence upon theoretical rights. But it also shows[6] how in practice dependence was bound to become attenuated and wither away, as the descendants of patron and freedman lost personal contact and went their different ways.

(iii) *Deditio.* This is, for our purposes, perhaps the most important way of becoming a client, as it embraces defeat in war.

Premerstein's view that manumission originally conferred only *de facto* freedom; but the point, in any case, is of no importance for historical times.

[1] We must not forget that even the *ius uitae ac necis* is known to us by mere chance and, but for one quotation in Suetonius (Val. Max., l.c. (p. 3, n. 2), is not decisive without support), might well have been 'disproved' by modern scholarship. In the absence of evidence we ought to suspend judgement. But it is worth pointing out that even if *penal* re-enslavement was allowed, freedom was not thereby made precarious: for what is precarious can be withdrawn at will and without reason (see next note and text).

[2] Thus rightly Kaser, op. cit. 98; cf. also 68 f.

[3] Dion. xx. 13 (cf. Kaser, pp. 73 f.).　　　　　[4] Mommsen, *Str.* iii. 422 f.

[5] Cic. *de or.* i. 176.　　　　　　[6] Stressed by Mommsen and Premerstein.

Unlike the ways we have discussed so far, it is a voluntary arrangement: the weaker party may refuse to offer and the stronger to accept it. The relation of dependence is formed only by the acceptance of the offer, which must proceed according to a set form. Discussion has centred round the precise form of the arrangement. Premerstein[1] sees it too legalistically. According to him, it is a 'treaty' between the victorious Roman general and the vanquished community, by which the former acquires a 'durch fides modificierte potestas' over the latter. He sees, of course, that it is an unusual sort of treaty—for one partner legally ceases to exist by agreeing to it, and he therefore cannot have any claim under it. But he gets over this by making the conqueror responsible to the gods, who punish breaches of *fides*.[2] He takes Livy's description of the surrender of Collatia[3] as the standard form of *deditio*; and indeed, the dramatic dialogue may be genuinely ancient (as it may also be a later lawyer's idea of how it *ought* to have happened). But he notices that there is no mention of *fides*, and so he believes that there must be two kinds of treaty: one in which mere *potestas* is acquired (i.e. there is no *fides* and therefore no *clientela*), and one in which there is an express promise of *fides* included in the form of words.[4] However, all this is fundamentally mistaken. First, it has been shown[5] that a *deditio* cannot properly be called a treaty,[6] for the reason we have noted. It is the attempt to assimilate *deditio in fidem* to a proper treaty that leads Premerstein to search for a sanction and find it in heaven. And this brings us to a second and perhaps more important point: the 'Treuversprechen' assumed by Premerstein is an arbitrary invention, like that which he posited for manumission. Polybius, in an important passage,[7] informs us that surrender *in fidem* meant the same (ἰσοδυναμεῖ) as surrender

---

[1] Op. cit., col. 26.

[2] This idea of a 'Deditionsvertrag' is taken over by Täubler and, from him and Premerstein, accepted by many others—e.g. Heinze, op. cit. 152 f.

[3] i. 38, 2 f.

[4] Heinze (l.c.) even thinks that surrender *in fidem* is a later development of surrender *in dicionem* (*potestatem*, &c.)—on no evidence at all. He is thus forced to reject Pol. xx. 9, 10 f.—a conclusion that should at least have made him examine his premiss. For a criticism of this view, see Heuss (next note).

[5] By Heuss, *Völkerr. Grundl.*, whom in general I follow.

[6] Livy, xxxiv. 57, 7 is irrelevant (cf. Heuss, op. cit. 62, n. 1).

[7] See n. 4 (above).

B

in dicionem; the Aetolians, he says, did not understand this. There is no reason why we should follow them. There is only one kind of *deditio*, and that gives the recipient complete power. But by accepting it, he morally binds himself not to make extreme use of it.[1] Surrender is unconditional,[2] and the choice of phrase (*in fidem, in dicionem*, &c., or some combination of them) arbitrary, as indeed the sources show.[3]

Once a community had surrendered, its members were *in fide* —but whose? Premerstein thinks the *fides* was only that of the commander receiving the surrender:[4] and he supports this by pointing out that the Roman People is not usually called 'patron', or others its 'clients', in official parlance. However, the surrender is often said to be *in fidem p.R.* and is thus regarded by the Romans;[5] and there was, of course, a temple to Fides publica (or Fides p.R.) as early as the middle of the third century—or even in the time of Numa, as tradition maintained.[6] We must, moreover, distinguish the state of being *in fide* immediately on surrender—a temporary state, which must have recurred at all periods—from the permanent clientship that could arise therefrom, but seems to be a later development. The latter was probably the way in which educated Romans in the second century considered the relations of Rome with at least some other states:

---

[1] Thus surrendered towns should not be plundered like those taken by assault (Livy, xxx. 7, 2 *et al.*); though we know of some that were (cf. Livy, xlii. 7). Heuss has shown how much the content of *fides* could vary: as Heinze puts it, only the 'Gewissenhaftigkeit' of the conqueror protected the conquered. (Cf. Piganiol, 'Venire in fidem', tracing changes in Roman practice.)

[2] Of course the Romans might give specific pledges before accepting the surrender (e.g. Livy, xxxii. 24, *fin.*); but the example referred to shows that these pledges had nothing to do with the legal act of surrender, but were only, as it were, its psychological causes. (In this case some days elapsed between the two.) If the Romans had ignored them later, they would have broken *fides Romana*, but not any treaty.

[3] Heuss (l.c.) comes to the peculiar conclusion—for which he finds no evidence in the sources—that the full phrase ought to be 'in fidem dicionemque' or some such combination. But this obscures the very point that he succeeds in making (viz. that the two elements are inseparable): by insisting on the presence of both terms we admit them to be theoretically separable. It is no less 'correct', as far as we can tell from the sources, to use either term by itself: they imply each other.

[4] He quotes Livy, xxxvii. 45, 2 'in fidem consulis dicionemque p.R.' (on which, see further Ch. VII, p. 156, nn. 4 f. and text).

[5] e.g. Pol. xx. 9, 10 = Livy, xxxvi. 28, 1; cf. xlii. 7, 5–6.

[6] Cf. Wissowa, *Religion*, 123 f.

the avoidance of the term in official documents may be due to a desire to spare their feelings—for *cliens* usually implies inferiority;[1] though we shall not be able to follow Mommsen's extreme view that anyone who ever surrendered to Rome legally remained her client ever after.[2] As for the commander's personal *fides*, it would certainly be at stake in the actions consequent on surrender. Whether he then became the patron of the conquered for ever after, is a different question: Cicero informs us[3] that *more maiorum* he did—but there is no evidence of this before the case of Marcellus and the Syracusans in 212;[4] though later examples are frequent.

We can now leave the problems of *deditio* (some aspects of which will have to be further discussed as instances arise) and pass on to

(iv) *Applicatio.* This is the most obscure of all the forms of clientship. Premerstein again invests it with a ritual, similar to that of *deditio*.[5] Mommsen calls it 'a form of manumission'[6] and puts it into the same class as *deditio*. He also believes that it was confined to members of the Latin (perhaps even the 'old Latin') communities.[7] It is said to have given the patron complete power, which, however, could not *in practice* be exercised over a man of free birth as it could over a freed slave. Mommsen even maintains that this *applicatio* was originally compulsory for those members of the communities concerned who wanted to settle in Rome. Premerstein does not seem to go quite so far. He also lists the advantages (precarious land and protection in the law-courts being the most important) which the intending client hoped to derive from *applicatio*.

All this legal superstructure appears to rest on one obscure passage of Cicero,[8] which is worth quoting in full: in *de or.* i, Crassus is expounding the need for *iuris prudentia* in advocates;

---

[1] Cf. Gelzer, *Nobilität*, 56, n. 7. The polite term, of course, is 'amicus' (Premerstein, *Werden*, 15—cf. p. 12, n. 6, below).

[2] The problem of the legal and customary status of a community after surrender, whether or not this was followed by a treaty, will be noticed later, as important cases occur: the answer must be given by the facts. [3] *off*. i. 35.

[4] Livy, xxvi. 32, 8. On Fabricius' supposed Samnite *clientela*, cf. Forni, *Ath.* 1953, 177 f.

[5] Op. cit., col. 32. [6] *Röm. Forsch.* i. 360 f.

[7] *Str.* iii. 57. [8] See *Note B*, p. 291.

after mentioning various cases of intricate law, including that of the Patrician Claudii and the Plebeian Claudii Marcelli, he goes on (s. 177):

'Quid? quod item in centumuirali iudicio certatum esse accepimus, qui Romam in exsilium uenisset, cui Romae exsulare ius esset, si se ad aliquem quasi patronum applicauisset intestatoque esset mortuus, nonne in ea causa ius applicationis, obscurum sane et ignotum, patefactum in iudicio atque illustratum est a patrono?'

The *Thesaurus Linguae Latinae* quotes this passage[1] as the only one in which the words 'applicare' and 'applicatio' are thus used as technical terms. This is surprising, but might be explained by the fact that the custom obviously fell into desuetude. But we notice that there are many non-technical phrases in which the word is used in similar contexts;[2] it can usually be fairly rendered 'to attach (oneself)', and is equally general in its metaphorical meaning: i.e. it refers to the selection of a companion[3] and often to voluntary submission to a superior[4] whom one is prepared to follow. It is thus naturally the word used for the selection of a patron by a prospective client appealing for help;[5] help of some sort was what the client wanted from his patron. As such it implies neither ritual nor legal relationships. Thus we find that there is a very common and non-technical meaning of 'se applicare', in which no legal relationship is established and no ritual or form of words seems to be needed: it is simply an arrangement between two parties such as we might find anywhere and at any time. There is, however, especially under Roman notions of gratitude, a tendency for a benefit conferred (especially on one in

---

[1] s.v. 'applicare', col. 298, ll. 33 f.; cf. 'applicatio', col. 295, ll. 62 f.

[2] 'me ad Molonem applicaui' (Cic. *Br.* 316)—as a student; 'externo potius se applicet quam ciui cedat' (Livy, xxxiv. 49, 10); also with 'ad familiaritatem', &c. (Cic. *Cluent.* 46; Nep. *Arist.* 2, 3).

[3] Ter. *Heaut.* 393.

[4] Cic. *Br.* 316 (n. 2, above); Livy, l.c. (ibid.).

[5] Ter. *And.* 924 f.: 'ille egens forte applicat . . . ad Chrysidis patrem se'—without any implication that the latter gains *potestas* over him. Note that the benefactor is 'is . . . qui eum recepit': should we assume a formal *deditio* with its 'Geberden'? Similarly in *Eun.* 885 f. Chaerea commends himself to Thais' *fides* to get her help in his love-affair; he says: 'te mihi patronam capio'—there is no trace of the verb 'applicare'. Nor does it appear in lines 1039 f., nor in many other passages where a person adopts a patron. We have no justification for endowing it with an arbitrary 'ceremonial' meaning, which is never required.

need) to establish a permanent obligation;[1] moreover, the help and protection is likely to be needed at other times (e.g. in the cases, mentioned by Mommsen and Premerstein, of an alien or a poor citizen). Thus the man who has once appealed for help becomes a permanent 'client', with his full consent. It will be noticed that in all this there is no mention of *potestas*: you may entrust yourself to a man's *fides* in more ways than one, and it need not always mean the same as in the case of *deditio*.[2] It seems, therefore, that we have no reason for accepting the elaborate myth of the great jurists; 'applicare', in the passage of Cicero, is probably no more a technical term than anywhere else, and the 'patron' thus chosen is carefully described as '*quasi* patronus' to show that he did not fit into the strict category of *patroni* (i.e. patrons of freedmen). This alone should be enough to show the non-technical character of the phraseology. It may be said that 'ius applicationis' must be a technical term. But this is not so: it need not denote a special category of law, any more than 'ius stirpis et gentilitatis' in the preceding section does; it simply means 'the legal position with regard to . . .', or some such phrase. It is a pity that we have no record of learned counsel's argument, or of the decision, in the case Cicero records. For all we know, the barrister *may* have used an argument similar to that of the modern interpreters, and it *may* have won the day—but we cannot build an elaborate theory on this.[3]

The upshot of this long argument is that phrases like *in fide esse* (or *in fidem uenire*) do not at any time have a single, simple

---

[1] Cf. Gelzer, *Nobilität*, 52 f., for innumerable examples.

[2] In fact, though in the case of *deditio* 'fides' is often combined with words like 'dicio' or 'potestas', *TLL* (s.v. 'fides', *init.*) does not furnish a single example of such a combination in the case of a patron voluntarily chosen—as indeed we might expect. The numerous instances of an accused's being 'in fide ac potestate' of the jury or the magistrate (ibid. I A b β) do not belong here. Hirtius (*b.G.* viii. 44, 3) is the exception that proves the rule; Fraenkel (*TLL*, l.c.) says: 'nota *fidem* paene idem ualere atque *potestatem*'; but in fact the *potestas* is far from being due to the surrender *in fidem*!

[3] Cicero's wording ('ius obscurum et ignotum patefactum atque illustratum est') strongly suggests the sort of case in which new law is in fact made by interpretation and not old law applied. In any case, we have no reason to suppose that the looser form of voluntary *clientela* that we know in historical times is merely a degenerate form of a legal and ritual link originally of the same nature as *clientela* by status (cf. text). This link looks like an invention of jurists (ancient and modern); as we saw, Cicero's wording distinguishes the two.

meaning. They denote a close relationship on a moral (i.e. extra-legal) basis; the legal element may or may not be the sort of *potestas* the patron has over his freedman or the victorious general over the surrendered enemy. There is no reason, *a priori* or in the light of evidence, why we should expect all these different situations to produce identical results. In fact, *clientela* is not (in origin or in development) a simple relationship, but at all historical times a name for a bundle of relationships united by the element of a permanent (or at least long-term) *fides*, to which corresponds the *officium* (&c.) of the client who receives its *beneficia*. However, as was inevitable, there was always a tendency to assimilate the various *Treuverhältnisse*—a tendency that influenced even legal theory.[1]

We have glanced in passing at the duties of the freedman, and we need not go in any detail into what was expected of clients in general.[2] This naturally changed with changing times: in earlier days they accompany their patron into battle,[3] in later times to the Forum or Campus.[4] But at all times they must be ready to support him in any way he requires. Above all, they must give an impression of power, importance, and character. Gelzer has collected some evidence for this important function of theirs;[5] and Heinze[6] has shown how the display was not only one of power, but one of character and virtue—the number of a man's clients showed the trust placed in his *fides*, which was at all times considered one of the main attributes of a gentleman. The patron's duties were equally general:[7] an obligation to protect the client, perhaps to provide for him, and to render him any assistance of which he was in need. As we have seen, this help

---

[1] Later law puts the *libertus*, the *cliens* and the *mercennarius* together under some form of domestic jurisdiction (cf. Kaser, op. cit. 101 f.); but it is agreed that this is not 'primitive'.

[2] Cf., for example, Dion. ii. 9—for what it is worth.

[3] Thus in the case of the Fabii in 479 (Dion. ix. 15, 2 f. *et al.*)—cf. that of Scipio in 134 (App. *Hisp.* 84), discussed pp. 168 f.

[4] The change is, of course, essentially a mere change of emphasis due to changing social conditions. The older kind of service was later revived in a new form, when required in times of turmoil (cf. later chapters, especially Ch. XI).

[5] Op. cit. 83, n. 5; cf. Premerstein, *Werden*, 19-20.   [6] Op. cit. 151 f.

[7] The well-known passages on the place of the client in the scale of a man's duties (especially Cato *ap.* Gell. v. 13, 4) show how seriously the old Roman gentleman took his *fides*.

and protection was why men often chose to become clients. It was, of course, a matter of *fides*: the client had no claim in law. But we know that the moral and religious sense of the Romans long abhorred the abuse of the patron's position of power and trust: the Twelve Tables (whether for the first time or not, we cannot tell) pronounced the patron who abused it *sacer*, and Vergil places him in the blackest Tartarus.[1] That, however, was perhaps archaism: we have reason to doubt the persistence of these moral standards.

Here we may leave this subject for the moment: we shall have more to say on those particular (and very important) aspects of it that form the subject of our inquiry. This short sketch is meant only to place the latter in its context, and to propound some problems of relevance to it. Its main purpose has been to show that we must not expect foreign *clientelae* to conform to one pattern, as ultra-formalistic interpretation of the concept might have persuaded us to do. The relationship presided over by Fides is of a moral and political rather than a legal kind: where there are legal foundations, it is the superstructure that is the realm of Fides—and that matters. And this, we shall find, is true in the public as in the private sphere.

Moreover, we have hitherto discussed only those relationships which might, despite their different origins, be said to constitute *clientela* in the strict sense. But other (related) concepts are no less important. The various classes of *clientela* are united by the fact that they comprise relationships admittedly between superior and inferior. Not so *hospitium* and *amicitia*, typical relationships between equals. *Hospitium*—universally known (and necessary) in primitive societies—was essentially an undertaking to offer mutual hospitality if the need arose: an undertaking that originally implies, *ipso facto*, an equivalence and near equality between the hospitable arrangements awaiting each party. It must originally have its formal badge (the *tessera hospitalis*),[2] to prevent abuse; later, perhaps, that may not be quite so essential.[3] *Hospitium*, like *clientela*, could also be a relationship between an

---

[1] *Aen.* vi. 609 and Serv. ad loc.
[2] Cf. *CIL*, i². 2, nos. 23, 828, 1764, for early examples.
[3] Cf. Ch. VII, pp. 154 f.

individual and a state: he would be a *hospes* to all its official
envoys to his city, while he would be given *hospitium publicum* if
he visited it. Formally there was no difference, and the *tessera*
was still needed; but no doubt the engagement would be entered
into more elaborately (one party to it being a body politic), and
that elaborate 'treaty' would perhaps be recorded on the *tessera*.[1]
However, these relations of equality did not long continue. As
Rome increased in importance, the Roman *hospes* increased in
stature as against his foreign partner. In public *hospitia*, where
formal engagements are recorded, we have formal proof that
hospitium merged into *clientela*.[2] In the case of private *hospitia*,
the nature of the cases recorded, and the facts of Latin word
usage, make it equally certain.[3] Similarly *amicitia*: a vague term
(originally) in its private meaning, it has, perhaps, ritual actions—
like the handshake—to found it, but nothing for lawyers or epi-
graphists to seize on. Fortunately, a public form is again attested:
the *formula amicorum* (or *sociorum*), by the second century (and
perhaps earlier), recorded the *amici populi Romani*, both states
and individuals;[4] though again no treaty was (at least later)
necessary to establish the relationship,[5] and this record will have
served only as a reminder, having no legal status. Again there is,
by now, no question of equality: just as, in private usage within
Rome,[6] 'amicus' can now be a polite term for an inferior (or,
conversely, a superior)—i.e. a client or patron—, so in the wider
sphere, where there are no equals left to Rome as a great power—
or to a Roman senator[7] as an individual—, *amicitia* necessarily

[1] Cf. *CIL*, i². 2, no. 611: a fish, typical of *tesserae hospitales*, but recording a
whole treaty (early second century B.C.). Cf. next note.

[2] The document cited in the preceding note, while almost certainly establishing
hospitium, contains a *deditio in fidem*. This shows how the merging of the two
classes (recurring, of course, in later documents of this type) had been accomplished
by the second century B.C.

[3] Cf. Ch. VII, l.c. (p. 11, n. 3).

[4] Livy xliii. 6, 10; xliv. 16, 7; *FIRA*, 35 (*SC de Asclepiade*), ll. 7 f. L = 24 f. G.
Livy's term is 'formula sociorum'; but there is no reason to think that there were
two different lists. On *socii*, see Heuss, *Völkerr. Grundl., passim*; see also *TLL*, s.v.
'amicus', coll. 1909–10. Cf. Meyer, *R. St.* 220.

[5] Heuss, op. cit.

[6] *TLL*, s.v. 'amicus', col. 1907, ll. 77 f. ('saepe i.q. cliens', with examples); cf.
col. 1911, ll. 10 f.

[7] After the Hannibalic War the Senate was more than an assembly of kings
(Plut. *Pyrrh.* 19, 6): in the eyes of at least one second-century king—and in fact it

becomes another term for clientship, for which category its non-legal nature eminently fits it.

Thus, to the mixed and disparate category that may be called '*clientela* proper', there are added, as the rise of Roman power and prestige makes equality a pretence, other relationships formally of a different nature, but ready enough to fit into the requirements of *beneficium* and *officium* that form the moral basis of that category.[1] It will be the purpose of this study to treat client relationships in the wider sense that thus arises. For the period with which we are concerned, any narrower definition would be untrue to the facts of history and would obscure, rather than illuminate, developments.

This inquiry will naturally fall into two parts. The first section (Chapters I–VI) will trace the development of client relationships in foreign policy. This will necessitate a broad survey of foreign policy during the period; but, of course, it is not intended to make it complete or to write a history of Roman foreign policy. While it has seemed preferable to give too much rather than too little, the special point of view of this study as a whole has always been borne in mind and forms the basis of interpretation. The picture thus sketched is, I believe, more true to the facts of historical development—and to Roman character—than those often painted in modern works; though it is not, of course, wholly new, and does not claim to be. This part of the inquiry may conveniently stop (as a detailed survey) about the middle of the second century B.C.: Roman hegemony is now complete and unchallenged, and client relationships have hardened into a recognized part of the administrative system.[2]

The second part (Chapters VII–XI) deals with the *clientelae* of individual Roman families and Roman leaders. Here, as will be

---

was obviously true for most of them—it was an assembly of gods (Pol. xxx. 18, often repeated). Nor was this mere flattery: for it could make and unmake kings.

[1] Cf. Gelzer, *Nobilität*, 52 f. The German word 'Treuverhältnisse' describes the whole category better than any English expression known to me. On *beneficium* and *officium*, see Volkmann, *H*, lxxxii, 1954, 475 f.

[2] As such they are admirably treated, within the limits of that work, by Sands (*Client Princes*). This study does not claim and is not intended to supersede that work, but to supply it with the historical perspective which its static interpretation unfortunately lacks. Compare the Epilogue.

seen, the scale of treatment demanded is chronologically inverted: while always of 'background' importance, these *clientelae* only come into the centre of the political stage with the Gracchan reforms and henceforth continue to gain in significance. The natural *terminus ad quem* here would be the establishment of the Principate, which absorbs the *clientelae* of the *principes* into that of the *Princeps*.[1] But exigencies of space and time here demanded arbitrary curtailment, especially as the scale of treatment would have to increase (with the volume of evidence available) for the last forty years. Perhaps another volume will some day deal with those years. Meanwhile, the second triumph of Pompey provides (as will be seen) a terminal date corresponding to the end of an epoch; and if it also marks the beginning of another—and more interesting—one, that is necessarily true of every terminal date an historian chooses; and it becomes all the more true, the better he has chosen his date. Though it cannot be complete, and though other historical influences and points of view must always be considered in conjunction with it, this study as a whole will (it is hoped) at least throw some light on the importance for Roman history of a specifically Roman category of thought. Perhaps it will even be of some relevance to perennial problems of power.

---

[1] For the demonstration and evaluation of this, see especially Premerstein, *Werden*, 112 f. and Syme, *Rom. Rev., passim.*

PART ONE

FOREIGN POLICY

I

THE ORGANIZATION OF ITALY
BEFORE THE HANNIBALIC WAR

IT is not our purpose, in this study, to trace the development of Rome from a small township to the leading power in Italy. At the starting-point of our main investigation, this process is practically complete, and Italy, except for the Gauls and Ligurians, united under Roman leadership. But since we shall be concerned with the changes in the relative positions of Rome and the rest of Italy which accompanied and followed the further expansion of Roman power, and with the development of Roman ideas on imperial organization, we must briefly survey the organization of Italy in the late third century and the various ways in which Roman statecraft had attached the many cities and nations of ancient Italy to the leading state. For purposes of convenience, we shall consider the situation before the outbreak of the Second Punic War and discuss the various forms of association in turn.[1]

(i) *Ciues Romani*. The most direct form was incorporation in the Roman state, the mark of which was the conferment of citizenship. This was an old and unsophisticated way, which was bound to reach its natural limits soon, under the influence of increasing difficulties presented by distance and national differences. Originally it implied the transfer of the conquered population to Rome and the destruction of the town concerned: the new Roman citizen had to come to the city of Rome.[2] It is not certain when

---

[1] We need not give complete lists; they can be found, for example, in Beloch, *R.G.* and *I.B.*, and in Afzelius, *Röm. Erob.* On the subject as a whole the standard work is Sherwin-White, *The Roman Citizenship* (cited as *RC*). There is an excellent summary in Meyer, *Röm. Staat*, 205 f.

[2] Cf. the tradition about Alba (Livy, i. 28 f.) and Politorium (Livy, i. 33).

this primitive method was outgrown.[1] The discovery that alliance could also be used for subordination[2] certainly did not put an end to it where it was still practicable. Probably the compulsory transfer of the population was soon abandoned: it was only the city as a body politic that had to be destroyed. The inhabitants were no doubt received into the new tribes that were formed for Roman emigrants to the newly-conquered territories.[3] But the next major step was taken some time in the fourth century: it was the invention (or, more probably, re-application) of *ciuitas sine suffragio*. The origins of this concept, as of that of *municipium* (related to it), are wrapped in obscurity, which it is not our task to pierce.[4] The first part of Festus' confused note on 'municipium' makes it probable that the concept had always existed: 'municipium id genus hominum dicitur, qui cum Romam uenissent neque ciues Romani essent, participes tamen fuerunt omnium rerum ad munus fungendum una cum Romanis ciuibus, praeterquam de suffragio ferendo aut magistratu capiendo; . . . qui post aliquot annos ciues Romani effecti sunt.'[5] The category is probably that of aliens who had settled in Rome (under the *ius migrationis*) and were waiting for the censors to complete their enfranchisement. Their status was ambiguous,[6] but temporary; and there is no reason why the institution should not, like the *ius migrationis* itself, date back to the beginning. At some time in the fourth century this concept was applied in a new sense. The city of Caere had been more closely linked with Rome than any other

---

[1] Perhaps Gabii and Crustumerium provide the first examples (Dion. iii. 49, 6; iv. 58, 4—cf. *RC*, 18 f.); but it is very likely that these cases are 'a reflection backwards to a remote epoch of a system inaugurated later' (*RC*, 19). Otherwise we are left to explain why the new system was abandoned for nearly two centuries. Cf. Frank, *Rom. Imp.* 42, n. 10.   [2] On this, cf. p. 20, n. 3 and text.

[3] Cf. Afzelius, op. cit. 17 f.; though he perhaps overstresses the argument that the creation of new tribes was consciously designed to increase the influence of these settlers.

[4] A summary of the most important views is given in Manni, *Municipi*, Introduction and Part I; it is not always accurate. Cf. *RC*, ch. ii, and (on the words 'municeps' and 'municipium') Pinsent, *CQ*, 1954, 158 f.

[5] Festus, s.v. 'municipium'. I omit the examples he gives, as they have served to mislead more often than to illuminate. We may compare the position of immigrants to the U.S.A. who have taken out their 'first papers', but are not yet naturalized. (See, for example, E. Balogh, *World Peace and the Refugee Problem*, Paris, 1949, p. 10.)

[6] The ambiguity persisted after the concept changed, as is well shown by Sherwin-White (*RC*, 37 f.).

city in Etruria.[1] By its assistance in the Gallic crisis it earned the
special thanks of the Romans.[2] Later, Caere joined Tarquinii in
a war against Rome and was defeated.[3] On this occasion, according to Livy,[4] the memory of their old friendship earned the
Caerites lenient treatment: they were given *indutiae* for 100
years and (apparently) not further punished. Bernardi[5] rejects
the Livian account and thinks that Caere was incorporated *sine
suffragio* at this time; and there is much to be said for such a view.
Livy, or his source, may simply be applying to Caere the scheme
of limited truces which was Rome's normal method of dealing
with Etruscan states;[6] and the Horatian scholiast actually informs us[7] (on what authority, he neglects to say) that Caere got
its *ciuitas sine suffragio* after a defeat. The Etruscan War had
made clear to the Romans the desirability of firmly controlling the
territory north of the city, as far as the 'natural boundary' of the
Ciminian Forest.[8] An independent Caere might be a dangerous
neighbour in the case of a *coniuratio Etruriae*. It is, as Fraccaro
points out, at least likely that the Romans saw this need for
protecting their northern flank—and if not immediately, then
certainly as soon as they were engaged in the major wars in the
south that followed a decade later. It was necessary to eliminate
Caere as a potential enemy; and a truce (or even a *foedus*) would
fail to give the necessary security. The only alternative, on
accepted policy, was the destruction of the city. But this is where
the *uetus meritum* of the Caerites—and the close ties that bound

---

[1] Cf. Bernardi, *Ath.* 1938, 240 f. On the *Caerites tabulae*, cf. also *RC*, 50 f.; but
that view is not followed here. I find it quite possible to accept both the connexion
with the Gallic invasion and the belief that the Caerite franchise was *ignominiosum*
(*RC*, 53). The *Caerites tabulae* (for which see Gell. xvi. 13, 7 and Hor. *ep.* i. 6, 62
with scholia) seem to prove the fact that Caere was the first city in a state of *ciuitas
s.s.* that was corporate and not temporary. Livy, xxviii. 45, 15 tells us nothing about
the status of Caere.

[2] Livy, v. 50, 3.   [3] Livy, vii. 19, 6 f.
[4] vii. 20, 8 f.   [5] Op. cit. 255 f.   [6] *RC*, 116.

[7] ad *ep.* i. 6, 62. Alternatively, of course, the truce may have been converted into
the new settlement during the following ten years. It is, at any rate, worth noting
that the defeat of Caere (reported to be the first city to receive *ciuitas s.s.*) precedes
by such a short time the main series of such grants, which begins either in 343 or
in 338. This makes it all the more dangerous to reject the tradition without good
reason.

[8] Fraccaro, 'L'Organizzazione', 199. For the Ciminian Forest and its terrors, see
Livy, ix. 36, 1.

the city to Rome—may have moved the Romans: they could not simply be sold into slavery, like the Veientines.[1] On the other hand, they could not—even if incorporation *optimo iure* had already been invented, or was then considered—simply receive the franchise: Rome's problem was that of dealing, for the first time, with a largely non-Latin city that yet had sentimental claims. The solution was *ciuitas sine suffragio*: the city remained in existence, but the inhabitants were made Roman citizens—except for the two main privileges of citizens (that of voting and that of holding office). Their status, in fact, was assimilated to that of resident aliens waiting for enfranchisement—but there was no promise that enfranchisement was ever to follow. The censors were bidden to enrol the new citizens in a special list, the *Caerites tabulae* (the resident aliens—the original *municipes*—had, of course, not been on any census list: for when they *were* enrolled, it was on the list of citizens and completed their enfranchisement). In return for this inferiority, Caere was probably granted a certain degree of local autonomy.[2] This case, then, provided the pattern that Rome was to follow extensively during the next half-century,[3] in particular in the case of Campanian and Volscian communities, where the situation was very similar to that of Caere—Rome wanted direct control, but the cities, though non-Latin, had strong claims to consideration.[4]

Thus the principle of receiving whole communities into the citizenship (or a form of it) was established. Its application was soon extended. The non-Latin city could not be given full citizenship immediately (and it is idle to inquire whether the *ciuitas sine suffragio* was meant to be 'permanent'—it was certainly not

---

[1] Livy, v. 22, 1.

[2] Exactly how much is doubtful, though later we know of a dictator and an aedile there (*CIL*, xi, p. 534). Their functions are most uncertain. (Cf. *RC*, 60 f.)

[3] For a list see Bernardi, op. cit. 276. At what precise time various communities (especially Capua) were thus incorporated is of no importance for our purpose. Satricum, for which there is no good evidence, should be deleted from Bernardi's list.

[4] Cf. Livy, viii. 14, 10 f. There is no need to invoke the Greek concept of ἰσοπολιτεία to explain these grants—any more than it can be made to explain *Latinitas* (thus Rosenberg, *H*, 1920, 352 f.): see Bernardi, *Ath.* 1942, 98 f. It is indeed 'a specially Roman principle' (*RC*, 45). The autonomy of the cities concerned should not be overstressed (thus Konopka, *Eos*, 1929, 596 f.); against the *cippus Abellanus* we must set *CIL*, i². 2, no. 611 (Fundi).

meant to be a short-term status); but when Rome decided to annex the territory of some Latin cities, for strategic reasons, after the great Latin War, the communities were received into the full citizenship. The difference—though important—was one of degree;[1] the Latin was related to the Roman: he spoke the same language and could make an intelligent voter. This is probably the simple explanation of the difference in treatment between the Latin and the non-Latin *municipium*. But both were communities of citizens, with autonomous organization, within the Roman state. The principle of Caere, when applied to Latium, led to the *municipium ciuium Romanorum optimo iure*.[2] And many of the *municipia ciuium sine suffragio* attained this full status in due course—though unfortunately we often do not know the precise date and circumstances.[3]

By the end of the fourth century, then, Rome was much more than a city-state: she had recognized the principle of autonomous local organizations of her citizens within the state, even to the extent of making treaties with them.[4] The possibility of the

---

[1] Cf. the definition of 'municeps' attributed to 'Servius filius' (?) by Festus; and that of 'municipium' (Festus, s.v.) as 'quorum ciuitas uniuersa in ciuitatem Romanam uenit'—whether *sine suffragio* or *optimo iure* (for this is the later definition of the word), as Festus' carefully selected examples show ('Aricini, Caerites, Anagnini'; for the Latins in 338 received *ciuitas optimo iure*—*RC*, 56).

[2] The case of Tusculum has suggested an alternative view: according to Livy it received its citizenship soon after 381 (vi. 26, 8; confirmed in 338: viii. 14, 4). But there seems to be no reason for the isolated earlier grant, and the difficulties raised by Livy's account (cf. Beloch, *R.G.* 318) are such that it should be abandoned. In any case, Livy's source did not state the exact date ('nec ita multo post') and may have referred—though Livy does not take it that way—to a grant a generation later. It is by far the easiest hypothesis that Tusculum received its citizenship in 338, together with other cities in Latium.

[3] The Sabines reached it soon (Vell. i. 14, 7); the cities of Formiae, Fundi and Arpinum in 188 (Livy, xxxviii. 36, 7 f.). This latter instance will be in part responsible for the request by Cumae for permission 'ut publice Latine loquerentur' (Livy, xl. 42, 13). But we do not know when Cumae succeeded in its evident purpose of attaining the full citizenship. (The inscription reported in *BCH*, vi, p. 45, is irrelevant.) However, it was probably before the Social War (*RC*, 65), and if so, almost certainly before the Gracchan troubles, which increased Roman exclusiveness.

[4] Lavinium may have had a treaty in 338 (Livy, viii. 11, 15). Once the Lanuvini are recognized (Livy, viii. 14, 2) as a corporate body distinct for *some* purposes from the Roman People, we need hardly quibble at a *foedus*. (On its meaning, cf. Beloch, *R.G.* 379.) It seems neither necessary nor possible to explain away the well-attested *municipia foederata*; though we need not follow Beloch's constructions all the way. The existence of these *foedera* is very important as an illustration of a new point of view (cf. text): we have so little evidence on their nature that we cannot go farther.

'Roman world' had been created. But the body of Roman citizens was—and for centuries remained—only a small part of the population of Italy, and *ager Romanus* a small part of its area. We must therefore go on to consider the relation of Rome to those communities not incorporated in her state.

(ii) *Latini*. The nearest to Rome, in every way, were the Latins. Rome herself had once been no more than one of the numerous Latin *populi*, and both ancient and modern scholarship has been much concerned with her rise to hegemony and rule.[1] It is generally accepted, nowadays, that about 500 B.C. Rome was already in control of a considerable part of the Latin coast. In the first treaty with Carthage,[2] several 'peoples' in that area are described as ὑπήκοοι of Rome; and, what is perhaps even more interesting, Rome claims, by implication, a protectorate even over the independent cities of Latium. As Polybius notices, there is as yet no mention of any states outside Latium. How the protectorate over the ὑπήκοοι was obtained and exercised, is not clear. Most probably we may assume treaties that in some way assured Roman superiority.[3] In any case, the 'peoples' concerned were still regarded as politically independent: they could still, it appears, be members of the council of Ferentina.[4] This was the political body corresponding to the League of Aricia, in which Rome (according to tradition) obtained the leading place under the last of the kings: it was probably this position that gave Rome the right to regard the Latin cities which were not ὑπήκοοι as also under her protection, and Latium as her sphere of influence.

With the Etruscan domination removed, this claim was contested by the Latins, who in a large measure regained their full independence. But with the appearance of invading hill-tribes in the fifth century, the need for coalition became plain: in some

---

[1] On the early history of Latium nothing has superseded *RC*, 5 f. Gelzer and Steinwenter (*RE*, s.vv. 'Latium' and 'ius Latii' respectively) give a detailed treatment of different aspects of the problem, with references.

[2] Pol. iii. 22; cf. *RC*, 15 f.

[3] Gelzer, op. cit., col. 952—but the developed form he gives is incredible. (Further discussion of such treaties will fit into our treatment of the *socii*—see below.)

[4] Cf. *RC*, 14 f. The fact that this is 'a shadowy anticipation of the system of the fourth century' (*RC*, 17) is a good reason for suspecting our sources; but Sherwin-White's case seems convincing. All that is required for the present purpose is the antiquity of Rome's claim to some form of protectorate over independent states.

form, Roman hegemony was recognized in what is traditionally known as the treaty of Sp. Cassius.[1] This was followed by a treaty with the Hernici—Rome's first extension of her hegemony beyond Latium. To supplement these treaties, which gave her a general position of pre-eminence in her small world, Rome probably again began to make special treaties with various smaller Latin states, perhaps making them ὑπήκοοι again.[2] At any rate, by the middle of the fourth century, these 'subjects' again appear, and again do not include all Latium.[3] Unfortunately, we know little of developments in Latium between these two dates. We do know that other states—notably Tibur and Praeneste—built up their own leagues of ὑπήκοοι,[4] and consequently sometimes clashed with Rome. And we know that the Latins and Hernicans became restive as they saw federal armies used to increase the Roman *Hausmacht* in the north, while they themselves were insufficiently protected against the hill-tribes.[5] But the threat of a new Gallic invasion again united the Latins: the treaty of Cassius was renewed[6] and, whatever it was before, it now became a treaty on equal terms between Rome and the rest of the Latins. In the second treaty with Carthage, Latium is again a Roman sphere of influence.

With the Volsci and Aequi warded off, the Latin League faced the Samnite Confederacy. The clash was bound to come, and it was precipitated by the Roman alliance with Capua.[7] The Latins had probably again become restive under what was becoming the Roman yoke: even the Volsci could now be regarded as friends.[8] It seemed advisable to the Roman leaders to confront their luke-warm allies with the Samnite danger, before the Latin League was too disunited to be able to deal with it—especially as this danger would strike the allies first and not approach Roman territory immediately. However, this time Rome miscalculated.

---

[1] See *Note C*, p. 291.

[2] *RC*, 25 f.   [3] Pol. iii. 24, 5.

[4] Livy, vi. 29, 6 (Praeneste); vii. 19, 1 (Tibur). His phrase is 'sub dicione', which (with its variants) denotes—where we can check it—'subject allies' and not annexed cities.   [5] Livy, vi. 10, 6 f.

[6] In fact, perhaps first cast in the form in which Cicero saw it and in which it has come down to us (see *Note C*, p. 291). For the events, see Livy, vii. 12.

[7] Livy, vii. 29. On events between 343 and 338, see especially Afzelius, *Erobe-rung*, 143 f. The status of Capua between those dates does not matter for the present purpose.   [8] Livy, vii. 27, 5.

The citizen army thought the war unnecessary;[1] the Volsci attacked, and the Latin allies, as Rome's reverses proved her weakness, prepared to revolt.[2] But the Samnites too were facing difficulties, especially in the south, where Archidamus might be dangerous.[3] The result, after much diplomatic intrigue, was the Latin War: Rome had been unable to protect her allies in Latium and Campania against the Samnite danger, which moreover (in the case of Latium) she had wantonly brought upon them; thus the reason for acknowledging the hegemony of Rome had disappeared, and with it the fear of her. The Latins and Campanians, in their elation, thought they could both attack their fallen leader and continue the war against the Samnites. This was their fatal mistake. They were defeated by the combined forces of Rome and Samnium,[4] and the settlement of 338 saw the end of the Latin League and of the independent political importance of the Latin states. Rome had begun, perhaps, by protecting her Latin neighbours against the Etruscans (though we cannot safely build on the quicksands of the prehistory of Rome and Latium), and certainly by representing and safeguarding them, after freeing herself from Etruscan domination, against the Etruscans' great Punic ally. She had borne the brunt of the Gallic invasion, and organized the Latin defence against the Gauls in the north and the hill-tribes in the east. In times of peace and apparent security the Latins had been restive at the growth of Rome's private power; but in times of danger the allies, on the whole, had held together and had looked to Rome for leadership. Rome, on the other hand, might claim (until 343) to have played her part fairly. If she had expanded her power in Etruria, she did thereby help to keep the threat of an Etruscan return from the Latins—and that might seem more important than the prevention of a Volscian raid. She had successfully led the Latins in their wars of defence and brought them rich booty. She had turned over parts of the conquered territory to their citizens in the form of Latin colonies;[5] and she had not unwarrantably interfered with their freedom.[6] She had not confiscated any of their territory as a

---

[1] Livy, vii. 39 f.
[2] Ibid., *ad fin.* and viii, *init.*
[3] Afzelius, *Eroberung*, 143 f.
[4] Ibid.
[5] Cf. *RC*, 22 f., 34 f.; and see below.
[6] For instances of that freedom, see *RC*, 22.

result of their revolts, nor destroyed (or annexed)[1] any of their cities. But her very success both increased her power and made her protection seem unnecessary to the Latins; and their consequent restiveness seemed faithless to Rome[2] and helped to drive her to the unwise decision that was meant to show her allies the need for continued unity. The settlement of 338 marks the failure of Rome's first protectorate—the first of such failures that turned out to be the steps to her greatness.

Fortunately, as we have seen, by 338 Rome had worked out the principle of incorporation that enabled her to deal with her late allies. The whole of Latium was annexed, except for the larger states of Tibur and Praeneste, Ardea (which must have remained faithful), and probably Lavinium.[3] Roman citizens were sent to occupy positions in Latium and Campania,[4] and the key city of Antium received a Roman colony.[5] And for the first time, as we have noticed, *ager Romanus* and *ciuitas Romana* were extended over large areas and important cities outside Latium.

The effect of the settlement on the concept of *Latinitas* was before long to dissociate it from the geographical concept of Latium and, in a different sphere, to begin the assimilation of 'Roman' and 'Latin' in meaning. Sherwin-White has traced and illustrated the development of this 'intangible bond',[6] and we shall return to it in so far as it falls within the limits of our inquiry. Meanwhile we need only notice that by the beginning of the second century A. Albinus could call himself 'homo Romanus natus in Latio'[7] and Ennius could talk about 'rem Romanam Latiumque augescere'.[8] This (given, of course, the initial kinship) was due to the fact that the geographical unit called Latium was now mainly *ager Romanus* and, with the swift extension of the latter, came to be regarded as its 'home territory'. On the

---

[1] On Tusculum, often regarded as an exception, see p. 19, n. 2. If the city became a 'subject ally' of Rome around 380, that would explain its incurring the dislike of the other Latins (Livy, vi. 33, 6); but, as we have seen, all is uncertain.

[2] 'infidum iam diu foedus' (Livy, vii, *ad fin.*); the charge is often repeated and may be based on fact.

[3] The settlement of 338 is given by Livy (viii. 14), on the whole credibly. Afzelius, op. cit. 55 f., returns to the view of Beloch that Lavinium received *ciuitas s.s.*; his arguments are not conclusive. The *foedus* does not make *ciuitas o.i.* impossible (see p. 19, n. 4).

[4] Livy, viii. 11, 13.

[5] Ibid. 14, 8.

[6] *RC*, 91–96.

[7] Gell. xi. 8, 1.

[8] *ann.* 466 V.

other hand, *Latini* were, on the whole, members of Latin colonies (which continued to be sent out on an increasing scale to safe-guard new conquests), many—or most—of them of Roman stock, and none of them (except accidentally) born or living in Latium. Thus *Latinitas* came to be regarded as a status[1] in-dependent of residence and beyond treaties:[2] though based on the Cassian treaty, which does not appear to have been formally abrogated, it was derived in fact from the unilateral declaration of the Roman government by which a Latin colony was estab-lished, or (in the case of the few states in Latium) that by which, in 338, they had had *res suae redditae*. This status could be con-ferred on anyone not born into it, if it so pleased the Roman People: at some time it was conferred on the Hernici,[3] and in due course on other men who were legally *peregrini*, but of partly Roman stock.[4] As Sherwin-White remarks,[5] the effect of the settlement of 338 resembles the punishment inflicted on the Campanians[6] in that a group of people were attached to (but not incorporated in) the Roman state by mere decision of the latter; though, as we have seen, a vague contractual basis seems to have remained. As we shall see when discussing the second century,[7] Rome thus came to acquire a new idea of her position as 'protect-ing' state: the settlement of 338 led to the 'freedom of Greece' and to the *ciuitas libera*, the 'client state' proper. At the same time, the peculiar precedent of a (now) unimportant treaty serving as the foundation for a complex moral and sentimental super-structure was to shape Rome's position in Italy in the second century.

The detail of the rights and duties of the Latins need not occupy us for long. Unfortunately, owing to the loss of the second decade of Livy, little is known of developments during the next century, and especially in the crucial period between the Pyrrhic and the Hannibalic Wars. Much has been written about the *duo-decim coloniae* mentioned, in an excruciating passage, by Cicero. But the judgement must ultimately be 'non liquet', until further evidence is found.[8] That the Latins were satisfied with their

[1] *RC*, 91–96. [2] See *Note D*, p. 291.
[3] Livy, xxxiv. 42, 5. [4] Livy, xliii. 3, 4. [5] *RC*, 91.
[6] Livy, xxvi. 34, 6. [7] Cf. Chs. III–VI, below.
[8] *Caec.* 102. Bernardi, 'Ius Ariminensium', gives the most important views

status[1] is shown by their unwavering loyalty in all the major wars of Rome after 338. How Rome regarded and exercised her rights and fulfilled her duties with regard to them in the second century (to which practically all our evidence refers), we shall discuss in due course.[2]

(iii) *Socii*.[3] The making of alliances outside Latium was, in early Roman history, almost unknown. At the time of the first treaty with Carthage there are none; the Hernici provide the first example, and it remains the only one till the middle of the fourth century:[4] the second treaty with Carthage, though it knows peace treaties and Roman subjects beyond Latium, mentions no Roman allies there.[5] The first properly Roman alliances outside Latium date from the time of Rome's entry into major Italian politics, i.e. the time of the first Samnite War. Whether or not Capua was the first case does not matter for our purpose: and after 338, at any rate, alliance is the normal way of attaching a foreign community. Citizenship, with or without the vote, had its geographical limits,[6] as involving direct supervision of some sort. Latinity was but slowly acquiring its new meaning. In general, Rome could operate only with alliances.

The nature and form of these alliances, however, is not at all clear. Since Täubler's great work on Roman treaties[7] it has been usual to regard the *socii* as attached either by *foedus aequum* or by *foedus iniquum*. The characteristic of the latter is said to be the clause in which the ally 'is bidden *maiestatem populi Romani comiter conseruare*' and that by which he 'is bound to assist Rome in wars where the allies' own interest is not at stake'.[8] The latter is even called 'the clause providing for assistance in aggressive

advanced by earlier writers. His own views are not convincing. As Sherwin-White has unanswerably pointed out (*RC*, 98), we know of no differentiation in the concept of Latinity down to 167—or, we may add, after.

[1] That the prohibition of *conubia* and *commercia* (and even of *concilia*) in 338 was only temporary is now generally accepted. Cf. *RC*, 107 f. (with references); Göhler, *Rom u. It.* 8 f.   [2] Ch. VI, below.

[3] We are not here concerned with the meaning of this term in the second century. It will be used, in this chapter, quite arbitrarily but conveniently, to mean 'Rome's non-Latin allies in Italy'.

[4] On all this, cf. the discussion above. The absence of *socii* until so late a date supports the view that the Hernican War was a federal Latin war and the treaty a treaty between the Latins and the Hernici.

[5] Pol. iii. 24, 6.   [6] Fraccaro, 'L'Organ.', 200 f.

[7] *Imp. Rom.* i (only).   [8] *RC*, 114–15.

wars'.[1] It is the *foedus iniquum* that Sherwin-White considers 'the chief instrument in the formation of the federation of allies' and a 'specially Roman institution'.[2]

All this goes far beyond our evidence and needs re-examination. We may start by noticing that, so far from the *foedus iniquum* being a 'specially Roman institution', the Romans are not known even to have had a name for it. While 'aequum foedus' is common enough, its opposite is expressed by various circumlocutions; nor is this surprising: 'iniquum' was hardly a suitable diplomatic term.[3] As for the 'characteristic' *maiestas* clause, Mommsen long ago observed that it was a late development and is not known to have been in any Italian treaty.[4] Altogether it is known for certain only in two instances (both in our literary sources)—the treaty with the Aetolians and that with Gades—and has been conjecturally restored in two epigraphical documents (Mytilene and Cnidos).[5] There is certainly no mention of it as early as the time when the Italian Confederacy was being built up. Indeed, it is doubtful if the phrase 'maiestas populi Romani' would be used so early.[6] We know that Rome, as early as the time of the first treaty with Carthage, considered some states as subject (in some way) to her authority.[7] But this is found in the Greek world too, and is indeed a natural development of a common situation: where a small state is made to sign an alliance with a large neighbour, it is bound to suffer a *de facto* curtailment of its independence, whatever the wording of the alliance. We can to some extent trace this development in the Delian League, and we can see

---

[1] *RC*, 114–15. [2] Ibid. 113.

[3] The only Classical instance I have found is Livy, xxxv. 46, 10, where, far from being a technical term, it has (as it ought to) a strongly emotive significance. Cf. Ch. II, p. 53, n. 2 and text. As a modern term it is convenient, if used with due caution and with no pretence of precise technical meaning.

[4] *Str.* iii. 664 f.

[5] Cf. Täubler, op. cit. 62 f. and 450. It appears to have been first used at the time of the Aetolian treaty; at any rate, its use was not at that time an accepted institution (see Ch. IV, pp. 84 ff.).

[6] Originally an attribute of gods (Wagenvoort, *Rom. Dyn.* 123), 'maiestas' does not appear as applied to the Roman People before the first century B.C. When the *lex Appuleia de maiestate* first made its use common at Rome, it was not at all clear what the term meant (Cic. *part. or.* 105 *et al.*).

[7] Cf. p. 20, nn. 2 and 3 and text. Gelzer (cited there) gives these Latin *populi* fully-developed first-century treaties, complete with *maiestas* clause. This is only the *reductio ad absurdum* of the view here controverted.

there how *de jure* recognition of the fact follows.[1] Modern examples also spring to mind. There is no reason to believe that these earliest treaties contained any clauses reducing one partner to inferiority. Sherwin-White presents the treaty with the Lucani[2] as a typical example of the working of a *foedus iniquum*.[3] This is not impossible, as by that time the insertion of clauses giving the Romans some kind of control over the ally concerned was already practised. But we must not assume it as a matter of course.[4] The Lucanians did, according to Livy, surrender *in fidem*: but it was not the surrender of a conquered community, but that of one seeking Roman help. And it is quite likely that in such cases the treaty was *aequum*. Thus Naples, Livy thought, had not been fought into surrender: the form of the treaty suggested this; yet it was considered to have come *in fidem*.[5] Another example of a *foedus* known to be *aequum* is that of Camerinum[6]—voluntarily concluded, possibly even without *deditio*. Nor could treaties like that with the Picentes[7] easily be other than *aequa*. Thus there is no reason to think that, when the Marrucini, Marsi, Paeligni and Frentani, quite undefeated, asked for a treaty in 304, it was not *aequum*.[8] Now we know that, when the Marsi had to be fought soon after, their defeat was followed by the confiscation of some territory and the 'restoration' of the treaty.[9] This instance makes it possible that, to the cities that concluded their alliances with Rome without being defeated, we may add at least some of those that had originally done so and then rebelled: 'foedus restitutum' (or 'renouatum') is a common phrase in such a case; and we

---

[1] Cf. Meiggs, *JHS*, 1943, 33 *et al.*

[2] Livy, x. 11, 11 f.   [3] *RC*, 115.

[4] Livy, x. 18, 8 is no evidence for interference with Lucanian autonomy: on the contrary, it was help asked for by the allied government.

[5] Livy, viii. 26, 6. (Cic. *Balb.* 21 shows how favourable a treaty Naples must have had.) Livy's argument from the form of the treaty seems to show that voluntary friendship was usually followed by a *foedus aequum*. Being one of the very few indications we have, this passage should not be neglected. We know (Livy, xxiii. 5, 9) that an *aequum foedus deditis* [*datum*] was possible. It seems that Velia can now be added to the small list of communities the nature of whose *foedus* is known: it appears to have had a *foedus aequum* (Bengtson, *Hist.* 1955, 457 f.).

[6] Livy, ix. 36, 8; xxviii. 45, 20; Cic. *Balb.* 46.

[7] Livy, x. 10, 12. Rome was only too glad of the alliance.

[8] Livy, ix. 45, 18; *RC*, 114.

[9] Livy, x. 3. Sherwin-White comments (l.c.): 'hardly a *foedus aequum*.' Why not, in view of the other evidence?

have no right to deny that it is accurate. To warn us against over-generalization along these lines, we have the case of the Apulian Teates:[1] the Apulian tribes had made a *foedus* with Rome in 326.[2] Under Samnite pressure they seem to have denounced the alliance.[3] In 318–17 the Romans used the opportunity afforded by a truce with the Samnites to conquer Apulia.[4] The Teates soon asked for and obtained an alliance, 'neque ut aequo tamen foedere, sed ut in dicione p.R. essent'. This, in the circumstances, was clearly exceptional, and seems to surprise Livy. Perhaps, in the case of an unreliable tribe so far from the City, the Romans thought it safer to take legal precautions. The upshot of this is simply that we must not be too dogmatic. There were treaties that were considered *aequa*, and they were perhaps the rule in certain circumstances. There were others that left the other signatory *in dicione populi Romani*—they also may have had their peculiar use. In what the *dicio* consisted, and what—at this period—were its marks, we do not know.[5] Nor does it matter very much. Mommsen's ruthless logic regarded all *socii* as 'reichs-angehörig'.[6] Technically he was wrong,[7] and at least the *socii* with *foedera aequa*—and probably all *socii*—were, in international law, independent.[8] But in practice, with the growth of Roman power, the result must before long have been what he saw.

(iv) *Socii nauales.* We need not follow the story of the conquest of Italy during the seventy years that followed the Latin settlement; it has often been told,[9] and though details might be discussed, there is little to be added for our purpose. We are concerned only with the organization of the conquests, and this, in essence, remained within the scheme we have surveyed: *ciuitas s.s.*

---

[1] Livy, ix. 20, 7 f.

[2] Livy, viii. 25, 3—almost certainly *aequum*: as Livy insists, there had been no previous contact and the treaty is part of the Roman policy of encirclement against the Samnites.   [3] Livy, viii. 37, 3 f. (very uncertain).

[4] Livy, ix. 20 (from two sources).

[5] It may have been a clause forbidding the ally to wage war or, as Sherwin-White supposes, one requiring him to have the same friends and enemies. Most probably, in view of Roman practice, it was (or contained) a military clause of some sort.

[6] *Str.* iii. 653.

[7] Though, as Horn (*Foed.* 15) has shown, Täubler's case (op. cit. 6 and *passim*) is not convincing. But the inscription Horn quotes, and Festus (s.v. 'postliminium'), are decisive.

[8] Festus (l.c.—quoting Aelius Gallus) makes no distinction.

[9] Cf. the relevant chapters of *CAH*, vii, and De Sanctis, *Storia*, ii.

where strict control was useful and the distance not too great; the *foedus* in all other cases; and we must add the planting of colonies, as from time immemorial, as *propugnacula imperii* in newly-subdued lands. The forms of organization which produced the *Wehrgenossenschaft* had been fashioned by 338, and no major development took place down to the war in Sicily. There is only one change that deserves mention; for it was to help in producing that development.[1] The duties of the *socii*, like those of the Latins, were mainly military, and it seems that they supplied troops *ex formula togatorum*.[2] Polybius gives us the roll-call of Italy a few years before the Hannibalic War[3]—there are allies from the whole Peninsula, with one significant omission: there is no mention of the Greek cities. Mommsen[4] thought to explain this by positing for them the special status of *socii nauales* (thus also explaining this rather peculiar term), i.e. confining their contribution to Italian defence to the furnishing of ships and men for them; this status, he thought, was inferior to that of the *togati* who contributed land forces. This view has been attacked by Horn,[5] who seeks to prove that the Greek cities were on exactly the same footing as all the other *socii*. Horn is right in stating firmly that, fundamentally, the position of the Greeks was the same as that of the others: it rested on the *foedus*. But he goes too far. Whether they were originally included in the *formula togatorum* we cannot know: it is *a priori* most unlikely and no late evidence will prove it.[6] But that they did not provide troops for the army of the Confederacy, but originally, on the whole, supplied its navy instead (as Mommsen saw), must be acknowledged;[7] and the difference—based as it probably was on the

---

[1] Cf. Ch. II, pp. 36 and 41.

[2] It is not known when this term came into use, though it sounds ancient—or archaizing. It is found in the *Lex Agraria* of 111, where it is confined to the Italian allies. Cf. Mommsen, *Str.* iii. 674; Horn, op. cit. 86, n. 37; also Ch. VI, p. 143 (below).

[3] ii. 24.   [4] *Str.* iii. 676 f.   [5] Op. cit. 83 f.

[6] At a time when Italiot Greeks in the East were called 'Ρωμαῖοι (see Ch. VI, p. 152, below), it would not be surprising if they were included. But in the early third century it would have been absurd to call them 'togati'. The contempt of civilized Greeks for the toga is well brought out in Appian's story of the Roman envoys' reception at Tarentum (*Samn.* 7), the spirit of which can hardly be rejected, whatever we think of its historicity.

[7] Horn (op. cit. 85–86) cites the case of the Neapolitan *turma* (Livy, xxiii. 1,

weakness of the Italiot citizen levy—is worth noting: had Rome not wanted a navy and been unwilling to provide it herself, and had they not been naval powers, there would hardly have been any worthwhile contribution they could have made to defence.[1] In any case, as far as the land army was concerned, the *formula togatorum* was now closed.

(v) *Italia.* Yet the Greeks, as Horn stresses, were full members of the Confederacy. In fact, the name they gave to their country —'Italia'—was taken up by the Romans and soon applied to the whole Peninsula; even in the third century, it was beginning to include the territory north of the Rubicon, and the Cisalpine Gauls became 'the Gauls in Italy'. It thus came to designate the country that mustered the grand alliance united under Roman leadership.[2] The members of that alliance were welded together in sentiment by a series of wars felt to be defensive.[3]

The Roman system of alliances beyond Latium began in the fourth century, when the courageous Latin state seemed the champion of the small peoples against the aggressive Samnite Confederacy.[4] The case of the Lucani[5] shows how, right down to the final check suffered by the Samnites in 290, Roman protection against this particular enemy was invoked, at least by those to whom the Samnites remained the immediate danger. The same instance also shows the pattern of Roman policy, which had not changed since the appeal of Capua prepared the way for such great advances: Rome claims, and successfully exercises, the right to extend her alliance to any free state and to protect it against its enemies, even if the attack actually preceded the

---

7 f.). This is beside the point. Quite apart from the fact that Naples had a *foedus aequum*, which was not universal practice, we must not forget the special circumstances of the time nor ignore the difference between a militia for self-defence and the furnishing of troops to the Confederacy. Thus, e.g., the Mamertines later had to furnish troops *in praesidio et in classe* (Cic. 2*Verr.* v. 52 f.): would Horn regard this as coming under the *formula togatorum*?

[1] See *Note E*, p. 292.

[2] Cf. Klingner, *Röm. Geisteswelt*, 13 f.

[3] In spite of what has sometimes been maintained, there can be no 'aggressive' clauses in Rome's treaties: under fetial law all wars had to be defensive, at least in appearance. Rome could fight only for her own protection or that of her allies. That this claim should have been given up in Roman treaties at such an early date is unthinkable. Up to the end of the third century, the interests of the Italian allies usually were at stake in Rome's wars. On the second century, see Ch. VI (below).

[4] Cf. Afzelius, *Eroberung*, 136 f.   [5] See p. 27, n. 2 and text.

alliance. Thus the principle of fetial law which prohibited aggressive wars was overcome and the legal form was developed which later permitted the conquest of the Mediterranean without clear infringement of this principle. And thus, also, Rome was to an increasing extent to acquire the reputation of the strong protector to whom weak nations most naturally appealed in their danger. It was thus, in particular, that Rome first came into close contact with the Greek world: when Thurii was in trouble in 282, knowing by bitter experience the ineffectiveness of the Tarentines and their royal mercenaries, it decided to call in the Romans and found efficient protection.[1]

The field of Roman protection thus gradually came to include the whole of the Peninsula. In the north, she was the champion against the Gauls,[2] in the south against Pyrrhus, the foreign invader.[3] And (as had once been the case with the Latin League), although in times of peace the allies might become restive, against the common enemy the alliance proved its solidity.[4] We shall see how this field of protection spread beyond Italy—to Sicily, where the Italic Mamertines appealed for help;[5] to Illyria, where (it seems) expansion had never been intended: Italy could no longer be safe without bridgeheads beyond the seas. Through all this, the allies remained contented: there is no trouble within the Confederacy during the First Punic War (except for the revolt of Falerii, isolated and soon defeated), and the Illyrian War was brought about immediately by the allies'

---

[1] Livy, *per.* xi *fin.*; App. *Samn.* 7; *et al.*; cf. Pl. *n.h.* xxxiv. 32. On earlier Roman contacts with Magna Graecia see Hoffmann, *Rom u. d. gr. Welt*, 1–60 (too uncritical of annalistic tradition). Naples, in fact the only ally for over forty years, being wise enough not to break with Rome, was left to live her own life (cf. Hoffmann, op. cit. 35 f.). As for Tarentum, the only fact we know is the treaty about the Lacinian promontory: a *modus vivendi* based on mutual lack of interest. Hoffmann, without scrutinizing the tradition, even accepts the 'war between Rome and Cleonymus' (ibid., p. 53).

[2] This was the view, e.g., of the Picentes (Livy, x. 10, 12); and the circumstances make it quite credible. The war that led to the battle of Lake Vadimo began with the protection of Arretium (Pol. ii. 19).

[3] In this war the principle of 'no negotiation with an invader on Italian soil' first appears—an historic occasion.

[4] In the Pyrrhic invasion the older allies in central Italy remain faithful, although some of them had recently rebelled.

[5] ὁμόφυλοι, as they call themselves in Polybius (i. 10, 2); yet they were Oscan. On the Etruscans, see Göhler, *Rom*, 33 f.

demands. When the Gauls mustered their forces in 226, Italy was united in the feeling of common danger—and this same union, unbroken for many years, was to meet the more dangerous invader who appeared a few years later.[1] The Hannibalic War, with its disasters and temptations, almost broke the Confederacy. But success made it emerge stronger than ever. It was only in the second century, with Italy secure under the Roman peace, that this sense of dependence on Roman leadership, confirmed by the Hannibalic War, began to weaken: Roman views as to respective rights and duties changed under the influence of power and experience, and the allies finally came to demand a revision of their status.[2]

[1] Pol. ii. 23, 13; iii. 90, 13 f.
[2] On these developments, see Ch. VI (below).

II

ROMAN RELATIONS OUTSIDE ITALY
BEFORE THE HANNIBALIC WAR

ROME had had some contacts outside Italy from very early times: we shall notice the more important of them below; but not until the Pyrrhic War, traditionally more than two centuries after the establishment of the Republic, was she brought into close contact with extra-Italian powers. The result of this war was therefore a noticeable widening of the political horizon. A mere two generations earlier, the Latin city, concerned only with local politics in a small strip of territory enclosed by natural boundaries, had suddenly found herself a great power—soon the leading state—in the Peninsula. Now, with equal abruptness, she was plunged into the deeper stream of Mediterranean affairs, where Eastern monarchs and peoples had long been steering their rival ships. Their interest in the upstart is well known from a characteristic anecdote, almost certainly genuine. When Ptolemy Philadelphus, after sending an embassy to Rome, received a counter-embassy, he followed diplomatic custom by giving rich gifts to the envoys. The latter had no precedent to guide them, and a special decision of the Senate was called for, in order to enable them to accept. This incident[1] conspicuously refutes those who—on slight and scrappy evidence—posit extensive contacts between Rome and the East before the Pyrrhic War. Contact with the Greek cities in Italy had led to contact with Pyrrhus, and this in its turn was followed, after the final conquest of Southern Italy, by the beginning of the struggle with Carthage.

(i) *The birth of the ciuitas libera.* Rome and Carthage had been friends since the beginning of the Republic, allies since the Latin

---

[1] Reported extensively; e.g. Dion. xx. 14, 1; Zon. viii. 6, 11. Cf. also the embassy from Apollonia, after 270; perhaps not the only one from across the Adriatic, as we hear of it by mere accident (Zon. viii. 7, 3; Livy, *per.* 15). The Romans did not bother to send counter-embassies (cf. Pol. ii. 12, 7): they were not yet schooled in diplomatic courtesy. On the 'treaty with Rhodes', see Holleaux's discussion (*Rome*, 30–36).

troubles of the fourth century.[1] When Pyrrhus proved a common danger to them, they signed a further alliance against him,[2] and after his return to Greece they were free to resume their activity in their respective spheres of influence—Italy and Sicily.[3] But Rome, having no enemy as strong as Syracuse to contend with, soon overcame all resistance. At the same time she took the opportunity of demonstrating to her allies the integrity of her *fides*: a group of Campanian adventurers who had seized Rhegium was exterminated and the city returned to its Greek population:[4] Rome could protect those who trusted in her, as (e.g.) Syracuse could not;[5] for Hiero, who had just seized power there, could defeat the Mamertines and stop their raids, but not (it seemed) take their city.[6] But the Mamertines were afraid, and, knowing Syracuse inexorable after their outrage on the Messenians, they called on the Carthaginians (their allies at least since the time of Pyrrhus) for aid. The latter seized their chance and occupied the citadel. But (it appears) the Mamertines had at the same time sent to the Romans for help, surrendering the city into their *fides*.[7] The dilemma of the Romans is graphically described by Polybius. But perhaps this *locus* on the Right and the Expedient is largely the result of later reflection: to the Roman of that

[1] Literature is extensive; see all the standard works. I see no reason to reject the traditional dates (though the first, of course, may not be precise): they fit in with what we know of political conditions at the times concerned, and Polybius comments on the difference in language between the first and the second of the treaties. The second, as has often been recognized, must be a treaty of alliance in the face of (for Rome) a Latin war; we may compare Pol. iii. 24, 5 with the Aetolian treaty of Laevinus (Livy, xxvi. 24, 11; and cf. Ch. III, p. 56).

[2] Pol. iii. 25.

[3] The supposed treaty of 306 (cf., e.g., Meyer, *Kl. Schr.* ii. 363) cannot be defended against Pol. iii. 26, 3 f. While Rome, with the capture of Tarentum, completed the conquest of Southern Italy, Carthage again extended her influence in Sicily from her strongpoint of Lilybaeum (cf. De Sanctis, *Storia*, iii. 1, 91).

[4] Pol. i. 7, 10 f. The motive is given by Polybius who, whatever we think of him, was quite capable of seeing it for himself and need not be regarded as thoughtlessly copying it from his Roman source.

[5] The Mamertines were originally in the Syracusan service, as their fellows in Rhegium were in that of Rome (Pol. i. 7).

[6] The battle of Mylae, success though it was, only τὴν τῶν βαρβάρων κατέπαυσε τόλμαν (Pol. i. 9, 8). The failure to follow it up is satisfactorily explained by the difficulty of besieging Messana and by the instability of Syracusan internal affairs.

[7] This seems the most likely order of events (from Pol. i. 10 f.). It is unwise and unnecessary to abandon Polybius for the inferior sources: he had read Philinus and knew what to think of him (i. 15).

day the problem would be simpler. There was not really any ἐξ-όφθαλμος ἀλογία between their behaviour towards Rhegium and that now contemplated towards Messana. The former city had been their ally and their own *fides* demanded its restoration; the Mamertines, again, had opposed Pyrrhus and thus (apart from being Italians) had a concrete claim on Rome: there is no conflict between the two cases. For it was not for the Romans to inquire how the Mamertines had gained their city (we may doubt if Rome was sufficiently φιλάνθρωπος to do so), and Rome as yet had no special protectorate over the Greeks; if any inquiry *was* made, it probably elicited the fact that the Greek exiles from Messana had joined their Syracusan supporters in acclaiming Pyrrhus! In Roman eyes there would be no moral obstacle to the alliance with the Mamertines. If the Senate hesitated and the People did not (and the fact, reported by Polybius, need not be doubted), the explanation will simply be that the Senate would realize the risk of a war with Carthage more clearly.[1] We may ask why the Mamertines transferred their allegiance and appealed to Rome. The simplest answer is again likely to be correct: Rome and Carthage had been allies against Pyrrhus, and therefore against Syracuse; it was natural to appeal to both of them. The Mamertines, merely eager to protect themselves, were simple mercenaries who little knew what they were stirring up.

Thus the Mamertines were received *in fidem* and the alliance was voted. It was a momentous step, as it turned out; but to the Romans, at the time, it was no more than the continuation of a familiar policy. We have seen in outline—and, if tradition were more reliable, we could have shown in detail—how Roman power had expanded through Rome's readiness to protect small states against powerful neighbours. The cases of the Campanians in 343, of the Lucanians in 299, and of Thurii in 282, are among the best examples[2] and show the present technique with almost paradigmatic clearness: the hard-pressed small state appeals to Rome and (probably) puts itself in her *fides*; it is accepted as an ally, and the power attacking it is warned off; war follows, and the client state is ultimately defended and well treated after victory.

---

[1] De Sanctis (op. cit. 99) sees this, but rejecting Polybius *a priori*, he has to embody it as best he can in a topsy-turvy account. Cf. also Frank, *Rom. Imp.* 85 f.; 107.
[2] See Ch. I for discussion of these cases.

The Mamertines, if they knew fairly recent Campanian history —as they probably did—, had reason to hope for Roman help and trust it. And events at Rhegium (so far from discouraging them) might confirm them in their reliance on *fides Romana*. This is probably why they finally expelled the Carthaginian garrison and received the Romans: with their two allies in conflict, the Carthaginians seemed mysterious strangers and not so trustworthy. Perhaps they were already negotiating with Syracuse; for the treaty between the two followed with suspicious swiftness,[1] and the interests of the two civilized powers were ultimately at one against the nest of brigands.[2] It was *fides Romana* that won Messana from the Carthaginians.

Thus the First Punic War began; its course, if we but knew more of it, would show the pattern repeated and the cities of the Punic part of Sicily voluntarily joining Rome and being received by her.[3] But we cannot, and need not, follow the details: we must consider the end of the War and its consequences. There, unfortunately, our evidence is poor: one scholar[4] has even said that we cannot know anything. This, however, is an overstatement. It is true that the *Verrines*, our best source on the organization of Sicily, show us the state of affairs that was finally established by the *lex Rupilia*; but it is possible to come to one or two conclusions about the earlier times we are here studying. The most remarkable fact is that the Romans did not treat Sicily as they seem to have treated Italy. In Italy, it appears, conquered and friendly communities received *foedera*,[5] which obliged them to make specified contributions to the armed forces led by Rome. Originally there seems to have been no intention of limiting this traditional instrument of administrative policy to the Peninsula; when the Mamertines surrendered their city to the Romans, it seems that they received a treaty of such a sort: they had to supply and equip one bireme and to furnish a contingent of troops.[6]

---

[1] Pol. i. 11, 7.   [2] De Sanctis, op. cit. 97.

[3] Cf. Cic. 2*Verr*. ii. 2 f.; Pol. i. 20, 6.

[4] Ziegler in *RE*, s.v. 'Σικελία', col. 2501.   [5] Cf. Ch. I (above).

[6] Whether the *foedus* was considered *aequum* is not an important matter, once we rid ourselves of the ultra-schematic view of *foedera*. Cicero, of course, tries to make out that it was not (2*Verr*. v. 50 f.; cf. Horn, *Foed*. 39 f.). But that is special pleading. There was certainly no *maiestas* clause; else he could not have failed to mention this obvious support for his argument. The contribution of one bireme was not

Like any other city with a treaty, Messana had *ius exilii*.[1] Thus the position of the Mamertines seems to have been much like that of the cities of Southern Italy.

But the interesting fact, as we have said, is that this system was not extended in the same form to the rest of Sicily: we know of no other city in Sicily—and there were many that went over to the Romans[2]—that received a *foedus*.[3]

The other cities that joined the Romans were declared *liberae* (*et immunes*).[4] There were five such cities in Cicero's day, and there were probably more before the revolt in the Second Punic War, which must have cost many cities their privileges.[5] In modern works of scholarship the position of these cities has not found the prominence it deserves. They are ignored by scholars who make the principle of the *ciuitas libera* begin in 197 B.C.[6] Yet the concept must date back to the First Punic War: there is no way in which a faithful community like Segesta[7] could have lost its *foedus*, if it had ever had one. Though the term 'libera et immunis' may be later, the status—freedom without a treaty—must be primitive. The question is how this status arose and what it involved—a question that will be specially important when we come to discuss the 'freedom of the Greeks'.

The task of investigation is again made more difficult by the scarcity of evidence and the nature of what we have: the latter (for Sicily) deals with the state of affairs at the time of Verres; but it is only reasonable to believe that, with the development of Rome from the uneasy mistress of Sicily to the secure ruler of the Mediterranean, some changes must have occurred. In Cicero's time Sicily was administered under the *lex Rupilia*, imposed as

a *munus graue*: Locri had to furnish at least two triremes, another city (Thurii?—the reading 'Uria' is unacceptable) as many as four (Livy, xlii. 48, 7). For the troops furnished (*in praesidio et in classe*), see 2 *Verr.* v. 52 f.

[1] Horn, op. cit. 41 (based on 2 *Verr.* v. 160).   [2] Cf. p. 36, n. 3.

[3] The only other *ciuitates foederatae* in Cicero's day were Tauromenium and Netum, and they received their treaties in the Second Punic War (Diod. xxiii. 6; cf. App. *Sic.* 5). It is barely possible that some other small communities had *foedera*: it has often been pointed out that in his summary (2 *Verr.* iii. 13) Cicero omits Netum, of whose *foedus* we happen to hear in other connexions (e.g. ibid. v. 56). But this is not important for our argument.

[4] Cic. ibid. iii. 13. On *immunitas* we shall have more to say.

[5] Livy, xxv. 40, 4; xxvi. 40, 14.   [6] e.g. *RC*, 150.

[7] Cf. *RE*, s.v. 'Segesta'. Her *cognatio* assured her favourable treatment and, on the other hand, kept her faithful (Cic. ibid. v. 83).

recently as 132.[1] Of the early period we know nothing directly (perhaps largely because the relevant books of Livy are lost and Polybius was less interested in Sicily)—as we have seen, modern scholars even ignore, or at best lightly glide over, the birth of the *ciuitas libera*. When it presents itself to us, fully grown, at the Isthmian Games of 196, they tend to call it a 'first experiment' and one that Rome 'first learned from the Greeks, and then twisted . . . to her own purposes'.[2] But the *ciuitates liberae* of Sicily precede the close contacts of Rome with any of the Hellenistic kings except Pyrrhus; and there is no reason to think (if we judge by his treatment of the cities) that he proclaimed the 'freedom of Sicily'.[3] Thus, unless we want to assume a Carthaginian origin (an assumption not absurd, but unsupported), we can explain the phenomenon only in terms of Roman ideas. Nor will it do to allege that the origin may be simply the subject condition of the cities concerned, which presented no legal possibility of a bilateral treaty:[4] this is legally doubtful in both Greece and Sicily—in the latter, since we do not know the *precise* status of (say) Segesta in the Carthaginian Empire; in the former, since the sovereignty of the city was, in Hellenistic times, usually recognized *de jure*.[5] Besides, there would have been no difficulty about signing a treaty with any city *after* its freedom was recognized, and we have at least one certain example of this.[6]

The explanation must lie elsewhere. Part of it has often been stated: the fighting qualities of the Sicilian cities were not such as to make them necessary—or even desirable—allies.[7] In one way the absence of a *foedus* is a mark of Roman disdain[8]—but not wholly so. As Cicero makes clear whenever he mentions these

[1] Sources in *MRR*, i. 498. Cf. the salutary warning of Accame, *Dom. Rom.* 48.

[2] *RC*, 150.

[3] Cf., e.g., Plut. *Pyrrh.* 23. The status of cities in Hiero's kingdom—whatever it was—is not to the point: the kingdom was not annexed, and in the early days of the War, when the status of a good many cities was settled, the Senate is unlikely to have known much about its internal affairs.

[4] Thus, cautiously, *RC*, 151.

[5] Cf. Heuss, *Stadt u. Herrscher*, 180 f. and *passim*.

[6] Sherwin-White (*RC*, l.c.) admits this possibility. But, though Utica is doubtful (Cic. *Balb.* 51 may be wrong), I see no doubt about Netum, which Sherwin-White does not mention: it was in Hiero's kingdom (Diod. xxiii. 4, 1), and after the Second Punic War it became *foederata* (see p. 37, n. 3).

[7] De Sanctis, *Storia*, iii. 1, 114 f.; *RC*, 155.

[8] 'Avversarî troppo deboli per essere rispettati dai vincitori' (De Sanctis, l.c.).

cities, they were regarded as privileged; and they were indeed so, as compared with the rest of the island. Segesta subtly flattered the Romans by claiming common descent from the Trojans— a claim that would impress and gratify the victors.[1] It seems reasonable to think that Segesta might have had a treaty, if she had wanted one. Besides, we know that Rome did make some use of the armed forces of these cities—and not only in Cicero's time, but (it seems) from the beginning.[2] Contempt for the fighting strength of their new friends might be in the minds of the Romans; but it does not by itself account for the creation of the *ciuitas libera*. Was the Sicilian Greek, after all, so much more contemptible than his kinsman in the Peninsula?

It may be argued, on the contrary, that the position of 'free state', without a formal alliance with a great power, was originally a special privilege. The 'alliance' of a small state with a strong protector had long been familiar in the Greek world; and it was known to be a cloak for Empire. Examples—the Athenian confederacies; the Symmachy of the Macedonian kings—spring to mind. More recently, Sicilians had no doubt watched the fate of the cities of Southern Italy, which found that alliance meant subjection.[3] There could (one should have thought) have been no prouder and happier position for a city at the time than to be

---

[1] See p. 37, n. 7. She was rewarded with extensive grants of land (Cic. 2*Verr.* v. 125). Malten (*ARW*, 1931) maintains that the Elymaeans were the first to transmit the legend to Rome. But the coins of Segesta (Head, *H.N.*[2] 166–7) presuppose it and play on *existing* feelings. It seems probable (cf. Picard, *RA*, 1944) that in some form the legend was known in fifth-century Veii.

[2] Cic. 2*Verr.* v. 86 *et al.*; cf. Pol. i. 40, 1 (the Panhormitani are σύμμαχοι), not decisive by itself. But Horn begs the question in maintaining that 'die Waffenhilfe . . . wird in gleicher Weise [wie von den foederatae] auch von den liberae geleistet' (*Foed.* 48). Surely not, since that of the former was, precisely, *ex foedere*! The contribution of the *ciuitas libera* (and of the *rex socius et amicus*) was originally voluntary and based only on moral obligation. As late as 171, when the Romans 'hoped for' ('speratus', not 'imperatus') the whole of the Thessalians' cavalry, they in fact got only 300 men (Livy, xlii. 55, 10).

[3] It would help if we knew more about the organization of the Carthaginian Empire, not to mention that of Agathocles. The former probably rested on alliances and tribute; though nothing is definitely known except that the Carthaginians did not directly administer the cities they controlled. Cf. Meltzer, *Gesch.* ii, ch. v; for Segesta, especially, ibid. 100. (Where he believes in direct control—e.g. Heraclea— the evidence is quite inconclusive.) About Agathocles we know even less; but at one stage he certainly seems to have been the ἡγεμών of a symmachy (Diod. xix. 71, 7).

free—free from the tribute, which probably all the cities in Sicily had been paying;[1] free (as they now were, once the war was over) from foreign garrisons; free from treaties with overpowering 'allies'. It is quite likely that in the Hellenistic East the form of the Symmachy was also to some extent discredited: Heuss has noted its avoidance, which contrasts with the policy of Alexander (at least in Europe and the Islands), inherited from Philip.[2] That the Western development must have been independent (as far as we can see), we have already noticed; but politics, like science, knows discoveries made, when the time is ripe for them, simultaneously in many places, giving rise to fruitless disputes as to priority and connexion.

If we rid ourselves of all the knowledge gained *ex post facto*— if we try to avoid being blinded by the light the *Verrines* cast on the development of the *ciuitas libera*—, the conclusion is inescapable that the 'freedom' the Romans conferred on a few chosen cities must have seemed to the latter (whatever the motives of the donors) a boon beyond their dreams. Nor can we validly maintain,[3] on evidence drawn from much later times, that the freedom of these cities was originally limited and precarious: as we shall see when we come to consider the 'freedom of the Hellenes',[4] the freedom conferred by Rome was originally a freedom without definitions and limitations; we have no reason to assume that the freedom of the specially favoured Sicilian cities was inferior to that given (when Rome was already a much greater power) to the Greeks.[5]

It is obvious that this grant was not, on the part of the Romans, an act of disinterested generosity. We have already noticed that,

[1] Cf. Carcopino, *La Loi*, 50 f.

[2] *St. u. H.* 178 f.; cf. Arr. ii. 1, 4; Diod. xvii. 49, 4; Tarn, *Alexander*, ii. 202 f.

[3] 'Donate per beneplacito . . . d'una parziale autonomia, che non le francava però dalla giurisdizione di Roma e che poteva revocarsi o menomarsi ad arbitrio di chi l'aveva concessa' (De Sanctis, *Storia*, iii. 1, 196)—an extreme example. None of these statements applies to the Greeks in 196 (cf. below): why, then, to the Sicilians in or before 241 ? At the most these disabilities were embryonically present in the original grant; but that is not to say that either party foresaw the development at the time. Cf. also p. 53, with n. 2 (below). On the original extent of this freedom we now have the welcome evidence of the Coan documents (Bengtson, *Hist.* 1955).

[4] See next chapter.

[5] Statements like Frank's (*Rom. Imp.* 102), that *commercium* with Segesta had been prohibited by Rome, are quite arbitrary.

for one thing, Rome could perhaps afford to dispense her new friends from treaties, as their armies were not worth considering except for purely local defence.[1] We must also remember that Rome did not even employ the armed forces of her Greek allies in Southern Italy in the army of the Confederacy: the list of the *formula togatorum* was closed.[2] Nor had the cities concerned been strong naval powers: there is no record of their warships before the *Verrines*, while (e.g.) the Italian Greeks played an important part in the First Punic War.[3] As for what resources they had, Rome knew that, with or without a treaty, she would be able to count on them. And this brings us to the main point: Rome could afford to be generous and refrain from imposing formal obligations, because she knew that she would have a strong *moral* claim on the states concerned—and the power to remind them of it. Just as, after 338, the Latins had been left in a state of moral and practical, rather than strictly legal, dependence,[4] so the *ciuitas libera* had no legal link with Rome: much less so than the Latins, who had once been in treaty relations with her and were still vaguely haunted by the ghost of the Cassian Treaty. In this, its position is like that of the client as against his patron—and indeed, these cities had probably surrendered *in fidem populi Romani* and were free *beneficio populi Romani*—as it always to a large extent remained in Roman life: an extra-legal dependence of the weak on a strong protector, founded on gratitude, piety, reverence, and all the sacred emotions—and the patron's power to enforce them. Just as scholars of legal cast of mind and training have tried to base private *clientela* on legal claims,[5] so they have often tried to find legal bases for every kind of international dependence.[6] But Rome's international relations

---

[1] See p. 38, nn. 7 and 8 and text. The same motive can be conjectured for the similar policy of Hellenistic kings (cf. Heuss, *St. u. H.* 141 f.); but they usually wanted tribute, while Rome did not. Cf. p. 40, n. 2 and text.

[2] See Ch. I, pp. 28 ff. [3] Pol. i. 20, 14 *et al.*

[4] See Ch. I, pp. 23–24. [5] e.g. Premerstein—see Introduction, *passim*.

[6] e.g. Täubler, *Imp. Rom.* i, *passim*, limits the application of the term 'client state' to those with 'foedera iniqua'. Sherwin-White (*RC*, 162) enters an emphatic protest against this ignorance of the concept of *clientela*. Mommsen (followed by most scholars—e.g. De Sanctis, quoted p. 40, n. 3) made the mistake of trying to base the position of the *ciuitas libera* on law—incidentally of rather a dubious kind. In law the *ciuitas libera* was a free state (originally), just as the client was a free man. Beyond this stretches the penumbra of custom, and of power to enforce it.

cannot be analysed in terms of law alone: whatever their legal position, *all* states dependent on her become client states.[1] And the relation of *clientela* is essentially extra-legal.[2] If any state can, however, be called the *paradeigma* of the client state, it is the *ciuitas libera*—a state with no legal obligations at all. As we shall notice, the logical Greeks at first could not see beyond the law; in the same way, we may imagine, Centuripa and the rest must have rejoiced overmuch at their new freedom. Perhaps that partly accounts for the fact that legal dependence soon developed—though in any case (as we see in the case of private *clientela*) custom tends to harden into law.[3]

Here we must leave the *ciuitas libera* for the moment: it will occupy us more in due course. There are other third-century examples of it (and we shall turn to them soon); but its future was really in the second century and in the East. Meanwhile—as we must remember—only a handful of favoured cities received their freedom. The rest of Roman Sicily (and, later, Sardinia and Corsica) was kept in close and direct dependence, finally being organized as the first 'provinces'.[4] With that organization, and the problems it presents, we are not directly concerned. Hiero retained a modest, but wealthy, kingdom in the eastern part of the island,[5] and remained a faithful friend of Rome.[6] At the same time, while taking care not to offend his powerful friend, he discreetly pursued a foreign policy of his own, keeping up close relations with other Hellenistic states (especially Egypt) and vigorously supporting Carthage in her troubles after the First Punic War.[7] Although entirely surrounded by Roman territory

---

[1] Thus rightly Sherwin-White, *RC*, 162.

[2] See Introduction, *passim*. Sherwin-White (l.c.), in one of the most valuable passages of his book, makes the very misleading inference that, because 'clientela' is not a term of international law, it is, in the international sphere, only a metaphor. In civil life also it is for the most part outside law: it is, at home and abroad, a habit of mind and a philosophy of society.

[3] See Introduction, *passim*.

[4] Solin. 5, 1; cf. Cic. 2*Verr*. ii. 1. On the organization, see Frank, *Rom. Imp.* 95 f. There is no evidence for the view that Hiero regarded all land as his property, or for the suggestion that he had 'free cities' in his kingdom. All that we really know is his method of tax-collection. On Sardinia, see below.

[5] Diod. xxiii. 4, 1 f.: the list is not complete (cf. Livy, xxiv. 30, 2: Herbesus), but probably substantially accurate.

[6] e.g. Livy, xxii. 37, 10.

[7] Polybius (i. 83, 2 f.) comments on his motives. Sources in *RE*, s.v. 'Hieron II'.

and at the mercy of Roman arms, he did not become a mere puppet king.

The success of their venture in Sicily seems to have set the Romans, for a while, on the course of conscious imperialism; though there were probably political differences within the Senate, which alone account sufficiently for such hesitation as was shown in the case of Sardinia,[1] the expansionists finally prevailed: Rome accepted the *deditio* of the Carthaginian mercenaries in Sardinia—thereby, perhaps for the first time, violating a treaty without equitable pretext—and made the Carthaginians cede that island and Corsica.[2] The *guerrilla* with the natives lasted for generations; but, with no other great power to compete, the conquest of the islands was only a matter of time; the Romans, safe enough in the cities, did not bother to complete it, except perhaps in the lowlands.[3] But in theory the islands became a 'province', and for the present we need not take any further notice of them. No experiment in freedom was tried there, and relations of dependence were brutally undisguised.[4]

(ii) *Freedom and ingratitude.* We need not follow the wars with Ligurian and Gallic tribes that went on year after year and slowly pushed the frontiers of the Confederacy farther north:[5] nothing of interest to our inquiry emerges from them. Instead, we may turn to the next major field of operations of Roman arms and diplomacy—Illyria. For, as Sicily was destined to be the stepping-stone to the conquest of the West, so Illyria was to draw the Romans, to some extent against their will, to the conquest of the East.

Little is known of Roman relations with Greece and the East before the First Illyrian War. There are stories of early contacts; but whatever truth there may be in them, there was no permanent

---

[1] The chronology of the mercenaries' rebellion is so obscure that no certain reconstruction is possible. (Cf. De Sanctis, *Storia*, iii. 1, 398, n. 33.)

[2] Pol. i. 79; 88, 8 f. *et al.* For the treaty violated, see iii. 27, 4. The pretext will have been that Sardinia was no longer in the power of Carthage and the war in which Rome intervened was merely one between the mercenaries and the natives (cf. Pol. i. 79, 5; thus Meltzer *ap.* Täubler, *Vorgeschichte*, 21, and Meyer, *Kl. Schr.* ii. 383–4). Attempts to explain the change in Rome's attitude solely by the change of Carthaginian fortunes (thus Meyer and De Sanctis, ll.cc.) are most unconvincing. Ignorance of sufficient facts makes a proper explanation impossible.

[3] Details in De Sanctis, *Storia*, iii. 1, 283 f.

[4] Cic. *Scaur.* 44.

[5] Details in De Sanctis, l.c.

friendship or close association. We have seen[1] how the Pyrrhic War first made Eastern nations interested in the Western barbarians; but there is no sign of more than passing curiosity. Holleaux[2] has demolished—once and for all, one hopes—the extravagant theories, once fashionable, of Roman interventions in Eastern politics and Roman treaties of 'friendship' or 'alliance' with Greek monarchs and republics. Little remains of these conjectures but a state of 'friendship' with Egypt and perhaps with some other countries; a state not taken very seriously by anyone and amounting to no more than mutual awareness.[3] It was not out of relations like these that Roman intervention in the East finally developed.[4]

It arose directly out of the protectorate Rome had now assumed over Italy and her usual fear of dangerous neighbours. The states of Italy were by now firmly united under her hegemony and in practice could not defend their own interests: just as the Latins had once depended on Rome for protection against the hill-tribes, the whole of Italy now depended on her for protection against aggressors from outside. Yet Rome, as her own security increased, was already less willing to meet her moral obligations. Thus, though many complaints had been made about interference by Illyrian pirates with Italian trade, the Senate had turned a deaf ear to them.[5] It was only when a major power seemed to be developing east of the Adriatic that it decided to take action. We have seen how Rome commonly used the protection of weaker

---

[1] See p. 33.

[2] *Rome*, chs. i and ii. Nothing of importance emerges from his long argument with Walek, who attacked his views (*RPh*, 1925–6).

[3] Heuss's researches into *amicitia* (in *Völk. Grundl.*) established the conclusion, already reached by Matthaei (*CQ*, 1907), that it was normally merely a state of *de facto* diplomatic recognition established by means of embassies. Holleaux's argument against the 'letter to Seleucus' (op. cit. 46 f.) is thus destroyed: a nodding acquaintance with the Seleucids, similar to that with the Lagids, is quite possible, and Rome may well have attempted to spread the legend of her Trojan origin— recently taken up by Segesta—in the East. But the existence of *amicitiae* in this sense does not affect Holleaux's political conclusions.

[4] For Rome's lack of interest in overseas expansion, see also Thiel, *Hist.*, ch. i. The first 'Roman' of whom we hear in Greece is Λούκιος Ὀλκαῖος, on an Aetolian proxeny list about the middle of the third century (*IG*, ix. 1, 17, 51). He is quite isolated, and his name suggests Etruscan origin (cf. Schulze, *Lat. Eig.*, Index, s.vv. 'Volcei', 'Volceius', f., and 'Ulceius', f.). The city of Vulci had been defeated in 280 and the colony of Cosa founded in 273 (see Brown, *MAAR*, xx, 1951, 16 f.).

[5] Pol. ii. 8, 1 and 3; cf. Holleaux, *Rome*, 26 f., 99 f.

states as a means of furthering her own policy. It was in this way that she used the complaints of the Italians as soon as she deemed her interests to be involved east of the Adriatic, and began a preventive war against the Illyrian kingdom under Teuta.

I have tried elsewhere[1] to discuss in detail the causes and the effects of the First Illyrian War, that turning-point in Roman history to which modern historians have in general paid so little attention. It marks the first extension of Roman influence east of the Adriatic; and—what is no less important—the further development of the principle of association without treaty, the genesis of which we have noticed in Sicily. After a rapid campaign, a chain of states dependent on Rome in this elusive way was established in Illyria: the cities of Corcyra, Apollonia, Dyrrhachium (Epidamnus) and Issa, and probably the tribes of the Parthini and Atintanes, became informal friends of Rome; another 'friend', Demetrius of Pharus, was made (or soon became) *de facto* ruler of the Illyrian kingdom.[2] During the years that followed, the strongest of these friends, Demetrius, convinced of the reality of his freedom, adopted an entirely independent policy. Rome had so far taken no interest in the distant kingdom of Macedon.[3] And as it happened, the death of Demetrius II of Macedon had prevented that kingdom from taking any interest in the Roman action in Illyria. But during the following years, Antigonus Doson succeeded in again establishing Macedonian supremacy over the greater part of Greece and in renewing the old Symmachy under his leadership.[4] It was probably at this point[5] that he turned his attention to Illyria and followed in his predecessor's footsteps by making an alliance with Demetrius of Pharus. Rome did not interfere. Antigonus was not regarded as a potential enemy, and Demetrius was left free to conduct his own foreign policy. Had the Senate been interested, it would have acted (at the latest) in 222, when the Gallic danger was conjured—and when Rome could have done the king and his

---

[1] *PBSR*, 1952, 72 f., where the evidence for the present account is discussed in detail.   [2] Pol. ii. 2, 2.

[3] On its western frontiers, see Fine, *TAPA* 1932, 126 f.

[4] See *CAH*, vii. 751 f.; Beloch, *G.G.* iv². 1, 638 and 706 f.

[5] Holleaux (*Rome*, 131), basing himself on Pol. iii. 16, 2 f., puts the alliance in 226–5. But Polybius' account is not to be followed too closely. 224 is the earliest date probable.

new ally a great deal of harm. A remonstrance might have been
enough to recall Demetrius, who had seen Roman power crush
Teuta in a few weeks;[1] a word of encouragement enough to rouse
the Aetolians, who were restive under the conditions they had
accepted from Macedon[2] and with whom, a few years before,
Rome had established *amicitia*.[3] But the Senate showed no
interest in the East. It was not pursuing an anti-Macedonian
policy during these years, any more than it had before and during
the Illyrian War;[4] nor did it take any action that might have made
its Illyrian friends consider themselves 'in entire dependence
upon the Republic'.[5] In this case we can see clearly what we
deduced in the case of the 'free' Sicilian cities: Rome did nothing
to limit the freedom of her friends. Demetrius was given no
reason to fear Roman intervention.

Yet intervention finally came. With a Carthaginian War loom-
ing up in the West, the Senate suddenly realized that the eastern
flank of Italy was again insecure; Demetrius' policy had made
such progress that, as in the days of Teuta, Rome was faced with
the threat of an independent power established on the Adriatic.
In 219, on a thin pretext and without much ceremony, a Roman
army invaded Illyria and after a short struggle drove Demetrius
into exile. The situation in Illyria was re-established. There was
no extension of the Roman sphere of influence (except that
Demetrius' two main strongholds joined the list of Rome's
friends) and no action against the new king of Macedon or against
Scerdilaidas, an Illyrian dynast who had just made an alliance
with him.[6] Rome's purpose had been very limited and was fully
achieved: she had destroyed the rising power of Demetrius and
at the same time given her friends a warning as to the limitations
of their 'freedom'. The example of Demetrius, the ungrateful
client, showed them the importance of remembering Rome's
beneficia. The nature of political *clientela* was becoming clear: the

---

[1] Such a remonstrance is duly supplied (for a later date) by an annalist (Dio,
fr. 53).

[2] Cf. Pol. iv. 3.

[3] Pol. ii. 2, 4 f. On the limited importance of these embassies cf. Holleaux, *Rome*,
113 f.; but they had opened a way for future action, had any action at all been
considered.

[4] See art. cit. (p. 45, n. 1).   [5] Thus Holleaux, *CAH*, vii. 837.

[6] Pol. iv. 29, 2; cf. Holleaux, *Rome*, 142 (and n. 2).

client must not forget his station and the benefits he had received from Rome.[1]

(iii) *Fides and spheres of influence*. We must now turn our attention to those events in the West that preceded and led to the Hannibalic War. The corner-stone of Roman policy in the West, after the defeat of Carthage, was friendship with Massilia. This Greek city, the centre of Greek culture in Gaul and Spain, had been friendly with the Roman Republic for a long time.[2] Tradition reports that she helped Rome to buy her freedom from the Gauls; and it was probably the common Gallic enemy that brought them together, then or at some later time. It is known that a Roman offering to Apollo stood in the Massiliot treasury at Delphi,[3] and there are other indications of friendly intercourse. The common Carthaginian and Ligurian enemies were added to the Gauls and helped to make the friendship ever closer. If Rome had once, perhaps, been the barbarian protégée of the great Greek city, the latter soon found herself turning to Rome and her confederacy for protection of her commerce and her territory.[4] We do not know when relations culminated in a formal alliance. It has been suggested that this must have been after the First Punic War, since Carthage and Rome then fought their naval battles without Massiliot intervention. The argument has probability, but not by any means certainty: for the battles of that war were fought far from Massilia's sphere of influence and interest; and in any case, the silence of our sources is not conclusive.[5] All

---

[1] On all this, cf. art. cit. (p. 45, n. 1), especially p. 86. Polybius (iii. 16, 2) gives us (from the Roman point of view) the illuminating characterization of Demetrius of Pharus as ʿἐπιλελησμένον τῶν προγεγονότων εἰς αὐτὸν εὐεργετημάτων ὑπὸ ʿΡωμαίων'. Oost (*Rom. Pol.*) independently arrives at rather similar views on the importance of the 'freedom' of the Illyrian allies and the Greeks' difficulty in understanding the Roman concept (cf., e.g., p. 13).

[2] The evidence can be conveniently found in *RE*, s.v. 'Massalia', col. 2132.

[3] Last (*CAH*, vii. 514) accepts the traditional date, though rejecting the traditional story of the occasion, of the offering. Similarly De Sanctis, *Storia*, ii. 146 f. (with discussion). Holleaux does not mention it. Hoffmann (*Rom u. d. gr. Welt*, 129 f.) rejects it entirely. (He also gives a useful bibliography of the question.) No final decision is possible: it depends on whether we decide to believe Appian's statement (*Ital.* 8) that the base still stood at Delphi, and if so, what we believe was engraved on it.

[4] On what follows, cf. Kramer, *AJP*, 1948, 1 f. But his views on Roman internal politics are over-simplified, and he tends to presuppose Massiliot influence in far too many cases (e.g. the Ligurian wars in and after 238—p. 5).

[5] Little was known about Massilia's contribution to the victory of the Ebro in

we know is that in the Second Punic War Massilia played an important and active part and that later she had a treaty of alliance with Rome.[1] Their interests, quite apart from the fact that they had common enemies, were complementary: to Massilia, Rome was that godsend—a power without serious commercial interests; to Rome, Massilia was a centre for information about events in Gaul and Spain and (later) for supplies going there. There can be no question that Massilia helped to make Rome interested in Spain and gave warning of events there (as she probably did of Gallic movements). But the detail of Roman interest in Spain is very obscure.

That there was none before 231 is certain. In that year Rome is said to have sent an embassy to Hamilcar who was building up the new Carthaginian Empire there.[2] Whether the notice is trustworthy, we do not know. Meyer thinks it is supported by the fact that 231 was the year in which the final instalment of the war indemnity was due.[3] The connexion is not obvious; and Hamilcar's reported quip seems to exclude it. To this very dubious embassy Täubler has assigned the conclusion of a treaty with Saguntum; but this is a mere guess, supported by no evidence.[4] On the other hand, the 'argument from silence' is here very strong: could Dio *possibly* have merely said that the embassy went ἐπὶ κατασκοπῇ, if it in fact concluded the treaty that was so important in bringing about the Hannibalic War? If the embassy itself is uncertain, the conclusion of the 'treaty with Saguntum' on the occasion of it is certainly false.[5] Rome, in 231, had no clients or interests in Spain.[6]

It was only the Gallic peril that again turned Roman eyes towards the Far West: with the Gauls known to be arming against them, the Senate sent an embassy to Hasdrubal in Spain to inquire about his intentions: it succeeded in extracting from him an

the Hannibalic War before the discovery of the Sosylus fragment (most conveniently printed in Bilabel, *Kl. Hist.-fragm.*, no. 10). But Pol. iii. 95, 7 does suggest that the Hannibalic War was the first in which the two powers fought side by side.

[1] Cf. last note; Pl. *n.h.* iii. 5, 4.   [2] Dio, fr. 48; the text is corrupt.

[3] *Kl. Schr.* ii. 393, n. 2.   [4] See *Note F*, p. 292.

[5] See *Note F*, p. 292.

[6] This, if my argument is followed thus far, disposes of Kramer's attempt (op. cit.) to make the treaty the work of the 'Aemilian party', which he credits with wider views than the 'Fabian party'. Such precise 'party' differentiation, hazardous at any time, is simply fanciful at this early date, where our evidence is so poor.

assurance that he would not move armed forces across the Ebro.[1]
Whether this was in the form of a treaty has been endlessly debated. But it hardly matters. It is clear that it was a formal assurance—and one, moreover, which the Carthaginians, though they
denied that in principle the mere word of a general was binding
on the State, respected until after Rome had declared war. The
crossing of the Ebro was neither an αἰτία nor an ἀρχή of the war.[2]
Had Massilia anything to do with this treaty? She had lost all her
colonies in the southern part of Spain—indeed, it seems as if at
the time only Emporiae and the little town of Rhode were surviving, both of them well north of the Ebro.[3] These, of course,
were protected by the new treaty, and it has been suggested that,
but for Massilia's claims, Rome might have drawn her line at
the Pyrenees.[4] It is quite possible that Rome asked for the Ebro
line partly in order to satisfy the ally whose watchfulness was so
important to her. But Rome (despite Täubler) did not think in terms
of strict geopolitics: if Hasdrubal *could* be persuaded to stop at
the Ebro, there was no reason why one should let him advance to
the Pyrenees; especially as this would have given him direct contact
with the dreaded Gauls. It was not only Massilia that profited.

We now come to Rome's relations with Saguntum—a subject
as important to our study, and to the study of Roman history,
as can be found. For as Rome's 'protection' of Messana led her to
conquer Sicily, so her 'protection' of Saguntum (at the time less
effective) led her to conquer the Western Mediterranean. In the
circumstances it is a pity that we are so ill informed about the date
and nature of the first connexion. The uncertainties surrounding
Messana are clouds in the noonday sky compared with the black
night enveloping Rome's early relations with the Saguntines.

We must start with Polybius—again our only good source.
From him we learn[5] that in 220 they were in the *fides* of Rome

---

[1] Pol. ii. 13. Polybius, for one, did not think that a treaty with Saguntum was
signed in 231 (see p. 48 and cf. *Note F*, p. 292): he says that it was only Hasdrubal's (not Hamilcar's) achievements in Spain that made Rome interested (ὃν καὶ
θεωροῦντες . . . ὥρμησαν ἐπὶ τὸ πολυπραγμονεῖν τὰ κατὰ τὴν Ἰβηρίαν).

[2] See *Note G*, p. 293.

[3] De Sanctis, *Storia*, iii. 1, 412 (and n. 64); there is no reason to assume a
separate treaty with Emporiae so early.

[4] Thus Scullard, *Rom. World*, 179. Kramer (op. cit. 18) seems to follow this view.

[5] iii. 14, 9 f.; 21, 5 f.; 30, 1 f.

and had been so for some years before 'the time of Hannibal'. In evidence (σημεῖον) of this he records that the Saguntines, in a time of στάσις, had called in the Romans as arbitrators; and the latter had put to death the leaders of one faction. (But in 241, we are told—nor could we ever have doubted it—the connexion had not yet been established.) The Saguntines, alarmed by Hannibal's activity, sent frequent messengers to Rome, but in vain, until in 220 the Senate decided to send an embassy to Hannibal. Hannibal took the wind out of their sails by charging the Romans with a breach of faith in their arbitration, and at the same time sent to Carthage accusing the Saguntines of attacking a tribe under his protection. Next spring he moved against Saguntum.

That is all. The questions are obvious. Was there a formal treaty with Saguntum? Did the connexion, whatever it was, exist before the appeal for Roman arbitration—i.e. does Polybius give the appeal as a σημεῖον of an *anterior* connexion, itself admitted by the Carthaginians, or does he only mean that by admitting knowledge of the appeal to Rome they *by implication* admitted that Saguntum was in the Roman *fides*? Was the connexion established before or after the 'Ebro treaty', and how were the two related? These are only the most important questions; and perhaps no certain answer is possible to any of them. The date of the first connexion is almost beyond conjecture; 231 seems impossible, as we have tried to show; 220 is too late; perhaps between 224 and 221 (with an earlier more likely than a later date) is as near as we can get to it.[1] The Roman interest in Saguntum probably (as might have been expected) *follows* the Ebro treaty and marks an extension of Roman influence. That as such, and as likely to bring Rome into conflict with Carthage, it was not unanimously approved in the Senate is shown by the events of 219. It was probably a violation of the spirit, though not the letter,[2] of the

---

[1] See p. 48. De Sanctis (*Storia*, iii. 1, 417, n. 75) thinks that Pol. iii. 30, 1 (πρότερον τῶν κατ᾽ Ἀννίβαν καιρῶν) must mean 'before H. became commander'. But, as many scholars have taken it, it may equally well mean 'before Saguntum had these dealings with H.'; though he is perhaps right in rejecting the years when the Gallic crisis was acute.

[2] That there was no definite Roman obligation is clear from Polybius (cf. *Note G*, p. 293), though scholars both ancient and modern have tried to find one. But if you bind yourself not to go beyond a certain point, you clearly *expect* to be free within these voluntary limits.

Ebro treaty, and Saguntum is one of the series of states over which Rome assumed a protectorate in order to use them as a lever against another power.

The precise nature of the connexion can, however, be established with fair probability: it is likely that Saguntum had no formal treaty. Had the city been formally allied, there could hardly have been such hesitation about aiding her in 219. In the case of a 'free' city, Rome's obligations depended on her *fides*— and it might be debated whether this included assistance where a major war might ensue, especially since the protégé was perhaps the aggressor: 'non temere mouendam rem tantam.'[1] We shall see later that Roman *fides* did in fact sometimes permit Rome to refrain from rendering armed assistance where a treaty would have made the obligation inescapable. If there *was* a treaty providing for mutual assistance with all forces, the deliberations of 219 become inexcusable—and unintelligible: for no similar case is known. Besides, Polybius says that the city was in the *fides* of Rome, but nowhere mentions a treaty; yet his case for Rome would have been much stronger, if he had: there would have been no need for the obscure indirect argument from the σημεῖον of the Saguntine appeal for Roman arbitration,[2] if there had been an engraved treaty to point to. And Polybius had looked up the documents bearing on Rome's relations with Carthage.

The last question we asked (whether Saguntum was in Rome's *fides* before the arbitration) now loses much of its importance. It is, perhaps, likely that she was not; indeed we cannot even tell whether a formal *deditio* ever took place or whether Rome considered Saguntum in her *fides* through the mere fact of the appeal.[3] But this hardly matters: for as we have noted, the relationship entails no legal obligations; and as for the moral obligations consequent on a *beneficium* (such as the arbitration was), we know that the Saguntines fully felt them. Where both parties agree, the details of how the relationship was established are a minor matter.

Did Rome finally go to war for the sake of Saguntum? The question is as absurd as to ask whether in 1939 the Allies went to war for the sake of Poland. In each case there were obligations,

---

[1] Livy, xxi. 6, 7. Cf. *Note H*, p. 293. [2] iii. 30, 1–2.
[3] Cf. Meltzer, *Gesch*. ii, 428 f. The *beneficium* of the arbitration would certainly suffice to found a 'Treuverhältnis'.

yet in each case there was a party that wanted to minimize and ignore them; in each case war was finally forced on the power concerned by the fact that it had staked its prestige by what amounts to an ultimatum at a time when the enemy still seemed able to be persuaded—and by the still more important fact that war was seen to be ultimately inevitable.

(iv) *Retrospect.* We have come to the eve of the war that was to establish Rome's position as unchallenged mistress of the Western Mediterranean; we must therefore review the results of her warfare and diplomacy from the time when she first seriously ventured beyond the Peninsula to the day when Fabius, against his will, shook out war from the folds of his toga; and we must see what conclusions emerge for our particular inquiry.

Rome had conquered Sicily, Sardinia and Corsica in the West and had completed the conquest of Italy by subduing (for the time being) Liguria and Cisalpine Gaul. In the whole of these territories there was but one independent state of any importance —Syracuse—and that by the grace of Rome. In the East, an extended bridgehead across the Adriatic and some territory in Histria was under Roman control. In the Far West, Massilia was a firm ally, becoming more and more dependent on Rome, and points of vantage had been secured in Spain. Yet Roman territory extended over only a fraction of Italy and Sicily; and only part of the remainder of Sicily (as well as the other islands) was a 'pro-uincia'—territory over which Rome claimed control (though not yet ownership)[1] by right of conquest and which, without any niceties of theory, she felt entitled to exploit. The rest of these lands—not by any means negligible in population and resources —was in theory independent. Thus we still find Rome, as we did at the end of the last chapter, only the leader of an alliance. Yet there are significant changes.

The most noticeable of them is the increase in the power of Rome at the expense of her allies. About the turn of the century, when Rome already controlled most of Italy, *ager Romanus* had not extended much beyond Latium and Southern Etruria. By the

---

[1] See Frank, *JRS*, 1927, 141 f. As he suggests (*Rom. Imp.* 97), Rome probably did not worry very much about the legal theory underlying her actions. What the legal theory of Hiero and of the Carthaginians had been, we do not know (despite Frank, *Rom. Imp.* 93 *et al.*); this fact makes all argument pointless.

time we have now reached, it was so extensive that it can no longer be compared with that of any other single Italian state.[1] Apart from this land owned by the Roman People, there were its provinces, directly dependent upon it and bringing no public profit to the allies. It is in the period we have just surveyed that Rome's private power first becomes such that revolt against her is unthinkable. What is more, the disproportion could only increase; for any further gains must also go to the Roman People, while its allies had no hope of expansion. Besides, Rome's importance as the organizing centre had correspondingly increased. First in the case of Latium, then in the case of Italy, Rome had been the centre of a confederacy and had given union to an otherwise unorganized body of states. This function, of course, became more important with each extension of the alliance. But now the alliance, at least as a permanent *Wehrgenossenschaft*, had reached its limits; and Rome had discovered the principle of the free client state. It is the great political discovery of the period, and its consequences are manifold. For the first time (apart from the ambiguous status of the Latins) there are now states without legal obligations to Rome, but bound to her by moral obligations —and power. They stand apart from the allies proper, and their orientation is directly towards Rome. They stand outside the bonds of unity which constant companionship in arms was forging in Italy. They look down on the subject allies from their free status;[2] and they form, in a sense, Rome's private *clientela*.[3]

We have seen, in our sketch of Roman expansion, how Rome acted as the protector of the weak and often used this role to strengthen her power. This continues in the period we have discussed; but with the development of the 'free state' Rome's

[1] According to Afzelius's calculations (*Röm. Erob.* 133 f.: for 225 B.C.), about one-fifth of the Peninsula; *ager Latinus* was a further twelfth.

[2] This is best shown by the proud answer of the magistrates of Chalcis (Livy, xxxv. 46, 10: from Polybius, and probably accurate), so often misinterpreted (cf. Ch. I, p. 26, n. 3 and text): 'nullam ciuitatem se in Graecia nosse quae . . . foedere iniquo alligata quas nolit leges patiatur.' The treaty imposed by a superior power was a recognized sign of bondage, and they were free from it.

[3] It is well worth noting that there is no reason to suppose that in private law the freedom of *liberti* was precarious (cf. Introduction, pp. 3–4): there was no precedent for regarding freedom once conferred as legally revocable, and this must apply to public as to private law. That in fact the law could be circumvented is no doubt true in both spheres, though there is no clear proof of it.

E

position in this respect further improves. For she now has more freedom to decide how much protection to accord. We see in the case of Saguntum that the 'free state' has not the same security and claim for assistance as the ally with a treaty. We have also, in the case of Demetrius, an alarming lesson in the real meaning of this 'freedom': the 'free' friend of Rome is free as long as Rome does not care. When she wishes to interfere, there will be formal pretexts—and above all, there will be the charge of ingratitude, justifying extreme measures. For the interpretation of the client's obligations rests largely—as in private *clientela*—with the patron. But the full realization of this was yet to come.

III

THE PROTECTORATE OF THE HELLENES

WE left the Romans in 219, firmly established in Illyria, but with no desire for expansion. Yet half a century later, as Polybius notes, they were the acknowledged masters of the East as of the West, and by 146 the Greeks, at least in Europe, knew that the yoke (light as it generally was) could not be shaken off. It is this change—which decided the cultural history of Europe—that we must now trace.

(i) *Prelude: Praeda Populi Romani.* The Romans, busy in the West, refrained from intervening in the Social War in Greece; they did not send the few ships that might have been decisive.[1] It is sometimes said that they must have incited Scerdilaidas to revolt against Macedon in 217[2]—there is no proof, and it is not very probable. But it is certain that the Senate must have seen with some apprehension how quickly and thoroughly Philip dealt with him after the Peace of Naupactus.[3] Early in 216, Philip's new fleet of a hundred *lembi* appeared in the Adriatic; he no doubt planned to attack Scerdilaidas by sea and secure a bridgehead on the coast. But Scerdilaidas, who had informed the Romans of the building of this fleet, had prevailed on them to send ten ships from their fleet at Lilybaeum to watch the situation; when they appeared, Philip's dream was shattered.[4] Philip now turned to Hannibal; as ill luck would have it, his messenger was seized at a most awkward moment, and the Romans, learning of the treaty about to be concluded, could take counter-measures.[5] But still they were not prepared to provoke him: Laevinus with his forces was

[1] Cf. Holleaux, *Rome*, 153 f.

[2] Holleaux, *Rome*, 165 f. (strangely enough!). For the facts, see Pol. v. 95, 1 f.: he does not mention the Romans. Cf. *PBSR*, 1952, 88 f.

[3] Pol. v. 108. Cf. Holleaux, *Rome*, 167 f.

[4] Pol. v. 109 f. This has been taken as proof of an earlier Roman understanding with Scerdilaidas (e.g. Holleaux, l.c.); but when the Senate received the report that its work of 219 was undone and a potentially hostile fleet about to appear in the Straits of Hydrus, it could hardly do less than send ten ships for observation. We hear nothing of positive help to the dynast (cf. art. cit. (n. 2)).

[5] On Philip's motives and policy, see Walbank, *Philip V*, 70 f.

stationed in Italy, and it was only when the attack on Oricum and Apollonia in 214 showed that the King's purpose was fixed that they at last moved to prevent his complete success. Thus, reluctantly, they became embroiled in Greek affairs.[1]

But even then they tried to minimize their commitments. For two more years they sought no allies beyond Illyria, where Scerdilaidas and his son Pleuratus naturally joined them.[2] It was only in 212 that Laevinus, after the ground had been suitably prepared, approached the Aetolians, and only in 211 that the notorious treaty between the two powers was finally concluded; and it was not ratified in Rome for over a year.[3] The event that probably decided the Romans to take this step (apart from the dangerous deterioration of their position in Illyria) was the capture of a Syracusan envoy to Philip, perhaps hinting at some plan by which Philip was to invade Italy: the capture of Tarentum was believed to have prepared a port for him, and it seemed that strong measures would at last have to be taken to keep him occupied.[4] The treaty actually concluded shows that Rome still had no 'Hellenic policy' and wanted to keep out of entanglements: the main operative clause—probably fetched and polished up from a forgotten corner in the Roman diplomatic arsenal—provided that all towns captured in the North-West were to go to the Aetolians, the Romans retaining only the prisoners and movable booty, or a share of it.[5] This clause, as we know, shocked the

---

[1] Cf. Holleaux, *Rome*, 187 f.

[2] This appears from Livy, xxvi. 24, 9. Whether they ever had a formal alliance is very doubtful (cf. below); that they were 'verbündet und tributpflichtig' (Zippel, *Röm. Herrschaft*, 71) is clearly false.

[3] Livy, xxvi. 24; cf. xxv. 23, 8. Cf. Holleaux, *Rome*, 208 f.; Walbank, *Philip V*, 82 f. and 301 f. (adopting De Sanctis's chronology, which seems the easiest). I have discussed the delay in ratification in a forthcoming article in *Latomus*: too much has often been made of it. Klaffenbach (*Röm.-ätol. Bund.*) reaffirms his belief in 212; see now McDonald, *JRS*, 1956, 153 f., for a new analysis.

[4] Pol. viii. 26 f.; Livy, xxiv. 13, 5; xxv. 23, 8: it is clear, whatever Philip's (and Hannibal's) plans in fact were, that the Romans seemed to have every reason to fear his invading Italy and that they did fear it. (Cf. Walbank, op. cit. 81 f., and, on Illyrian events, art. cit. (p. 55, n. 2).)

[5] Livy, xxvi. 24, 8 f., especially §. 11. The treaty is discussed in all the standard works; see Walbank, op. cit. 83–84, n. 8, for references. Cf. Klaffenbach's publication and discussion of the newly-found fragment of the treaty; this raises new difficulties and cannot be discussed here: it does not affect the picture here presented. Walbank strangely misinterprets Heuss's view and rejects it; it is here accepted. I cannot see how De Sanctis (*Storia*, iii. 2, 415) and Holleaux (*Rome*, 237)

Greek world, which had left such customs behind in the development of its civilization.[1] But it amply confirms the impression gained from Roman policy as a whole and the temporary and limited nature of this alliance in particular: for not only did Rome abandon in advance any territorial claims she might win, but by her brutality she made it clear that she had no interest in winning Greek friendship; and her whole conduct of the war that followed showed her prepared to apply this clause with characteristic ruthlessness.[2]

Whether the Aetolian alliance was followed by any further treaties, we cannot discover for certain. It has been much discussed whether the states mentioned by Livy as given the option of joining the alliance[3]—Elis and Sparta (Messene must be accidentally omitted), and the kings Attalus, Pleuratus and Scerdilaidas—ever formally did so or were content to remain in a relation of informal *amicitia* with Rome.[4] For Elis we have no evidence except Pol. xviii. 42, 7, where (at the end of the Second War) she and Messene are described as σύμμαχοι of the Romans. It is unlikely that this refers to a new treaty, signed during that war.[5] But in any case, it cannot be *direct* evidence for a treaty in the First War, as this treaty would naturally come to an end with the end of that war. For Messene, however, there is more evidence: in his reply to Nabis, Flamininus describes her as 'uno atque eodem iure foederis quo et Lacedaemonem in amicitiam

can turn the promise not to make a separate peace into a 'perpetual defensive alliance'.

[1] See *Note I*, p. 293.

[2] Holleaux, op. cit. 219 f., especially 231 f.

[3] Livy, xxvi. 24, 9. Cf. Holleaux, op. cit. 211, n. 1; 213, n. 4. It is not as certain as modern commentators think that there was not a 'rex Thracum' in the same position (whether or not his name was Pleuratus, as Livy says). At any rate, on hearing of the treaty, Philip made a raid on the Thracian Maedi (Livy, xxvi. 25, 6 f.), even though this left his Greek allies open to the attack that inevitably developed. After Attalus' arrival, with the forces of the coalition mustering for a combined attack, we again find the Maedi preparing to invade Macedon (Pol. x. 41, 4).

[4] Petzold (*Eröffnung*, 15 f.) denies that they were even invited to join and does not admit more than *amicitia* with Rome for any of them. At the other extreme, Larsen (*CP*, 1937, 17 f.) tries at some length to prove that they all had treaties. It is best, with Heuss (op. cit. 39 f.), not to be dogmatic where there is so little evidence. We can only make reasonable conjectures by examining the context of Roman policy.

[5] Petzold, op. cit. 24, n. 50.

nostram acceptam'.[1] This is decisive, for Messene as for Sparta.
For the *foedus* cannot be that with the Aetolians, by which in fact
neither state entered the Roman *amicitia*.[2] But for Sparta there
is further evidence still, in the altercation between Nabis and
Flamininus: Nabis refers to a 'uetustissimum foedus', and Flamininus cannot deny it: all that he can say (misleadingly) is that it
was made with the rightful king and not with the tyrant.[3] Thus
Sparta and Messene did have treaties with Rome; and we have no
reason to doubt that Elis did too. The Illyrian kings probably
did not sign a formal alliance (as we shall see when we discuss
the Peace of Phoenice); as for Attalus, we do not know, but there
is some reason to think that he did not.[4]

Rome, as is well known, showed no relish for the war;[5] and
after 'neglecting the affairs of Greece' to such an extent that the
Aetolians were forced to accept Philip's terms, Rome herself
made peace at Phoenice in 205. It is this peace that we must
discuss next.

The terms are given in Livy (P.) xxix. 12, 13–14: the Romans
were to receive the Parthini, Dimale, and two other Illyrian
towns, but Philip might keep Atintania, if the Senate allowed it
(as it seems to have done); and several kings and cities were
adscripti to the Peace. The authenticity of the list of *adscripti* and
the implications of the treaty have been discussed *ad nauseam*;[6]

[1] Livy (P.), xxxiv. 32, 16.

[2] Livy, xxvi. 24, 9: it only gave them the option of joining. The result can certainly not be called 'amicitia iure foederis'.

[3] Livy, xxxiv. 31 f., especially 31, 4–5 and 32, 1 (the reply). Cf. Heuss, op. cit.
44 f., and Larsen, *CP*, 1935, 210 f. I have limited myself to the most important
points. Petzold's attempt to deal with the case of Sparta (op. cit. 19 f.) is very unconvincing. When Nabis talks of a 'uetustissimum foedus', I cannot understand
how the *noun* can be 'not taken literally', though it is easy to see that the *adjective*
is rhetorical; as for the 'Tatsache, daß [Flamininus] ihm das Vorhandensein eines
solchen foedus zu bestreiten vermag', Petzold is guilty of a plain equivocation:
Flamininus does not deny the existence of a treaty.

[4] On the Illyrians, see below. On Attalus, cf. Petzold, op. cit. 16, n. 24; Polybius'
reference to his co-operation as κοινοπραγία (xvi. 25, 4), in a passage where the links
are very much stressed, suggests that there was no treaty. In his review of Petzold's
book Larsen admits (*CP*, 1943, 59) that there is really no decisive evidence (retract-
ing *CP*, 1937, 17 f.).

[5] Cf. Holleaux's detailed study in *Rome*, 236 f. Balsdon (*JRS*, 1954, 31–32), arguing
on the other side, cannot deny or disprove Rome's neglect until it was too late.

[6] The most important contributions are cited by McDonald, *JRS*, 1937, 181,
and Petzold, op. cit. 12 f. To these we must now add (especially) Balsdon, art. cit.

I can only present my own views, without discussing all modern proposals in detail.

There is fairly general agreement that Athens and Ilium were inserted by Roman annalists. No one has satisfactorily defended Ilium; and whether or not Athens should be struck out does not matter much for our purpose.[1] There remain (on the Roman side) the three Greek states which—as we have just seen—had signed treaties with Rome after the Aetolians, as well as the Illyrian and Pergamene kingdoms. Sparta, Elis and Messene were inserted simply in conformity with the Aetolian treaty and (no doubt) with the similar treaties signed with those states individually. Holleaux has denied this;[2] but he has no reasons deserving of any attention. In fact, he has only two arguments: first, that the states concerned must have joined the Aetolians in their separate peace, as they could not have fought on by themselves—and this, he believes, is supported by the fact that there was no war in Peloponnese after the Aetolian peace and that in 201 the alliance of the three states with the Aetolians was still in existence; secondly, that the Roman envoys sent out in 200 B.C. (cf. below) did not call on any of those states. The latter argument has often been refuted:[3] they called mainly on allies of Philip whom they hoped to win over. The former, however, is also valueless: the fact that there was no war in Peloponnese after 206 does not prove that there was a peace treaty; nor is the continued alliance with the Aetolians of any relevance. It does, however, suggest the true answer: the Aetolians, obviously, had not deserted their Peloponnesian allies—else the alliance would not have been deemed to continue —and had duly included them (as *adscripti*) in their peace treaty; this gave them *de facto* peace and accounts for there being no further fighting. But this alone clearly did not dispense the Romans from their obligation to do the same; for it did not mean that those states, like the Aetolians, had themselves signed a peace without regard for the Romans. The three states, although out of the war, remained Rome's allies on the old terms and were duly provided for at Phoenice. Attalus and Pleuratus were added simply as *amici* of Rome: they may have had their own treaties

[1] For an attempted defence, see Balsdon, art. cit.
[2] *Rome*, 259 f.
[3] Most clearly by Larsen, *CP*, 1935, 210 f.

with Philip besides; for no details are mentioned with regard to them.[1]

What were the implications of the treaty and the position after it? Rome had no formal allies east of the Adriatic; for her alliances there had been temporary arrangements for the war. But she retained many *amicitiae*—in Illyria (where a long stretch of southern coastline was now under her control); in Peloponnese and perhaps Athens; and even in Asia—and she had acquired the hatred of the rest of the Greek world: Rome was no longer unknown, and only the future could show whether friendship or enmity would predominate. She had no definite commitments: for *amicitia*, as we saw in the case of Saguntum, was elastic. We have no right to assume that *adscriptio* in the Peace implied any Roman guarantee: it was only a public announcement that the states concerned were friends of Rome and that, if they were attacked, the aggressor would have to consider that. How elastic Rome's interpretation of her obligations towards her friends could be, was at the same time made clear to Philip by the case of Pleuratus: for it seems that although Pleuratus was an *amicus* of Rome, Philip could now retain most of the territory he had taken from him during the war. Clearly Roman *amicitia* was no guarantee except when it suited Rome. If the Saguntines had at least been posthumously defended, the Peace of Phoenice marks a new stage in Roman interpretation of moral commitments.[2]

What Rome's purpose was, in concluding this inglorious peace to end an inglorious war, we cannot discover with any certainty. Later it was believed that she meant it only as a respite, to enable her to complete the defeat of Carthage, after which war was to be resumed.[3] This is probably argument *ex post facto*, and Holleaux

---

[1] On Philip's extensive conquests in Illyria, cf. Zippel, *Röm. Herrschaft*, 69 f., as corrected by Holleaux, *Rome*, 199 f.

[2] Cf. last note. Pleuratus' treatment is fair (though it cannot be quite decisive) evidence for the view that he had no treaty, but depended on Roman *fides*. On Rome's attitude to her *amici*, as revealed by the Peace, cf. *PBSR*, 1952, 90 f.

[3] Livy, xxi. 12, 16; Zon. ix. 15, 1; Just. xxix. 4, 11; App. *Mac.* 3. Petzold (op. cit. 24) is inclined to accept this view, mainly because its ascription to the annalists' imagination (thus Holleaux, *Rome*, 284 f., followed by most scholars—for some sound modifications, see Larsen, *CP*, 1937, 28) would clash with his own notions of their tendencies.

has shown its weaknesses.[1] But he goes too far in the other direction: for, as we have seen, Rome did keep her *amici*, and she was now in control of a continuous strip of Illyrian coast such as historians commonly assign to her as early as 228. And though her will to live at peace with Philip cannot be doubted, it is clear that his 'stab in the back' had not been forgotten: the embers of suspicion remained. Moreover, there was a useful grievance against the Aetolians, who had failed to sacrifice themselves on Rome's behalf.

The events of the next few years have been obscured by the attempts of annalists to find a plausible justification for Roman bellicosity in 201/200.[2] There is mention of complaints by allies of Philip's disregard for the treaty; of Roman and Macedonian embassies about the matter; and even of actual fighting, in which Romans took part. It is difficult to determine how much of this is true and how much invention or distortion.[3] It seems, however, very probable that the Roman embassy is not imaginary and that the 'allies', on whose appeal the mission is sent and whose defence Cotta organizes 'ne ad regem deficerent',[4] are Illyrians. This, of course, is not excluded by the fact that Philip's main interests were then in the East: there is, in any case, no question of more than frontier pressure and, above all, diplomatic attempts to make Rome's 'free' friends the allies of Macedon.[5] Philip had, as he believed, learnt the lesson of Phoenice: the Romans would not defend their 'friends'.[6] It seems, indeed, that in spite of Cotta's

---

[1] Cf. last note. Balsdon (art. cit.) tries to revive the view here rejected, but does not argue his case in sufficient detail to refute Holleaux's weighty arguments.

[2] The most detailed study (to be used very cautiously) is Petzold's (op. cit.), where an attempt is made to separate the Polybian narrative from 'annalistic accretions'. His criteria are too coloured by his theories on the annalists' tendencies (quite undifferentiated); nor will it do to use 'Polybian' and 'annalistic' purely as emotive labels, without looking into the merits of each case. Cf., e.g., next note.

[3] Livy, xxx. 26, 2 f.; 42, 2 f. The contributors to *RE* (Klebs s.v. 'Aurelius' 103, Münzer s.vv. 'Mamilius' 5 and 'Terentius' 83) accept the outline of the story without discussion. Balsdon (art. cit. 35—cf. *CQ*, 1953, 162 f.) accepts it after some discussion. Cf. my notes in *PBSR*, 1952, 91. Broughton (*MRR*, i. 313 and 315) accepts the names of the envoys. Bickermann (*CP*, 1945, 143) disbelieves it entirely, but fails to account for it. (Cf. also Petzold, op. cit. 44 f.) I do not see (despite Balsdon, l.c.) that much can be done for the 'Macedonum legio'. (See now Dorey, *AJP*, lxxviii, 1957, 185 f.)

[4] Livy, xxx. 42, 5.

[5] Cf. *PBSR*, 1952, 90 f.

[6] Cf. p. 60, n. 2 and text.

efforts Philip made some progress: for among the peace terms offered by Flamininus in 197 there is the demand 'τοὺς κατὰ τὴν Ἰλλυρίδα τόπους παραδοῦναι Ῥωμαίοις, ὧν γέγονε κύριος μετὰ τὰς ἐν Ἠπείρῳ διαλύσεις'.[1] But this time, at least, in spite of their withdrawal in 205, the Romans had not lost interest in the East: they intended to make sure of their bridgehead in Illyria this time, as they had failed to do in 228 and done half-heartedly in 219.[2] We also see that this is done, not by armed force or any claim to sovereignty, but merely by sending an envoy, and with full recognition of the independence of the 'free' friends. Rome still showed due regard for their freedom: it spared her the obligation of armed assistance. The patron would advise and protect his clients; but while he did not rule them, he was bound to them only by moral obligations, the interpretation of which depended on himself.[3]

(ii) *Iniuriae in socias urbes.* We now come to the outbreak of the Second Macedonian War; and the events that led up to it are surpassed in obscurity only by its causes. The former—fortunately—do not concern us as such; at the latter we must glance before proceeding.[4]

We have seen that the Peace of Phoenice did not, as Holleaux thought, mark the end of Roman interest in Greece and the East. He has, indeed, only one main argument in support of his view: the treatment of the Aetolian embassy that came to ask for

---

[1] Pol. xviii. 1, 14 = Livy, xxxii. 33, 3. I have discussed this in *PBSR*, 1952, 91, as supporting my interpretation of the events of these few years. (Cf. Balsdon, art. cit. 35.)

[2] Philip, readier to decide than to ponder, did not notice the difference. As in the case of Demetrius of Pharus before and of so many others after him, the logical Greek mind was baffled by Roman political and moral ideas; the conflict had finally to be resolved by force of arms.

[3] On the events of 205–201, see Balsdon, art. cit. I would stress, against his scepticism, the annalists' general desire to ante-date the 'protectorate of the Hellenes', the origin and development of which I have here tried to trace. (Cf. Petzold, op. cit.—not to be lightly cast aside.) This explains how events in Illyria—and especially events affecting the Greek fringe of coastal cities there—could be transferred to 'Greece'. Balsdon admits that there is evidence for trouble in Illyria, while there is none for Greece—and little room for it.

[4] The chief work in English is the article by McDonald and Walbank in *JRS*, 1937, 180 f.; but Petzold (op. cit. 75 f. and 111 f.) has raised grave doubts about their use of Pausanias and the Cephisodorus inscription (*Hesperia*, 1936, 419 f.) and dating of the Acarnanian raid. Cf. the careful re-examination of the evidence by Balsdon, art. cit. 35 f.

Roman support, probably in 202. But, even if this embassy is historical—which is far from certain—, we know nothing about its outcome except that Rome did not help the Aetolians, probably on the grounds that the alliance no longer existed.[1] This, however, is not surprising, especially considering that Roman attention must have been concentrated on North Africa, where (before Zama) the war was not by any means decided. To involve herself, at this critical time, in a war with Philip, by the side of allies who (apart from all else) had already shown themselves unable to stand up to him, would be inexcusable folly and might well endanger the situation in Illyria which Rome was so carefully maintaining; for the Hannibalic War had strained Italian manpower to the utmost and, until the war was finished, there was no certainty that the strain would not again increase.[2] The historian knows that there was no danger: the Senate knew only the past.

Roman interest in the East was limited to securing Illyria and merely watching Greece. The Senate had wanted peace with Philip. But now Philip had shown that peace with him was dangerous: if he were allowed to continue his activities, the whole of Illyria might change its allegiance. This was the state of affairs when Rhodes and Attalus sent envoys in 201, reporting Philip's aggression in the East and his 'pact' with Antiochus. Action was quick and bellicose.[3] Galba, a 'Macedonian expert', was elected consul, and in the spring of next year a Roman embassy crossed to Greece and visited Philip's most important Greek allies, proclaiming the new Roman policy, a statement of which they finally handed to the King's general, Nicanor. They met Attalus at Athens and seem to have given him some assurances; but they had to be careful, especially as the Roman Assembly had not yet voted for war. They then stayed in Rhodes, where they were informed that this vote had at last been passed; thereupon

[1] Livy, xxxi. 29, 4; App. *Mac.* 4, 2. Cf. art. cit. (p. 56, n. 3).

[2] For the Roman manpower problem, see De Sanctis, *Storia*, iii. 2; thus in 203, with the War almost finished, Rome had 20 legions in the field (p. 540).

[3] On what follows, see McDonald–Walbank, art. cit. Except as regards Athens, I have seen no alternative to their picture of events, which is here followed. Balsdon fails to establish (or even to indicate) a satisfactory chronology (op. cit.); Lepidus at Abydus is precisely a non-senator delivering the declaration of war, as required by the first alternative in Livy, xxxi. 8, 3 f.: as he was there anyway, he was used, and there is no real mystery about it. (Rightly Walbank, art. cit. 195 f.)

they sent Lepidus (one of their members) to deliver the formal declaration of war to Philip, and proceeded to Syria and Egypt— for what purpose and with what results is uncertain, but certainly in connexion with the war about to begin. This quick decision to attack Philip need not surprise us as much as it surprises those[1] who attribute to the Fathers a complete lack of interest in the East between 205 and 201. But it is, in any case, a change and needs explaining. No one line of explanation, though, is enough. Holleaux[2] attributes it to fear of the pact between Philip and Antiochus, which the Rhodian and Pergamene envoys announced in Rome;[3] Rome, he thinks, tended to believe that all kings were the natural enemies of the Republic. Though there is little evidence for such a belief—only of anti-Roman propaganda attributing it to Rome[4]—and it is indeed absurd to imagine anything of the sort at a time when Rome was about to wage war in defence of Attalus, it is no doubt true that rumour of the pact with the remote and famed Antiochus must have made Philip seem a potential threat. But we must not overstress this: for Philip had not fared too well in his Eastern campaign,[5] and there had been little trace of any help for him from the Seleucid. Attalus and Rhodes knew this, and the Romans must have heard of it before their army crossed the Adriatic. Yet they decided to prosecute the war. Nor did they at any time fear an invasion of Italy: for no preparations (such as we shall later meet before the war with Antiochus) were made to counter such a threat. Griffith,[6] recognizing the insufficiency of this motive, has added to it Roman fear of Philip's renewed naval power. This can hardly have been very important: in 201 Rome had no interests in the Aegean, and a fleet operating there was not the sort of thing to frighten the

[1] e.g. Holleaux, Griffith, McDonald, Scullard. (See McDonald–Walbank's bibliography.)   [2] *Rome*, 320 f. (cf. *CAH*, viii. 157 f.).

[3] That this pact did not in fact exist has been very persuasively argued by Magie, in *JRS*, 1939, 32 f. It is easy, but methodologically dubious, to meet all his evidence by making more and more *ad hoc* assumptions about Philip's Macchiavellian craftiness (not a quality for which he is usually conspicuous) and the two monarchs' treacherous selfishness. Zeuxis may well have aided Philip—as far as he did so—without the existence of any pact, in order to oblige him at small cost and avoid his depredations (Pol. xvi. 1, 8; 24, 6).

[4] Pol. xxi. 9, 2 and 6 f.—we need not consider Cato's quip (Plut. *Cat. Mai.* 8, 12 f.) as political doctrine.

[5] Holleaux, *Rome*, 315 f.   [6] *CHJ*, 1935, 1 f.

Senate into war—especially as that fleet had shown its inability to master those of Rhodes and Pergamum,[1] and as it had, in any case, contained only fifty-three cataphracts even before the battle of Chios[2] and ceased to be a danger after it.[3]

These and other reasons[4] may in varying degrees have influenced the Senate—but none of them seems sufficient to justify a major war at a time when Roman manpower and economic resources needed nothing more than recovery. And we are driven to recognizing that the Illyrian situation contains a main part of the answer to our question: the Senate had tried a policy of peace with Philip and failed, and now war seemed inevitable. Besides, more irrational motives must (as so often) have played an important part. Philip had tried to stab Rome in the back when she was, he thought, on the point of defeat by Hannibal. And the Romans did not forgive their enemies, especially those whom they thought treacherous. We shall see, in the case of the Third Punic War, how the spirit of stark hatred could intervene in Roman politics, even against political interest. In the same way, we may well believe, many senators in 201 may have felt that the time for their revenge had come: Philip was in trouble in the East and had made powerful enemies; Rome had defeated her only great antagonist—it was time to pay the King back in his own coin.[5] Who were the propounders of this policy, we cannot tell with certainty. It has been suggested that Scipio was opposed to it.[6] But there is no evidence for this, and indeed it is

[1] McDonald, following Griffith, calls Philip 'the victor of Lade and Chios' (art. cit. 180); this is more flattering than Philip himself would have expected.

[2] Pol. xvi. 2, 9. Even the island of Cos could resist him (Ditt. Syll. 568–9).

[3] Its losses in the battle included 26 cataphracts (Pol. xvi. 7, 1 f.). That Polybius' Rhodian sources were guilty of exaggeration is very likely; but he knew their faults (cf. xvi. 14 f.), and if he here followed them, it was because he saw that later events showed them to be in substance (i.e. in reporting the practical elimination of Philip's fleet) correct.

[4] For some other views, see Scullard, Rom. World, 441 f.; McDonald, art. cit. 206, n. 155. Oost (Rom. Pol. 40 f. and notes) offers nothing new on this question.

[5] Philip's treacherous attack on Rome was obviously in men's minds during the Second Macedonian War. Though it is hard to penetrate later elaborations, it does seem as though his aiding Hannibal assumed, if anything, greater importance after the event (cf. Petzold, op. cit. 55 f.). On Illyria, see PBSR, 1952, 90 f.

[6] McDonald, JRS, 1938, 154 f.; Scullard, Rom. Pol. 86 f., rightly stressing the absence of Scipio's name; but it does not follow that he opposed the war. It has also been suggested that Scipio engineered the policy (Oost, Rom. Pol. 117, n. 4, and works there cited). In fact we ought to remember that between 205 and 201

not certain that he, with experience only of war and diplomacy in the West, had any set Eastern policy on his return. Galba and Tuditanus, the principal Eastern experts, supported it: Galba was made consul and sent to Greece; Tuditanus was on the mission which presented the ultimatum and visited Syria and Egypt. Cotta, the other consul, was related to M. Cotta, whom we found in Illyria: the aggressive policy, it seems, had the support of the 'Eastern lobby'. It was these men, no doubt, who knew Philip's weakness and who had discovered how the Greeks could be turned against him, especially at a time when his treachery and cruelty had already made a strong impression upon them. It was they, moreover, who knew that Illyria would only be safe when Macedon had been humbled.

The method chosen to achieve this appears in the ultimatum which the Roman mission proclaimed to the principal leagues of Greece and finally handed to Nicanor.[1] Philip was not to wage war on any Greeks and was to submit his dispute with Attalus to arbitration; only on these conditions could he live in peace with Rome. The subtlety of these conditions is greater than has sometimes been seen: for some historians have thought them brutal demands, running counter to all justice to such an extent as to ensure rejection and war.[2] But it is clear that Rome did not want war, if the same result could be achieved peacefully: it was perhaps unlikely that the terms would be accepted—for Rome had no legal *locus standi*,[3] and Philip would see their long-range implications; but if they were, so much the better. The caution of the Roman embassy at Athens is not due *entirely* to the fact that they 'had to drive two unwilling parties into conflict, the Roman people and Philip':[4] it may have been partly due to hopes of a peace with honour and advantage. For the real aim, as is seen in the peace made after the war, was to make Philip into a

(when all these events were preparing) Scipio was rather busy in the West. Nor was foreign policy necessarily on 'party lines'.

[1] Pol. xvi. 27, 2 f.

[2] Thus Holleaux, *CAH*, viii. 160: 'an intolerable provocation . . .; in plain contradiction to the facts, Philip was represented as the aggressor. . . . The destruction of all that Macedon had achieved in Greece since Philip II was in fact what the Senate demanded.' This outburst is generally followed by other historians.

[3] Of modern writers only Bickermann (*RPh*, 1935), with his theory of a 'common peace', has held the contrary. His views are generally rejected. (For a clear statement, see Petzold, op. cit. 23–24.)   [4] Scullard, *Rom. World*, 232.

client prince and (as an inevitable consequence) Greece into a protectorate.

There is nothing harsh in the request that Philip's differences with Attalus should be discussed ἐν ἴσῳ κριτηρίῳ:[1] Holleaux, and those who follow him, must not be allowed to usurp the function of the court that never sat and—without evidence—persuade us of Philip's innocence. Much—even the respective chronology of the battles of Lade and Chios—has been made to hinge on this assertion; yet, on investigation, we must suspend judgement. For all we know is that Attalus' fleet was present at Chios, but not at Lade; that Philip invaded Pergamene territory; and that Theophiliscus of Rhodes persuaded Attalus to take strong action.[2] We do not know the order of these events, and we do not know what action is referred to. We have only Philip's word against the Senate's (i.e. that of Attalus' envoys). And in any case, it is more than likely that Rhodes and Attalus could make out a *prima facie* case. The Senate's proposal, whatever the true facts, was not 'in plain contradiction' to what facts it was likely to know. Nor does the other demand go as far as has been suggested; for it only means that Philip should cease attacking Greek states. It is wildly extravagant to claim[3] that this simple demand 'by implication . . . declared unjustified all former wars waged by himself or his predecessors against Greeks, and thus denied validity to the result of their victories'. It might as easily be claimed that present-day demands that certain powers should stop their policy of aggression seek to confine the powers concerned to their frontiers of several hundred years ago. In fact there is not even the more moderate claim of the 'freedom of the Hellenes': Rome had not yet moved quite as far as that.[4]

---

[1] Pol. xvi. 27, 2 f. That his actions are called ἀδικήματα does not prejudge the issue: judgement is still to come. The word may well be due to Polybius.

[2] Ibid. 1; 2 f.; 9, 4.

[3] Holleaux, l.c. (p. 66, n. 2). That passage is a classic example of *ex post facto* misinterpretation of a document. For a reasonable view, see Aymard, *Premiers Rapports*, 278, n. 14.

[4] Petzold (op. cit. 37) not only asserts (without evidence) that this claim was then made as a definite part of Roman policy, but even specifically that it was made 'nach dem bewährten Vorbild des Polyperchon und Antigonos'. He gives no reason for believing that the Senate of 200 was guided by Hellenistic political experience, and there is (as we shall see) good reason to think that it knew very little about Eastern affairs and learnt only gradually. The method of forbidding

In fact the Roman ultimatum is only a further extension of an old Roman political idea, which we have seen at work quite often:[1] just as, originally, Rome had invented a method of evading the requirements of fetial law—that wars must be waged only in defence of one's own or of allied territory—by making alliances with, and thereby assuming 'legitimate' protection over, states actually facing attack, so now states were unilaterally taken under Roman protection without even the formality of a treaty. This is a natural consequence of the greater elasticity that Roman diplomatic categories had acquired since 264, though its practical effect was, of course, to do away with the last restrictions (except purely formal ones) which fetial law imposed upon policy. In the two generations since Roman armies first crossed the sea, the system of the Confederacy, already made less rigid by the ambiguous status of the Latins after 338, had—as we have seen —been practically abandoned as far as further expansion was concerned. Instead, there had grown up a system of informal connexion with free states, beginning in Sicily and further tested in Illyria, the elastic obligations of which fitted into the Roman habits of social thought which we know as 'clientela' and, while thus acquiring moral sanction, also fitted in well with the practical requirements of power politics. As this system was extended and became firmly established, it even transformed by its influence the earlier concept of *amicitia*—which Rome knew well, e.g. in the case of Massilia or Egypt—until the Romans could no longer imagine the co-existence of genuinely equal states: her *amici* could only be her clients.[2]

a power to make war on certain (often newly-chosen) allies of Rome is, as we have seen, thoroughly Roman. See next note.

[1] Cf. Ch. II, p. 35. Oost (op. cit. 43 and n. 25), without any discussion, denies that it could be Roman. Admitting the unlikelihood of the Fathers' studying Artaxerxes and Polyperchon, he thinks the Romans learnt it from the Aetolians in 211. But the Aetolians in 211 made no such pretence—nor (as we have seen) did the Romans. Oost also maintains (ll. cc. and *passim*) that the 'freedom of Greece' was already stipulated in the ultimatum to Philip. But he misinterprets that document and has to have recourse to an odd quibble (120, n. 24).

[2] Cf. the extremely valuable paper by Matthaei in *CQ*, 1907, 182 f. But she sees a clash only between Greek φιλία and Roman *societas* (with *foedus*) and fails to notice the growth of the new system of free (client) *amici* from Roman roots, and the transformation it brought about in the Roman idea of *amicitia*: that the latter was originally not so very different from that of the Greeks is shown by Roman practice in earlier times.

But this was still in the future. In the meantime, Rome presented her ultimatum on behalf of her new friends, the Greeks.[1] If Philip rejected it—as was likely—it meant war; and Rome was prepared and had a fair cause and good allies. If he accepted it— and, as we have seen, it was not so intolerably harsh as to preclude this—and withdrew from his new conquests, he would cease to be a danger and become dependent on Rome, though to all appearances still a powerful monarch. For his schemes of expansion in the East would have gone the way of those in the West; and to the Greeks he would be the humbled aggressor and Rome the champion—a reversal of roles which his influence even among his old Greek allies could not long survive. However, despite all this it might have been better for him to accept humiliation and wait for his chance—Rome's clash with Antiochus, and the reversal of Greek feeling, both of which he might have promoted. But he was outraged by Roman arrogance and faithlessness and decided on war.

The war thus arose from a complex of causes: principally Roman fear and Roman hatred, but also Philip's decision not to submit. Rome, though she had no legal justification for it, created a pretext by an extension of traditional practice—an extension which, though legally perhaps unwarranted, is historically quite comprehensible in the light of the development of Roman diplomatic categories since 264. And this, in the course of war, led to that important event, the 'liberation' of the Greeks.

(iii) *Patrocinium orbis Graeci.* Considering the paucity of reliable sources, we are fortunate in being able to trace fairly clearly the origins and development of the idea of 'the freedom of Greece'. At first, as we have seen, Roman ideas did not go beyond the 'protection' of Philip's recent victims: in 200 he is asked only to stop waging war on Greeks—the fact, and the manner of it, had turned Greek sentiment against him, and the

---

[1] Frank suggests (*Rom. Imp.* 146 f.) that the vague and originally non-legal term 'amici et socii' was used to veil the fact that Rome had no treaty (*societas*) with the states concerned. But the term may well be older than the second century (we have no relevant evidence): it must surely be as old as the system of the 'free' client ally. For these allies, as they did fight by the side of Rome, were 'socii' (= σύμμαχοι) in fact, while legally 'amici' (= φίλοι) having no treaty. At any rate we find the term 'socius' (= σύμμαχος) used of them later (e.g. Pol. i. 40, 1, where it probably derives from an early source).

F

request was bound to be popular. There is no thought of freeing (say) the Thessalians or the Corinthians, or even—except by diplomatic means—of detaching the Achaean League: when Lepidus, in the interview before Abydus, mentions the victims Rome is protecting,[1] they are only those of Philip's recent campaigns. Philip remembered this, and when he saw his hopes fading, tried to make peace more or less on these terms: he offered to give up all he had ever conquered and asked if that was enough.[2] But by then (198) it was not. For Flamininus, with whom he then negotiated, was the bearer of the Senate's new policy. This new policy demanded (apart from reparations) the evacuation of the whole of Greece. When Philip, at the conference on the Aous, asked what cities he was required to liberate, Flamininus began with the Thessalians. And at the conference at Nicaea, though Flamininus here may have played a double game, it is clear that Philip had no real chance of peace on any other terms: the first question the Senate later asked his envoys in Rome was whether he was willing to give up the 'fetters of Greece'.[3]

Precisely how the new policy arose, between 200 and 198, we cannot tell. It is not likely to have been Flamininus' own invention: a young man of no position, he must have had powerful backing to gain his command.[4] But he was, as it turned out, the right man for the situation, and the comparative failure of his predecessors—for when Flamininus took over, Philip still held the Aous gorge, and Rome's allies had been severely defeated and had lost interest in the war—must have made it clear to many senators that a new approach was advisable. That is probably why a talented and ambitious young man was sent out and given

[1] Pol. xvi. 34, 3 f. This disposes of Holleaux's rhetoric.

[2] Livy, xxxii. 10, 4 f.; Pol. xviii. 7, 1 f. Scullard (*Rom. World*, 240) says that at the Aous conference Philip was 'clearly ready to sacrifice much.' But in fact his sacrifice was negligible: by 198 he retained (as far as we can judge) very little of his early conquests. Philip's offers were a return to the terms of the ultimatum of Abydus in the light of the new military situation, first at the Aous and then (after it had worsened) at Nicaea.

[3] Pol. xviii. 11, 12 f.

[4] Cf. Scullard, *Rom. Pol.* 97 f. What really emerges from that discussion is that we cannot even reasonably conjecture the composition of his support. That a Patrician could, for practical purposes, be a *nouus homo* is clear enough: cf., for example, the case of M. Scaurus.

good veteran reinforcements[1] and a good propagandist policy.[2] The effect was immediate. The Aous conference served as the stage for the dramatic announcement of the policy (Flamininus was an adept at *coups de théâtre*), and the battle of the Gorge was Philip's first serious defeat. And by November of that year we find the greater part of Greece fighting by the side of the consul:[3] in particular, the Achaean League had been won over.[4] But the new policy was not only propaganda, designed to impress the Greeks: it represented solid Roman interests. For it had become clear to the Senate that the demand that Philip should give up his conquests was strategically as well as politically insufficient. The Greek allies demanded Philip's complete withdrawal from Greece, and in particular from the three 'fetters of Greece': unless Demetrias, Chalcis and Acrocorinth were given up, they could not feel secure[5]—and thus Rome learnt that, unless she too insisted on this condition, the war might turn out to have been fought in vain. It is thus likely that the new policy arose out of the lessons learnt in the course of the war. In any case, the demand that Philip should evacuate Greece was formulated by Flamininus and the Greek allies into a common platform.

But this platform was not yet the 'freedom of the Greeks': it is given by Polybius, more modestly, as ἁπάσης ἐκχωρεῖν τῆς

---

[1] Nearly 9,000 men, mostly veterans of the Spanish and African campaigns (Livy, xxxii. 8, 2; 9, 1).

[2] That the policy was the Senate's as well as his own is likely on general grounds (see text) and is made quite clear by the fate of Philip's embassy of 198–197 (Pol. xviii. 11, 12 f.). On the negotiations at Nicaea, cf. Holleaux, *RÉG*, 1923, 115 f., arguing that Flamininus may have been prepared to give up the new policy for the sake of personal advantage—not, perhaps, untrue to his character, but not a necessary assumption. See Feyel, *RÉG*, lvi, 1943, 235 f.

[3] Pol. xviii. 1, 3–4 (for the date see Walbank, *Philip V*, 321).

[4] Livy, xxxii. 19 f.; Pol. xviii. 13 f. Aymard (*Prem. Rapports*, 76 f.) shows the absence of Roman diplomatic activity in Achaea (and this no doubt holds for the rest of Greece) in the years 200 and 199, and the intense diplomatic activity that must have followed the Aous battle.

[5] Pol. xviii. 2, 6 *et al.* It is likely that the Aetolians had a great deal to do with the formulation of the new policy: the first knowledge we have of it is the demand that Philip should give up Thessaly, and the Aetolians were particularly interested in Thessaly (ibid. 3, 9 f. *et al.*). For the allies' views on the 'fetters of Greece', see Pol. xviii. 11, 4 f.—Flamininus (if not the Senate) must have been thoroughly familiar with these views by that time. Aymard (op. cit. 130, n. 59) makes the peculiar suggestion that this point was first put to the Greeks by Roman senators! For the common platform, see Pol. xviii. 9.

Ἑλλάδος.[1] This, then, is the stage Roman plans had reached by
198: in 200, Philip was to stop attacking the Greeks; now he was
to withdraw from the whole of Greece. But there was still no
mention of what was to happen to Greece after his withdrawal.
For at the time one had to take care not to offend the allies, who
were all hoping for some of the spoils: even if the Senate's mind
was made up—and nothing suggests that it was: the Senate was
not given to facing problems of organization before they arose—,
the new policy could have propaganda value only in its negative
form.[2]

It is only after the war has been won at Cynoscephalae that we
at last come to the 'freedom of the Greeks'. And again, the
implications are not yet those of the Isthmian declaration. By
now the question of organizing the territory Philip was to give up
had to be faced, especially as Antiochus was approaching Europe
with an army. And now for the first time Flamininus informed the
Aetolians that cities which had surrendered to the *fides* of Rome
would not be given up to them. The Aetolians were enraged at
what they considered deceit; but the rest of the Greeks approved:
for it was now clear to them that the 'liberated' Greek cities could
expect not to be handed over to new masters.[3] The attitude of
the Romans themselves to their conquests, however, remained in
doubt even after the Senate's commissioners arrived bearing its
decree. It began: 'All the Greeks not under Philip's rule in both
Asia and Europe are to be free and live according to their own
laws', and went on to stipulate that those under Philip's rule were
to be handed over to the Romans before the Isthmian Games,
except for (in practice) those too far distant to be occupied by the
Romans; these were to be free. It was obvious that the
Romans would permit no other masters in Greece, European
and Asiatic—the warning to Antiochus was plain, and it was

---

[1] Pol. xviii. 9, 1; cf. 1, 13; 2, 6. Livy's account of the Aous conference mentions
only the withdrawal of garrisons (xxxii. 10, 3—the word 'liberare' in ss. 4 and 7 only
means 'free from Philip's control' and is probably Livy's translation, perhaps
coloured by later events, of Polybius' ἀφεῖναι).

[2] Flamininus—no doubt in accordance with instructions—was particularly
attentive to the Aetolians as long as they were needed; cf. p. 71, n. 5, and see,
for example, Pol. xviii. 8, 9.

[3] Ibid. 38, 9 f. (Cf. now Klaffenbach, op. cit. 14 f., and McDonald, *JRS*, 1956,
91 f.) Yet even so the Senate wanted to give Oreus to Eumenes (Pol. xviii, 47, 10),
and he kept Aegina.

underlined by the request to Prusias to free Cius.[1] But it was not by any means obvious what the Romans were going to do with the cities over which they could claim rights of conquest from Philip. The Asiatic ones were declared 'free'—this was convenient for Rome, and indeed no good alternative was possible. But were they going to occupy those in Europe? The Aetolians, despite Polybius' prejudiced account, had good reason to fear it. For, as we hear, the Senate itself had not made up its mind about the 'fetters of Greece': the Greeks were now within an ace of reaping the harvest of their excessive insistence on the importance of these places. Only after a good deal of discussion did Flamininus convince the ten commissioners that for Rome they were not worth retaining: the goodwill of the Greeks (especially the Achaeans) would be a greater asset, particularly as the Aetolians were offended beyond remedy.[2] But this decision, in the meantime, was kept secret, while Flamininus staged his greatest *coup de théâtre*—it was only the proclamation at the Isthmian games that assured the Greeks that (in theory, at least) they were all to be free, and that the Romans would not assume any of the burdens and privileges of sovereignty.[3]

Much has been written about the proclamation and what it implied. Subtle webs have been spun about the difference between the Greeks declared free directly by the *Senatus consultum* and those freed by the proclamation; and Polybius, who knows no such difference, has been accused of misunderstanding it.[4] It has been said that the declaration of freedom was drawn from the Hellenistic political arsenal, and even that Rome cunningly adapted it to her purpose.[5] It cannot be denied that by 197/6 the Senate *may* have been influenced by the history of Polyperchon and Antigonus: Flamininus would certainly have known it. But I hope to have shown that the 'freedom of the Greeks' is not, as

---

[1] Pol. xviii. 44. (Probably ineffective.)

[2] Ibid. 45. McDonald (*JRS*, 1938, 155) believes that the Senate had wanted Greek autonomy right from 201 and was now changing its mind. I hope to have shown that this is not the most likely interpretation of the evidence.

[3] Pol. xviii. 46. The ultimate evacuation of the 'fetters', implied in the proclamation, must by then have been decided on (cf. Aymard, op. cit. 180 f.).

[4] Pol., l.c. (s. 15). Cf. Täubler, *Imp. Rom.* i. 437 f.; *RC*, 150 f.

[5] Täubler and Sherwin-White, ll.cc.; Jones, *Buckler Studies*, 103 f.; Scullard, *Rom. Pol.* 100 f.; and many others.

is sometimes thought, a new idea in Roman diplomacy, for which foreign origins have to be posited, but a natural development of Roman policy, due to strategic and political experience. The idea itself is thoroughly Roman: if we subtract the pomp and grandiloquence—which alone we may safely ascribe to Flamininus' knowledge of Greek history and ideas, as much as to his character—, the declaration that the Greeks were to be free does not differ from the (less spectacular) earlier decisions that Segesta or the Illyrian coast were to be free: it was a declaration of *nolle episcopari*. Nor is there any real difference between the Greeks 'originally free' and those once 'under Philip's rule'. Both groups were in the same class: free *amici* of Rome. The differences noticed by Täubler were as unknown to the Senate as to Polybius: for it sent its commissioners to 'establish firmly the freedom of the Greeks'—without distinction.[1] Thus the idea is Roman, and (as this whole account has tried to show) its application is the result of four years of fighting and diplomacy, during which we can see Roman policy gradually leading up to it. Nor was there any cunning adaptation: when the Senate declares the Greeks 'free', it really means them to be legally free—except in so far as gratitude would oblige them to respect Rome's will. The limitation turned out to be severe; but it was extra-legal. And it was the only limitation. Also, such as it was, it applied to *all* the Greeks: for they all had their freedom by a *munus populi Romani*.[2] The legal theory of those who maintain that a 'unilateral' declaration of freedom was necessarily precarious, because it could be 'unilaterally' withdrawn, is fundamentally vicious: the freedom of (say) the Thessalians could not be withdrawn by the Senate any more than that of New Zealand or India can be withdrawn by the British Parliament, which 'unilaterally' granted it. As we have seen, even the freed slave did not hold his freedom precariously. Where the Senate meant a benefit to be precarious, this had to be unequivocally stated.[3] And no one ever mentions such a provision even in the cases—e.g. those of the Sicilian cities after the *lex Rupilia*—where freedom is at its lowest and our information at its best.

---

[1] Pol. xviii. 42, 5.

[2] Cf. Livy (P.), xxxiv. 49, 11 f. The commissioners' instructions were to βεβαιοῦν τοῖς Ἕλλησι τὴν ἐλευθερίαν (Pol. xviii. 42, 5).   [3] Cf. App. *Iber.* 44, *fin.*

How Rome regarded her position with respect to her Greek friends became clear immediately. Flamininus and the commissioners went about adapting constitutions, arranging leagues, and being generally helpful. In Boeotia Flamininus even became involved in party intrigues to the extent of (perhaps unwittingly) lending help in a political assassination.[1] This instance, discreditable as it is, provides the best proof of the fact that Rome did not regard herself as sovereign and the Greeks as subjects: for if Flamininus had been able to make direct demands, the whole unsavoury business would have been unnecessary. Later again, when war is declared against Nabis, to complete the work of liberation, no one thinks of ordering the Greeks to join in it: Flamininus expounds the situation and politely asks for their decision—which can, of course, be taken for granted.[2] After the war, Roman troops are withdrawn from the fetters of Greece, and with a paternal speech Rome leaves the Greeks to their freedom. The paternal attitude is requited by the Achaeans with a splendid example of a *pium officium*: the relationship of Rome and the Greeks is settled.[3]

(iv) *Protection and power politics.* As we have seen, the decree of the Senate about Greek freedom had applied to Asia as well as to Europe. And the Roman commissioners hastened to supervise the freeing of Bargylia—probably the only one of the Asiatic cities occupied by Philip which had not yet fallen into the hands of Antiochus.[4] The Romans were afraid of Antiochus and thus— as by writing to Prusias about Cius—warned him to keep off.[5] This was made quite clear to his envoys who saw Flamininus, and also by the Roman envoys sent to him.[6] The latter suffered a severe diplomatic defeat: when they insisted that Ptolemy's possessions must be returned to him (a point, incidentally, not

---

[1] Pol. xviii. 47, 5 f.; 43, 7 f. Notice again that the fault of the Boeotian lower classes is ἀχαριστία (s. 8)—not a crime, but the client's sin towards his patron (cf. Demetrius of Pharus—Ch. II, p. 47, n. 1 and text). Cf. also Ditt. *Syll.* 674; Livy, xxxiv. 48, 2.   [2] Livy, xxxiv. 22, 4 f.; Aymard, op. cit. 198.

[3] See *Note J*, p. 294.

[4] Pol. xviii. 48, 2; 50, 1; Holleaux, op. cit. 179; 181. Thasos and other Thracian cities were also quickly freed.   [5] Pol. xviii. 39, 3 f.

[6] Ibid. 47, 1 f.; as the Romans emphatically put it: οὐδένα γὰρ ἔτι τῶν Ἑλλήνων οὔτε πολεμεῖσθαι νῦν ὑπ' οὐδενὸς οὔτε δουλεύειν οὐδενί—he was not to bring back war and royal domination to the Greek world. The conference of Lysimachia (Pol. xviii. 50, 5 f.) is treated in all the standard works.

easily reconcilable with the policy of 'freedom'), he retorted that
Ptolemy was about to become his son-in-law; as for the freedom
of the Asiatic cities, they could have it—but as his free gift, not
at the Romans' command; and if Lampsacus and Smyrna (who
had appealed to Rome) had any grievances against him, he would
submit to the arbitration of—Rhodes! The implications of this
were clear:[1] if Rome wanted war, she could begin it, but the
diplomatic advantages of a fair pretext she could not use against
him as she had against Philip. She would have to fight for the
return to Ptolemy of possessions which he had surrendered and
for the freedom of cities which Antiochus had declared free! On
these terms, she could not hope for much support or sympathy
in the Hellenistic world. Rome accepted defeat, and the matter
was not pressed. For the moment the war against Nabis kept
Roman troops in Greece, while Antiochus strengthened his position by diplomacy. But in 194, against Scipio's advice, the Senate
finally voted for evacuation.[2] To the Greeks this was to show the
Roman conception of their freedom (meant to contrast with Antiochus' practice in Asia), and to Antiochus that the Roman action in
Greece was not intended to prepare aggression against him. At
the same time, preparations were made against a possible landing
in Italy (for since Hannibal had taken refuge with the King—perhaps another motive for Rome's reluctance to plunge rashly into
war—, this seemed a possibility): colonies were planted on likely
sites on the Italian coast.[3]

Antiochus, on the strength of the Roman gesture, sent envoys
to ask for a treaty on the basis of the *status quo*. But this Rome was
not prepared to grant. She did not intend to make her diplomatic
defeat permanent. Flamininus, now the chief expert on Eastern
affairs, whose advice the Senate had followed since his consulship,
was put at the head of a committee of the House entrusted with
the negotiations. Relieved of the need to think of a wider audience,
he dropped all claims to be protecting Greek freedom. The envoys
were told frankly that if the King withdrew from Europe (i.e.
Thrace), he could have Asia to himself; if he did not, Rome

---

[1] On the legal background to Antiochus' claims, see Bickermann, *H*, 1932, 47 f.
—too legalistic (especially as regards the Roman point of view); cf. Heuss, *Völkerr.
Grundl.* 86. See now my treatment of the whole question in *CP*, 1959, 81 f.
[2] App. *Syr.* 5–6; Livy, xxxiv. 43, 3 f.   [3] Ibid. 45; cf. Frank, *Rom. Imp.* 170.

would continue to be interested in the cities of Asia. Antiochus had not expected this: his envoys had no instructions on this matter. He probably expected Rome to strike some face-saving bargain about the Greek cities, but he had no reason to believe that there would be demands in terms of pure power politics. When the envoys hedged, complaining that the King's honour was at stake in Thrace, the Roman bluntly informed them that Rome's honour was committed to defend the freedom of the Greeks, in Asia as in Europe: if Rome departed from her code of honour, the King might do likewise; if he refused, the Roman point of honour was much more honourable than his—it would be a struggle for freedom against enslavement! It is fortunate that Polybius and the Polybian tradition enable us to follow this brutal cynicism. The greatest *coup* was still to come. With deadlock certain, Flamininus reported to the House in the presence of all the Greek delegations, including those from Asia: Rome, he said, would liberate them from Antiochus, as she had liberated their cousins from Philip. Antiochus' envoys were paralysed: if they exposed the lie, they feared an immediate declaration of war, which they had no authority to precipitate. They could only entreat the Senate not to break off negotiations. Flamininus had played his hand well, and the defeat of Lysimachia was avenged.[1]

The King, however, though he did not want war, was not afraid of it. And the envoys' report on the talks in Rome must have served to embitter him. He refused to admit Rome's claim to interfere in his lawful possessions, whether in Thrace or in Asia; thus a Roman embassy sent to pursue the object of Flamininus' policy failed, probably to some extent owing to the intrigues of the only person of any consequence on the Roman side who wanted war—Eumenes.[2]

[1] Livy, xxxiv. 57, 4–59, 8. Livy (or his source) has misrepresented the facts in making Flamininus say, in his final report to the House in the presence of the Greek envoys, that Rome would liberate the Greek cities from Antiochus 'nisi decedat Europa'. This is inconceivable, but fortunately can be refuted from Livy's own account; see art. cit. (p. 76, n. 1). It is sometimes said that the Senate exploited the looseness of the term 'Hellenes' (which might, but need not, apply to Asia). But there was no looseness: the Greeks in Asia had been explicitly declared free as well (Pol. xviii. 44, 2). Roman policy has not even this defence.

[2] Livy, xxxv. 13, 4–17, 2. Antiochus may have offered slight concessions (App. *Syr.* 12).

On their return journey, the King's envoys now called at Delphi. This interest encouraged the Aetolians to foment war: they sent envoys to Antiochus, Philip, and Nabis. Only Nabis took their advice and attacked the coast towns which, in the peace of 194, Flamininus had placed under Achean protection. The Achaeans sent to Rome to inform the Senate and at the same time took up arms. Both they and the Roman squadron sent to help them—for the Senate could not ignore this challenge to its prestige—were successful; meanwhile Flamininus and other Roman envoys had come to Greece to counteract Aetolian propaganda. Flamininus also tried to prevent the Acheans from fighting Nabis before Roman support arrived; but in vain. In the end, however, their success was not decisive, for they could not take Sparta.[1]

The Roman mission was, on the whole, successful: their very presence was enough to confirm the loyalty of their allies and give the wealthy party, whom Flamininus had done his best to leave in charge in the cities, the chance to crush their opponents, who were anti-Roman;[2] though at Chalcis armed force was necessary[3]—but not Roman force. Rome scrupulously refrained from armed intervention, which would have cancelled out the effect of the policy of 194: she used her *auctoritas*, and it usually sufficed. It failed only in Aetolia and at Demetrias. The Aetolians were too incensed for negotiations and were now full of hope because of the King's promises: though Flamininus himself attended their meeting and Athenian envoys pleaded for Rome, he had no hope of success. Antiochus was invited 'to liberate Greece'.[4] At Demetrias Rome reaped the harvest of her cynical policy. A rumour had been spread that the city was to be returned to Philip as the price of assistance against Antiochus; this caused a split in the wealthy party whom Flamininus had left in power there, and he was asked to deny the report officially. The report, however, was not, perhaps, altogether unfounded: Rome was hoping for Philip's help, which was bound to be important in the war; and even if there had been no promises, it would not do to offend him with a denial. Flamininus did not deny it; instead, he

[1] Livy, xxxv. 12, 1–13, 3; 22, 1–2; 23, 4–5; 25, 1–30, 13.

[2] Ibid. 31, 1 f. On the class conflict, ibid. 34, 3. On the aristocratic sympathies of Flamininus, xxxiv. 51, 4 f.   [3] Id. xxxv. 37, 4 f.

[4] Ibid. 32, 2–33, 11. On negotiations between the League and Antiochus, and the conflicting attitudes of the two powers, see art. cit. (p. 76, n. 1).

impressed on the people their debt of gratitude for Rome's past action in freeing them—a poor argument, if they were to be enslaved again. The presence of Flamininus, invoking the gods to witness the ingratitude of the Magnesians, saved the situation for the moment; but with Aetolian help the anti-Roman party soon gained power, and Villius, sent to plead the rights of the patron again, was not admitted. It was, in fact, this revolt of Demetrias—an opportunity that might not be repeated—which decided Antiochus to land there and join the Aetolians in 'liberating Greece'.[1]

The revolt of Demetrias—one of the cities 'freed' from Philip—provides the final answer to those who talk of Roman suzerainty over those cities. If Demetrias was more bound to Rome than other cities, it was only because Philip's oppression had been harsher and the Roman *beneficium* correspondingly greater; but the charge against Demetrias was not rebellion, but ingratitude.[2]

Thus began the war waged by both sides for the 'liberation of the Greeks', with the Greeks themselves inclining now to the one, now to the other, of their liberators, according to the fortunes of war and to the parties in power. Antiochus soon lost ground: he failed to support the forces of social revolution, which might have been at his disposal, without—on the whole—winning over their opponents, who indeed had cause to be satisfied with Rome: for to them Rome's 'freedom of the Greeks' meant real freedom and security—their party firmly in power, and no unwanted outside interference in their affairs. Thus, when Antiochus added military incompetence to his diplomatic faults, no one but the Aetolians stirred a finger for him.[3] The war now breaks up into two separate parts: that with the Aetolians and that with Antiochus. Of the former we shall speak in the

[1] See my article (cited p. 76, n. 1).

[2] Livy, xxxv. 31, 4 f.; 34, 5 f.; 39, 3 f.; 43, 2 f. The *whole* of Greece, 'freed' or 'originally free', was *beneficio libertatis obnoxia* (ibid. 31, 8).

[3] For the history of the war, see Holleaux in *CAH*, viii. For the attitude of the aristocratic Greek governments the *locus classicus* is Livy, xxxv. 46, 5 f. (Chalcis). The Epirots (Pol. xx. 3, 1 f.) show the indifference of the Greeks in general: they would follow the stronger. Even the Boeotians, democratically governed and remembering the murder of Brachyllas, received the King only when his superiority seemed apparent (Livy, xxxv. 50, 5; Pol. xx. 7, 3). For the attitude of the Greeks after Thermopylae, see Livy xxxvi. 20, 1 f. *et al.* It was the only rational attitude; but it confirms the absence of any enthusiasm that might have overcome reason.

next chapter. The latter, after the Scipios' crossing into Asia, was won at Magnesia, and Antiochus was given terms which ensured his inability to harm Roman interests. These terms, already decided upon long before the battle, were later confirmed and elaborated into the final peace treaty, signed by Manlius (the Scipios' successor) and the King. It is this treaty, and the settlement of Asia consequent upon it and Manlius' campaigns, that we must now consider from the point of view of our study.[1]

The claim to be fighting for the freedom of the Greeks was completely abandoned: it had served its propagandist purpose and would not be needed again. Rome had no intention of creating in Asia a host of independent cities whose freedom her prestige might force her to protect and whose quarrels and difficulties she would have to settle. Only those cities were left free which had been either free or subject to Antiochus and had joined the Romans and kept faith with them; the others (in general) were ordered to pay tribute to Eumenes, who also received Antiochus' European possessions (including Lysimachia) and a large expanse of country. The Rhodians were given suzerainty over Lycia and Caria, in terms which later led to conflict. Antiochus was ordered to withdraw behind the Taurus, and his army and (especially) his navy were limited; he was left free to repel attacks, but was not allowed under any circumstances to attack Roman allies, or to receive exiles from, or hire mercenaries in, their territory, or to make alliances or peace treaties with them.[2]

The settlement, together with the contemporary settlement of Greece, contained the seeds of the decline of the 'free' communities

---

[1] The Scipios' terms: Pol. xxi. 14, 7 f. (Cf. 17, 3 f.) The treaty (which, despite some modern views, Polybius does not pretend to be quoting *verbatim*): Pol. xxi. 43; the preceding negotiations in Rome: ibid. 18 f.; Livy, xxxvii. 52 f.; the campaigns and settlement of Manlius: Pol. xxi. 33 f.; 41 f.; Livy, xxxviii. 12–17; 37–40, 2. The evidence of inscriptions now becomes important and abundant. (Bibliography: Holleaux in *CAH*, viii. 731–2.) Particularly important a Roman treaty with Cibyra (*OGIS*, 762), usually dated *c.* 188 and, if so, the oldest Roman treaty surviving (but in fact probably later—see below); and Roman letters to various cities (Heraclea, Colophon: Ditt. *Syll.* 618, *Riv. Fil.* 1924, 29; Delphi: *BCH*, 1930, 39).

[2] Pol. xxi. 42 f. He does not mention the class of cities fully independent before the war, perhaps because there were few. They were no doubt treated like those subject to Antiochus: thus Smyrna is mentioned together with some of that class.

in the Roman world. This aspect we shall consider in our next chapter. For the present we need only notice how it marks the climax of the Roman policy begun in 201, when the idea of defending Greek cities against the power of kings first occurred to Senatorial politicians. Within a few years, as we saw, this idea developed into the *patrocinium libertatis Graecorum*—a powerful weapon against Philip and Antiochus. It is strange that this diplomatic manœuvre has ever been ascribed to sentimentality about the Greeks and Flamininus presented as a Roman Byron.[1] For it is clear to the historian (even if perhaps to some of the Greeks it was not) that Rome and her representatives had no genuine concern for the Greeks. The precedent of permitting her friends to retain Greek cities is set at once: Eumenes retains Aegina and probably Andros, and he very nearly gets a foothold in Euboea to which he has no right at all;[2] the tyrant Nabis is maintained on his throne to be a thorn in the side of the Achaeans, who are not allowed to annex the 'maritime cities' conquered from him.[3] In Asia, too, while freedom is claimed for the Greeks, the same embassy asks for the restoration of Ptolemy's cities. Then, when the bargain proposed by Flamininus fails (owing to the King's refusal to fall in with Roman methods of power politics) and Rome's declared war aim is to free the Greeks from Antiochus 'with the same *fides* as from Philip', the final settlement shows that Roman *fides* can be very elastic: for most of the Greeks thus 'freed' are left subject to Eumenes.

Nor can we even discern 'party differences' on the issue in Rome. Scholars have written of the 'liberal policy of the Scipios', as contrasted with the 'imperialistic policy of the Senate'—or, again, of Scipionic 'realism', as contrasted with Flamininus' doctrinaire hankering after Classical Greek 'autonomy'.[4] Yet there

---

[1] Frank's chapter in *Rom. Imp.* is the stock example—though even he has to recognize that the 'sentimental' phase was extremely short.

[2] Pol. xviii. 47, 10; Larsen, *CP*, 1937, 17.

[3] Aymard's defence of this part of Flamininus' policy is very feeble (op. cit. 251 f.): we have no evidence whatever of any anti-Achaean feeling or Spartiate nationalism in these towns and it is useless paradox to suggest that, if they had been attached to the League, it could not have guarded them as securely. To leave them fully independent (op. cit. 254, n. 20) was impossible, as they would have become a battlefield and given rise to continual disorder. Flamininus did achieve order (Rome's chief aim) with the minimum of Achaean aggrandisement.

[4] De Sanctis, *Storia*, iv. 1, 206 f.; McDonald, *JRS*, 1938, 153 f.

is no good reason for believing that such opposition as there was between the Scipios and the Senate majority was due to differences on foreign policy: the spirit of the Scipios' armistice terms is the same as that of the Senate's peace treaty.[1] And what we know of Scipio Africanus and Flamininus does not point to any fundamental difference: we have Scipio's letter to Prusias and Flamininus' Isthmian proclamation—but also Scipio's letter giving freedom to Heraclea and Flamininus' efforts to preserve Nabis. What we know of Flamininus—his attitude to the Achaean League, whose expansion he controlled and restricted; his Boeotian intrigues and settlement of constitutions; his tortuous policy towards Nabis; his treatment of the Aetolians; finally his cynical bargaining with Antiochus' envoys—all this does not add up to the picture of a doctrinaire phil-Hellene. Yet for no one have such principles been more persistently claimed, both in antiquity and in modern times—mainly because, in his own day, there was no one who successfully challenged his motives.

There is no change in Roman motives—only a shift of emphasis in Roman methods. The 'freedom of Greece' was a piece of (by that time) traditional Roman diplomacy. Rome had (partly by accident) discovered the value of the 'free' friend, especially in the cases of Saguntum and the Illyrians: he acted as a centre for gathering information and also as an outpost and a shock-absorber; if he was attacked, Rome was in the pleasant position of being able to decide whether and when to assist him—Saguntum had not been helped till it was too late and the Illyrians not at all (except by means of an envoy), and little attention had been paid to the Illyrian kings at Phoenice. Thus this policy of solid advantages combined with elastic liabilities was now applied to the Greeks, with a propagandist twist to suit their traditions. It was soon found (if it had not, indeed, always been known) that it could not be extended to Asia; and so the Romans, demanding a concession from Antiochus in return for their not occupying European Greece, fell back on another diplomatic category they

---

[1] Against De Sanctis (l.c.) we must remember that Polybius' account of the Scipios' terms is incomplete, and that it was common for the final terms to be harsher in detail. It is not true that the Senate's terms left the Seleucids unable to defend themselves: for a fair account, see Holleaux, *CAH*, viii. 233 f. Nor should we ascribe geographical vagueness to sinister motives: Roman ideas of geography were not precise.

knew well: the demarcation line. This again is often described as a Hellenistic and un-Roman concept; yet Rome had been practising it for centuries: ever since the first treaty with Carthage the demarcation line—against Tarentum, against Pyrrhus (who was requested to leave Italy), against Hasdrubal—had been a stock device of Roman diplomacy. Now the Senate demanded that, as Hasdrubal had once undertaken to remain beyond the Ebro, so Antiochus should undertake to remain beyond the Hellespont. This would have given Rome security. The Hellespont, like the Ebro, was a perfect 'natural' demarcation line—not in the sense that it was easy to defend, but in that any violation would be patent and undeniable. An arbitrary line through Thrace, wherever drawn, would not have offered this advantage —and Philip's intrigues after the Peace of Phoenice[1] had warned the Senate of the danger of such lines.

Antiochus rejected these terms, and the resulting war showed the Senate that the traditional policy of the small 'free' allies was not enough, especially if these allies were politically conscious Greeks: they would not always be satisfied with the position of Saguntum and the Illyrians, and even at the best they would, in case of conflict, be content to become *praemia uictoris*. Thus the method was adapted, perhaps under the influence of experience gained in the Hannibalic War,[2] and beyond the free states of European Greece there was created the great free kingdom of the Attalids, combining for Rome the known advantages of the 'free' friend with the new advantages of strength sufficient to be of independent military value, but not sufficient to be able to cut itself loose entirely from the Roman connexion. Roman diplomacy had learnt its lessons well. It was twenty years before this new policy failed.

[1] See pp. 61–62.

[2] This has often been recognized, but the policy then tends to be ascribed to P. Scipio personally—rather perversely, as he himself (*ap.* Pol. xxi. 11, 3 f.) does not confine his examples to his own actions, and as he, of course, so far from dictating the settlement of Asia, was not even allowed to sign the peace treaty.

IV

PROTECTORATE TO DOMINATION

(i) *Greece and Macedon down to the Third Macedonian War.* We left the Aetolian War[1] after the battle of Thermopylae, in order to follow events in Asia. Meanwhile the Aetolians were bravely resisting, though attacked by both Roman and Macedonian forces. Rome tried to fit them into the scheme of her Greek arrangements: successive commanders, as well as the Senate, demanded *deditio*, and the consul Glabrio (in a famous scene—not, as is sometimes thought, a wanton display of arrogance) made it clear to them that this involved complete abandonment of legal rights. There is not much doubt that, had they agreed to this, Rome would have left them 'free' like the rest of the Greeks—what else was there to do? But they were too proud to agree, and too conscious of their past insults to Rome to trust her *fides*. One might even argue, after the treatment they had received from Flamininus, that they did not think highly of Rome's good faith. Twice a truce was arranged, but the Aetolians did not obtain a tolerable peace; Rome, however, gained time for her war in the East. Finally Fulvius gave them peace on condition that they should pay a reasonable indemnity and 'have the same friends and enemies' as the Roman People, and also give up Cephallenia and all the cities they had lost and never attempt any expansion. It is doubtful whether the consul had instructions to do this—it looks as though he acted on his own responsibility (doing what was sensible from the point of view of the state and would give him the distinction of finishing the war) and trusted to his supporters in the Senate to secure ratification.[2] In any case, the treaty

---

[1] See Holleaux in *CAH*, viii. 216 f.; 226 f. Sources: Pol. xx. 9 f. (the *deditio* to Glabrio); xxi. 2 f. and 25 f.; Livy (P.), xxxvi. 22–35 (Flamininus' intervention: 34–35); xxxvii. 1, 1–6; 4, 6–7, 7; 49; xxxviii. 1–11. The Senate's alternative was not very seriously meant: a fine of 1,000 talents was added, which the Aetolians clearly would not be able to raise (Pol. xxi. 5, 3). Scipio made it as clear as he could that, if they did surrender to his *fides*, they would be well treated (ibid. 4, 10). Formal guarantees were, of course, not admitted by the nature of *deditio* (cf. Heuss, *Völk. Grundl.* 60 f.). Cf. Piganiol, *RIDA*, 1950, 339 f.

[2] This is suggested by the complicated negotiations both in his camp and at

was ratified more or less on his terms: the only noteworthy addition was the clause (which we here meet for the first time, but which was destined to become a familiar instrument in Roman treaty-making) that the Aetolians should faithfully observe the power and empire of Rome.[1] Its purpose, as Täubler saw,[2] was to establish a legalized *clientela*.

At the time the new clause aroused no comment: neither Polybius nor (it seems) the Aetolians display any interest—any consciousness of the fact that, as modern scholars unanimously believe, the whole nature of the treaty had been radically changed from an 'equal' to an 'unequal' one. For the Senate also, we may imagine, the chief operative clauses were that the Aetolians should have the same friends and enemies as Rome and that they should pay an indemnity: on these clauses the Fathers had insisted from the start, and it was these that reduced the League to real dependence. Yet it is interesting to investigate the background of that clause, which was to attain such importance.

We have seen that it was Roman policy to leave the Greeks attached to Rome by the moral bonds which, to the Roman mind, constituted the obligation of the client towards the patron. The Greeks, on the whole, were well satisfied to be left free and, if they noticed their dependence, did not greatly care. But there were two exceptions to this: the two powerful leagues of the Aetolians and the Achaeans—the only Greek states of the mainland which had played an important part in Eastern power politics. The Aetolians had always proved troublesome to Rome: they seemed quite incapable of pious clientship. First, they had (in the official Roman view) shown 'ingratitude' as early as the First War with Philip, when they made peace on their own; later they had requited Roman benefits to Greece by calling in Antiochus;

Rome. The great speech of Damis (?) probably produced a genuine effect upon a Senate not yet surfeited with Greek oratory (Pol. xxi. 31 f.). On Fulvius' *factio* in the Senate, see Scullard, *Rom. Pol.* 135 f.: he always took full advantage of his legal rights and got away with it—cf. Livy, xxxvii. 47, 7, with Scullard's discussion (l.c.); xxxviii. 35, 1; xxxix. 4–5.

[1] Pol. xxi. 32, 2. What precise Latin phrase he is translating we cannot tell. Livy, in his retranslation, has 'imperium maiestatemque p.R. . . . conseruato'. This is the famous '*maiestas* clause', which Täubler and his followers think characteristic of a *foedus iniquum*. I have treated this matter in Ch. I. Cf. *JRS*, 1952, 76 f.

[2] *Imp. Rom.* i. 62 f. He is wrong in making this the only form of international *clientela*, or indeed proper *clientela* at all.

and, if they had what to them—as perhaps to us—seemed good reason for these steps, the Senate could hardly be expected to see it. Moreover, they would insist on their treaty rights, without submitting to Roman guidance,[1] and—correspondingly—they went to extreme lengths to secure formal guarantees, not showing any wish to trust Roman *fides*. The intangible links of moral obligations—that reverence of the weaker for the stronger, which was the essence of *clientela*—were quite alien to this proud and embittered people. The Achaeans,[2] too, though they had for some time been meek and dutiful, had always desired the formal guarantees of a treaty. For many years, it appears, the Senate hesitated; for it would not commit itself to definite obligations.[3] But at length (probably early in 191, when the Achaeans had shown, by the decree passed in declaring war on Antiochus, that they were content with their position of clients) it yielded to their requests and gave them a treaty *aequo iure*. But the Achaeans misunderstood this new *beneficium*. Led by Philopoemen, they proceeded to consider themselves henceforth the equals of Rome and showed no obedience to Roman advice and admonition. This probably helps to explain why the Senate, having had bad experiences with formal treaties, insisted on an Aetolian *deditio* and persisted in offering a treaty—and a most unfavourable treaty at that—only on conditions the Aetolians could not fulfil.

But the war, as Fulvius no doubt saw, had to be ended and the Aetolians somehow converted into dependents. For, besides the physical difficulties of prolonged *guerrilla* and siege warfare, the final annihilation of the League was politically impossible: direct annexation, with its reverberations throughout Greece and its difficulties of administration not even (in this case) compensated by any material rewards, the Romans would not even consider; and the alternative was to leave the field to Philip, who, as Flamininus knew, was only too willing to step in. The solution —discovered by the Senate, it seems, only in the debate on the ratification of Fulvius' treaty—was to give the Aetolians the treaty they insisted on, but insert a clause trying to express in

---

[1] Thus they had considered the treaty of 211 to be still in force when the Romans (exploiting the misunderstanding) called on them for renewed assistance, and they made full claims under it (cf. last chapter).

[2] On their policy and attitude, see the masterly study by Aymard (*Prem. Rapp.*).

[3] On this, see *JRS*, 1952, 76 f.

pseudo-legal terminology that obligation of clientship which they would not otherwise recognize: that was the '*maiestas* clause', preserving all the convenient vagueness of the extra-legal bond. Thus the Aetolians were fitted into the pattern and the 'free' Greeks shown their unwritten duty. As we have seen, the new diplomatic instrument thus created was to make history.

At the same time the meaning of *libertas* was entering upon a radical transformation. As we saw in the case of the Illyrians and that of the Greeks freed from Philip,[1] the Romans' conception of the freedom of their client states had involved a voluntary moral subordination of those states, based on gratitude and *pietas*, but had not known any legal restriction of that freedom. In Roman eyes such restrictions would have been impossible, for a state (like a man) either was or was not free—it could, if free, be bound by contract (like the Italian *socii*) or attached by moral bonds (like the free 'allies' without treaties), but its freedom as such was indivisible and unconditional. But the Greek concepts of αὐτονομία and ἐλευθερία had long passed beyond this simple stage: bandied about as political catchwords ever since the fifth century, they had markedly deteriorated with use; by now, their meaning was worn down to something like 'local autonomy', though careful kings would preserve polite fictions in their dealings with cities. This kind of 'freedom' was quite reconcilable with garrisons, tribute, and what would normally seem multiple signs of domination.[2] The Romans had probably first met this strange conception of freedom during (and particularly at the end of) the Second Macedonian War. In the Senate's decree brought by the commissioners in 196, the Greeks in Asia and Europe (excluding as yet those in Philip's power) were simply proclaimed 'free'; but in the Isthmian proclamation, composed in Greek for a Greek audience in familiar Hellenistic terminology, the Greeks once in Philip's power are proclaimed 'free, free from garrisons, free

---

[1] Chapters II and III above. We must repeat the point that for Sicily, where the *ciuitas libera* was born, most of our information comes from the *Verrines* and cannot be used as evidence for the third and early second century. Yet some scholars make no distinctions and notice no evolution. Statements like Henze's (*Civ. Lib.* 1), that *libertas* was always 'certis legibus circumscripta' are quite false for early times. (See also Jones, *Greek City*, 118 f. and 321, n. 45.)

[2] On the two Greek concepts, as used in Hellenistic times, see Jones's essay in *Buckler Studies* and Heuss's careful study in *St. u. Herrscher*.

from tribute'. Then, if not before, Flamininus must have learnt that the first simple term did not *ipso facto* include the others. But the lesson had no immediate consequences.[1]

Throughout the war that followed, Rome never thought of limiting freedom by decree. Thus in the Scipios' letter to Heraclea-by-Latmus we have the old policy clearly expressed: συγχωροῦμεν δὲ ὑμῖν τὴν . . . ἐλευθερίαν καθότι καὶ ταῖς ἄλλαις πόλεσιν ὅσαι ἡμῖν τὴν ἐπιτροπὴν ἔδωκαν.[2] In Europe, too, the consul Glabrio writes to the Delphians promising to see to it that they should get αὐτονομία:[3] he had no doubt said 'libertas'.

The beginning of the change may with some confidence be assigned to 190/189 B.C., when the Senate had to resettle European Greece and settle Asia, and Rome was full of embassies from the states concerned. The Senate knew very little about Asia—it had frankly called on Eumenes for expert advice to assist it in the settlement.[4] It was probably now that the majority of the *Patres* were first made aware of the fact that ἐλευθερία and αὐτονομία in Asia (and to some extent among the European Greeks) had a very different meaning: there had been 'free' cities that paid tribute to Antiochus! The acquaintance with this conception of freedom was no doubt improved by Manlius' and the commissioners' long and thorough work in Asia. For the first time a Roman document takes notice of 'free' cities that pay tribute, and in Europe for the first time (as far as we know) a people (the Delphians) is—at its own request—proclaimed *liber et immunis*.[5] The innovation is significant; and although for the moment there is no Roman attempt to dissociate *libertas* and

[1] The *SC* is summarized in Pol. xviii. 44, 2 f. The use of ἐλευθέρους (= 'liberos') simply is confirmed by later evidence as to spontaneous Roman usage (cf. below). The proclamation (ibid. 46, 5 f.) has 'ἐλευθέρους ἀφρουρήτους ἀφορολογήτους νόμοις χρωμένους τοῖς πατρίοις'; for Roman acquaintance with the Hellenistic diplomatic style, cf. the *asylia* decree for Teos (Ditt. *Syll.* 601).

[2] Ditt. *Syll.* 618, 9 f.—a better text by Holleaux in *RFIC*, 1924, 39 f.

[3] *BCH*, 1932, 3 (l. 10—there is no possibility of expansion or definition).

[4] On the settlement, see Ch. III, p. 80, n. 1; Eumenes as expert adviser: Pol. xxi. 18, 9.

[5] For the Asian commission's final settlement, see Pol. xxi. 46, 2 f. (the wording is based on the document). For Delphi (given ἐλευθερία καὶ ἀνεισφορία at its *own request*) the documents are conveniently reproduced by Holleaux, *BCH*, 1930, 39: the date, as he shows, is after April 189, i.e. after the long and difficult business of Asia had been settled; with both the consuls in their provinces, the praetor would preside over the Senate and communicate its decision.

immunitas and thus follow the Hellenistic kings, the possibility of this dissociation is henceforth present. And it is not long before we see an indirect effect of this deterioration in the concept of *libertas*: when, in 187, the Ambraciots are again given their freedom, the Senate for the first time adds a condition: 'portoria quae uellent . . . caperent, dum eorum immunes Romani ac socii nominis Latini essent.'[1]

It is not our task to engage in a detailed study of events in Greece in the two decades following the settlement. It is a story of local feuds and appeals to Rome, followed (as far as we know) by a tolerable compromise and uneasy peace. Nor is our evidence sufficient to make a thorough study possible—Polybius and his tradition give us practically nothing beyond the concerns of Achaea and Macedon; and there is little other evidence. We cannot clearly distinguish the motives of Roman foreign policy, nor the men who advocated different courses of action. From what evidence we have, it seems that the Senate was out to affirm and insist upon Rome's claims to keep a friendly eye on Greece— to send commissions for inspection and investigation and pass decrees calling on the Greeks to follow certain courses—, but unwilling to threaten force where the Greeks took their freedom literally; and it seems, moreover, that there were no 'party differences' over Eastern policy. It is sometimes asserted that Roman policy hardened (for a short time) after 185, and this has been ascribed to the influence of Cato which then ousted that of the Scipios.[2] There is no evidence for such a view; before and after 185 there is the same mixture of officious haughtiness and unwillingness to use force against those embittered by it: before and after, there is the unedifying record of the Roman noble's ineptitude at diplomacy. Thus Fulvius tries to tell the Achaeans where they should hold their assemblies, and to be vocal but non-committal over the Spartan question; Metellus wants to appeal to a general meeting of the Achaean League against a

---

[1] Livy, xxxviii. 44, 4. Whether such a condition henceforth appeared in other declarations of *libertas*, we do not know. (*FIRA*, 11, ll. 31 f., suggests that some similar clause may have.) Scullard (*Rom. World*, 346–7) strangely speaks of a 'treaty' between Rome and Ambracia.

[2] Frank, *Rom. Imp.* 190 f., followed by Scullard (l.c.), who, however, ascribes the 'sudden stiffening' to the 'middle group'. This shows the uncertainty of such speculations.

decision of the Achaean *principes* and is deeply offended when this is not permitted; Appius finally loses his temper and threatens force,[1] as is only to be expected in a member of that *gens*—but there is no fundamental change in attitude, and his blustering has no more consequences than the sulking of Metellus. Nor need we think Cato (or, for that matter, the 'middle group') responsible for the tone adopted by a Claudian. When Frank advanced his view of the 'hardening' of Roman policy under Cato, he was influenced by the fact that he believed in a 'sentimental' Eastern policy by Rome in the first years of the century, and that by the middle of its second decade the evidence against such a view is altogether overwhelming. If we reject—as we must —his first mistake, we are dispensed from imitating the second. Roman policy might seem to us more or less ineffectively brutal according to the personality of the commissioners sent out, but fundamentally there is no change where he seeks it. The commissioners sent at various times belong to all the 'groups' and 'parties' that scholars have distinguished in the Senate: the only general tendency we can notice is the appointment of 'experts'. Thus Flamininus, Metellus, and Ap. Claudius are asked to decide the Spartan question at a time when, with four mutually hostile groups of Spartan exiles and envoys in Rome, its intricacies must have been past understanding.[2] Yet Roman methods of arbitration were superficial and based too much on Roman interest, and judgement[3]—often, as in the case of Sparta, delivered in the tactless and hectoring way in which great powers will address the small—was bound to drive the party against which it went to extremes of bitterness.

A change does finally come; but it is due not to any 'party', but to Roman political experience as guided by a Greek: Callicrates the Achaean, opponent of Lycortas, finally—as Polybius clearly tells us[4]—succeeded in eliminating that alternation between

---

[1] Livy, xxxviii. 30, 1 f.; 32, 3 f.; Pol. xxii. 10; 12, 5 f.; Livy, xxxix. 37, 18. The Senate's decree in the case of Metellus (Pol., l.c.) shows clearly that, for all their officiousness, the Fathers were not claiming suzerainty over Greece. Yet they were apparently quite willing to upset the political structure of the League by treating with individual member states, and even its social structure by appealing to the Assembly against decisions of its magistrates.

[2] Pol. xxii. 4, 1 f.   [3] See Matthaei, *CQ*, 1908, 241 f.

[4] xxiv. 8, 9 f. Scullard (*Rom. World*, 265) says that as a result of Callisthenes' policies

high-handedness and weakness which was keeping Greece in a state of turbulence. He told the Romans that they must make up their minds: if they wanted to have their injunctions carried out, there were men willing to undertake the task; but it was bound to make them unpopular, and they could not do it without Roman support. At present, as he rightly pointed out, it was almost becoming a point of honour in Achaea to do the opposite of what the Romans advised; and this was responsible for keeping dissatisfaction alive in Peloponnese, fostered by hope and frustration.

The Romans acted on his advice and henceforth (we are told) were outspoken in supporting their supporters. Callicrates, in the eyes of most modern historians, was 'reckoned by later Greeks as one of the most infamous of traitors'.[1] We may, however, reduce 'later Greeks' to the son of his enemy Lycortas; though it is likely enough that there were others who disliked him, there must have been some (in Sparta and Messene, and perhaps elsewhere) who blessed him for the era of peace he initiated in the troubled peninsula. We need feel neither contempt nor admiration—his motives were no more unselfish than those of many other politicians, but his vision was clearer. There is, in fact, no doubt that he was right, and that his policy (carried out, with the moral support of Rome, during the rest of his life) was the only way of ending the increasing tension. And it is relevant to remember that the Romans had begun to use the weapon of direct interference before this. We may feel regret for the few hundred members of the Achaean ruling class who suffered in consequence, and no doubt the price was higher than it need have been. But we must not ignore the achievement of Callicrates in at least making the Senate define that political tendency which it had initiated in the case of Macedon. The Roman προστασία—which had perhaps been courteously recognized, but practically ignored, by the Achaeans and had always been appealed to by those dissatisfied with their present lot[2]—was henceforth a fact.

Rome had 'many flatterers but few friends'. Whatever we think of the sincerity of politicians, then or earlier, the fact is that Achaea, without real loss, henceforth had undisturbed peace for a generation, based on co-operation with Rome.

[1] Frank, op. cit. 199. The judgement is typical of many; but see Cary, *Greek World*, 198, for a somewhat fairer view. Most recently, Oost (*Rom. Pol.* 68–69) —not usually deceived by propaganda—repeats the usual sneers.

[2] On Roman interference, see below and compare what we have already seen. The

In Southern Greece the Romans had tried to assert their superiority and weaken the Achaean League as far as possible without open threats.[1] But the League was not strong enough to call forth a Roman display of force in order to curb its independence, and it was—fundamentally—Roman indifference that permitted it to ignore Roman pretensions. In Macedon matters were different. The Romans, never quick to forget such things, had not forgotten the two bitter wars against Philip, and his help against Antiochus had failed to pacify them completely. He had, indeed, been admitted into alliance and had rendered valuable services; but even before the end of the Aetolian War we see Roman efforts to prevent him from reaping the benefits he had expected.[2] As soon as the settlement of the East was completed, Philip's neighbours began to complain that he was wrongfully occupying some of their cities. The Romans sent out a commission to investigate, and this commission ordered him to evacuate all the contested territory and withdraw his garrisons from Aenus and Maronea, which Eumenes had accused him of holding by force and fraud. This order was confirmed by the Senate and another commission was sent to see if he had complied with it.[3] It has often been discussed whether the decision was just, and since we have not the evidence put before the commissioners, they are usually given the benefit of the doubt.[4] But it seems that

term 'προστασία' is used by Polybius in connexion with the massacre at Compasion (xxii. 3, 1). Büttner-Wobst (following a previous editor) changes the ''Ρωμαίων' of the manuscript to 'Λακεδαιμονίων', which makes the passage pointless, if not untranslatable. The Spartans may well have believed in a Roman προστασία over Sparta since their *deditio* to Fulvius (Livy, xxxviii. 31, 5 f.), if not ever since the war with Nabis. (For the meaning of the term, cf. Ditt. *Syll.* 685, 97.) Whether the Achaeans recognized such a thing, we are not told; in any case, they had ignored it in practice.

[1] Cf. pp. 89–90. The most shameless example in our abundant evidence is the case of Messene (Pol. xxiii. 14, 8 f.; 17, 3).

Philip as an ally: Livy, xxxiii. 35, 5 f.; xxxvi. 4, 1 f.; 14, 1 f.; 25, 1 f.; *et al.*, especially xxxvii. 7, 13 f. For the Roman attitude, xxxvi. 25, 7; 34, 8 f. Philip probably did not get a treaty of mutual assistance: his help seems to be voluntary (Livy, xxxvi. 4 *et al.*).

[3] Livy, xxxix. 24, 5–29, 2; 33, 1 f.; 34, 1 f. Fragments of Polybius' account: xxii. 6; 11; 13–14.

[4] e.g. Cary, op. cit. 198–9; Benecke in *CAH*, viii. 244 f. For a very fair discussion, see Walbank, *Philip V*, 232 f. Scullard (*Rom. Pol.* 175 and note) seems to assume that the Romans were right. Frank (op. cit. 196) finds it difficult to understand how Philip had 'dared to risk a contest with Rome'. That ought to have made Frank examine his premiss.

on general grounds our judgement must go against them. We are informed of all the places about which there was any dispute and we are told that Philip was ordered to evacuate them all, and a rider to the decision stated that 'the kingdom of Macedon should be confined to its ancient boundaries'. The Senate confirmed this, and in particular ordered the evacuation of the Thracian coast.[1] This, coming as it did after an official proclamation promising protection to all those who complained against Philip,[2] cannot be reasonably interpreted as anything but a manœuvre to weaken Philip with a show of justice—as indeed Philip understood. We shall find the same technique—the invitation to bring complaints, followed by an outright judgement in favour of the complainants —employed in other cases where there is not a shadow of doubt as to Roman motives; and they help to cast light on this first example. It is quite likely that there were legal doubts in the case of some cities; and that Rome should be called in to decide was only natural, whatever the legal position.[3] But it must surely arouse our suspicions to hear that in every single case the decision went against Philip: it is hardly probable that only those cities which had in fact been unjustly occupied would avail themselves of the chance to complain. Yet this is what the apologists expect us to believe. Much is sometimes made of the fact that the commission of 186/5 referred the case of Aenus and Maronea to the Senate.[4] But they merely had no mandate for goading Philip into war. The Senate itself, free from such limitations, calmly decided against him and risked the consequences. Moreover, the decision confining the kingdom to its ancient boundaries declared all conquests invalid in principle—since what date, was left undefined. This, of course, simply invited new complaints, and we know that they were not slow in coming: when Philip, in despair, sends Demetrius to Rome, he has a long charge-sheet to answer.[5]

[1] Livy, xxxix. 25, 3 f.; 26, 14; 33, 3–4 = Pol. xxii. 11, 3–4.

[2] Pol. xxii. 6, 5.

[3] Rome had not in any legal sense 'guaranteed' the freedom of the Greek states (Heuss, *Völk. Gr.* 84 f.; Aymard, *Prem. Rapp.* 273 f.), and if Philip held some cities by right of conquest after 196, it seems that Rome had no right to interfere. Philip certainly thought so. But, as in 201, such a right was simply assumed, and with better reason: Rome now regarded all the Greek states as her clients.

[4] Livy, xxxix. 28 f. Benecke (op. cit. 250) believes that Philip's case impressed them.

[5] Pol. xxiii. 1 f.

The mission of Demetrius marks a turning-point in Roman policy towards Macedon in particular and towards client kings in general. Hitherto Rome had arbitrarily restricted their foreign policy when it suited her, but had refrained from open interference in their internal affairs. Demetrius, however, guileless and gullible as he was known to be and again proved himself, presented the Senate with a chance of destroying the power of Macedon by one bold blow, instead of whittling it away by a series of judgements with the constant risk of goading Philip into war. On the advice of Flamininus (still, no doubt, the chief Eastern expert) it was decided to declare the petty persecution of Philip at an end, but show by exaggerated public honours heaped on Demetrius, as well as in private conversations with him, that the Senate regarded him as the 'Roman candidate' for the kingship of Macedon. It is, as far as we know, the first occasion on which such a step is taken in the case of an established kingdom. This ostentatious favour was kept up after his return home and seems to have split the kingdom into two factions, until Philip, afraid for his throne and for the future of the country which he was trying to restore to strength, decided to execute Demetrius.[1] If this is the first, it is not the last time we shall meet with such Roman intrigues—the whole course of Roman policy towards Macedon in the eighties is strikingly paralleled by that towards Pergamum in the sixties, and in the latter case, fortunately, our evidence is too clear to permit a 'non liquet'. The Senate had discovered a new weapon of policy.[2]

But the plan failed: Demetrius was executed and, when Philip died in the midst of his schemes for the regeneration of Macedon,

[1] The tragedy of the Macedonian royal house (cf. Walbank, *JHS*, 1938, 55 f.) is told in some of Livy's most artistic passages (xxxix. 53 f.; xl. 5 f.; 20 f.), adapted freely from Polybius (cf. Pol. xxiii. 3, 7 f.; 7; 11). Polybius, who hated Philip and was given to moralizing (e.g. xxiii. 10; cf. Walbank, op. cit.), naturally believed the version most unfavourable to him. For an excellent discussion, see Edson, *HSCP*, 1935, 191 f. I suggest, however, that a faction hostile to Perseus and favouring the succession of Antigonus engineered the posthumous rehabilitation of Demetrius.

[2] The charge against Demetrius was not only (as a hasty reading of Livy suggests) that he was trying to oust Perseus (thus most moderns—even Edson, op. cit.), but that he was aiming at supplanting Philip. The later Attalid example (see below) supports this charge against both him and his Roman friends. On this see Pol. xxiii. 3, 8. Livy's dishonesty is shown beyond redemption by his omission of this passage. Callicrates had no doubt carefully watched these events (see above): we know the interest that they aroused in Achaea (see Walbank, op. cit.).

Perseus succeeded to the throne.[1] We need not go into his policy in detail.[2] It is clear that, suspect from the beginning as the enemy of Demetrius, he increased Roman suspicions by his dynastic policy and by taking the other side in the class struggles in Greece; he may also have been guilty of intrigues in Illyria, though our evidence proves only that he was willing to cultivate useful friendships there. When Eumenes finally paid a personal visit to Rome in order to accuse the King, the Senate decided to act. Troops were sent to Illyria, and a mission was dispatched to Greece to ensure the supremacy of the pro-Roman party in all states.[3] The mission, led by the astute Q. Marcius Philippus, had one outstanding success. It broke up the Boeotian League, which, under its democratic leadership, had long been ill at ease in the new order imposed by Rome and had, at some time before the war was foreseen, made the mistake of signing a treaty with Perseus (then recognized as a friend of the Roman People). It was now quite prepared to support Rome; but Philippus insisted on dissolution.[4] The absolute power of Rome, regardless of legal rights, appears in its true light in this first—and immediately successful—attempt to break up a friendly state by the mere command of an envoy.

Meanwhile more peaceful missions had secured promises of loyalty from the few relatively important powers of the East.[5] Thus the war was confidently begun, and finally won despite the mistakes of successive Roman commanders. But these mistakes and the resulting setbacks had been enough to make most of the Roman allies in the East reconsider their position: if Perseus were destroyed, they would be left wholly subservient to a

---

[1] On Philip's last years, see Walbank, op. cit. and *Philip V*, 255 f.

[2] See Benecke, Cary, Walbank, opp. citt. Cf. Sands, *Cl. Pr.* 184.

[3] Livy, xlii. 18, 2 f.; 27, 5 f.; 31, 1 f.; 37, 1 f.; 43, 4 f. That the Senate had long been suspicious is shown by the succession of envoys sent to Macedon and Greece. We need only consider the decisive mission headed by Marcius.

[4] Pol. xxvii. 1 f. Scullard (*Rom. Pol.* 198) imputes the war to 'the new plebeian clique of magistrates' and believes (on the strength of Plut. *Cato*, 8) that Cato was opposed to it; there is no good evidence for this. It is hard to see any significant difference in the policy of Philippus as compared, say, with that of the Patrician Flamininus (cf. p. 82). The particular time of the outbreak of war is sufficiently explained by Eumenes' visit.

[5] Livy, xlii. 6, 4 f.; 26, 2 f.; 45, 1 f.; Pol. xxvii. 3, 1; also some of doubtful authenticity. Cf. *MRR*, i. 412 f.

henceforth unshakeable Roman power; there were many men who thought that Perseus' successes gave them a chance to avoid this. Our sources do not permit us to reconstruct the details of anti-Roman activities; but it seems that in all the important Greek states in Europe, as well as in Rhodes, there were anti-Roman parties, which gained in strength as the war dragged on. While the war lasted, Roman diplomacy had to be cautious. C. Popillius and Cn. Octavius were sent on a mission to three troubled leagues; and (to judge by Polybius' hostile account) they showed remarkable tact:[1] unofficial warnings in private talks were in each instance followed by a conciliatory public address and (it seems) a genuine attempt to heal discord within the states, even at the expense of protecting anti-Roman leaders. Rome did not need active Greek support for the war, and the Greeks could serve her best by simply causing no trouble. It was probably mainly to this end that some well-known Aetolian trouble-makers had been removed to Rome,[2] though other leaders of the hostile party were not touched. Rhodes was treated with even greater courtesy.[3]

(ii) *After Pydna.* But as soon as the war was won and Rome had no one to fear, diplomacy was dropped and Rome stood forth as the ruler of the world,[4] tolerating neither opposition nor indeed anything but unquestioning compliance with her wishes. Greece, Macedon and the East—friends, enemies and neutrals—all immediately felt the consequences of Roman victory. The most liberal treatment was (as so often) reserved for the humbled enemy: Macedon was divided into four republics and declared 'free', though with certain restrictions (to prevent its resurgence as a nation) and a small tribute.[5] It was difficult to know what to do with the country: Rome, as always, was reluctant to assume

---

[1] Pol. xxviii. 3 f.

[2] Pol. xxvii. 15, 14; xxviii. 4, 6. We do not know how it had been done; but the *maiestas* clause (or its equivalent) in the Aetolian treaty gave the Romans wide powers of interference, and thus it is not surprising to see this policy first applied in the case of the Aetolian League.   [3] Pol. xxviii. 2, 5 f.; 17, 1 f.

[4] Polybius, who was personally so much affected by this change, saw the importance of the victory (iii. 1, 9 *et al.*). But we must bear in mind (as this study has attempted to show in outline) that the roots of the new policy go back to well before the war with Perseus.

[5] On the settlement, see Larsen, *CP*, 1949, 73 f., and Aymard, *CP*, 1950, 96 f. Its details do not concern us.

the burden of directly controlling a hostile population; yet the country could not be left to become an enemy again, for it was difficult to conquer. An alternative had, however, to be found, which would yet leave it strong enough to hold off the barbarians in the north. We know that there was a debate in the Senate and that Cato voted for freedom;[1] whether he was responsible for the details of the final arrangement, we do not know. But we have seen how the meaning of 'libertas' had changed, until it could conveniently be hedged about with provisos: this concept is here first applied on a large scale; in particular, we encounter for the first time the dissociation of *libertas* and *immunitas*, which later became general. Many attempts have been made to explain it: it. has even been claimed that the tribute was too small to be meant as a sign of subjection.[2] But the simplest explanation is probably the correct one: as once in the first 'province' of Sicily, Rome found a country used to paying a tax, and the Senate simply decided to go on collecting it. Only, in this case—after the historical developments we have traced—it could be done even though the country was not officially annexed; and as the country had to be economically weakened for political reasons, the tax had to be reduced correspondingly.

Illyria—the realm of Perseus' ineffective ally Genthius—was treated similarly.[3] Rome was prepared to be generous to harmless ex-enemies. But in Greece her tone suddenly changed from the tactful diplomacy forced on her by the war to revengeful and brutal interference. In all the states Roman commissioners suddenly appeared with open accusations against all leaders who had not followed the line of total subjection. And, as had been done in Aetolia during the war—only this time without a shadow of legal justification—, all these men were deported to Italy: a thousand, as we know, came from Achaea; and we have no reason to suppose that other states received different treatment. Despite

---

[1] Malcovati, *ORF*², 61. The wording, corrupt as the text seems to be, shows that 'libertas' did not mean 'freedom from a king' (as some modern scholars propose), but 'freedom' in the Roman sense. We do not know who (if anybody) spoke on the other side.

[2] Frank, op. cit. 210 (I am not sure what he means). For another theory, see Scullard, *Rom. World*, 273.

[3] Cf. Zippel, *Röm. Herrsch.* 95 f. Cotys, another ex-enemy, also received generous treatment (Pol. xxx. 17; Livy, xlv. 18): perhaps because he would be a useful friend and an uncomfortable enemy.

constant appeals by their states, they were kept in Italy without trial and not allowed to return, until only few of them were left.[1] Such was Rome's action against those not guilty of the crime of opposing her; those who were did not meet with such leniency: they were massacred and their cities plundered. In Epirus alone, we are told, Paullus destroyed seventy cities and sold 150,000 men into slavery—we do not quite know why.[2] Henceforth there was no question of Greek 'freedom'; the history of the next seventeen years shows no further development and need not delay us. There remains only the dismal account of the Achaean revolt, which we shall briefly discuss in due course.

We must now turn to Rome's treatment of the rest of the Greek and Eastern world, which we left in 188, duly organized by Roman commissioners, but too far from Rome to be directly under her control. Eumenes, as we saw, was the champion of the Roman peace in this area; and the republic of Rhodes, though never subservient enough to be beyond suspicion, retained its power and wealth. During the next twenty years there is little Roman intervention. There are only two major wars, in both of which Rome intervenes (at his request) on Eumenes' behalf: that against Prusias and that against Pharnaces. Prusias, who had attacked Pergamum, made peace at Rome's bidding—perhaps, as has been suggested, because Pharnaces was already proving a common danger to him and Eumenes.[3] But Pharnaces was less

---

[1] Polybius and Livy report many such embassies. Scullard again ascribes this measure to 'the more extreme plebeian leaders' (*Rom. Pol.* 213) and believes that Paullus opposed it. But we need not be prepared to take the word of his son's protégé for this (Pol. xxx. 13, 11—claiming to argue from later events), and there is no reason to believe that such 'extremists' wielded any great power in 167. As in other similar cases, we have no evidence for 'party differences' based on principle in matters of foreign policy. The Senate's refusal to let the men return until 151 shows that it was not a matter of a momentary success by a clique.

[2] Pol. xxx. 15; Livy, xlv. 34. It is often assumed that Paullus was an unwilling instrument—e.g. Scullard (l.c.). Oost's analysis (*Rom. Pol.* 83 f., with notes) disposes of that. Livy is based on the biased Polybius and himself prevaricates further; even so, some valuable indications of Paullus' character and policy survive. Cf. xlv. 27 (some penal measures); 28, 6 f. and 31, 1 f. (the Aetolian massacre); 34 (the Epirot massacre). In the last of these it is worth noting that the Patrician Paullus wrote to the Plebeian Anicius warning him to keep his hands off the destined booty of his own men (34, 1). We are pleased to hear that he failed to win their favour by it (s. 7).

[3] Pol. iii. 3, 6; xxiii. 1, 4; 3, 1; Livy, xxxix. 51. (Cf. Cary, op. cit. 214.) It is not clear what part Prusias played in the war with Pharnaces. Polybius' report of the

amenable to Roman mediation: though he sent envoys to Rome, he would not at first take part in negotiations under a Roman mission to Asia and in the end refused to accept its terms, though it seems that he was politely treated throughout. Rome did not enforce her terms: as we know, she did not regard herself as obliged to support her free 'friends and allies' by armed force, where this was not in her interest. Luckily, the allies were strong enough to defeat their enemy; but the result must have been to strengthen Pergamum's own position by showing that her strength was not merely a reflection of the Roman name. The proud Pharnaces never became a client of Rome.[1]

Rome's intervention in the dispute of Rhodes with her new subjects was neither glorious nor effective. Lycia and Caria, as we have seen, were Rhodes' share of the spoils of Antiochus—a small enough reward for her services. The Rhodians proceeded to tax their new subjects and issue orders to them, and they soon encountered resistance—to some extent, probably, fanned by Eumenes, whose interests now generally ran counter to those of the Republic.[2] The dispute was referred to Rome, and the Senate, not unwilling—after a recent display of Rhodian naval strength—to cause the Republic some embarrassment, yet unable to cancel the decision of its own representatives, left the issue (in practice) undecided, merely reminding the Rhodians that the Lycians had been assigned to them οὐκ ἐν δωρεᾷ, τὸ δὲ πλεῖον ὡς φίλοι καὶ σύμμαχοι.[3] This encouraged the Lycians, just defeated, to rebel again, but probably to no effect, as the Senate, of course, would not use force on their behalf. The only effect of the incident was to strengthen the anti-Roman party in Rhodes.

Thus, down to the end of the Third Macedonian War, the hand of Rome lay lightly upon the East. Eumenes and Rhodes, the chief 'friends' of Rome, generally had as much freedom as

---

treaty implies that he was an ally of Eumenes and Ariarathes (xxv. 2, 3); but he is never mentioned in the war itself (iii. 3, 6; xxiv. 15, 1 f.; xxv. 2, 2 and 15).

[1] Pol. xxiii. 10, 1 f. *et al.*; xxiv. 15. For Rome's politeness, cf. xxiv. 15, 7. It looks as though the Romans tried to prevent Eumenes from being too successful on his own (ibid. 4 f.)—the outcome must have been a shock for the Senate. For the coins of Pharnaces, whose dynasty claims the succession to the Achaemenids, see Head, *HN*[2], 500. On the policy of the dynasty, see also Reinach, *Mithr. Eup.* 35 f. It is likely that Roman interests were officially safeguarded in the treaty (*RE*, s.v. 'Pharnakes', col. 1850).

[2] Pol. xxii. 5; xxiv. 15; xxvii. 7, 5 f.; cf. xxx. 31, 4.   [3] Pol. xxv. 4, 1 f.

they wanted; Ariarathes and Prusias were loosely attached to the Roman sphere of influence—probably voluntarily, as an insurance against Pergamene power; the Galatians had been bound over to keep the peace and, assigned to Eumenes' general supervision, remained more or less quiet down to the time of the Macedonian War.[1] The victory over Perseus completely alters this. As soon as, with the end of the war, the need for diplomacy had disappeared, Roman intervention became brutally direct, and even those not immediately affected were quick to acknowledge Roman hegemony. The change was made easier by the fact that Eumenes and the Rhodians had compromised themselves before the end of the war, though they had given loyal help through most of it. But Rome was eager to seize the chance and ensure their complete dependence.

The Rhodians, according to our sources, had indeed been unwise as well as unfaithful. They undertook to mediate between Perseus and Rome and (we are told) threatened to fight against the power that refused; this could only be Rome, as Perseus had probably asked them to take this step and in any case was always ready to end the war. Rome could never have accepted such an ultimatum. But, as it happened, the messengers presenting it arrived after the news of the victory of Pydna and were consequently treated almost as enemies.[2] We need not accept the whole of this account: the form of the ultimatum appears to have been invented by an annalist, and the Rhodians' crime may safely be reduced to what they had done in so many other wars: an offer to mediate, as they said, in a war which was causing much suffering to the Greeks. It is clear that their envoys foresaw no danger in their mission: they did not even disguise it when the news of Pydna was announced. But the Senate, seizing its opportunity and wishing to make an example of the Rhodians[3]—for the

---

[1] On Prusias II see Livy, xlii. 29, 3; xliv. 10, 12; 14, 5 f. (his vacillation in the Macedonian War). On Ariarathes, overawed by Manlius (Pol. xxi. 41, 4 f.; Livy, xxxviii. 39, 6), see above and Livy, xlii. 29, 4: he was a firm friend of Eumenes. For a constitutional peculiarity see Strabo, xii. 2, 11 (cf. Tarn, *JHS*, 1909, 269 for Macedon). On the Galatians see Livy, xxxviii. 40, 1; cf. Pol. xxiv. 14; xxv. 2, 4; and *Note K*, p. 294 below. On Seleucids and Ptolemies see below, pp. 107 f.

[2] Pol. xxix. 5 f.; 19. Cf. Livy (A.), xliv. 14, 8 f.

[3] These words are used by Polybius (xxix. 19, 5). We shall see that the 'example' was certainly successful.

client had no business to offer arbitration to the patron, who had come to expect nothing but unquestioning support—gave a crushing reply. The quarrel dragged on till 165, though the Rhodians at once gave up all thought of independence, wiped out their anti-Roman faction and asked for nothing but a treaty recognizing them as allies. There was a party in the Senate which wanted a declaration of war. It consisted mainly of those who had held commands in Greece and Macedonia and thus had occasion to know the prestige of Rhodes in the Greek world. But the majority (led by Cato, who no doubt realized that war was totally unnecessary at a time when the prospective enemy was begging for his own humiliation) opposed such rashness. All that the Senate did was to declare Lycia and Caria free and, when this led to a revolt by Caunus and Stratonicea, order the Rhodians to withdraw from these cities as well. At the same time Delos was turned over to Athens as a free harbour, and it is hard to escape the conclusion that the Senate had some idea of the effect this measure would have on Rhodian commerce. Finally, with Rhodes humbled beyond hope of political revival, the alliance was granted (165 B.C.). It marks the end of Rhodian independence: as a 'free' ally, the proud Republic had not regarded itself as a client even at quite a late date; but henceforth Rhodes remained a faithful client—fully accepting the Roman point of view—and was even allowed to reoccupy Calynda.[1] Yet the Senate had a long memory for the crimes of its allies, and Rhodes' chief crime had been her naval strength. Thus, when in 155 Rhodes became involved in a war with the pirates of Crete, the Senate— in spite of the alliance—does not seem to have stirred a finger.[2] This war—which was probably indecisive—is the last independent act of Rhodes that has come down to us. And the Senate— to its cost, as it was to discover—would rather encourage the

---

[1] Pol. xxx. 4 f; 21; 23; 31 (cf. Livy, xlv. 10, 4 f.); xxxi. 4 f. That the 'liberation' of Delos was aimed against Rhodes (though not chiefly meant to profit Italians—cf. Hatzfeld, *Trafiquants*, 372) is very likely, and the effect was immediate (Pol. xxx. 31, 12—Büttner-Wobst's emendation is not convincing). It is unprofitable to theorize about the legal justification of some of the Roman decrees against Rhodes: the decree freeing Caunus and Stratonicea shows that force was the only argument used (Pol. xxx. 31, 6 f.; cf. Heuss, *Völk. Gr.* 107 f.).

[2] Pol. xxxiii. 15, 3 f.: Callicrates persuaded the Achaeans to remain neutral, referring to Roman wishes. Rhodes was quite desperate (ibid. 17). Cf. Trog. *prol.* 35.

pirates than the remains of a spirit of independence in its allies. The existence of treaties, as we see, had by this time ceased to matter: the condition of the 'free' *amici* had begun to affect that of allies with treaties.

Eumenes had been the chief agent, if not in bringing about the war with Perseus, at least in causing it to start when it did; and throughout its duration his forces gave the Romans valuable help, even to the extent of denuding Pergamum of adequate protection. As a result, he had to face a dangerous Galatian invasion about the time the war was approaching its end.[1] After Pydna he sent his brother Attalus to Rome, to convey his congratulations and present his claims (probably to Aenus and Maronea, which he had hoped to acquire twenty years before), and in particular to ask for Roman help against the Gauls. But meanwhile Rome's attitude to him had changed from friendship to suspicion. The reason for this Polybius found in secret negotiations said to have taken place between the King and Perseus, in which Eumenes—at a price he did not obtain—had offered either to desert the Romans or even to procure Perseus a tolerable peace.[2] It is difficult to know what to make of this strange conspiracy. Scholars' judgements have ranged from complete rejection to complete belief.[3] That Perseus' chief enemy should offer to sell his ally (to whom he had shown unwavering loyalty) to him for a financial consideration; that the King who was considered πανουργότατος should engage in negotiations which he could not hope to conceal for any length of time, yet which, if they came to the Senate's knowledge, were bound to endanger the position he had so carefully built up for himself over two decades—these suggestions are indeed hard to believe without damning evidence. Yet we must join Scullard[4] in reluctant and cautious belief. For Polybius gives a detailed and circumstantial account of the affair, quoting Perseus' friends as his sources and assuring us that he himself was as astonished at it as any of us,[5] i.e. did not lightly

---

[1] For the evidence, see De Sanctis, *Storia*, iv. 1, 357 f.

[2] Pol. xxix. 5 f.; xxx. 1 and 6.   [3] Cf. De Sanctis, l.c.; Frank, op. cit. 212.

[4] *Rom. Pol.* 286–7: this seems to me the best discussion.

[5] xxix. 5, 3; 8, 10. Cf. xxix. 9, where he makes it quite clear that the whole affair was little short of incredible. De Sanctis (p. 359, n. 320) ignores xxix. 8, 10 (Polybius' sources of information) and misinterprets xxix. 6, 2 f. to mean that Polybius convinced himself of Eumenes' guilt to exculpate the Romans.

believe or (as he makes clear) decide to report it. In the circumstances we must believe Polybius. It remains to ask whether we can make sense of Eumenes' motives; and this is not impossible. The strain of the protracted war was beginning to tell on Pergamum; the King no doubt knew that the Gauls, with whom Perseus had perhaps been intriguing,[1] were restive and awaiting their opportunity. The expense of the war must have been considerable, and there seemed to be no immediate hope of victory. Knowing this, and foreseeing that he would soon be forced to withdraw his troops in order to defend his kingdom, Eumenes may well have thought it a stroke of genius to persuade his enemy to pay him for it. And, suspecting that Rome shared his own (and Perseus') desire to be rid of the war, he went farther and offered to advise Rome to make peace—provided he was paid even better: for, once his troops were out of it (as they would soon be in any case), it did not matter to him whether the war continued. Thus Eumenes may have aimed at these two advantages: to be paid (at a time when he needed money) for withdrawing his troops, since he knew he would have to do it anyway; and to be paid more for advising a peace which Rome would gladly make. Perhaps, too, even Eumenes had come to realize that Rome, if she did win the war outright, would not be a comfortable neighbour.

That this does not amount to treason is obvious. But the Senate, following almost invariable Roman custom, once it had made up its mind that it did, was never after willing to listen to explanations. When Attalus, as we have seen, came to Rome as his brother's envoy, he was secretly advised to claim the Pergamene throne or at least part of the kingdom; in expectation of his acceptance, the Senate promised him Aenus and Maronea. The authors of the scheme were, according to Polybius, 'some prominent men'; we do not know their names, but cannot help suspecting that he is shielding his friends in a disreputable affair. Flamininus was dead, but his policy over Demetrius had apparently impressed some circles and was now taken up and applied to another allied kingdom. It failed again: Attalus wavered, but

---

[1] As with the European Gauls (Pol. xxv. 6, 3; 9, 13; cf. Diod. xxxi. 19). There is no reason to believe that the Romans encouraged the Galatian invasion of Pergamum.

did not fall; and the Senate was left to make its motives clear to all by declaring Aenus and Maronea free.[1] From now on down to Eumenes' death the old ally is treated as a potential enemy, and the system of 188 is supplanted by one of direct contact between Rome and Asia and direct and frequent interference in its affairs. Instead of remote hegemony, depending on the power and fidelity of one or two allies, Rome now aims at establishing a balance of power in Asia and making the kings and peoples composing it directly dependent upon herself. This may be simply due to the fact (as the Senate considered it) that the two allies who were the props of the old system had shown their instability; but the effect far surpasses the dubious cause, and it is legitimate to think that, with the final downfall of Macedon, the East has simply been brought much nearer, and Rome, though still unwilling to undertake the burdens of direct administration, is determined to forbid the growth of any power not wholly dependent on her favour within the geographical limits she can control.

The establishment of this balance of power was the work of the next few years. Pergamum was left exposed to Galatian attacks by a mission which, officially sent to end the war, in fact encouraged the barbarians in secret negotiations.[2] The war dragged on for some time, until the King set out for Rome in order to try to regain favour. But in vain: the Senate, which had received his self-abasing enemy Prusias II with every mark of honour, sent him home from Brundisium unheard. This published his disgrace to the world; and in the following year the Gauls, just defeated by Eumenes, sent a delegation to Rome and were duly granted 'autonomy', provided they kept the peace;[3] thus Eumenes was cheated of the fruits of his victory. The Greek cities of Asia, for whom the Gauls were the dreaded enemy, celebrated him as their saviour—perhaps all the more

[1] Pol. xxx. 1–3. If Philippus had given the advice, Polybius would have shown no more hesitation in mentioning his name than he shows in mentioning Flamininus in the affair of Demetrius (xxiii. 3, 7) and Philippus himself in connexion with some other shady actions (xxiii. 10, 8 f.; xxvii. 1, 3 f.; xxviii. 17, 4 f.).

[2] Pol. xxx. 3, 7 f.; Livy, xlv. 34, 10 f. Livy disguises it.

[3] Pol. xxx. 18 f.; 28. For the Pergamene victory, see *I. v. Perg.* 165; cf. next note. It is sometimes asserted that the Senate freed the Gauls from the overlordship of Eumenes, under which they had been since 188 (e.g. Sands, *Cl. Pr.* 187 and 212). But their 'autonomy' was probably only a return to the *status quo*: what concerned the Senate was the removal of Eumenes' garrisons. Cf. *Note K*, p. 294.

eagerly, as he was no longer the instrument of Rome.[1] But
Prusias now began to stir up trouble for him, and the stream of
embassies to Rome to complain about him and of Roman envoys
to investigate the complaints is reminiscent of the fate of Philip
twenty years before, when Eumenes had been in the happier
position now occupied by the Bithynian. Finally, a Roman embassy established itself at Sardis and—as another embassy had
once done at Tempe—listened, under guarantee of safety to all
comers, to anyone who wished to complain. Nor, it seems, were
complainants slow to come.[2] But we do not hear of any decisive
action on the part of Rome. We cannot help suspecting that the
situation—with Pergamum weakened and disgraced, but not
destroyed—suited the Senate very well: if it had decided to
destroy Pergamum, Prusias would have been the only one to
benefit and Rome might no longer have been able to keep the
balance in Asia. When, after Eumenes' death, Prusias decided to
attack Pergamum, a Roman commission ordered him to desist;
and when he refused, Rome promoted an alliance of her friends
against him to which he succumbed; and she then imposed a
settlement, by which the balance was restored.[3] Though the
Senate by now had no intention of taking up arms on behalf of
a threatened ally, it could still—as we see—act quickly and decisively in other ways, where it cared to. It is significant that it
cared to only in those cases where the balance of power was in
danger of being upset.

We need not enter in any detail into the tangled history of
Roman relations with other kings in this area. But it is worth
noting that the success of Rome decided the ruler of Pontus to
become an ally,[4] and that this period sees the beginning of two
important customs. First, we see kings voluntarily sending their
heirs apparent to Rome to be educated and acquire useful friendships there.[5] This, no doubt, was meant to secure the succession

[1] *OGIS*, 305, 7 f. and other surviving inscriptions, especially *OGIS*, 763. Pol.
xxxi. 6, 6; cf. Holleaux, *RÉG*, 1924, 305 f.   [2] See *Note K*, p. 294.
[3] Pol. xxxii. 15 f.; xxxiii. 1; 12 f. For the coalition, see xxxiii. 12, 7 f.; cf. 13, 1 f.
for the result. Territorially the *status quo* was re-established, as usual; but Prusias
had to pay heavy damages (xxxiii. 13, 6 f.) and his 'rebellion' was never forgiven,
as is clear from Rome's failure to support him against his son (Pol. xxxvi. 14).
[4] App. *Mith.* 10 (not dated).
[5] Livy, xlii. 19, 3 f. (Cappadocia)—at the outbreak of the Macedonian War;

for the young men concerned both against rival claimants at
home and against the possible hostility of the Senate: the kings,
no doubt, had not forgotten the lesson of the Senate's favour for
Demetrius (who had, by accident, been brought up at Rome as
a hostage) and its hostility to Perseus. The other custom, closely
related to it, is that of seeking Roman recognition. It was natural
enough that a king succeeding to the throne should 'renew
friendship' (and any treaty that might exist) with the Senate:
that was only a public proclamation that he intended to continue
his predecessor's policy.[1] It is doubtful whether Perseus or
Antiochus IV did more than this at the beginning of their reigns.[2]
But when Ariarathes V succeeded his father, he awaited the return
of his envoys from Rome with obvious anxiety, and when they
reported that the Senate had renewed the Roman friendship
his father had obtained, he clearly showed his elation.[3] We do
not know the circumstances of his accession, but he obviously
did not regard the renewal of friendship as a mere diplomatic
formality. This development, due (no doubt) to the increasing
power of Rome after Pydna and the traditional insecurity of
Eastern kings, comes to a head in the case of a 'king' with a very
bad claim to his throne and a *damnosa hereditas*—Demetrius I of
Syria. For he is not entitled to the name of king at all and wants
(*inter alia*) to be addressed by the Senate as 'king': this is the first
main object of his endeavours.[4] His failure soon led to his downfall, as Rome encouraged another pretender. Henceforth it is the
aim of every king within Rome's orbit to be 'called king' by her:
it is better to be 'called friend and ally', but it is not by any
means useless merely to have been 'rex appellatus'. Thus the
Senate made full use of the inherent superiority of oligarchic
government over monarchic in the matter of succession.

xlv. 44, 4 f. (Bithynia)—just after Pydna. Prusias no doubt thought it wise to imitate
his neighbour's more timely action! On Masinissa (Livy, xlv. 44, 15) see below. Cf.
the 'presentation' to the Senate of the younger Attalus (Pol. xxxiii. 18, 1–3).

[1] Cf. Heuss, *Völk. Gr.* 46 f.

[2] Livy, xl. 58, 9 (Livy's wording must not be strictly interpreted—cf. Pol. xxv.
3, 1); xlii. 6, 6 f. (on Antiochus).   [3] Pol. xxxi. 7, 1.

[4] Pol. xxxi. 33, 3: πάντα ποιήσειν Ῥωμαίοις ἀναδεχόμενος, ἕως ἐξειργάσατο [?]
βασιλεὺς ὑπ' αὐτῶν προσαγορευθῆναι. Such *appellatio* later became the object of
much bribery. In the isolated earlier instance of Masinissa (Livy, xxx. 15, 7;
cf. 17, 6 f.) the account is so rhetorical (and from bad sources) that we may
probably ignore it. See *Note M*, p. 295.

We must complete this picture of royal dependence by glancing at the affairs of Syria and Egypt. Here, too, Roman power had barely been felt before the war with Perseus, and here, too, Pydna marks the turning-point. Egypt had settled its native revolts and pursued an independent policy, being on friendly terms with the Greek world. The Seleucid monarchy had overcome the uprisings following upon the defeat of Antiochus the Great and, thanks to the capable administration and unifying policy of Seleucus IV and Antiochus IV, had steadily regained strength.[1] About the time the Third Macedonian War broke out, these two old enemies clashed again, as the ministers of Ptolemy VI tried to regain Coele Syria. The Senate was too busy to attempt effective intervention: Philippus, to whom the war was referred for action, asked the Rhodians and the Achaeans to mediate. Only T. Numisius Tarquiniensis could be spared to represent Roman authority in the task of mediation.[2] But all this changed with the news of Pydna: at once C. Popillius, a consular renowned for diplomatic success, was sent with two others to end the war; for Antiochus was besieging Alexandria. Popillius, who in Rome's danger had shown a good deal of tact in negotiations, now insolently ordered Antiochus to evacuate Cyprus and Egypt. The King obeyed: Rome's authority was unquestioned.[3]

The decades that followed saw the disintegration of the kingdoms of both the Seleucids and the Ptolemies, and in each case the Senate did its best to further it. Syria remained strong until Antiochus' death (163), and Rome found no cause for overt interference, though commissions of inspection could be sent on thin pretexts.[4] On Antiochus' death, Rome refused to let Demetrius

---

[1] See *CAH*, viii. 495 f.

[2] Pol. xxviii. 1; 17, 4; xxix. 25, 3 *et al.* For the course of the war, cf. Livy, xlv. 11, 1 f. Antiochus seems to have done his best to keep Roman friendship (Livy, xlii. 26, 7—if true; cf. Polyaen. iv. 21). Egypt, though not so helpful, was formally correct (Pol. xxviii. 1): M. Lepidus, the patron of the Ptolemies, seems to have prevented his client from committing the *faux pas* for which the Rhodians later suffered (ibid.). This seems to provide a *terminus ante quem* for his patronate.

[3] Pol. xxix. 27; Livy, xliv. 19, 13 f. For Popillius' tact at a critical time, cf. Pol. xxviii. 3–5; for his insolence after victory, see also Livy, xlv. 10, 7 f. It is clear (Livy, xliv. 29, 1 f. and xlv. 10, 1 f.) that the embassy had instructions to proceed to Egypt only after victory. Their stay in Delos was not only prudent delay (thus Scullard, *Rom. Pol.* 210): they had a task to perform there while military operations lasted.   [4] Pol. xxx. 27, 1 f.; 30, 5 f.; xxxi. 1, 6 f.

(who was a hostage in Rome) return to occupy the throne and preferred to support the claims of Antiochus V, who was still a child: for his weakness could be used with great profit. A commission led by Cn. Octavius was sent to Syria to burn the navy and hamstring the elephants, on the pretext that the treaty of Apamea had been transgressed by the rearmament policy of the Seleucids. The claim was weak, for Antiochus IV had been an obedient ally, and Rome had never enforced the treaty against him, so that (at the least) its restrictions had lapsed by usurpation. But the Senate was not concerned with legal niceties; and when Octavius was murdered and Demetrius escaped from Rome to occupy the throne (aided, we suspect, by the Aemilii and their friends), Rome used the grievance to best effect, accepting—in the Senate's traditional way—neither apology nor compensation.[1] Indeed, the Senate went on to foment trouble in the unhappy kingdom by making treaties with—and thus giving moral support to—its rebellious subjects and sanctioning the attempts of pretenders:[2] again there was no question of legal rights, as there was no one to sit in judgement. As the kingdom was weakened by the misfortunes of prolonged civil war and war with the Parthians, Roman interest naturally ceased: we do not know of any Roman intervention between the accession of Alexander Balas and the Mithridatic Wars. The Senate had long ceased to protect its friends, and there were no enemies strong enough to invite intrigue.

Egypt was in the happier position of being governed, till 145,

[1] On these confused events, see Pol. xxxi. 2; 8; 11–15; 33; xxxii. 2 f. Polybius' Roman friends cannot have been quite unconcerned in the events that he abetted. That the Senate was prepared to look on is not surprising: the complications now bound to arise in the East were to its liking. This is proved by its cynical support for Orophernes (Demetrius' candidate) against Ariarathes (Rome's recognized *amicus*) in Cappadocia (Pol. xxxii. 10; App. *Syr.* 47; Zon. ix. 24, *fin.*). That Demetrius ever gained official Roman recognition (thus Scullard, op. cit. 230; Cary, op. cit. 221) cannot be proved. (In Pol. xxxi. 33, 3, if the text is sound, 'αὐτῶν' refers to the envoys.)

[2] See 1 Macc. viii. 17: the famous treaty with the Jews. (Cf. Täubler, *Imp. Rom.* i. 239 f.; Accame, *Dom. Rom.* 79 f. It is a 'Senatorial treaty'—see pp. 111 f.) There may well have been more such treaties, as this one is preserved for us well outside the main stream of tradition. The comment of Justin on such acts is apposite: 'facile tunc Romanis de alieno largientibus' (xxxv. 3, 9). On Roman support for Alexander, see Pol. xxxiii. 18, 6 f. (with his comment). This behaviour towards the Seleucid kingdom contradicted the assertion that Antiochus had been a 'friend and ally'.

by a king superior in ability to any since the great figures at the beginning of his line. What Ptolemy Philometor would have achieved, had he reigned a century before, we can but conjecture; what we know is that, in the changed conditions of his day, he retained his kingdom by war and diplomacy as the only Hellenistic state *de facto* independent of Rome.[1] We have seen how it was Roman intervention that saved his country from becoming part of the Seleucid Empire. Philometor drew the right conclusion. When, in 164, he was expelled by his brother (known as Physcon), who had pretended to the throne ever since Antiochus' invasion and had apparently been recognized by Rome as a joint ruler— a constitutional experiment as unjustifiable in theory as bound in practice to profit Rome by weakening Egyptian power[2]—, he appeared in the Senate as a suppliant and was restored to Egypt and Cyprus, his brother being sent to rule over Cyrenaica. But his brother objected to this and himself came to Rome, pointing out that Cyprus plus Cyrenaica was more nearly equal to Egypt. Struck by the justice of this—for such a division would go even farther towards preventing the Ptolemies from retaining dangerous reserves of power—the Senate gave him Cyprus.[3] But Philometor refused to hand it over; the Senate showed some vigour in renouncing its friendship with him and sending another mission,[4] but apparently with no result. For some years the deadlock was complete. Then Ptolemy Physcon had a brilliant and hitherto unheard-of idea; unfortunately we have no evidence as to whether it was his own or was suggested to him by Roman friends. He made a will, leaving all his possessions to Rome, if he died without direct heirs. After publishing this will, he went to Rome again and accused his brother—incredibly enough, as it turned out—of plotting against his life: a charge that the will was no doubt intended to underline. The Senate affected to believe the charge,

[1] For the history of Egypt during this period, see the standard works, especially Otto, *6. Ptol.* On Philometor, cf. Pol. xxviii. 21, 4–5; xxxix. 7, 1 f.

[2] Pol. xxix. 27, 9; xxx. 16, 1. Pol. xxxi. 10, 8 applies to this as to the rest of Roman policy towards the two kings. It is difficult not to accept (in outline) Otto's view of the Senate.

[3] Despite what is sometimes asserted, Pol. xxxi. 10, 4 f. proves that the first partition had been made by order of the Senate through its two commissioners.

[4] Pol. xxxi. 17 f. Philometor may well have counted on his Roman friends to protect him (Scullard, op. cit. 230, n. 3—we should add Lepidus, the greatest man in Rome).

expelled Philometor's envoys from Italy (an ominous approach to a declaration of war) and sent out five envoys of its own, with a token naval force, in order to promote a coalition against Philometor and establish Physcon in Cyprus.[1] But what succeeded in the case of Prusias failed against the King of Egypt. For whereas the former was generally unpopular, none of Rome's allies had any quarrel with Philometor, and they would not fight where Rome herself would not. The Senate could not use its clients to carry out a policy in which neither they nor—it must have seemed to them—the Romans themselves were much concerned. The only result was that Philometor captured Physcon—and restored him to Cyrene, treating him with great friendliness.[2] Henceforth Egypt could recuperate, and the King began to see to the succession (and at the same time, no doubt, offered the Senate a compromise) by making his son Eupator 'King of Cyprus'. Unfortunately the young man died in 150;[3] Philometor then resumed control of Cyprus and turned his attention to Syria. There he intervened in the civil war to such effect that he was even himself offered the crown at Antioch.[4] But, on consideration, he declined the offer, for fear that it might call forth Roman intervention.[5] Whether Rome was considering action against him, we do not know; for he died immediately and Egyptian influence in Syria ceased (145).

We have now surveyed Rome's policy towards the kings of the East down to the middle of the second century, and it is time to summarize our conclusions. It is not the defeat of Antiochus the Great, but—as Polybius well knew—only the victory of Pydna

---

[1] Pol. xxxiii. 11. The will has been discovered (see Otto, op. cit. 97 f.). As its date is 155 and that of his visit to Rome 154, and the connexion is easy to find, it is otiose to assume that it was drafted earlier. The 'frenzy' that made various kings after this sign such documents (Accame, *Dom. Rom.* 54) was anything but madness: such an act secured the favour of Rome and discouraged domestic assassins.

[2] Pol. xxxix. 7, 5 f.

[3] I have followed Scullard (op. cit. 237) against Otto: it had been customary ever since the days of the first Antigonus to make the son king in his father's lifetime, and in this case the existence of a potential claimant (Physcon) made that course imperative. The territorial designation was a device used ever since the Persian Empire. Otto cannot be right in making Lepidus *tutor* only of this 'King of Cyprus': Lepidus' connexion with Egypt is attested much earlier (see p. 107, n. 2); and the famous *denarius* certainly suggests, by the personification of Alexandria, that the moneyer thought the young king a Ptolemy ruling at Alexandria.

[4] Pol. xxxix. 7, 1; Just. xxxix. 1, 5 f.; 2, 1 f.   [5] Jos. *Ant.* xiii. 113 f.

which reduces these kings to true dependence on Rome. All the kings round the shores of the Mediterranean, and many farther inland, become her 'allies'—whether by treaty or not is by now immaterial—and in every case this is taken by the Senate to give it wide powers over them: they are forced to accept its arbitration; their very title to the throne comes to depend on its recognition; and they are expected to fight against Rome's enemies at her command.[1] Yet they get little in exchange: they can hope for no protection by Roman arms—at the most, Rome's other allies will be encouraged to support them; they are safe against pretenders only as long as they are reasonably successful against them, yet not so strong as to threaten Rome's balance of power; and the Senate is on the watch for chances of weakening the kingdoms of even its most faithful allies, and ready to transfer its support (without provocation) to their enemies, as soon as it suspects them of excessive power. Yet it is not willing to risk armed conflict for this aim—for it knows that none of the kings is a real danger; and in any case, the Republic need only wait for the inevitable problem of the succession.

Rome's relations with Eastern cities[2] naturally develop, in a general way, along similar lines; but as the size of the cities made their strength not worth considering, the closer contacts after Pydna reveal the Senate in a better light. Before Pydna there is little direct contact. Only two treaties are known or even suggested, neither of them securely datable.[3] And what embassies we know of come mainly on formal business. After the war (and especially after the 'freeing' of Lycia and Caria, Caunus and Stratonicea) the cities hasten to pay homage to Rome.[4] It is doubtful whether many of them were even now granted treaties— this (as the case of the Rhodians shows) was a special favour;[5] but all were no doubt called 'friends and allies'. To this time, too, we must (as far as our evidence goes) assign a new kind of

---

[1] Evidence collected (not exhaustively) by Sands, *Cl. Pr.*, *passim*.

[2] Best discussed by Magie in *Buckler Studies*, 111 f. The case of Rhodes presents special features and has been separately treated above.

[3] See *Note L*, p. 295.

[4] Livy, xliii. 6 (cf. *Note L*); xlv. 20, 4.

[5] Magie (op. cit. 179) wants to date the treaty with Methymna (Ditt. *Syll.* 693) before 154; this is as possible as the commonly accepted date (*c.* 133), but no more so.

treaty, obscuring *de jure* the boundary between merely 'free' and
'federate' ally, already obscured *de facto*: the treaty not signed by
the Roman People. This device, fashioned—as we shall see—in
Rome's dealings with the less civilized communities of the West,
now becomes general, as there is no one left—at home or abroad
—to challenge the Senate's actions.[1] Rome did not, however,
interfere in the cities' affairs: the Senate had more important
things to do. Even disputes between cities, when brought before
it, were referred to other cities for arbitration. But the cities,
unlike the kingdoms, could normally be sure of protection: for
their protection was the humiliation of the kings.[2] (When it was
not, the Romans did not perhaps care quite so much.[3]) In return,
those powerful enough were expected to assist Rome—but they
were no doubt weak enough to be forgiven if they did not take
very much trouble about this.[4] The life of the 'free' cities at this
time was probably more peaceful and on the whole freer than it
had been under the kings' protection: there was as yet (except
once or twice during war) no exploitation, and the Senate's lack
of interest in the cities themselves, combined with its desire for
their safety and goodwill as a weapon against the kings, secured
them the best condition they ever knew.

With the farther East subservient, Macedonia divided and dependent, and Greece ruled by Rome's protégés practically in her
name, peace seemed assured. The Senate relaxed some of the
restrictions on the Macedonian republics, and in 151 at last sent
home the survivors of the Achaeans (and perhaps other Greeks)
deported to Italy.[5] But Macedonia, already politically unsettled,[6]
had been weakened too much: Andriscus, a pretender whom no

---

[1] Cf. the careful analysis of Accame (*Dom. Rom.* 75 f.), defending and strengthening Täubler's conclusions (cited there). Cf. pp. 118 f., 122 f.

[2] Magie, op. cit. 181 f.

[3] Thus we do not hear of any Roman help for Siphnos, sacked by the Cretans
(Diod. xxxi. 45).

[4] Magie, l.c.—but the cities that helped to humble Prusias no doubt had their
own quarrels with that unbeloved monarch. There was no rush to help against
Philometor (see above).

[5] Macedonia: Diod. xxxi. 8, 5 f. is the main source. Cf. Larsen and Aymard in
CP, 1949 and 1950. Achaeans: Pol. xxxv. 6. For other Greeks a similar date may
be assumed (the Aetolians were ultimately allowed to go home: see Just. xxxiii.
2, 8).

[6] Cf. Pol. xxxv. 4, 11.

one at first took seriously, defeated what armies the young republics could muster, and it took a regular Roman army to overcome
him.[1] At the same time the Achaean League, under the influence
of his successes, of Roman difficulties in the West and (no doubt)
the agitation of the anti-Roman party strengthened by the return
of the exiles, began—for the first time for twenty years—to defy
Roman orders: a new generation had grown up, which could not
remember the troubled times to which Callicrates had put an
end; and when the old man died on an embassy to Rome, the
conflict became inevitable. The details are obscure, as our main
source is Pausanias. But it seems that, after Athens had aroused
suspicion of the Achaeans in Rome in connexion with her differences with the League over Oropus and the Delians, the Spartan
troubles flared up again and the League decided to coerce Sparta
in spite of a Roman interdict. The Senate replied by declaring
Sparta as well as Argos, Corinth and Oetean Heraclea 'free' and
independent of the League. The envoys reading this decree at
Corinth barely escaped with their lives, and the Senate, to its
astonishment, saw that Corinth (for one) could only be coerced
into 'freedom' by armed force. With Roman armies already engaged in so many theatres of war, this seemed futile, and Roman
envoys at once became more conciliatory, omitting all references
to the cities 'freed' and confining their attention to the Spartan
problem. But the leaders of the League, sure of support in the
greater part of Greece, failed to strike their bargain and thought
they could achieve genuine independence. The result—as was
foreseen by all sober men—was the quick defeat of the League
and the sack of Corinth.[2] Thus ended the last attempt to secure
real freedom for Greece, bringing little glory to either the victors
or the defeated.

(iii) *Imperium Romanum.* The year 146 brings to their inevitable conclusion the developments begun—as we have seen—even

---

[1] Pol. xxxvi. 10; 17, 13 f.; Livy, *per.* xlix–l.

[2] Paus. vii. 11 f. We have some fragments of Polybius (xxxviii. 1 f.; 9 f.; xxxix.
1 f.), probably exaggerating Roman patience and the madness of the Achaean
demagogues. Dio (fr. 72) adds the thin excuse that the cities now declared 'free'
were those once taken by Rome from Philip. This statement, which often gets into
modern works as a serious point of law, may have been made (if it derives from
Polybius); but that does not render it either valid or even true: force was once more
the relevant argument.

before the victory over Perseus: it sees the end of proper international relations and proper international law over the Roman world. Henceforth all allies—'free' or 'federate'—are clients, in the sense that their rights and obligations are in practice independent of law and treaties and are entirely defined and interpreted by Rome. There is thus no need, for our purpose, to take this study any farther: the conflict[1] between Greek and Roman notions of law and morality—a conflict that we were first able to follow (where it has usually been ignored) in the case of Demetrius of Pharus and have watched down to its final convulsion in the Achaean War—has been resolved in the only way it could be: by force. In the process, as we have seen only too clearly, the political morale of the Greek world, already undermined by the emergence of the Hellenistic kingdoms, was crushed and the Greek political genius finally destroyed. Whether or not this was ultimately unfortunate, it is not our concern to judge. In fact it was to lead to arbitrary exploitation, and sufferings in war unsurpassed in Greek history. It took a century before universal weariness produced the Roman Peace.

There is not enough evidence, after the fading out of our chief historical sources, to enable us to follow in detail what steps still remained to be taken to bring nearer the equalization of Rome's subjects. It is interesting that the term 'socii' now comes to be used practically to mean 'subjects'.[2] That the equalization was never complete is true and important; and great scholars have carefully analysed what evidence we have in particular instances.[3] The gaps cannot all be filled. We should like to know precisely how the *ciuitates liberae* of Sicily sank to the status they occupy at the time of the *Verrines*;[4] or how and when the free city of Utica comes to be the residence of the governor of Africa.[5] But the fact of the extinction of law and the substitution for it of custom as interpreted by Rome—and interpreted (as it often was) arbitrarily enough—is clear and inescapable: henceforth what limits there are to Roman power are those that the Senate chooses

---

[1] This conflict is noticed, as far as it concerns *amici* without treaties, by Oost, *Rom. Pol.*, *passim*.

[2] Accame, op. cit. 54, n. 3 (with references).

[3] Notably Accame, well beyond the modest claim of his title.

[4] That it was settled by the *lex Rupilia* is clear from Cicero.

[5] Cf. p. 139 (with n. 4).

to impose (and is able to enforce against its own members) and what Roman obligations exist are those that the Senate chooses to assume. That this state, after 146, exists in the West as in the East has already been implied; it will next be our purpose to see briefly how it developed there.

V

ROME AND THE WEST (218–133 B.C.)

IT was the Second Punic War that founded Roman control over the Western Mediterranean: the rival power which by 238 had been driven from the Tyrrhenian Sea was now reduced to subjection and its new Spanish empire taken over by the victors; there was no great power left in the West to dispute Roman predominance. The decades that follow mark the natural working out of the process thus begun, a process centring in Spain: Rome slowly extends her control over those who had not yet recognized it, and she has to face difficulties of quite unexpected magnitude. The chief stage of the process is completed in 133, when, with the destruction of Numantia, Spain is at last secure; and it is this stage that we must now proceed to examine, not indeed with the detailed scrutiny of the general political or economic historian, but in so far as it affects our study.[1]

(i) *Spain.* When war was declared, it was the intention of the Senate to fight it in Spain—even when it was known that Hannibal was invading Italy, the consul P. Scipio did not abandon the original plan, but sent his brother to Spain with part of the army; and after the end of his consulate he joined him in Spain.[2] The next six years are taken up with the vicissitudes of battles and alliances, the Romans on the whole making steady progress, though it is difficult to disentangle the truth from the conventional annalistic accretions.[3] But that persuasiveness in winning allies that had been largely responsible for the Scipios' success[4] finally caused their downfall. Deserted by their Celtiberian mercenaries, they were defeated and killed, and it was with difficulty that

[1] The subject is treated at some length in all the standard works. On the governors of Spain and their exploits, see Goetzfried, *Annalen* (down to 154 B.C.); and now *MRR*, i. Schulten's *Numantia* (vol. i) is essential for the history of the Celtiberi and contains much valuable discussion of more general scope. Sutherland, *The Romans in Spain* (referred to, henceforth, by the author's name only), though unreliable in detail, gives a very useful general picture.

[2] Livy, xxi. 17; 32, 1 f.; 60; xxii. 22, 1 f.

[3] Livy, ll.cc.; xxii. 19 f.; xxiii. 26–29; 48–49; xxiv. 41–42; 49.

[4] App. *Iber.* 15, *fin.*

the Roman knight L. Marcius saved the remnants of the armies and the Roman hold on the coastal strip north of the Ebro.[1]

It was this situation that young P. Scipio (the later Africanus) was sent out to retrieve. The story of his success, from his brilliant capture of New Carthage to his failure, on dubious technical grounds, to obtain a triumph, has lost nothing in the telling by our ancient sources.[2] But though we must try to discount their bias, and, in particular, to give due credit to his colleague Silanus (whom they have done their best to ignore) and to the ability of the Senate at home, it is clear that Scipio's personality[3] was an important asset to the Roman cause. Here we must only consider Scipio's policy towards the Spaniards and the organization he created in order to link them to Rome. The evidence (as usual for the barbarian West) is scarce and unsatisfactory; but some conclusions can be reached. Most Spaniards at this time lived in a tribal organization, and it is mainly of Scipio's relations with these tribes that we are informed. We know that he tried to impress the simple tribesmen, and especially their kings and nobles, with his *magnitudo animi*;[4] but he took good care to see that the profit of this prestige, like that of his military successes, was permanently safeguarded for Rome. He continued the policy, pursued by his father and uncle, of binding the barbarian chieftains by definite treaties and solemn oaths. Indibilis, one of the kings about whom we know most, was given a treaty binding him to accept the orders of Roman commanders;[5] and we have no reason to suppose that Scipio dealt differently with other tribal chieftains who joined him. The Spanish auxiliaries who served in the Roman army[6] were probably furnished under such treaties. Yet we may doubt whether these treaties were ever formally referred to Rome. For his treatment of Iberian cities we have no evidence; nor is their previous constitutional status at all clear. Thus, for

---

[1] Livy, xxv. 32 f. (critically discussed by Goetzfried, op. cit. 4 f.).

[2] Pol. x. 2 f.; 34 f.; xi. 20 f.; Livy, xxvi. 18 f.; 41 f.; xxvii. 17 f.; xxviii. 1 f.; 12–38. Cf. Goetzfried, op. cit. 17 f. Detailed discussion in Scullard's *Scipio Africanus*.

[3] On Scipio's flaunting of far-flung *clientelae*, with the *inuidia* it engendered, cf. p. 166.

[4] Pol. x. 19, 3 f.; 40; *et al.*

[5] Pol. x. 38, 4–5; Livy, xxviii. 32, 5 does not disprove this. (Cf. Livy, xxi. 60, 3 f.)

[6] e.g. Livy, xxviii. 13, 3 f.

I

example, we are told that Culchas ruled over twenty-eight *oppida*,[1] but we are not told which (if any) of the Iberian cities taken by the Romans in these years were independent and who ruled over those that were not. Accordingly, we cannot tell how these cities were dealt with: though there is no evidence of any treaties with them (only of capture or surrender and, at the most, 'res suae redditae'),[2] most of them will in fact have been covered by the treaties signed with chieftains. But in at least some cases Scipio, perhaps following a preference for dealing with individuals, attached cities to himself and Rome by personal links: at Castax, we are told, he installed a tyrant;[3] and as we do not hear anything about his constitutional arrangements elsewhere, it is reasonable to believe that he may have done so in other cases where he was lenient towards a city.

The civilized Greek and Phoenician cities of the coast had to be treated differently. Emporiae and Rhode, then Massiliot colonies, were Roman allies of long standing.[4] It may be presumed that, like their parent city,[5] they sooner or later got treaties, and it seems they never broke them. Saguntum, counted a Greek city, was Rome's oldest ally in Spain, and it may have been now that she was rewarded with an honourable treaty.[6] For the treatment of the Phoenician cities we have the example of Gades, the most important of them. Unfortunately, its case is not quite clear, as the detailed evidence of the *Pro Balbo* relates only to the treaty it got from the Senate in 78 B.C. Cicero indeed suggests that this may have been a renewal of its original treaty granted by L. Marcius in 206; but he is not sure, and he clearly does not know much about this original treaty.[7] That there was such a treaty is confirmed by the Gaditane petition in 199: the passage reporting it makes it clear that the treaty provided for the imposition of a Roman prefect.[8] We also know that the treaty was not (as might

---

[1] Livy, xxviii. 13, 3.   [2] For this, cf. Orongis (Livy, xxviii. 3, 15).

[3] App. *Iber.* 32, *fin.* Cf. Pol. xxi. 11, 5; McDonald, *JRS*, 1938, 160.

[4] Emporiae was the chief Roman base from the beginning of the war (Pol. iii. 76, 1; Livy, xxi. 60, 1), and was to remain so in later times of trouble (Livy, xxxiv. 8, 7). Rhode, although less important, also played its part (Livy, xxxiv. 8, 7).

[5] See Ch. II, pp. 47-48.   [6] Cf. pp. 49 f.

[7] *Balb.* 34 f. That Marcius, in 206, was a centurion is improbable; cf. Livy, xxv. 37; xxviii, *passim.*

[8] Livy, xxxii. 2, 5. Cf. *CP*, 1954, 250 f. That the '*maiestas* clause' was used as early as this is unlikely, as I have tried to argue in Ch. IV.

have been expected) ratified by the Senate or the People: it was a military convention[1]—hence the prefect—and, with the military situation changed, the Senate took no action other than to stop the sending of the prefect; thus it was not certain how far Rome was officially bound by it. The status of Gades (and, no doubt, of most of the other Phoenician cities) is in fact intermediate between the *ciuitas libera* and the *ciuitas foederata*. And it is quite likely that the Spanish chieftains were left in the same condition. It was another way of binding a foreign state without committing Rome too precisely, similar to *libertas* as used in the East, but perhaps better adapted to the West, where it was safer not to rely entirely on the allied community's sense of moral obligation—and where 'freedom' had less propaganda value.

Before leaving Spain, Scipio probably organized the whole Roman sphere of influence after a fashion, though, as he was pressed for time, it is doubtful whether he did it very thoroughly.[2] He also took one other step that was to have important consequences: he settled some Roman and Italian veterans unfit for service in a small community on the lower Baetis, which he called 'Italica'.[3] He then left the new 'province' to lesser commanders.

After his departure his system was faced with immediate collapse. To the Spanish chieftains loyalty was a personal thing, and, with Scipio removed, they felt free to ignore their treaties. Besides, they had no doubt joined the Romans in the hope of securing independence from Carthage with their aid; and after the expulsion of the Carthaginians, they saw no reason for letting the Romans stay on. Yet the yoke had been light, and this first revolt aroused no enthusiasm. It was not till 197, in changed circumstances, that the Romans were faced with a serious war, and Cato had to be sent out with a consular army.[4] Even after Cato's exploits (much exaggerated by legend) fighting continued, and it was only Ti. Gracchus who, in 179/8, closed the first stage of the long war for Spanish independence.[5]

---

[1] Cic., l.c.: what Täubler (*Imp. Rom.* i. 132 f.) calls 'Feldherrnvertrag'.

[2] Pol. xi. 33, 8 (cf. Zon. ix. 10)—see Goetzfried, op. cit. 25.

[3] App. *Iber.* 38. The name sufficiently shows the inclusion of Italians.

[4] Livy, xxix. 1, 19 f.; xxxi. 49, 7; xxxiii. 27; 43 f.; xxxiv. 8, 4 f.

[5] Id., xxxv. 1 f.; 7; xxxvi. 39; xxxvii. 46; 57; xxxix. 7; 21; 30; 42; 56; xl. 1; 16; 30 f.; 39 f.; 47 f. (Gracchus); xli. 6 f. and *per.* xli (his settlement and return); App. *Iber.* 41-43; Pol. xxv. 1. The wars are discussed in the standard works.

Much had happened in the forty years since the Romans began the war for Spain, and Roman influence and power there had, despite some setbacks, been steadily expanded and consolidated. Naturally enough, relations of dependence and methods of government had become clarified. Before Cato's campaign there was little regular organization. The edifice built by Scipio had been left in charge of two commanders with small armies and ill-defined duties. They were no doubt meant to keep a general watch over the loyalty of the new allies and to collect the contributions which Rome had imposed. There is no detailed record of any tribute for this first period. The *stipendium* doubled after the revolt of 205 was probably not regarded as a permanent imposition: it was collected by Scipio as a contribution towards the up-keep of the Roman army[1] and perhaps as a war indemnity after a previous rebellion; and Polybius, in his brief reference to the treaty with Indibilis, gives only his military obligations, which must have included the furnishing of supplies.[2] There is no evidence in all this of any particular desire for economic exploitation[3] or of a deliberate experiment in the form of government to be adopted. It was only in 198/197 that this was changed.

At this time it was decided to organize the new conquests on the model of Sicily and Sardinia. As in the case of those islands, a permanent tribute now seems to have been imposed. Only thus can it be explained that, while in 198 L. Manlius Acidinus—after some warfare, as the Senate's grant of an ovation shows—brought back 1,200 pounds of silver and 30 of gold, Blasio in 196 brought home 20,000 pounds of uncoined silver, 34,500 silver coins, and 1,515 pounds of gold, and Stertinius 50,000 pounds of silver[4]— neither of them, as far as we know, with any greater military achievements to his credit than Acidinus; and later figures, where Livy gives them, never again reach the latter's low level.[5] Soon after, in time for the elections for 197, it was further decided to elect two more praetors to govern Spain, and the first two appointed were given armies to relieve those that had been in Spain since the Hannibalic War and were asked to delimit the

---

[1] Livy, xxix. 3, 5. Cf. Pol. xi. 25, 9.   [2] Pol. x. 38, 5.
[3] Schulten, *Gesch. v. Num.* 28; Sutherland, 45 f.
[4] Livy, xxxii. 7, 4; xxxiii. 27, 1 f.
[5] e.g. xxxiv. 10; 46, 2; xxxvi. 21, 10 and 39, 1; xxxix. 42, 3 f.

borders of two 'provinces' in the Peninsula.[1] The government of Spain had been permanently organized and the Romans proposed to enjoy the fruits of their victory.

The result of this organization was a major war. The Iberians, restive under the light yoke of Roman supervision in the war (and immediate post-war) years, now found themselves under a harder master than the Carthaginians had ever been, and they at once took up arms. They were joined by some (at least) of the Phoenician cities, and, apart from the Greeks, the Romans had few allies left. When the seriousness of the situation became apparent, Cato had to be sent with a consular army to restore the situation, and he seems to have been temporarily successful.[2] Legend has exaggerated his exploits, but on the whole obscured his significance. For it is only after Cato that we can speak of a stable provincial organization in Spain. We know that, with his interest in economics, he first organized Spanish mining for the profit of Rome;[3] and that same interest seems to have been used in organizing the assessment of tribute,[4] a task which cannot have been satisfactorily completed in the short time before the outbreak of the insurrection and must indeed, as we have argued, have been its cause. We know that Cato's organization was ratified by the Senate and made binding on future governors.[5] And, although our sources are too much taken up with anecdotes and campaigns to give us any details about it, we must not join them in failing to see its importance.

From the military point of view Cato's campaigns had not been decisive; in fact, his attack upon the Celtiberi only succeeded in turning them into open enemies of Rome. For many years fighting went on, sometimes on quite a large scale, until Ti. Gracchus, in 179, imposed a more lasting settlement on the Celtiberi.[6] We are not concerned with the details of the fighting.

---

[1] Livy, xxxii. 27, 6; 28, 11. The number of the Roman troops seems to have been omitted, either by a copyist or by Livy himself. It may have been one legion each (the later permanent strength). For the borders of the two provinces, see Sutherland, 48 f. and map 2 (where, for '206 B.C.' read '197 B.C.').

[2] Livy, xxxiii. 19, 7; 21, 6; 25, 8 f.; 43 f.; xxxiv. 8, 4 f.; 46, 2 f.; App. *Iber.* 39 f.

[3] Livy, xxxiv. 21, 7.   [4] On the collection of the tribute, see Sutherland, 53 f.

[5] This much truth must underlie Plut. *Cat. Mai.* 11, and it perhaps forms one of the bases on which that story arose.

[6] On the wars, see the standard works. Gracchus' settlement was at last a *uera pax* (Livy, xl. 50, 5).

Whether any general policy can be discerned through the inadequate information given by our sources is a difficult question. We are told that Culchas, a tribal chieftain, had seen his kingdom reduced from twenty-eight to seventeen 'cities' between the first appearance of the Romans and the revolt of 197. This is further generalized into the statement that 'communes and towns were encouraged at the expense of larger tribal units, while native chiefs were no doubt controlled'.[1] Yet there is no evidence for all this. Even if Livy's figures for the number of 'cities' under a barbarian chieftain can be trusted, there is nothing in the sources to justify the belief that his territory had been diminished, or that the Romans had encouraged such a tendency. Sutherland mentions the possibility of synoecism, as peace returned and civilization progressed:[2] if some of his 'cities' united into stronger communities, the ruler would not thereby be weakened. Moreover, we happen to know that it was not easy to count the number of 'cities' in Spain: in a famous passage, Polybius is accused of counting every little πύργος as a πόλις in order to glorify Gracchus.[3] Thus the example of Culchas, so often abused, tells us nothing. On the contrary, the Scipios in their letter to Prusias used Culchas as an example of a chieftain made into a great king by Roman aid.[4] And although the letter is a propagandist document, it must at least be true that down to the time of his rebellion Culchas' kingdom had not been diminished. Nor can we discern any general principles in L. Aemilius Paullus' letter to the people of Hasta,[5] from which Mommsen and others draw completely unwarranted conclusions:[6] for we do not know the circumstances leading up to the decision.[7] There is thus nothing on which to base conclusions as to Roman policy in Spain during the period between Cato and Gracchus.

The Gracchan settlement does not seem to mark any violent change; Gracchus, we learn, made treaties with the Celtiberian

---

[1] Livy, xxxiii. 21, 8, compared with xxviii. 13, 3 (206 B.C.). Sutherland, 65; Scullard, *History*, 288.

[2] p. 61. Strangely enough, he thinks that this led to a 'persistent decrease' in Culchas' territory.   [3] Pol. xxv. 1.

[4] Pol. xxi. 11, 7.   [5] *ILS*, 15.

[6] *Str.* iii, p. xvii, n. 1; also Sutherland, 73 f.

[7] e.g. whether it is penal (plausibly suggested by Goetzfried, op. cit. 76); or what was the precise previous state of the *serui* mentioned.

tribes, carefully laying down their duties and (by implication, at least) defining their rights. This is merely an extension to Celt-iberia of the method that had been used in Spain ever since Scipio. We do not hear of any ratification of these treaties by the Roman People: it is Gracchus who takes the oaths, and later they are 'the treaties of Gracchus'.[1] It may be assumed that the Senate ratified the settlement of Gracchus, as it had that of Cato; and we know that, though some of the communities were granted precarious exemption from the more burdensome provisions of their treaties (as Gades once had been),[2] the 'treaties of Gracchus' henceforth became the official constitution of Celtiberia, referred to by both sides in cases of dispute. Gracchus seems also to have tried to win the support of the poorer classes for Rome—a sound, and indeed obvious, policy in a country where they would otherwise be a constant threat to peace.[3]

The Gracchan system brought relief to the troubled Peninsula; but it could not last, as it had the fatal fault (common in Roman institutions) of being static. The duties of each tribe were deemed to be fixed for ever, without adjustment to changing condi-tions; and the clause forbidding the Celtiberians to found new cities—a clause apparently contradicting Gracchus' own policy of founding Graccurris[4] and revealing complete indifference to the advance of civilization and prosperity in Spain—is typical of the spirit of the settlement. But the effect of peace was bound to go beyond the vision of its maker, and the town founded as a monu-ment to proud achievement was to play its part in spreading Roman civilization. Nor is the age of the Gracchan Peace, or at least the greater part of it, marred by that cruelty, treachery and exploitation rightly charged against Roman rule in Spain at so many other times. In 171 the communities of both the Spanish provinces sent petitions to the Senate to protest against certain abuses; and though the main culprits had sufficient influence to escape punishment, recurrence of abuses in the collection of tri-bute was prevented and the towns were protected against the imposition of Roman prefects.[5] This care of the Senate for peace in Spain, and its avoidance of excessive exploitation, is also shown

---

[1] App. *Iber.* 43 f.; cf. 48, *fin.*
[2] Ibid. 44. For Gades, see above.
[3] Ibid. 43.
[4] Livy, *per.* xli.
[5] Id., xliii. 2.

by the case of the Belli, who at some time after Gracchus—and, it seems, a sufficiently long time before 154 for the privilege to be by then regarded as a right—were exempted from the payment of tribute and the furnishing of troops.[1] This is not the action of unbridled avarice. We may conclude that for a short time the provinces knew relative peace and prosperity.[2]

The synoecism of Segeda in 154[3] marks the beginning of the next series of wars, one disfigured by as foul a record of faithlessness and cruelty on the part of the Romans as history has to show. A few men, like Marcellus (152-151), stand out as examples of honesty and political foresight; it is due to him that for eight difficult years the Romans did not have to face the hostility of some of the most warlike tribes; and had his conduct and his policy been followed, the disgrace of Numantia would have been unnecessary.[4] But in fact the war dragged on, through several treaties disowned by the Senate, even after the murder of Viriathus, the great Iberian leader, until Scipio Aemilianus starved Numantia into surrender in 133.[5]

With the war ended, Scipio took certain preliminary measures, which were followed by the sending of the usual Senatorial commission to settle the territory reconquered or newly occupied.[6] Of the nature of this settlement we know little, except that Roman control seems to have been tightened and the 'allies' unmistakably turned into subjects. The cessation of the silver coinage of Citerior is probably rightly put at this time: it had become economically unnecessary, as the Roman *denarii* introduced by the legions, the silver coins already in circulation, and the bronze, which was (it seems) reorganized, were sufficient for the needs of the still primitive province; and its stoppage, like the reorganization of the bronze, may well be part of the work of the Senatorial commission.[7] It is permissible to guess that new

---

[1] App. *Iber.* 44.

[2] That there was *some* fighting cannot be denied—at least until the Gracchan system settled down. Cf. Livy, xli. 28, 3; *Fasti triumph.* for 174 (Ap. Claudius Centho); *Fasti Cap.* for 175 (M. Titinius Curvus).   [3] App. *Iber.* 44.

[4] Ibid. 48 f.   [5] Ibid. 96 f.

[6] Ibid. 98 *fin.*-99 *init.* For the extent of the new conquests, see Sutherland, map 2.

[7] Hill, *Notes on the anc. coinage of Hisp. Cit.* (New York, 1931), 122 f.; Sutherland, 110 f.

treaties, on the model of those of Gracchus, were concluded—
we have no evidence, but the Senate's methods were not likely to
change violently. This may also explain the absence of any trace
of increasing urbanization: for Gracchus had forbidden the
building of cities. However, the mere presence of the commission
suggests that this time the Senate no longer hesitated to commit
itself; the new system was no longer the work of an individual
commander, of doubtful legal status and (despite general Senatorial sanction) liable to be upset by his successors.

Here we may leave Spain, now probably provincialized at least
as far as Roman conquests went. We shall have more to say about
the progress of citizenship there in a later chapter.[1]

(ii) *Africa.* In Africa, after the War, the Romans had to deal
with constant differences between Masinissa and Carthage.
Masinissa had recovered his throne and enlarged his kingdom
through the help of Scipio: it was Scipio who (we are told)
addressed Masinissa as king,[2] and who gave him the territory
Rome had conquered from Syphax;[3] and we know that the close
relations between the houses of the ruler and the dynast continued.[4] More than any other king, Masinissa was the creature of
Rome, and indeed of one Roman. It is not surprising that he
remained conspicuously loyal to Rome and willing to execute,
and even anticipate, her wishes.[5] Carthage, on the other hand,
was the defeated enemy, and hatred and resentment towards her
seem to have smouldered in the minds of the Senate, although
right down to the fifties there was never any reasonable doubt of
Carthaginian loyalty:[6] for the commercial and land-owning
aristocracy would not permit any more political and military
adventurers to gamble away their returning prosperity.[7] Carthage,
however, had become a client state: her treaty, we are told, forbade her not only to wage war outside her own frontiers, but to

---

[1] Ch. XI, below.
[2] See *Note M*, p. 295.
[3] Livy, xxx. 44, 12.
[4] See below.
[5] Livy, xxxi. 19, 3 f.; xxxvi. 3, 1; 4, 8; xlii. 35, 6 f.; 62, 2; xliii. 3, 6; 6, 13; xlv.
13, 13 f.; App. *Iber.* 46.
[6] Livy, xxxi. 19, 1 f.; xxxiii. 49, 4; xxxiv. 60, 1 f.; xxxvi. 3, 1; 4, 5 f.; 44, 5 f.;
xliii. 3, 7; 6, 11 f.
[7] Cf. Livy, xxxi. 19, 1 f.; xxxiii. 45, 6 f.; xxxiv. 60, 1 f.

wage war against allies of Rome in any circumstances;[1] and though we need not accept this clause—contrary as it was to *ius gentium*[2]—, Rome now had the moral responsibility of protecting her. The history of the relations of Carthage and Masinissa during the fifty years following the peace is, as far as we can trace it, that of the attitude of Rome to her two client states; and it is, to some extent, the experience of their subservience that moulded Rome's attitude towards her Eastern friends and allies.

Trouble began not long after the end of the War. The peace treaty had guaranteed Carthage her old African boundaries, but provided for the cession to Masinissa of everything that had belonged to him or his ancestors.[3] Thus the boundary fixed in 201 (the Φοινικίδες τάφροι)[4] was not a frontier between Carthage and Masinissa, and it is doubtful if such a frontier ever existed. There was bound to be continual dispute as to what constituted the ancient boundaries of Masinissa's kingdom—a state of affairs that suited Rome so well that she soon tried to copy it in the case of another old enemy, Macedon.[5] The stages of Masinissa's encroachment on the remaining territory of Carthage are, owing to the state of our sources, not easy to follow; but modern historians have tried to reconstruct them from geographical probabilities.[6] They do not concern us in detail. We are concerned only with the Roman attitude to them. Differences are mentioned as early as 195 and again in 193; the next dispute we hear of is an isolated one in 182. In 174 relations are strained, and this is followed by another attack by the King.[7] Then Livy unfortunately gives out: the only further evidence on actual disputes

[1] This clause, usually accepted and made much of, seems to rest on a sentence in a Livian speech in 172! (xlii. 23, 3–4.) Cf. Scullard, *Scipio*, 253 f.: a thorough and scholarly discussion. Livy, xxx. 37, 4 is patently false—and contradicts xlii. 23, 4.

[2] For this, see Livy, xlii. 41, 11: a similar attempt on the part of Rome to forbid self-defence.

[3] Pol. xv. 18, 5.

[4] App. *Lib.* 54 (cf. 32 and 59). There is no mention of these trenches in Polybius or Livy, and some scholars thus reject them as annalistic fabrication (e.g. Kahrstedt, *Gesch. d. Karth.* iii. 591, n. 1). But a passage quoted from Eumachus (*FGrHist.* ii B, p. 906) seems to prove their existence. (Cf. Gsell, *HAAN.* ii. 102.)

[5] Livy, (P.), xxxix. 26, 14; cf. Ch. IV, p. 93.

[6] See Kahrstedt, op. cit. 590 f.; 606 f.; map II; Schur, *RE*, s.v. 'Massinissa', coll. 2158 f.; Gsell, op. cit. iii. 314 f. The most important text is Pol. xxxi. 21 (161 B.C.); but it deals only with the dispute over the *Emporia*.

[7] Livy, xxxiii. 47, 8; xxxiv. 62 f.; xl. 17, 1 f.; 34, *fin.*; xli. 22, 1 f.; xlii. 23 f.

about territory, before the final one that led to the last Punic War, is a Polybian passage, two references in the *Periochae*, and Appian.[1]

German scholars, in dealing with the history of these wars, have on the whole admired Masinissa as the unifier of his country; but his skill, his success, and even his political achievements, must not blind us to the barbarian immorality of his methods. There was room in North-West Africa for the peaceful coexistence of a demilitarized Carthaginian republic and a Numidian kingdom educated and civilized by it; and the course of history might have been different, if Masinissa had restrained his lust for expansion. As it is, in spite of his imitation of Hellenism, he must remain to us, as Schur accuses the ancients of depicting him, 'der barbarische Bedränger des schwach gewordenen Kulturlandes',[2] and the man responsible for the Roman annexation of Africa.

We have noticed that the Romans did nothing to put an end to the situation created by the terms of their treaty; it seems, in fact, that they tried to ensure its continuance. In 195 we are not told of any decision: Livy reports only the flight of Hannibal. In 193, after Carthage had given proof of her loyalty by refusing to intrigue with Hannibal and Antiochus, a mission was sent to arbitrate; but although it was headed by Scipio Africanus himself, it gave no clear decision—as Livy notes, bad faith is the only possible reason.[3] In fact this must have meant that Masinissa gained his point; for he had superior armed forces, and in any case the Carthaginians were forbidden to attack him and thus could not expel him from territory he had occupied.

In 182 a Roman commission refused to decide on the status of some territory that at one time had been taken from the Carthaginians by Masinissa's father: it was the sort of dispute the settlement of 201 had encouraged, especially as Masinissa's ancestors had been raiding barbarians. It was referred back to the Senate, whose decision we are not told, unless it was a Senate decision which in the following year 'secured Carthage peace

[1] For Polybius, see p. 126, n. 6. Livy, *per.* xlvii (157 B.C.) and xlviii (153 B.C.); App. *Lib.* 69. Saumagne ('Prétextes') is guilty of some very arbitrary reconstruction of the sources.

[2] Op. cit., col. 2160.

[3] See *Note N*, p. 295.

from Masinissa'.[1] In any case, it is clear that Masinissa retained the contested land. In 174 the King seems to have used Roman fears of Perseus to accuse Carthage of conspiring with him—and, indeed, it would not be surprising if a section in Carthage favoured the cause of Perseus. Having, he thought, prepared his ground, he launched a major attack on Carthaginian territory, occupying more than seventy cities. In 172 the matter came up for discussion in the Senate. With the war against Perseus imminent, it did not want to drive Carthage to desperate measures; thus decision was postponed and the principle of the 'ancient frontiers' was reasserted—we do not know with what effect on the actual situation in Africa. Nor do we know what happened when the affair came up for discussion in the following year, as Livy's text breaks off.[2]

Roman protection for Carthage had not, as we can see, been very effective, and it is clear that Rome had favoured her faithful watchdog Masinissa. Yet Masinissa realized that Rome did give Carthage protection of a sort:[3] it is as clear to us as it is said to have been to him that, had the Roman power been removed, he could, at that time, have conquered the remaining Carthaginian territory without much difficulty and might even have taken the city, especially with the support of the faction friendly to him.[4] This is not due to any moral scruples on the part of Rome: had there been any, it would have been easy to fix a definite frontier somewhere and guarantee it.[5] Carthage was being protected mainly to keep a balance of power in Africa and to remind Masinissa of his dependence on Rome, partly because her annual instalment of the indemnity was a welcome addition to the Roman budget; although fear and hatred of her persisted and were

---

[1] Livy, xl. 34, 14. The anecdote in App. *Lib.* 68 may refer to the same occasion, but does not give a decision by the Senate. Livy's 'pacem [Carthaginiensibus] praestitit' (l.c.) and 'possessionis ius non mutarunt' (ibid. 17, 6) suggest the commission which (in Appian) orders both parties to keep the peace, without taking the disputed territory out of Masinissa's possession. The two Livian stories may be doublets, or the second may refer to a decision by the Senate. Gsell (op. cit. iii. 317 f.— against Kahrstedt, op. cit. 608, n. 1) has seen the true implications of the second passage.

[2] After xliii. 3.

[3] Livy, (P.?), xlii. 29, 8 f. Cf. Kahrstedt, op. cit. 609.

[4] Cf. App. *Lib.* 68.

[5] Livy (xlii. 23, 6) makes the Carthaginians beg the Senate to do this.

responsible for the arbitrators' decisions. The sudden conspicuous pretence of fairness at the critical time before the Macedonian War shows as nothing else can how seriously Carthage was still taken at Rome.

After the victory over Perseus, Masinissa sent his son Masgaba to Rome to congratulate the Senate;[1] he, if we may believe Livy, announced to the Romans the King's own view of his clientship: he had only the *usus* of his kingdom, while the *dominium* belonged to Rome. But the Romans were not prepared to accept this theory of *clientela*: the Senate's reply, we find, praises him for his due gratitude and his performance of his *officia*, i.e. reasserts the traditional Roman view. While we must not attach too much weight to the details of this report, the points we have mentioned —the contrasted views of *clientela*—read genuine enough and seem psychologically and historically too sound to be the invention of an annalist. The passage shows how in the West, as in the East, *clientela* baffled the non-Roman. If we accept it, it is easy to understand that the Roman view, already sufficiently elastic in its assessment of Rome's duties, was bound to be influenced, sooner or later, by the non-Roman interpretation.

Masinissa even offered to come to Rome and sacrifice to Jupiter on the Capitol. But the Senate did not permit this: the King was over seventy,[2] and the journey to Rome might be too strenuous: nor would his own kingdom necessarily be safe in his absence.[3]

A few years later the King launched his final series of attacks on Carthage—still with Roman support. In 161, after a prolonged dispute, he was awarded the *Emporia*, in a decision which Polybius acknowledges to be quite unjust.[4] A little later he launched an attack on the rich plain round Thugga, and (we are told) a Roman commission under Cato did nothing. According to Appian, this commission wanted to decide περὶ ἅπαντα, which implies that it at last offered to fix a frontier; but this time it was the Carthaginians who would not have it. This is intelligible only if their strength was now equal to resisting Masinissa—and

---

[1] Livy, xlv. 13, 12 f.   [2] His age in App. *Lib.* 71; Pol. xxxvi. 16, 2; *et al.*

[3] Livy, l.c. The Senate's refusal was hardly meant as a slight to him. While in Rome, Masgaba tried to arouse suspicion against Carthage; unfortunately there is at this point a lacuna in Livy's text and we know nothing further.

[4] Pol. xxxi. 21; cf. *Note N*, p. 295.

what follows suggests that it was. We can understand why Cato convinced himself that Carthage was again a danger.[1]

This brings us to the events preceding the Third Punic War. According to Appian,[2] the Senate, after hearing Cato's report, secretly decided upon war, waiting only for a suitable pretext before beginning it; from this time forward Cato always pressed for the destruction of Carthage, Scipio Nasica for its preservation. This pretext was in due course provided by Carthage. The Carthaginians had expelled their pro-Numidian faction, and when Masinissa tried to intervene in their favour, his envoys were excluded and molested. He thereupon laid siege to a town on Carthaginian territory; the Carthaginians resisted by armed force, and after some fighting (in the course of which Rome intervened to no purpose) their army was defeated and the survivors treacherously killed. The Romans thereupon began to collect an army, and the Carthaginians, afraid of Roman attack, condemned the leaders responsible for the war and sent a mission of apology. The Romans expressed their dissatisfaction, but would not give a clear answer on methods of reparation. At this point Utica, the largest city still subject to Carthage, surrendered into the Roman *fides*; the Senate accepted the surrender and now openly declared war.

In the Livian *Periocha*[3] the Romans hear a rumour that Carthage is preparing an army under a grandson of Syphax; Cato advises war against Carthage, Scipio Nasica opposes him. A mission goes to Carthage to investigate and to settle a dispute with Masinissa. Masinissa offers to withdraw from the disputed territory and (it seems) peace is about to be made, when a demagogue incites the mob to violence against the Roman envoys. Gulussa reports further preparations for war at Carthage, there is another debate in the Senate between Scipio and Cato and ten more envoys are sent to investigate. The envoys return

---

[1] App. *Lib.* 68–69. Cf. Gsell, op. cit. iii. 320 f. It is usually assumed that Livy (*per.* xlvii) gives two missions, the first in 157 B.C. But the *Periocha* cannot be used for precise chronology, and he probably reports only one mission, which goes out to arbitrate, reports 'uim naualis materiae' at Carthage, and is identical with that given by Appian (l.c.) and Plutarch (*Cat. Mai.* 26) as headed by Cato. It may be put in 153–2. (Cf. Gsell, op. cit. iii. 321; Gelzer, *R. St.* i. 79; but the events connected, in App. *Lib.* 68, with the name of Carthalo were probably much earlier. See above.)   [2] *Lib.* 69 f.   [3] *Per.* xlviii and xlix.

accompanied by a Carthaginian embassy and Gulussa (who, it later appears, had not been admitted into Carthage) and confirm the reports. After another debate between Scipio and Cato the Senate decides not to declare war if Carthage disarms. This, apparently, is of no avail, and after another such debate war is declared.

Zonaras[1] makes the Carthaginians collect allies and ships against Masinissa; the Romans send Scipio Nasica to reproach them and prevail upon Masinissa to give up some disputed territory. The Carthaginians remain as disobedient as before, and the Romans, hearing that Masinissa has defeated them, declare war upon them.

Little remains of Polybius[2] on the subject; but he stresses the fact that the Senate had early resolved upon war and was waiting only for a pretext; and he also reports the declaration of war as following upon the surrender of Utica. It is therefore generally agreed that Appian's account is based on Polybius'. There is a slight difference: Appian makes the Carthaginians send πρέσβεις αὐτοκράτορας (who receive the demand for hostages—see below) only after hearing of the declaration of war, and he does not mention their *deditio*;[3] Polybius stresses the latter and says that it was the action taken by the πρεσβευταὶ αὐτοκράτορες when, after reaching Rome, they found war already declared;[4] the demand for hostages then follows. This, however, is probably due only to inaccuracy in Appian (or his immediate source), and Appian's account may be accepted as Polybian, though with mistakes in the transmission.

Livy, as reported by his epitomator, is clearly based on annalistic apologetics: the discussions between Cato and Nasica are multiplied; the Senate is painted as long-suffering under provocation; and the first embassy—with the violence against Roman ambassadors, which goes unpunished—is a poor doublet of the second.[5] The annalists had been busy inventing excuses for one

---

[1] ix. 26.   [2] xxxvi, *init.*   [3] *Lib.* 76.

[4] xxxvi. 3. Saumagne attempts to derive this part of the accounts of Appian and Polybius from antithetical sources; but this seems to be refuted by the factual correspondences in the accounts (as distinct from the judgements on them, most of which Appian has put into rhetorical speeches).

[5] Cf. Kahrstedt, op. cit. 620 f.; Gelzer, l.c. (p. 130, n. 1). Gsell (op. cit. iii. 334, n. 1) does not accept the view that Livy's two embassies are doublets: he thinks the whole account pure annalistic fiction. But this is extreme.

of Rome's most shameful actions. Zonaras (i.e. Dio) and Livy both draw on these apologies and may for our purpose be ignored. The course of events, then, was roughly that given by Appian from Polybius. Scipio Nasica's hereditary interest in Africa[1] may have led to his inclusion in an embassy—perhaps the one which also included Cato and which might have saved Carthage. On its return, impressed by its report on the Carthaginians' resources and perhaps on their returning independence of spirit,[2] the Senate was stampeded into its secret resolution to go to war as soon as a fair pretext could be found—a resolution not unparalleled in the annals of modern governments. Nasica's opposition continued, on moral (no doubt) as much as on politico-philosophical grounds,[3] while Cato tried to hold the Senate to its decision. Nasica was very close to success, as the first wave of feeling receded.[4] When it was learnt that Carthage was resisting Masinissa by armed force, an embassy was sent to investigate and to settle the dispute. It did nothing. Nor could the young Scipio Aemilianus, who happened to be in Africa and tried to act in the tradition of his adoptive family, persuade the Carthaginians to end the war by acknowledging the failure of their policy: the surrender of the deserters would have ended the war; but the Carthaginians, though willing to withdraw (it seems) from territory they had reoccupied in their pursuit of the Numidians, would not give up their most important weapon.[5] It was probably now that the Senate decided to have an army in readiness, in case Masinissa was defeated. This, and the sudden Carthaginian disaster, persuaded Utica to surrender to Rome; and with this favourable opportunity offering,[6] morality was forgotten and Cato had

[1] He was probably the senior member of the house of the Scipiones. Scipio Aemilianus' policy at this stage is essentially similar (see below). I cannot accept Astin's views (*Latomus*, xv, 1956, 159 f.), which presuppose an interrelation between internal politics and foreign policy for which I see no evidence at that period.

[2] Cf. pp. 129–30.

[3] For the latter, see Gelzer, l.c.   [4] Pol. xxxvi. 2, 4.

[5] App. *Lib.* 70 f. Appian's story of their 'secret instructions' is, of course, most probably developed *ex post facto*. On the importance of the deserters see p. 136 (with n. 2). In Appian the Carthaginians offer to cede τὴν περὶ τὸ Ἐμπόριον γῆν. If this is the district ceded in 161, the Punic armies had penetrated into it again in their pursuit of the Numidians (l.c.)—which makes good sense.

[6] We are told that in Rome the War was popular and generally regarded as a chance for easy booty (App. *Lib.* 75, *fin.*). At the time of its outbreak Nasica may have been on a mission to Greece and Macedonia and unable to prevent it (see *MRR*, i. 457).

no trouble in persuading the Senate to declare war. At this point the Carthaginian envoys arrived and made their surrender.

Events after this are (in outline) generally agreed upon, and we need not go into them in detail. It is known how the Romans used the rights which they considered *deditio* gave them in order to weaken Carthage by degrees,[1] until—with the city disarmed, the Roman army established in Africa, and hostages in Roman hands—it seemed that the order to evacuate the site of Carthage could not be resisted; it is also known how this reasonable belief turned out to be mistaken, and how a long and inglorious war was necessary to subdue the defenceless city. But before going on to the settlement we must discuss Roman pretexts and motives in undertaking the war.

A full statement of pretexts is given in the Livian *Periocha*:[2] possession of ships contrary to the treaty; the advance of an army beyond the frontier; an attack on Masinissa, friend and ally of the Roman People; and the exclusion of Gulussa from the city, when he had been accompanied by Roman envoys. This part of the Livian account must not be lightly rejected. We have seen the annalistic falsifications in his narrative of events—the attempt to justify and extol the Senate and put Carthage in the wrong—and the same tendency can be discerned in this part of his account. Thus the *deditio* of Utica is only made after war has already been declared—there is no mention of the cynical realism that Appian probably found in Polybius. Yet it will not do to reject the *Senatus consultum* declaring war as mere fabrication.[3] Of its four allegations, one (the second) is almost certainly true,[4] one (the third) is precisely what may be expected in a partisan interpretation, and the first and the last are not impossible as complaints, though one is not a just cause for war by Rome and the other may in fact have been untrue.[5] The absence of those charges that are

---

[1] Saumagne (op. cit. 19 f.) is perhaps right in thinking that the nature of *deditio*, at the time, was not as clear as the Roman tradition thinks (cf. Piganiol, *RIDA*, 1950, 339 f.). In any case, like other Roman institutions on the periphery of law, it would not be clear to non-Romans.

[2] xlix. Saumagne (op. cit.) takes no account of this text.

[3] As it is by Kahrstedt (p. 624): 'Senatsbeschlüsse gehören zum wertvollsten Bestand der Annalistik' (Gelzer, *R. St.* i. 84).   [4] See p. 132, n. 5.

[5] Kahrstedt (l.c.) denies that Carthage had a fleet: there is no reference to one in Pol. xxxvi. 6, 7 (admittedly fragmentary) or in App. *Lib.* 80 and Strabo, xvii. 3, 15; nor even in Livy, *per.* xlix among the munitions surrendered! But the evidence is

obviously annalistic inventions—such as ill-treatment of a Roman embassy, or contumacy in the face of Roman injunctions to disarm—and of any reference to the clause, smuggled into the treaty of 201 by some annalist, which forbade Carthage to defend herself against attack on her own territory, helps to confirm the essential authenticity of the decree.

But it is clear that, even if these are the pretexts actually given by the Senate, they were not the real causes of the war. Rome had been preparing the attack for some time, and the Carthaginians' breach of the treaty of 201 in pursuing Masinissa beyond their frontiers (for in this the Carthaginians had admittedly put themselves technically in the wrong) only furnished a fair pretext, just as the weakening of Carthage and the surrender of Utica provided a convenient occasion.

Ever since Kahrstedt advanced his revolutionary theory,[1] it has been widely held that the real reason was a very unexpected and Machiavellian one: Carthage had to be destroyed, not because she was strong enough to inspire fear, but because she was too weak to defend herself against Numidia; if Masinissa occupied the remaining Punic territory, he would become one of those strong neighbours whom Rome always feared. Thus the people of Carthage were sacrificed to protect Rome against her own client. This view has gained many adherents;[2] but not only is it completely unknown to antiquity, the Romans being always depicted as the constant supporters of Masinissa even beyond what morality would permit—it seems, in fact, absurd in itself. We have commented above on the King's conception of his clientship, and we shall see in the instance of his final dispositions that it had not changed as the years passed. If Rome wanted to maintain a balance of power in Africa, all she had to do was to stop favouring Masinissa's aggression—to send a commission with instructions to ensure a lasting peace. We know that Masinissa offered to submit to Roman arbitration even when Carthage was at last becoming suspicious of it.[3] If Rome had been

not decisive: the Carthaginians certainly had the few warships they were allowed by the treaty (Strabo, l.c.; cf. Livy, xxxvi. 42, 2), and these are not mentioned in this connexion either.

[1] Op. cit. 615 f. et al.

[2] e.g. Schur, RE, s.v. 'Massinissa', c. 2163; Gsell, op. cit. iii. 329 f.; Scullard, History, 302; Charlesworth, CAH, viii. 476.   [3] App. Lib. 69; Zon. ix. 26.

determined to show that the suspicion was no longer justified, the problem of Masinissa's excessive power would have ceased to exist. And the volte-face that was possible in the case of Pergamum[1] would have been easier still in the case of Numidia. Kahrstedt's far-fetched hypothesis is otiose. The only grain of truth we can salvage from it is—what we knew before—that, once the Romans did decide that Carthage ought to be destroyed, they determined to undertake the execution themselves and to avoid giving Masinissa any further increase in power and territory; and that Masinissa was a little hurt by this check to his ambitions.[2] But that is irrelevant to the question of Roman motives in taking the decision in the first place.

Adcock has pointed out[3] that we must not make the mistake of thinking of those motives as based entirely on cool calculation; the Romans, it seems, were predisposed to believe all evil of Carthage, and hatred and fear perverted their practical as well as their moral judgement.[4] We have noted how the decision to go to war was made after Carthage had begun to show some independence of spirit,[5] and we are told by all our sources that the one thing on which Cato and Nasica agreed in their long debate was the strength and resources of Carthage—there was never any suggestion that the city was weak.[6] The course of events, in fact, cannot be explained on the assumption that the Senate thought little of Punic strength: through the whole of the sorry recital of perfidy and cruelty there run the threads of fear and hatred—the fear that decided that Carthage must cease to exist and yet hesitated, at every step, to attack her with her resources undiminished; and the hatred that knew no claims of morality and no pity.[7] Nor was the fear, irrationally exaggerated though we must think it, as completely unfounded as modern historians would make us believe. As is stressed by our ancient sources, the strength of Carthage is shown, more than by the vast quantities of armaments

---

[1] See Ch. IV, pp. 102 f.
[2] App. *Lib.* 94.   [3] *CHJ*, 1946, 117 f.
[4] Cf. Gelzer, op. cit. 68 f. Velleius recognized this (i. 12, 2): 'magis quia uolebant Romani quidquid de Carthaginiensibus diceretur credere quam quia credenda adferebantur.' Cf. (s. 5): 'magis inuidia imperii quam ullius eius temporis noxiae inuisam.'   [5] Cf. pp. 129–30.   [6] Cf. Gelzer, op. cit. 88 f.
[7] Popular opinion in Italy did not give Carthage much hope after the surrender of Utica (cf. App. *Lib.* 75, *fin.*). But the Senate did not take any chances even then.

she surrendered, by her great achievement in producing munitions and withstanding immediate attacks and a prolonged siege,
even after being totally disarmed.[1] And the quantities of war
material handed in, after terrible losses in the war with Masinissa,
show that preparations for war had been proceeding for years.
This, of course, explains Punic hesitation in submitting to Cato's
mission, and the vigorous counter-attack against Masinissa:
Carthage had acquired some confidence in her reviving strength.
Moreover, Masinissa's policy of converting Numidia into a strong
centralized kingdom had made many enemies for him in his own
country, and it looks as though Punic diplomacy did not fail to
exploit this situation: the desertion of two Numidian chieftains
with their cavalry seems to have been prepared in advance;[2] and,
had Carthage been successful, their example might have been
widely followed. That was why, when Scipio tried to end the war
between Carthage and Masinissa, the surrender of those deserters
was the point on which negotiations finally broke down:[3] it was
the one point on which, in the interests of his future safety, the
latter had to insist, and which, as long as there was any hope of
future successes, the former could not grant. Once the last instalment of her old war indemnity was paid, Carthage, well prepared
for war, and with growing economic resources, could face Masinissa on more than equal terms; his kingdom might disintegrate
under pressure and diplomacy, and North Africa return to its old
allegiance. It is quite probable that Carthage, by the late fifties,
was aiming at nothing less than this. Roman fears, therefore,
though exaggerated by old memories (for it is clear that Carthage
knew that she could not resist Rome), may not have been as
absurd as we are usually invited to believe.[4]

---

[1] On the quick rearmament, see App. *Lib.* 93; Strabo, xvii. 3, 15; Zon. ix. 26; *et al.*

[2] The desertion came at the beginning of the battle and went quite smoothly
(App. *Lib.* 70). Livy (*per.* xlviii) mentions an Ariobarzanes (?), grandson of Syphax,
as leading Numidians in Carthaginian employ. Kahrstedt (op. cit. 624) believes
this is annalistic falsification—perhaps rightly. But this prearranged desertion at a
decisive moment suggests that there may be a kernel of truth in it. Even in the
sixties the Carthaginians had received, and refused to surrender, a Numidian
chieftain (Pol. xxxi. 21, 7).

[3] App. *Lib.* 72. The Senate, already worried by Cato's report, must have been
thoroughly frightened by Scipio's account: the army of 80,000 infantry and 4,000
cavalry (ibid. 75) was not meant for a small police operation.

[4] An extreme instance of the 'minimizing view' in Kahrstedt (op. cit. 615–16):

We may, then, accept the unanimous testimony of the Ancients and believe that Carthage was destroyed, not because she was weak, but because the Senate feared that she was becoming too strong. We must next, before closing our survey, discuss the result of the events of 149–146 on the state of affairs in Africa.

Long before the war ended, Masinissa had died—probably early in 148.[1] On his death-bed he showed that he held the same view of his position as he had throughout his life: he entrusted the disposal of his kingdom to Scipio Aemilianus. His ring, however, he gave to his son Micipsa; he, therefore, was probably marked out as his heir, if the Roman should agree.[2] Scipio does not seem to have given supreme power to any of the King's sons: we are told that he assigned the royal capital of Cirta to Micipsa, the judiciary to Mastanabal, and the army to Gulussa, giving the treasury and the royal title to them in common, while the other (illegitimate) sons received individual principalities.[3] This step clearly had the effect of weakening the kingdom created by Masinissa; but it is difficult to see how Scipio could have preserved its strength, even if he had deliberately tried to do so: if Micipsa had been made sole ruler, there would have been immediate revolts by the other two sons. As for the illegitimate sons, their principalities were no doubt similar to the many others existing in the country and remained under the suzerainty of the throne. Scipio's division seems to show that *fides* for which he was famous[4] and which we saw him exercising in the war between Carthage and Masinissa.[5] He succeeded in accomplishing his task to the greatest benefit of both Numidia and Rome. In any case, the two younger sons died before long, and Micipsa, *primus inter pares* through his possession of the royal capital, soon remained

---

'Daß die Fruchtbarkeit der paar Tausend Quadratkilometer . . . und die eifrige Produktion recht minderwertiger Ware in der Hauptstadt irgendwie von politischer Wirkung sein konnten. . . .' It is instructive to see how all the military and political facts we know are, in this description, completely ignored.

[1] Suggested by the Oxyrhynchus *Epitome* of Livy, 118 f.

[2] App. *Lib.* 105–6; Zon. ix. 27; cf. Pol. xxxvi. 16.

[3] Thus Appian. Zonaras' version differs in that Micipsa receives the finances: Cirta and the royal title are not mentioned. Appian's version, having passed through fewer hands in its descent (from Polybius), is probably better.

[4] Dio, fr. 70, 7; App. *Lib.* 101 (both from Polybius).

[5] See p. 132.

sole ruler, living in perfect amity with Rome.[1] We cannot accuse the Romans of disloyalty in their policy towards their Numidian allies. But there is, of course, never again any question of a Numidian foreign policy.

After the capture and destruction of Carthage, Rome was faced with the problem of how to deal with the city and its remaining territory. The Senate sent a commission of ten, to advise Scipio on its organization—a method that had become usual after a great victory abroad.[2] The commission decided to raze what remained of Carthage and pronounce curses against anyone who settled there or at Megara. The towns that had not abandoned Carthage were also destroyed, but there is no record of any prohibition against rebuilding them.[3] The towns that had joined Rome were declared free and granted increases of territory—above all Utica, which now possessed the coast from Carthage to Hippo.[4] The rest of the country became a 'province': a governor was to administer it and tribute was imposed. To avoid future frontier disputes, a trench was dug from the river Tussa to Thaenae, to mark the boundary between the province and Numidia—no doubt on the model of the old 'Phoenician trenches',

---

[1] Sallust (*Jug.* 5, 5–6) mentions the joint rule of the brothers only by implication, as an unimportant intermediate stage. The famous Thugga inscription (*Rec. des Inscr. Lib.*, no. 2) is dated in the tenth year of Micipsa (falsely explained—op. cit., p. 4—as 149 B.C.!): thus by then Micipsa was sole ruler. Numidian contingents and elephants continue to serve as Roman *auxilia*: e.g. App. *Iber.* 67 and 89; cf. Sall. *Jug.* 7 f. On the cultured court of Micipsa, see Diod. xxxiv. 35. The libraries of Carthage, divided by the Senate among the three brothers (Pliny, *n.h.* xviii. 22), no doubt all ultimately passed into his hands.

[2] App. *Lib.* 135. That Scipio had to send to Rome for instructions before destroying Carthage (Zon. ix. 30, *fin.*, with a doublet of the debate between Cato and Nasica!) is unlikely: it had, after all, been decided upon before the commencement of hostilities. On the *lex Livia* appointing the organizing commission of ten men, see Mommsen, *GS*, i. 129 f.; the whole matter is extremely doubtful, and we have no right to include (thus, for example, *MRR*, i. 466) a Livius in the tribunician *fasti* on the strength of it.

[3] Strabo, xvii. 3, 16 gives some names (cf. Gsell, op. cit. 403, n. 7).

[4] Utica is called *foederata* in Cic. *Balb* 51; but this, if not a mere error (cf. *Scaur.* 54), can at most refer to a treaty signed at some later time. The *Lex Agraria* decisively confirms Appian on the original arrangement (see Mommsen, *GS*, i. 125 f.). The land assigned to the free cities was different in status from their original territory (*Lex Agr.* 79 f.). The simplest explanation is that they were *possessores*: it is not recorded whether this land was *immunis*. The same will apply to the sons of Masinissa (ibid. 81). Scipio's *acta* were no doubt confirmed on his return, as those · of other commanders performing such tasks regularly were.

and perhaps even using part of them.[1] It was Rome's first recorded attempt to mark out an artificial frontier.

Thus ended the great struggle with Carthage. Another once powerful and hostile state had been eliminated. As in the case of Macedon, defeat was not enough and loyalty no guarantee: as soon as the old enemy showed renewed signs of independence, Rome was satisfied with nothing less than total annihilation. But Rome, unwilling to strengthen her Numidian client excessively, had learnt the lesson of the recent events in Macedon; thus annexation was the only course possible. That it was followed only from political necessity, and not from any desire for gain or expansion, is clear from the nature of the settlement. The frontier was drawn along the boundary of 150, and none of the territory occupied by Masinissa in his successive encroachments was—as it might have been—demanded back from his sons.[2] And though a tribute was imposed, the area subject to it was limited by the recognition of the freedom—and, if the separation of the two ideas was by then a conscious legal theory, the immunity[3]—of all the communities that had joined Rome, and by the assignation of part of the remaining provincial land to Rome's allies. It is often said that Utica became the seat of the governor of Africa. There is no evidence for this conspicuous example of the deterioration of *libertas* before 83,[4] and speculation on it unfortunately seems profitless. Meanwhile, as in Greece, so also in Africa, the organization of client states was, in 146, still the *preferred* policy, and 'provinces' were formed only where this course was forced upon Rome by the decisive failure of that policy. The lesson of Spain did not encourage future experiments in direct administration.

During the whole remainder of the period covered by our survey this preference never changed: it was only where the policy of organizing client states had decisively failed that, as a

---

[1] Pliny, *n.h.* v. 22 and 25: the exact interpretation is not clear. On land assigned to Masinissa's sons, see last note: it may (but need not) be the land later possessed by Hiempsal (Cic. *leg. agr.* i. 10 f.; ii. 58).

[2] Sall. *Jug.* 19, 7—reading like official phraseology.

[3] Some of these towns are later *liberae et immunes*; see Mommsen, l.c. (p. 138, n. 4).

[4] *MRR*, ii. 69. The sources are not unambiguous (e.g. Oros. 'apud Uticam'; and cf. the scholiast's comment, l.c.). This state of affairs is sometimes quite arbitrarily read into Sall. *Jug.* 104, 1. (Thus Accame, *Dom. Rom.* 60.)

last resort, Rome had to annex: Asia, originally intended as an appanage where Rome was to collect the rents once due to the king, flared up in bitter rebellion and had to be annexed and organized—though even then, it seems, it was done inefficiently and haphazardly; Gaul beyond the Alps, where a Roman colony and some garrisons guarding the vital road to Spain are a conspicuous mark of Roman unwillingness to govern directly, had to be taken over after the terrible German hordes had demonstrated its dangers; Cyrene, bequeathed to Rome in 96, was left to fall into anarchy, from which it was saved only in 74 by the personal exertion of its patron L. Lucullus; Bithynia, bequeathed to Rome in 74, at once became a theatre of war. Only Gallia Cisalpina may be claimed as a province organized without pressing necessity—but that, of course, is not a matter of annexation.[1]

[1] On Asia, see Magie, *Roman Rule*, i. 147 f. (with notes in vol. ii). The original intention was almost certainly to leave it as Cyrene was later left. On Cyrene and Bithynia, see the standard works. Cyrene was finally annexed in 74, in the consulship of L. Lucullus: he had seen the state of affairs there as a legate (Plut. *Luc.* 2, 5 f.) and no doubt prevailed upon the Senate to relieve it. On Gallia Transalpina—usually recorded, in modern (but not in ancient) works, as a 'province' from 120 (see Jullian, *Hist. de la G.* iii. 23 f., for its precise 'extent')—see Ch. XII, pp. 263 f. On the Cisalpina see Ewins, *PBSR*, 1955, 75 f.

VI

ROME AND ITALY (218–133 B.C.)

(i) *Law, custom, and power.* The Second Punic War was the supreme testing-time for the Italian Confederacy. On the whole it stood the test reasonably well.[1] It is an exaggeration to put the proportion of the loyal to the rebellious as high as 5 to 1—though all estimates of population figures are necessarily rather arbitrary, Livy's list[2] suggests that a total of over half the allies joined Hannibal;[3] and this does not include the Greek cities, the most important of which seceded. But the loyalty of even half the allies was an important fact, in view of Hannibal's tempting appeals supported by victories.[4] Yet if this could cheer the Romans, there was much to frighten them; for even among the faithful loyalty was not always secure. The Latins, though they never threatened secession (for racial and sentimental ties were too strong), were deeply split by the disobedience of the twelve colonies;[5] Etruria, in 209–208, was on the brink of revolt and its loyalty was secured only by prompt and high-handed action at Arretium; and even that was not the end of the matter:[6] Hasdrubal's approach inspired sections of Etruria and Umbria to rebellious plans and actual collaboration;[7] nor could terrorism prevent a repetition of this at the approach of Mago.[8] After the end of the War, the whole of the Peninsula had to be purged of 'collaborators' by measures that suggest (behind Livy's unemotional language) the grim reign of terror of a thoroughly frightened government. Moreover, the war was followed by a period of general lawlessness,

---

[1] Some facts and theories are collected by Göhler, *Rom*, 36, n. 181. References for those not specially documented here will be found there. The subject of this section has so often been competently discussed (notably by Sherwin-White in *RC*) that the facts need not be set out in detail.

[2] xxii. 61, 11—the Campani must be added in the calculation, if not in the text.

[3] This can be roughly calculated from the figures in Afzelius, *Röm. Erob.*, which suggest a total of at least 900,000 for Livy's list.

[4] Livy, xxi–xxiii, *passim.*   [5] Id. xxvii. 9, 7 f.

[6] Ibid. 21, 6 f.; 24; 38, 6.

[7] Id. xxviii. 10, 4–5.

[8] Id. xxix. 36, 10 f.; xxx. 26, 12.

said (no doubt wrongly, but perhaps with sincere belief) to be connected with plots by Carthaginian hostages.[1]

All this naturally led to a change in Roman relations with the allies. Just as in Roman domestic politics the prolonged state of emergency led to an increase in the power and authority of the Senate as the central directing body, so in Italy as a whole twenty years of war were bound to leave the central authority (i.e. Rome) in a much stronger position; and Rome's insecurity was bound to overcome any scruples she might have had in using that strength. As we have seen, the structure that we call (for convenience' sake) the Italian Confederacy was in law merely an agglomeration of bilateral treaties of various form between Rome and individual Italian tribes and cities.[2] It is very doubtful whether (beyond the levy) Roman powers as against each ally were clearly and uniformly defined from the start: at any rate, in such Roman treaties as we know, there are no precise provisions for procedure in cases of alleged breach of treaty—in fact, there are few provisions beyond those for mutual aid.[3] It is misleading to say that Rome, when taking executive action against an Italian city, did so 'as executive head of the Confederation'[4] (though, of course, such a phrase may often legitimately be used for the sake of convenience): there is no trace of an Act of Federation giving Rome the status of ἡγεμών with certain executive powers, and no scholar would seriously argue for the existence of such a document. When Rome took action against an Italian state, whether against a rebellious tribe in the fourth century or against Capua in the Hannibalic War, she did so as the wronged partner to a bilateral treaty; and when she used other Italian troops in such action, that use was based on the clause in each individual treaty which promised mutual support in case of attack. As there was (as seems obvious from the course of events) no procedure laid down

---

[1] Livy, xxxi. 8, 11; cf. xxx. 24, 4 (a dictator and mag. eq. on assizes in the ex-rebel cities); xxxi. 12; xxxii. 1, 7 (sacrilege at Locri and inquiries about it); xxxii. 26 (slave rising, incited by Carthaginians).

[2] Cf. Ch. I: the Latins occupied a special position, which is discussed there.

[3] McDonald (*JRS*, 1944, 11) speaks of 'well-established Confederate procedure'; but there is no reason to believe that there was any such thing before the Hannibalic War, except as regards the levying of troops. Polybius' account in book vi is, as McDonald agrees (ibid. 13, n. 11), at least strongly coloured by contemporary theory and practice. (See pp. 145 f., below.)

[4] McDonald, op. cit. 13. Cf. Gelzer's salutary remarks in *Gnomon*, 1941, 147.

for arbitration between Rome and other cities, it was ultimately left to each partner, in each of those treaties, to determine what constituted a breach of the treaty, justifying counter-action. The result of this was predetermined: what might, to the Romans, seem strict interpretation of their rights under a treaty, might appear arbitrary interference to an ally concerned; what, to the ally, would then seem legitimate self-defence, was by Rome regarded as violation of the treaty, calling for punishment. In view of the relative strength of Rome (supported by the other allies) and each individual ally, no city could normally risk that. This sufficiently explains why, once the Confederacy had embraced the greater part of Italy (early in the third century), there are no more revolts (except for the isolated case of Falerii) until the Hannibalic War, when special conditions promised impunity; and why, in the period we are now discussing, there are no revolts at all.

It will be seen that, though the mutual obligations of Rome and her Italian allies rested on carefully defined and (no doubt) carefully preserved treaties, the basis of the Confederacy was only in the formal sense the aggregate of those treaties. In a sense, Rome's power—and with it the effectiveness of the Confederacy —rested on the very fact that she was *not* the head of a Con-federacy, such as Sparta and (in theory, at least) even Athens had been. There was no common Council—in fact, strictly, not even a Confederate army: there was only the Roman army with its *socii*, each assisting according to its own treaty.[1] This elasticity, with its advantages for Rome, is particularly obvious in the case of the Latins, whose rights and obligations were probably still based on an outdated treaty deliberately not renewed.[2] We have seen how it was probably to some extent the model of the status of the Latins that helped the Romans, as soon as their power expanded beyond Italy, to embark on the experiment of doing away with the basic treaty altogether and leave some of their new allies 'free'.[3] What we must here notice is the converse: the fact that an extra-legal element, essentially similar to that which later

---

[1] We do not really know anything about the *formula togatorum* as such; it was certainly not—in any useful sense of the term—a 'federal' document, but merely, like (e.g.) the *formula sociorum* (Livy, xliii. 6, 10; xliv. 16, 7—cf. *FIRA*, no. 35 (p. 257), l. 7), a convenient list kept by the Roman People for its own use.

[2] Cf. Ch. I, pp. 25 f.

[3] Cf. pp. 24 and 41.

determined the relations between Rome and her 'free' friends, was inherent in the Italian Confederacy from the beginning and was fully brought out by the prolonged state of emergency during the Hannibalic War and Roman insecurity due to it. It is during that war and, after it, during the second century B.C. that we see Rome making use of her powers of definition in order, with the inevitable allied acquiescence, to extend her control from precedent to precedent, until what allied autonomy remains (and it is still considerable) is guaranteed not so much by treaty as by the Senate's ingrained unwillingness to assume avoidable administrative responsibilities.

It has been necessary, as against some misleading modern formulations, to stress the essential nature of the Confederacy and of Rome's power. It was, however, inevitable that a sense of unity should grow up among all the states so often fighting side by side. We have seen early traces of this and have tried to follow the way in which, from the very beginning, Rome consistently appeared as the protector of the allies of the moment; and we have seen that this was often (particularly in the early stages) what kept them faithful to the alliance.[1] This feeling was naturally strengthened during the Hannibalic War among those of the allies who remained loyal: it seems to be chiefly responsible for the loyalty of the eighteen colonies in 209,[2] for the enthusiasm that greeted C. Claudius Nero's march to the Metaurus.[3] Rome's success in the War and punishment of those who had joined the enemy—i.e. of those who had most strongly felt their grievances[4] —finally made this feeling paramount. Those who remained were, quite apart from considerations of law or even of power, by natural selection those more ready to acknowledge Rome's leadership and collaborate with her. While during the War we still have clear evidence of dissatisfaction even among the loyal allies and of attempts to influence Roman policy,[5] it is only to be expected that after victory there should be, not only no such

---

[1] Ch. I, *passim*. On the interesting history of the word 'Italia', see Klingner, *Röm. Geist.* 13 f.   [2] Livy, xxvii. 9 f.

[3] Ibid. 45, 6 f. Cf. also Varro's speech to the Campanians (xxiii. 5, especially ss. 11 f.); though, of course, it cannot be pressed as precise evidence. For the Gallic War, cf. Polybius' statements (ii. 23, 12; 31, 7).

[4] The *locus classicus* is Capua's treaty with Hannibal, making grievances clear by implication (Livy, xxiii. 7, 1 f.).   [5] Notably Livy, xxvii. 9.

evidence, but (probably) no such spirit among the allies. Their submission by now was voluntary, based not only (or not even chiefly) on fear, but on the habit of obedience and the desire for protection.[1]

Gradually Rome evolved a suitable vocabulary, legitimizing diverse kinds of interference by precedent and the need to keep order: Polybius' theoretical formulation of the kinds of situation calling for Roman intervention[2] can be fully documented from the pages of Livy. McDonald[3] traces the extension of the concept of 'coniuratio' to cover these various cases and shows how in similar cases the Senate also took it upon itself to suspend the Roman citizen's right of appeal. The parallelism is instructive and noteworthy; but perhaps the insistence on the importance of a single concept is unnecessary. Polybius, after all, mentions συνωμοσία as only one of several categories; and if we at times find the word (or its Latin equivalent) applied to instances that more properly fit into others, that only shows the arbitrary and legally unsatisfactory nature of the whole elaborate subdivision. We know that citizens were at times executed without right of appeal even though in no sense 'conspirators'—by the end of the century this was to become common practice. The real point is that these matters (both within Rome and in her relations with the allies) were *not* governed by law, but by custom—and power to enforce it. If Rome could send the allies detailed instructions on matters certainly not provided for in her original treaties (as she did, for example, in the case of the Bacchanalia),[4] it was not because the Senate had (or even claimed) a right to intervene in cases of *coniuratio*—there was probably no such provision in the original treaties—, but because it had become natural for the Senate to send instructions on matters of importance; we can be certain, for all

---

[1] This aspect is brought out particularly well in Göhler's book, though clothed in excessively mystical language. Polybius, when he speaks of κατάπληξις καὶ καταξίωσις παρὰ τοῖς συμμάχοις τοῦ 'Ρωμαίων πολιτεύματος (iii. 90, *fin.*), strikes a truer balance.

[2] vi. 13, 4 f. προδοσία, of course, is frequent and obvious. Of συνωμοσία the best-known example is the Bacchanalian conspiracy (Livy, xxxix. 8 f.). For φαρμακεία, see Livy, xxxix. 41, 5; for δολοφονία the best instance is probably the affair of the *silua Sila* (Cic. *Br.* 85), though some of the examples of *coniurationes* (of slaves or *pastores*) in Livy might be brought under this heading.   [3] Op. cit. 13 f.

[4] *SC de Bacch.* (*FIRA*, no. 30), ll. 7 f. Of particular interest is the small matter of the display of the decree (22 f.).

the various reasons we have discussed, that no excuse was given and that neither side felt the need for one. If the Senate summons the Tiburtes to defend themselves against some charge (unknown to us),[1] it was not because it had (or claimed) the right of ἐπιτί-μησις,[2] but because it had thought a rumour important enough to send for Tiburtine envoys and hear them; and we may be sure that neither in Rome nor in Tibur did lawyers look up treaties or even precedents before either one party gave the order or the other hastened to obey it.[3]

Allied willingness to accept Roman control can be seen particularly clearly in the known cases in which the allies asked for Roman intervention. The best known of these are the two expulsions of 187 and 177:[4] in the latter case Livy explicitly tells us that the allied states had been asking for action for a long time. These, however, are not instances of interference in the internal affairs of communities. Whatever the legal rights of the immigrants in Rome—and the case for expulsion seems legally very weak, except as regards those who (in 177) had been guilty of the kind of fraud Livy tries to describe—, their expulsion would be by virtue of Roman law and sovereignty, and even the order that they should be *censi* in their old communities (i.e. return to their old citizenship) was only a necessary complement of the revocation of their Roman *ciuitas*. While it is true that these two incidents must not be used as evidence for Roman ill-treatment of the allies,[5] we might almost add that they do not justify other conclusions either.

There are, however, cases better illustrating official allied submissiveness. It was obvious that, where Rome was (in any sense) a party to a dispute, the case should go to Rome: the imperial power could not submit to arbitration. Thus when (in 168) Pisa complained that land belonging to the city had been appropriated by the Roman commissioners for the colony of Luna, the complaint was made to the Senate, which appointed a commission of

---

[1] *FIRA*, no. 33.　　　[2] Pol. vi. 13, 4 f.; cf. McDonald, l.c. (p. 145, n. 3).

[3] The question whether laws passed in Rome could normally apply to allied cities is entirely theoretical. When it suited Rome, they did (e.g. Livy, xxxv. 7, 4 f. —cf. Göhler, *Rom*, 53 f., admitting the fact with verbose apologia). For a list of such laws known to us, see Niccolini, *RAL*, 1946, 112.

[4] Livy, xxxix. 3, 4 f.; xli. 8, 6 f.

[5] Rightly pointed out by Göhler, *Rom*, 63 f.

inquiry.[1] But cases of arbitration and settling of boundaries between two Italian states are attested,[2] and these must have been voluntarily referred to the Senate, which in each case appoints the arbitrators. Polybius[3] again gives arbitration as a recognized function of the Senate; but again it is unlikely that that was so from the start, in view of the limited legal basis of the Confederacy.

Most important, of course, was help and protection: in the military sphere, at least, this was one of the few things that we can be certain were stipulated by treaty. During the Hannibalic War military help, when asked for, was given whenever possible.[4] That was in Rome's own interest. But outlying places, still threatened by enemies, might at any time have to appeal for protection: the Senate would then decide what could be done for them.[5] More revealing is assistance in settling internal disputes—by armed force, if necessary, as happened at Patavium in 174: this, of course, was done at the request of the state concerned; it could be regarded as certain that the governing class (which had appealed to Rome) would be supported by the Senate.[6] This had not, perhaps, always been the case. It is difficult to make out whether Livy's account of class divisions in Italy during the War (with the upper classes favouring Rome and the lower classes Hannibal) truthfully represents a state of affairs due to political affinity and collaboration or is a second-century myth, invented to uphold oligarchy in Italy: on the whole, the latter seems more likely. Livy occasionally contradicts his own main thesis, and these counter-examples may all the more readily be accepted as

[1] Livy, xlv. 13, 10 f.

[2] Cic. *off.* i. 33; Val. Max. vii. 3, 4 (Nola and Naples); *CIL*, i^2. 633 f. (Ateste and its neighbours); and the *sententia Minuciorum* (ibid. 584), dealing with a dispute between a city and its dependants (perhaps not strictly Italian).

[3] l.c. (p. 146, n. 2). This whole question is lucidly discussed by Sherwin-White in *RC*, 120 f.

[4] e.g. Livy, xxiii. 14, 10; 15, 2; xxiv. 13, 10. In the worst years it was not always possible and requests for help had to be turned down (e.g. id., xxiii. 20, 4).

[5] Id., xliii. 1, 5 f.: Aquileia. The envoys are politely asked 'uellentne eam rem C. Cassio consuli mandari'. But the importance of this should not be overstressed: it does not (as is sometimes asserted) show any special regard for the independence of Aquileia. In fact, the Senate is trying to avoid taking any special measures in response to the appeal, and, to cover itself, it has to get Aquileian approval.

[6] Id., xli. 27, 3 (for the appeal by the Patavine authorities, note: 'quos . . . ipsorum legati attulerant'). Cf. McDonald, op. cit. 14. (It is convenient to use Cispadane illustrations along with Italian ones: the Cispadana had no separate administration.)

historical.[1] They strongly suggest that before the War there had
been little Roman interference on behalf of oligarchic governments.[2] In this respect, as in others, the Hannibalic War seems
to be a decisive influence.

Extension of Roman control and interference, aided by the
submissiveness of the allies who came to accept and even request
it, is, then, characteristic of Roman relations with the allies in the
second century. It is illustrated and underlined by the increasing
demands (both legal and illegal) of Roman magistrates upon allied
cities. The famous case of L. Postumius at Praeneste,[3] as Livy
reports, set a precedent, and, quite apart from the expense involved, the Roman magistrate in the allied city became the representative of a conquering power among its subjects. The same
year that saw this precedent also saw a Roman censor plunder a
famous Italian shrine;[4] and though the Senate returned the spoils,
the temple was permanently damaged—no doubt owing to the
submissive attitude of the priests, who would not incur the
hostility of a powerful Roman family by fully restoring it.[5] Here,
as in the case of Praeneste, we again see the inevitable effect of
the habit of Roman control and submission to it.[6] It was in this
way that relations of *hospitium* between Roman nobles and Italian
families necessarily lost their character of (comparative) equality
and became those of patron and client, as we find them in the late
Republic:[7] the Italian (like the provincial) city, for instance, was
de facto expected to aid the advancement of its Roman patron,[8] to
accept him as arbitrator in cases of dispute, and often to use his
services for diplomatic exchanges;[9] and as every city had such

---

[1] Livy, xxiii. 14, 7; xxiv. 13, 8 (Nola); xxiv. 2, 8 (Croton); and his general state-
ments that this state of affairs prevailed all over Italy. Yet at Locri (xxiii. 30, 8),
Arpi (xxiv. 47, 6), and apparently at Tarentum (xxiv. 13, 3), the People favoured
Rome and the aristocracy brought about defection.

[2] But see x. 18, 8 (if true) for an early instance.   [3] Id., xlii. 1, 6 f. (173 B.C.).

[4] Q. Fulvius Flaccus and the tiles of the temple of Lacinian Hera (ibid. 3).

[5] Livy's statement that no craftsman was found who could replace them is
patently absurd.

[6] Livy comments on the bad effect of excessive submissiveness (n. 3, above:
Praeneste).   [7] On this, see Ch. VII (below). Livy (l.c.) notices the change.

[8] Id., xl. 44, 12: as is implied, the Senate's limitation was not permanently
successful.

[9] e.g. the Minucii at Genua (p. 147, n. 2). Cf. Dion. Hal. ii. 11, 1 f.; App. *b.c.*
ii. 4 (not distinguishing between Italy and the provinces); Livy, xxxix. 17, 4 (*litterae
hospitum*).

patrons, these necessarily assumed *vis-à-vis* their Italian client cities an importance similar to that which they already had as regards foreign kings and cities:[1] it is a mark of the decline in status of the Italian communities, a decline that (as we have seen) came about without any changes in their legal position and in large measure with their consent.

The fact of this decline is patent: that Italy was Rome's immediate and proper 'sphere of influence' is recognized by foreign powers by the beginning of the second century[2] and is clear from the confusion between the designations of 'Romans' and 'Italians' in Eastern countries, where the Greeks do not even seem to know that an Italian is not *ciuis Romanus*.[3]

(ii) *The benefits of protection.* We must next briefly consider whether the Italians derived any profit from this situation.

In military service they were, of course, by treaty completely at Rome's orders. During the great wars of the second century, allied troops were freely used alongside the legions, and—as far as we can tell—their losses were frequently heavier. It has often been suspected that this may be due to Roman tactics, which exposed them to the greater risks.[4] Their territories had been ravaged by the Hannibalic War, and after it—as far as we can tell—they lacked the opportunity the Romans found of recouping themselves by indemnity and confiscation. At the most, they at times received a share in assignations—but, as far as we can tell, not always the share to which they were entitled.[5] It is no wonder that their cities and lands were gradually depopulated—a fact which, however, the Senate recognized by lowering their quotas: after 176—down to where Livy fails us—the normal allied

---

[1] See further in Ch. VII (below).

[2] Livy, xxxiii. 40, 2; cf. xxx. 30, 6 f. (not, of course, genuine).

[3] Throughout the century, it seems, all Italians there are normally called ʽΡωμαῖοι, though when writing in Latin they dare not usurp the title and remain 'Italici' (Hatzfeld, *Trafiquants*, *passim*, especially 243 f.). This may have started with the case of *municipes* (*ciues s.s.*), who were in fact citizens (cf. the ʽΡωμαῖος ἐκ Κύμης: *BCH*, xxxvi, 1912, 80); but it soon becomes general.

[4] Evidence collected and carefully analysed by Afzelius, *Röm. Kriegsm.* (especially 74-75).

[5] Livy, xlii. 4, 4: 'diuiserunt dena iugera in singulos, sociis n.L. terna.' Göhler's unconvincing attempt to prove that they were not legally entitled to more (*Rom*, 51–52) hardly supports his conclusion that Rome 'eine durchaus loyale und für die Bundesgenossen keineswegs ungünstige . . . Politik betrieben hat'.

complement for the legion of 5,200 infantry and 300 cavalry is 5,000 infantry and 300 cavalry; i.e. it is roughly equal in strength.[1] This is a reduction of one-third since the beginning of the century, when the figures had been 7,500 and 400. We have no reason to assume Roman generosity: as is known, some of the Latin cities in any case found it hard to meet their commitments, and the figures must be a measure of demographic change. In 225 the number of allies had been about double that of Roman citizens;[2] it is clear that fifty years later that proportion had changed considerably. From what we hear of the position in the age of the Gracchi—though it is very little, amounting to not much more than the complaints about depopulation among the allies, which are scattered through Appian's account—we have every reason to think that it did not improve in the following fifty years.[3] The Senate was not altogether blind to the dangers of the change. This, no doubt, was the reason for the law that forbade migration of those who did not leave sons at home—a law apparently passed between 187 and 177—and for Roman compliance with the requests to expel Latin immigrants.[4] The result of this care for allied manpower was that, as far as we know, after 177 the acquisition of Roman citizenship was closed to the allies. Henceforth the gulf between *ciues Romani* and their subjects is fixed. In the long run the allies did not profit.

As far as movable booty was concerned, the evidence on the treatment of the allies is scanty; probably they were, on the whole, fairly treated as regards their share of it (and this must have been a very powerful factor in keeping them contented)—but they were always at the mercy of an overweening Roman commander, and

[1] Afzelius, op. cit. 62 f.

[2] Id., *Röm. Erob.*, *passim* (summarized pp. 133-5).

[3] We begin to understand how inferior the forces of *Italia* must have been in the last desperate uprising, and also why the census figures do not leap up sensationally after Italian enfranchisement. (For other reasons see p. 242, with n. 2.)

[4] On the expulsions, see p. 146. The law is mentioned in Livy, xli. 8. As it does not appear in connexion with the earlier expulsion, it is usually rightly assumed that it was passed between these two dates. Our texts of Livy apply it (with the consequent possibility of obtaining *ciuitas*) to all the Italians (not only to the Latins), and there is no good reason for rejecting this. Whether, however, the complaints of 177 came from all the Italian communities or only from the *nomen Latinum* is perhaps impossible to decide with certainty, as Livy is often confused in his nomenclature (cf. Mommsen, *Str.* iii. 661 f.).

here, as in other spheres, their position as helpless dependants soon becomes marked.[1] Nor have we much reason to think that allied cities and their gods shared the prosperity that came to Rome and her gods as a result of successful war. Compared with the innumerable foundations of temples, and constructions and adornment of public buildings, in Rome by successful commanders, evidence of such things in allied cities is almost non-existent. The *tituli Mummiani* alone form a major exception, adding epigraphic weight to the testimony we have of the unusual honesty and high character of that *nouus homo*.[2] At the most, a few men like Scipio Aemilianus may have cultivated allied friendship by some generosity.[3]

It will now be clear that, though the allies had some profit to show for their faithful and arduous service—particularly in the viritane distribution of booty, which must not be underestimated as a means of keeping their individual loyalty—, we can hardly share Göhler's enthusiasm about Roman treatment of them.[4] Above all, just as we noticed that what independence was left to them—and we cannot deny that it was considerable, including most of the day-to-day working of their communities—was in fact retained by the grace of Rome (there being no noticeable hesitation in infringing it whenever, for any purpose, Rome saw fit to do so),[5] so it is clear that what profits they derived from their submission to Rome were precarious and in any case not proportionate to their services. In this their position is very close to that of the inhabitants of the provinces and of the 'free' and federate communities outside Italy. Yet it is worth noting that the old terminology continues: as in the days when Rome had protected them against foreign attack, she bases her hegemony on moral grounds: when the Senate absolves the Tiburtines from blame, it is careful to point out 'ea uos merito nostro facere non

---

[1] Evidence given and discussed by Göhler, *Rom*, 50 f. For C. Claudius Pulcher's reduction of their share, exceptional (it seems) and very unpopular, see Livy, xli. 13, 7 f.

[2] *CIL*, i². 2, 626 f. For Mummius' character, see Pol. xxxix. 6, 2 f. (and cf. Münzer, *RE*, s.v., coll. 1200 f.).

[3] Cf. his gifts to the Sicilians (Cic. 2*Verr*. ii. 3 *et al.*). Cf. *CIL*, i². 2, 625. Other isolated gifts ibid. 616 f.

[4] Quoted p. 149, n. 5.

[5] On the 'municipalization' of allied magistrates, see *RC*, 120 f.

potuisse, neque uos dignos esse quei ea faceretis'.[1] Thus the
actual words of the Senate confirm our conclusion that Roman
relations with the allies in the second century were far removed
from whatever was stipulated in their respective treaties: like her
relations with those 'friends' altogether without treaties—and like
the relations of patron and client within the body politic—, they
were based on duties owed in return for *beneficia*; and the interpretation of both was ultimately left, without appeal, in the hands
of the stronger partner.

There was, however, one sphere in which allied profits from
the Roman alliance were tangible and substantial: that of foreign
negotia.[2] Except for the *publica*, such things were almost wholly
in the hands of allied individuals and—before long—great dynastic families.[3] As we have already seen, these were collectively
known to Greek-speaking provincials as ʻΡωμαῖοι.[4] They were
indeed powerfully protected by the Roman name. The corollary
of Rome's claim to hegemony over Italy—which, as we have
seen, was by the second century recognized as her special sphere
of influence—was the necessity of validating that claim by protecting Italian interests abroad. Even in the third century the
Roman name had loyally protected Italian blockade-runners in
wars with which Rome had no concern.[5] This policy continued
in the second century.[6] At times—we have one example[7] in the
very small number of documents or references to documents that
we possess—special exemptions and privileges for Italians were
extorted from conquered enemies. But even apart from such
positive action, Roman prestige must have stood the *negotiatores*
in good stead. And these *negotia*—especially in the East—were
very important: the *negotiatores* belonged to the leading families,
particularly of Southern Italy, and most of those families that we
know had widespread connexions there.[8] It is perhaps not too

---

[1] *FIRA*, no. 33, ll. 7–8. What follows ('neque id uobeis . . . oitile esse facere') we
cannot interpret, as we do not know the facts of the affair. Cf. Meyer, *Röm. St.*,
214.
   [2] The word covers nearly every kind of commercial and financial activity, as
Hatzfeld has shown.
   [3] Hatzfeld, op. cit., *passim*; Gabba, *GS*, 40 f.   [4] See p. 149, n. 3.
   [5] Thus at Carthage (Pol. i. 83, 6 f.) and in Illyria (Pol. ii. 8, 2—cf. *PBSR*, 1952,
75 f.).   [6] Pol. xxiii. 9, 12.
   [7] Ambracia (Livy, xxxviii. 44, 4).   [8] Cf. Gabba, *GS*, 15 f.

fanciful to believe that, just as their lower classes were reconciled to the insecurity and inferiority of their position by their share in booty (regularly captured in large quantities, down to 146 B.C.), so these families were reconciled to their inferiority at home by their equality to Romans abroad and by the profits this brought them. However, in the long run it was inevitable that the benefits should be taken for granted and the burdens resented; in particular, equality abroad was bound to lead to demands for equality at home. As has been pointed out,[1] the families that had for so long, as *negotiatores*, profited by Roman protection provided the leaders of *Italia* in the Social War. But before this could happen, affronts and temptations were yet to be multiplied.

---

[1] Most recently, and in great detail, by Gabba (l.c.).

PART TWO

INTERNAL POLITICS

VII

THE NOBLE AND HIS FOREIGN CLIENTS

HITHERTO we have been concerned with the clients of
the *Populus Romanus*—the dependent states that, for
reasons of historical development and the categories of
Roman political thinking, stood to Rome in the relation of a client
to his patron, owing the Roman People *officia* in return for *beneficia* received. Within this survey we have already had occasion
to notice the importance of great Romans—a Scipio Africanus or
a Flamininus—as the executors of policy in their relations with
dependent states. We must now look in some detail at the network
of personal links between great Roman individuals and families
and individuals, families and states outside the City. This will
provide us with a valuable insight into the organization of
Roman supremacy in Italy and the Mediterranean, as well as giving
us the background to those later developments that made the possession of such connexions by Roman politicians an important
factor in domestic politics.[1]

Relations of *hospitium* between Roman families and private
families abroad go back to the earliest times and are, of course,
paralleled all over the ancient world. They were originally formally established and their token was the *tessera hospitalis*, of
which we have second-century examples;[2] but it is probable that
later, with increasing relations between prominent Romans and
prominent families outside Rome, the formality was abandoned
and *hospitium* said to exist where hospitality—its chief and

[1] The basis of any discussion of the subject must be Gelzer, *Nobilität* (especially
50 f., 70 f.). Cf. also Premerstein, *Werden*, 13 f. The general background of the
concept of *clientela* has been discussed in the Introduction.
[2] *CIL*, i²., nos. 23, 828, 1764.

original function—had been given. The prominent Roman, like Cicero, had *hospites* all over the world; and the prominent non-Roman would take pride in his *hospitium* with numerous great Romans.[1] Naturally, as Roman power became dominant, *hospitium*, originally a relationship between equals, developed into a form of *clientela*: the Roman senator would in fact be the patron of his Sicilian *hospes*. This is precisely similar to the change in the relationship between Rome and her partners in 'equal' treaties,[2] and to some extent in that between Rome and the 'free' cities.[3] Thus Sthenius of Thermae and Diodorus of Melita, when persecuted by Verres, relied upon the protection of their Roman *hospites*.[4] There is thus no need for us to distinguish *hospitium* from *clientela*: it is unlikely that the Roman senator in the late Republic felt any difference between them,[5] and, in any case, their practical effect was the same: it is idle to inquire whether the private armies of the last decades of the Republic were raised from among *hospites* or clients.[6]

More important still were the connexions between Romans and kings and cities abroad. These are a well-known and much-discussed form of *clientela*. They were founded (like all forms of patronage) by a *beneficium* conferred by the Roman on the state concerned, or by a formal treaty between the two parties.[7] The importance of these connexions increased with the expansion of Rome and the bitterness of the political struggles in the City. There is no evidence of their playing any noteworthy part before

---

[1] Thus Sthenius of Thermae was the *hospes* of Marius, Pompey, C. Marcellus, Cicero, and others (Cic. 2*Verr*. ii. 110 f., 117: also of Verres, who abused his hospitality). From the account of Cicero it seems that no formal 'treaty' had been made.

[2] See Ch. VI, above. Livy comments on the change (xlii. 1, 10 f.).

[3] Though here inequality was in fact present from the start; cf. Part I of this study, *passim*.

[4] Cic. 2*Verr*. ii. 96; iv. 41. Note that 'patroni atque hospites' and 'defensores atque hospites' are linked as natural pairs and almost synonyms.

[5] See last note.

[6] Henceforth the term 'client' and 'patron'—denoting the factual relationship—will be used to cover both.

[7] For details, see below, and cf. Introduction. As in the case of *hospitium*, the formal mode may have been the original one; and *hospitium publicum* cannot originally have involved *clientela*—a concept belonging to a different category. But the distinction is again of no practical importance for our purpose. (Cf. Introduction, pp. 11 f.)

the Hannibalic War. We can hardly doubt that they existed (for the effect of a *beneficium* was probably a deep-seated and ancient part of the Roman ethic)[1] and there is some evidence for it; but, significantly enough, the very evidence is late:[2] when such things became important, old connexions would no doubt be pulled out of the *Fasti* and ancestral *imagines* and *laudationes*, and polished up for the benefit of both protector and protected.

The origins of these connexions, as we have said, are manifold and can be reduced only to the one simple formula of a *beneficium* conferred. The best-known form of it was victory in war. Cicero mentions it as an ancestral custom that the Roman commander should become the patron of the enemy he had defeated[3] and this patronate was (like all such obligations) hereditary. It is common to regard this as the oldest form of this kind of *clientela* (i.e. the connexion between a Roman family and a foreign king or community) and to derive it from the surrender of the defeated enemy *in fidem* of the victor: this *fides*, it is thought, was that of the commander as an individual, and the relationship thus set up was not terminated by the settlement (treaty or whatever it was) between the Roman People and the defeated.[4] There are, however, no good grounds for accepting this explanation. The surrender was never *in fidem* of the commander as an individual but *in fidem* of the Roman People and its representative. The usual phrase is 'in fidem p.R.';[5] only rarely do we find a variant like 'in fidem consulis dicionemque p.R.',[6] and we have no reason to think it more precise than the common phrase.[7] However, even in these cases it is the commander in his official capacity ('consul'), not as a private individual (e.g. 'L. Cornelius Scipio'), who is mentioned and in point: the surrender is to the Roman People, and he is its representative and receives it as such. Nor is there any reason to think the relationship created by this surrender

---

[1] See Introduction, especially p. 13 (with n. 1). For international affairs this is developed in Part I.

[2] See *Note O*, p. 296.   [3] Cic. *off.* i. 35.

[4] Mommsen, *RF*, i. 361 f. (cf. *Str.* iii. 65); generally followed: e.g. Premerstein, *RE*, s.v. 'clientes', coll. 26 f.; Gelzer, *Nob.* 50–51. Cf. Introduction, pp. 6–7.

[5] e.g. Pol. xx. 9, 10 f. (the famous case of the Aetolians); cf. *Lex Repetundarum* (*FIRA*, no. 7), l. 1.

[6] Livy, xxxvii. 45, 3 (190 B.C.); cf. the old formula (if it is genuine) in i. 38, 2: 'in meam populique Romani dicionem'.

[7] The context in Livy (xxxvii, l.c.) has no pretensions to official precision.

permanent: it merely lasts until the fate of the conquered is settled by the Roman People (by treaty, declaration of *libertas*, &c.) and is then naturally at an end.[1] Mommsen, of course, realized this, and had to find various *ad hoc* explanations to maintain his theory—none of them more than *a priori* assumptions.[2] There is no need to believe that surrender *in fidem* ever created a permanent relationship based on *fides* between the conquered and either the Roman People or its representative, the commander, as an individual.

Nor is there much evidence—such as one might expect, if the custom were really primitive or at least ancient—that *mos maiorum* in this case goes back farther than the age of the great wars. It is commonly thought that the Samnite *clientela* of Fabricius is the oldest example and thus proves the existence of the custom in the time of the Italian wars.[3] But this *clientela* is a late invention, and the first genuine case that we know about is that of M. Claudius Marcellus (*cos.* III 214) and his promise to protect the Syracusans he had defeated.[4] It is a tempting hypothesis that this was the first instance and by its dramatic circumstances (emphasized by the skill of the Greek protagonists) created a precedent.[5] There is, indeed, something paradoxical in the idea of the conqueror's and his descendants' interest in the conquered, and it is unlikely that such an idea was primitive.[6]

In fact, this kind of patronate over nations and kings should not be dissociated from others based on some fortuitous official link: there is nothing unique about the relationship established by victory and surrender, and it is in every way parallel to that founded by (it seems) any official contact between a Roman

---

[1] There is no reason to think that *clientela*, where it later exists, is due to that original surrender *in fidem*: it is much easier (and quite sufficient) to refer it back to the *beneficium* of whatever dispositions (short of total destruction) the Roman People finally made. We find the same relationship where there has apparently been no surrender; cf. the case of the Achaean League (Chs. III and IV, *passim*).

[2] *Str.* iii. 65; 716.

[3] Thus Mommsen (*Str.* iii. 65, n. 1); Premerstein, l.c.; Gelzer, l.c. (p. 156, n. 4). This is based on an anecdote in Val. Max. iv. 3, 6, which is clearly spurious. See Forni, *Ath.* 1953, 177 f.   [4] Livy, xxvi. 32, *fin.*

[5] In any case, an automatic and obligatory (thus Premerstein, l.c.) patronate of the victor over the vanquished makes this whole scene unintelligible.

[6] Cf. the attitude of T. Manlius Torquatus—by no means benevolent—to the Latins in 216 (Livy, xxiii. 22, 7): not in spite of but because of, his ancestor's triumph over them, to which he alludes.

magistrate or representative and a foreign power, where there is no question of surrender *in fidem*. Thus M. Valerius Laevinus, as propraetor in Macedonia and Greece, had made Rome's first treaty of alliance with the Aetolians; his son Gaius, in 189, acted as the patron of the Aetolians in their peace negotiations.[1] C. Flaminius, as praetor, had governed Sicily: in 195 the Sicilians sent cheap corn to Rome to honour his memory.[2] These early examples are worth quoting as showing the widely differing types of original contact that could lead to a permanent connexion in all respects similar to that established by victory. Throughout the subsequent history of the Republic we find this kind of patronate flourishing and extending, and the bases of it—the original official contacts—as varied as we have seen them to be in these earlier instances. Victory in war continues to be an important one: thus the Minucii become patrons of Liguria; Domitii and Fabii become the patrons of the Transalpine Gauls,[3] and in Spain, where there was constant fighting, there are numerous examples.[4] These, however, merge into what is naturally by far the largest class: clientship founded by administration. It was swelled by a confluence of Roman ideas and Greek practice; for the cities of the East had long been accustomed to honour kings and powerful private individuals as their benefactors, and this and the ancient Greek institution of the proxeny naturally developed into patronate, until the Greeks even adopted the Latin word. These connexions, of course, given the Roman sense of tradition and their importance (which we shall see before long) in political advancement, became hereditary, and as a result, by the late Republic, all families of any importance (and some of not very much) had such connexions abroad, and particularly in the East.[5] Sometimes *clientela* could arise in odd ways. Thus a man might be assigned by the Senate the duty of in some way protecting the interests of a foreign community (e.g. by prosecuting one who had oppressed

---

[1] Pol. xxi. 29; Livy, xxxviii. 9, 8; cf. xxxi. 3, 3.

[2] Livy, xxxiii. 42, 8: his son, as *aed. cur.*, distributes it.

[3] See especially Ch. XI (below) for the development of this. Cf. Cic. *div. in Caec.* 67 (Domitii); Sall. *Cat.* 41, 4; Cic. *Pis.* 77; *Font.* 36 (Fabii); for Minucii, see *RE*, s.v., nos. 54–56.

[4] Traceable quite often through individual clients and the spread of names. This is fully discussed in Ch. XI.

[5] Examples are numerous and well known.

it.[1] This was probably done in most cases at the request of the community concerned: for foreign cities and peoples naturally seized every chance of attaching the great noble families to their interests.[2]

This brief survey of evidence ranging from the age of the great wars to the end of the Republic has shown that every kind of contact between leading Romans and foreign states could lead to the establishment of *clientela*: victory in war, administrative contacts, or the initiative of the state concerned (or of the Senate)[3] in establishing it. There is no evidence to suggest that formal action was necessary, though it could be—and no doubt often was—taken to make the matter more solemn.[4] The point is that any document existing would in any case not be binding in law; for *clientela* was an extra-legal institution, sanctioned by *mos maiorum* and supported by the realities of power.[5] The way in which the patron and the client community—whether they had themselves established the connexion or whether it was inherited —regarded their duties and rights was a matter for their own conscience and perhaps originally the gods (judging the demands of each particular situation), and not for a tribunal interpreting documents. The main point was that, in exchange for *beneficia*

---

[1] Cf. Cn. Domitius Cn. f. (Ahenobarbus), honoured at Samos as the son τοῦ δοθέντος ὑπὸ τῆς συγκλήτου πάτρωνος τῷ δήμῳ (*RE*, s.v. 'Domitius', no. 11).

[2] Thus a L. Calpurnius Piso (probably, despite Münzer, the later *cos.* 58) prosecuted P. Gabinius at the request of the Achaeans (Cic. *div. in Caec.* 64); no previous connexion is known. C. Caesar Strabo prosecuted T. Albucius in 103 at the request of the Sardinians (ibid. 63). This connexion was kept up: a L. Caesar, perhaps the great-nephew of Strabo, was considered a likely prosecutor of Scaurus in 54 (Cic. *Att.* iv. 17, 5). Cf. also the proxenies conferred at Delphi on distinguished visitors (Ditt. *Syll.* i. 585): it is possible that many Romans, without known cause honoured in the East as patrons, in the late Republic, are merely visitors.

[3] Or, of course, of the Roman concerned; but for this there is no evidence until the late Republic, when these *clientelae* assume a new importance (see Ch. XI).

[4] e.g. *CIL*, i². 611 (Fundi?), and treaties such as that between Balbus and the Gaditanes (Cic. *Balb.* 41 f.). Though negative evidence is naturally hard to find, it is most unlikely that a formal instrument existed (e.g.) in cases like those of n. 2 (above). What formal record there was, was often, no doubt, merely an adaptation of a Greek proxeny decree: in the relevant cases cited in nn. 1 and 2 (above) it is hard to imagine a *deditio in fidem* on Italian lines.

[5] See Introduction, *passim*. The legal sanction it had found in the Twelve Tables (such as it was) cannot have applied to the later and looser form of it that we are here considering. At least, it is hard to imagine what action could have been brought, and we hear of no instances.

received and expected, the community undertook the *officia* of a client.[1]

It will, however, be of interest to examine the normal working of such a connexion, as this will enable us to understand its importance in the State even before it was thrown into excessive prominence by the final convulsions of the Republic. The chief routine duty of the patron was to facilitate diplomatic relations between Rome and the client state concerned. Thus he would entertain its envoys in Rome and introduce them into the Senate;[2] and though on important occasions this might be done by the consuls or praetor, it was difficult for a small city to get a hearing without the efforts of its patrons.[3] It was understood that he would also support its pleas and use his influence to obtain a favourable settlement.[4] He would be asked to settle its internal difficulties requiring arbitration and, where there were differences between clients of one man, he might be requested (either directly by the states concerned or by the Senate) to settle them.[5] Indeed, it was quite common, where a mission abroad required particular tact, for the Senate to entrust it to a man with extensive local knowledge and influence in the area.[6] When a decree or law

[1] *b. Hisp.* 42 is a *locus classicus*. I shall choose some representative instances of this interplay; they could easily be multiplied.

[2] Flamininus introduces embassies from the whole of Greece and from Asia (Livy, xxxiv. 59, 4); Caesar prides himself on having scrupulously fulfilled this function (*b. Hisp.* 42). The Pergamene envoy stayed at Ti. Gracchus' house, as the elder Ti. Gracchus had become a patron of Pergamum (Ch. VIII, pp. 173–4). Pompey entertained his Eastern princes (Dio, xxxix. 14, 3; Strabo, xvii. 1, 11).

[3] The case of Abdera, which enlisted the support of Teos, is a classic (Ditt. *Syll.* ii. 656). Cf. the Massiliots' intervention on behalf of Lampsacus (ibid. 591). It is often said that no city *could* approach the Senate without such an introduction; but, as Mommsen saw (*Str.* iii. 597; 704; 741 f.—though with unnecessary distinctions), there is no evidence for this. Cf., for example, the letter of the praetor P. Cornelius Blasio to the Corcyraeans (*BCH*, 1924, 381 f.), *init.*, for correct procedure.

[4] Cf. last note and p. 158, n. 1. Note the efforts of Scipio on behalf of the Achaean exiles and the Rhodians' plaintive approach to their patrons (Pol. xxx. 4, 5).

[5] P. Sulla in the case of Pompeii (Cic. *Sull.* 60 f.—with other patrons, unnamed); Scipio Aemilianus in that of the Macedonians (Pol. xxxv. 4, 10 f.); also in the dispute between Masinissa and Carthage (App. *Lib.* 72—the Carthaginians had refused Cato's mediation: ibid. 69); the Minucii in a Ligurian dispute (*ILS*, 5946). Cf. p. 193 (below), and see next note. Cf. also Cic. 2*Verr.* ii. 122 (the new constitution of Halaesa—see *Note O*, p. 296). On all this, cf. Dion. Hal. ii. 11, 1.

[6] The best example is the whole career of T. Flamininus. See especially Plut. *Tit.* 15, 2 f. (cf. Livy, xxxv. 23 f.); Livy, xxxvi. 31, 5 (cf. Pol. xxiii. 5). Chs. III–V will furnish numerous examples.

affected a foreign community, it was often the patron's task to inform it.[1] Finally, he would protect his clients from extortion and oppression.[2]

It is clear that there was a great deal the patron could do for his client community. Naturally he had a right to expect a great deal in return. Just as in the case of his Roman clients,[3] he could expect its support in his public career and private difficulties. After 149, when L. Piso instituted the *quaestio repetundarum*, the praises of client states, hitherto a measure of a man's prestige,[4] became important in protecting him from the malice of his Roman enemies—or from the just resentment of a province.[5] If he was nevertheless condemned, his clients could at least offer him a place of refuge: the case of P. Rutilius Rufus, the victim of the moneylenders' spite, is (as eulogistic tradition proclaims) unique —but only in the fact that he actually settled in the province he was said to have plundered.[6] Nor would he live there in poverty: kings and peoples would see to it that he could live as became his station.[7] But it was not only in adversity that the patron could count on his clients' assistance. It was normally of use to him— particularly (but not only) in his aedileship—in providing him with the means for capturing popular favour. We have already seen how the younger Flaminius was enabled by his Sicilian clients (inherited from his father) to distribute cheap corn in his aedileship.[8] Tiberius Gracchus the father exploited his clients to such an extent that the Senate had to intervene to prevent such extravagance in future. It did not, of course, entirely stop such contributions; as Livy informs us at the same time, the consul

---

[1] Cf. Livy, xxxix. 17, 4 (the *SC de Bacchanalibus*).

[2] e.g. the case of the Spanish provinces in 171 (Livy, xliii. 2); also the names of the nobles supporting Cicero against Verres (and Cicero's own position—*div. in Caec.*, *init.*), and cf. the case of Roscius of Ameria (Ch. X, below, *fin.*).

[3] See Introduction, *passim*.   [4] See below.

[5] There are instances in Cicero's great *repetundae* cases: the *Verrines* (though Verres persuaded only Messana), *pro Flacco*, *pro Fonteio*, *pro Scauro*; also in other kinds of case where such support is relevant (e.g. *Sull.* 61). Ap. Claudius, Cicero's predecessor in Cilicia, thought such *laudationes* most important (Cic. *fam.* iii. 10; viii. 6). Prosecutor as well as defendant could make use of them to establish his character against opposing counsel: cf. Cic. *Flacc.* 74 f.

[6] Val. Max. ii. 10, 5; Dio, fr. 67, 4. C. Cato (*cos.* 114) went to Tarraco, where he had family connexions (see Appendix B), and became a citizen there (Cic. *Balb.* 28).

[7] Rutilius, like Job, grew richer than before his disaster (Dio, l.c.)—as the moralists would stress.   [8] See p. 158, n. 2.

Q. Fulvius Flaccus collected money from Spain for his votive games,[1] and later, as censor, the same Flaccus went so far as to strip the temple of Lacinian Hera of its tiles.[2] For this outrage, which the Senate could annul, but not punish, vengeance had to be left to the enraged gods.[3] African beasts first appear in Rome in large numbers in 169, in the aedileship of a Scipio and a Lentulus (nephew of the *cos.* 201).[4] If we hear less of this kind of contribution in the late Republic, it is probably not because it was no longer practised, but because it was taken for granted, and in the multiplicity of foreign connexions of the great houses it is no longer easy to trace it; but the lavish games of Pompey and of Caesar after their great victories will have owed something to this source.

Colonies of Roman citizens and (to some extent) Latin colonies perhaps deserve special mention: they consisted of men who had the vote. It seems that the *tresuiri* who had founded a colony became its (hereditary) patrons[5] and could thus call on it to support their political advancement. The importance of this is attested in the case of Flamininus, who, as a young man, had helped to supplement colonies: they later supported his claim to the consulship.[6] Though the Latins could only vote in one tribe, the support of the new colonists would no doubt bring about that of their families in Rome, and that may have swung a considerable section of the vote. Citizens of Roman colonies had the full vote of Roman citizens. While Roman colonies were small (300 men was the usual number), that did not matter. But in the second decade of the second century we suddenly find three

---

[1] Livy, xl. 44, 12 (182 B.C.; 179 B.C.).

[2] Id., xlii. 3. He could not do this by virtue of his office; it must be remembered that his famous father (*RE*, s.v. 'Fulvius', no. 59) had commanded in Bruttium.   [3] Val. Max. i. 1, 20 (putting the temple at Locri!).

[4] Livy, xliv. 18, *fin.*

[5] P. Sulla patron of Pompeii (p. 160, n. 5); cf. *FIRA*, no. 21 (*Lex Col. Gen. Jul.*), ch. 97.

[6] Plut. *Tit.* 1, *fin.*–2, *init.* (confused). Flamininus is mentioned by Livy as being on a commission to distribute land to veterans and on one to supplement Venusia (*MRR*, i. 322 and 325–6, with n. 7). He was not on the commission to supplement Narnia, whose members we know (Livy, xxxii. 2, 7). It can be argued that he was on that chosen for Cosa and that Plutarch has merely put 'Narnia' for 'Venusia'; but this is not very likely, for chronological reasons. Plutarch's source may have referred to support by veterans to whom he had given allotments; but some such reference there must have been, and the substance may be accepted.

citizen colonies (Mutina, Parma and Luna) founded with a population of 2,000 families each.[1] This change bears the mark of an individual policy, and we know that it is that of M. Lepidus, the great *Princeps Senatus*, who was chairman of the commissions for all three.[2] It is clear that the privilege of founding such colonies was jealously guarded, and in any case the experiment was not repeated. When this policy was resumed, it was by the *populares* at the end of the century; and the Senate's opposition to Junonia and Neptunia, and later to L. Crassus' Narbo Martius,[3] may well have been partly motivated by the fear of the political power that would be conferred by the patronate over such solid bodies of Roman citizens who could—though only in cases of extreme importance—be mobilized as voters, and who, in any case, would exert a great deal of political influence through their contacts in the City.

Thus *clientelae* abroad were of very real value to the prominent Roman wanting a public career. But beyond this concrete importance there was the reputation they gave him: for power, in Rome, was indissolubly linked with standing and prestige, and these were advertised by foreign *clientelae* as much as by the attendance of Roman clients.[4] Foreign envoys attending his *levée* no doubt added distinction to the crowd;[5] the introduction of envoys and even of kings into the Senate[6] was a public advertisement of his standing among the allies; and Roman senators serving in the provinces could see visible reminders, in stone and bronze, of the benefits he had conferred on cities, nations and kings, and of their fulsome gratitude.[7] These connexions also gave the Roman noble a great deal of personal power abroad—more than he had in the City, where the Senate jealously watched him. For the patron, as we have seen,[8] stood to his clients in the position of a father, and they were expected to ask his advice, as a son would ask a

---

[1] See Tibiletti, 'Ricerche', *Ath.* 1950, 219 f. (table p. 222).

[2] Tibiletti, l.c.; cf. *MRR*, i. 380, 399 (the composition here, despite textual corruption, shows that he was chairman).

[3] See Ch. VIII, *passim* (C. Gracchus); Ch. XI, pp. 264 f. (Crassus): I have not stressed this point again, as it is speculative and merely worth bearing in mind.

[4] See Introduction. On all this, see Gelzer, *Nob.* 81–82.

[5] Cf. Ditt. *Syll.* 656, ll. 21 f.

[6] See p. 160, n. 2.   [7] See *Note P*, p. 296.

[8] See Introduction, pp. 2 f.; cf. p. 164, n. 2; p. 253, n. 4.

father's, before taking decisions of particular importance. Naturally, as the passage of time led to the multiplication of patrons, this became less feasible; fortunately, with the expansion and consolidation of Roman power, it also became less important, as few weighty decisions would now ever have to be taken. Much depended, of course, on the personality of the patron: on how seriously he took his duties and his rights. The great Flamininus regarded himself as practically the guardian of the Greeks: having defended their 'freedom' (i.e. his personal Eastern policy) against those Romans who preferred reliance on force to trust in the effects of a *beneficium*, he constantly used his *auctoritas* to control their policy,[1] complaining when they omitted to consult him.[2] No less was his interest in the Macedonian dynasty: having obtained the recognition of Philip V as an ally,[3] he particularly attached the heir presumptive Demetrius to himself, becoming his political adviser.[4] Masinissa attached himself to the house of the Cornelii Scipiones to the day of his death, advising his successors to do the same: he even made Scipio Aemilianus his executor.[5] This, as Valerius Maximus observes, was a striking example of gratitude—particularly in one who had attained a position of such power: Jugurtha showed no such restraint and used his Roman connexions to his own advantage.[6] Much, as we have seen, depended on personalities. Sulla's envoy could stop the victorious Mithridates;[7] Pompey was suspected—whether justly or not does not concern us here—of using kings as pawns in his own political game.[8] M. Scaurus, the *Princeps Senatus*, was a man 'cuius . . . nutu prope orbis terrarum regebatur'.[9] Aemilianus fully used the power his connexions gave him. C. Gracchus made the most of his,[10] perturbing his enemies. Yet we hear nothing

---

[1] See Chs. III and IV, *passim*.

[2] Livy, xxxvi. 31 f.—a very illuminating passage, which we have noticed in its due place.   [3] Plut. *Tit.* 14, *fin.*

[4] Livy, xl. 20, 3 *et al.* Perseus calls him Demetrius' 'auctor omnium rerum et magister' (xl. 11, 2; cf. 23, 7). He probably introduced the prince into the Senate and moved the decree in his honour (xxxix. 47, 8 f.; cf. xl. 11, 1 and App. *Mac.* 9, 6). Cf. p. 94 (with notes).

[5] Val. Max. v. 2, *ext.* 4; App. *Lib.* 105–6; Zon. ix. 27. See p. 137.

[6] See Ch. IX, pp. 192 f.   [7] App. *Mith.* 66.

[8] Plut. *Pomp.* 49, 13. For his *clientelae* (down to 70 B.C.), see Ch. XI, *passim*.

[9] Cic. *Font.* 24—probably not only referring to his *auctoritas* in the Senate.

[10] See Ch. VIII, *passim*.

of any foreign influence exerted by that heir to a mighty name, T. Quinctius Flamininus (*cos.* 150),[1] or his son (*cos.* 123). Inherited power might get a man the consulship; his influence depended on himself.

We have now seen the kinds of services that client and patron could render each other during the century or so that passed between the Hannibalic War and the time of troubles preceding the end of the Republic. The evidence is fairly copious and examples could be multiplied; but enough has been said, with particular reference to well-known instances, to show the importance of *clientelae* (to both parties concerned) in the normal working of Roman institutions in the great age of the Republic. As we have incidentally seen from some of our examples, this normal function of *clientela* continued behind the more striking events of the half-century following. How various forces combined, round the turn of the first century B.C., to enhance its sinister aspects and mould it into an instrument of δυναστεία, will be the concern of later chapters. What is worth stressing at this point is the all-pervasive nature of this phenomenon and its extreme importance in fashioning and preserving the fabric of Roman rule through generations of trial and (often all but fatal) error in policy and administration. It was *clientela* in its private aspects that enabled Rome to assert and maintain that dominance over ostensibly independent states, which she claimed by virtue of the extension of this same category of Roman thought to the sphere of international relations. The career of Flamininus, with his interventions in Eastern affairs, provides the most striking, though not by any means the only, example. The 'Roman parties' that controlled Greece during the period of *libertas* were connected by personal ties with the leading families of Rome.[2] Chieftains and kings relied on their Roman *amici* for their power and their security.[3] In war, personal friendship with prominent Romans might overcome national policy and prevent defection or at least mitigate its consequences.[4] It is mainly due

[1] He headed a mission sent to return some Thracian hostages (Livy, xlv. 42, 11).
[2] On a prominent example (Charops the Epirot), see Scullard, *JRS*, 1945, 60 f.—perhaps a little exaggerated.
[3] Examples in Chs. II–V, *passim*, especially Ch. IV. Cf. Sands, *Cl. Pr.* 139 f.: a short list for the late Republic.
[4] Note the influence of personal connexions at Capua in 216 and following years

to this solid structure of personal relationships that the Empire of the Roman People survived the storms of the last few generations of the Republic; for amid the internecine campaigns of Roman war-lords and the depredations of Roman moneylenders and magistrates, the loyalty of the subject territories stands out as, on the whole, unshaken and all but incomprehensible.[1]

In Rome, however, power was bound to cause *inuidia*, and the great patrons of foreign states, not averse to displaying their connexions, were bound to suffer from it. This was so, particularly, in the ages of great wars—in the early second century B.C. and again at the end of the Republic. For the former time, Flamininus and the Scipios are the outstanding examples. We have seen how theatrically Flamininus advertised his patronate over the Greeks. The Scipios, however, surpassed all in tactlessness, adopting *cognomina* from the whole of the *orbis* they had conquered.[2] Flamininus at least avoided personal disaster, though he could not save his brother from disgrace in Cato's censorship.[3] The Scipios fell headlong—a warning to others of excessive pretensions; though in fact the affectations of P. Africanus had been harmless enough and he had not been a real power in moulding policy.[4] As the first generation of the great conquerors passed away, far-flung *clientelae* ceased to cause surprise and alarm: Tiberius Gracchus the Elder, with connexions in Macedonia and Greece, Asia and the kingdoms of the East, Spain and Sardinia, left the memory (heightened by contrast with his sons) of a great and wise man. Scipio Aemilianus, heir to the connexions of two great houses, becomes a respected figure beloved by his fellow-nobles —if we are to believe Cicero.[5] Yet even this virtuous man had

(Livy, xxiii. 4, 7 f.); though in this case the main link was *conubium*. The Epirot Nestor, who saved a Roman consul from a plot (Pol. xxvii. 16), is a good example of a loyal client's value.

[1] For a detailed investigation of these relationships and their pervasiveness in some provinces, see Ch. XI.

[2] Africanus, Asiagenus (if that is correct), Hispallus.

[3] Livy, xxxix. 42 *et al.* Whether T. Flamininus would have been entitled to the dignity of *princ. Sen.* by *mos maiorum* is not certain (Kienast, *Cato*, 74 and n. 72).

[4] Kienast, op. cit. 57 f. We need not examine the 'trials of the Scipios' in detail. The best treatments are by Fraccaro (now in *Opuscula*, i. 263 f.) and Scullard (*Rom. Pol.* 290 f.).

[5] On Gracchus, see the article in *RE* (s.v. 'Sempronius', no. 53), with Cicero's judgements there cited. On his attitude to his clients, see p. 161. On Scipio, see *RE*, s.v. 'Cornelius', no. 335, especially coll. 1460 f. (cf. p. 160, n. 5).

his *obtrectatores et inuidi*, and their machinations (we are told) brought disaster to the State.[1] We shall have occasion, in due course, to follow the further working of *inuidia* in this connexion. The great example, of course, is the lonely figure of Pompey, the conqueror of the East,[2] just beyond the limit set to this inquiry.

Dignitas, leading to concrete advantages and even *potentia*, and on the other hand *inuidia*—these are the two poles of the noble's foreign *clientelae*. It is in the last few generations of the Republic that they play an ever-increasing part in the tragedy of its civil discord, and we must now turn to a detailed investigation of that part—an investigation that will occupy the remainder of this study.

[1] Cic. *rep.* i. 31.   [2] Id. *Att.* i. 18, 6 *et al.*

VIII

THE ITALIANS—POLICIES AND POLITICS

HITHERTO our main study has been the development
of Rome's policy towards her subjects and the various
principles of organization she adopted: the different ways
in which her allies were associated with her. The personal influence of outstanding Roman families and individuals—of Flamininus, of Q. Marcius Philippus, of Scipio Aemilianus—had been
used in what one may fairly call the best interests of the State and
had supplemented and cemented the links binding foreign communities to Rome. At home, though the possession of far-flung
clientelae added to a man's prestige (always important in Roman
politics), and could bring him more concrete advantages (especially in his aedileship), his clients had no very direct influence
on his political progress, and excessive international connexions
might even damage the noble. All this did not change overnight.
Indeed, as I have already suggested, we shall find that, at the very
time when personal rivalries were destroying the Republic, personal connexions were holding the Empire together; and the
greatest of the Republican dynasts, Pompey, laboured most under
the *inuidia* of his own power. Both in its beneficent effects and in
its political limitations the history of *clientela* shows no dis-
continuity. But we have now come to a point at which the possession and cultivation of personal connexions and political support
outside the City of Rome begins to assume increasing practical
importance, until it becomes one of the main methods, and
therefore aims, of political ambition. We shall, therefore, first
study the origins of this tendency in the political struggles round
the work of the Gracchi.

For our study the tribunate of Tiberius Gracchus does not in
itself mark an epoch. In retrospect, we may consider the private
army that Scipio Aemilianus took with him to Numantia in 134[1]
much more portentous. Scipio had good precedent for his action,[2]

---

[1] App. *Iber.* 84.

[2] e.g. Scipio Africanus; cf. Gabba, 'L'esercito prof.', 183 f., showing how these
incidents resemble—and how they differ from—the old private levy of retainers

and, no doubt, contemporaries saw no dangerous implications in it. Yet we may well say that it was the prologue to a new era.

It was during the absence of Scipio, and, with him, of many of the foremost *iuuenes* of Italy, that Tiberius Gracchus was elected tribune. He was the eldest son of Ti. Sempronius P.f. Gracchus, censor and twice consul, one of the most powerful men of his age. The elder Gracchus had founded and maintained far-flung connexions in the East and the West; but while his methods towards competitors were ruthless, and while he made full use (as far as anyone could in his day) of his clients for his political advancement,[1] his *fides* towards them remained above reproach. It is well known how the younger Tiberius used the credit of his father's name in order to extricate the army of Mancinus, and how the Senate's repudiation of the treaty he had negotiated roused his anger and helped to turn him against the nobility.[2] It is true that his cousin Scipio saved him from extradition; but the disgrace aroused his *dolor*. Not for the last time the ruling faction had made the mistake of attacking the *dignitas* and undermining the *fides* of a proud and unyielding aristocrat. Tiberius could not save his paternal clients: to restore his *fides* and save his *dignitas* he turned reformer and later revolutionary. It is worth noting that the credit of the family in Spain does not seem to have suffered[3]—perhaps Tiberius' motives were not impugned, or perhaps his self-sacrifice and his brother's policy[4] redeemed his memory.

With the details of Tiberius' programme and career we are not much concerned. The only question we shall have to decide—and it is an important one—is whether his main agrarian proposal (or any other measure) applied to Italian allies or only to Roman citizens. This is a very difficult problem, on which neither the ancient nor the modern tradition is in agreement. The disagreement in the ancient sources is explicit—and it is between Appian, considered our best source for Tiberius Gracchus,[5] and Cicero, who, in the family tradition of the Mucii Scaevolae, must have

---

like that of the Fabii. We may add the obvious comment that the mere geographical extension of the new *clientela*, as compared with the compact *clientes* of old time, already introduced a significant difference: thus Scipio's, Appian tells us, included cities and kings.   [1] Cf. Ch. VII, pp. 161; 166.

[2] Plut. *Tib. Gr.* 5 f.; Cic. *Br.* 103; *har. resp.* 43.

[3] Cf. the Sempronii in Appendix B.   [4] See pp. 182 f.

[5] Taeger, *Tib. Gr.*, *passim*; Göhler, *Rom*, 100 f. Cf. below.

had first-rate sources. Appian (as Göhler has shown beyond reasonable doubt)[1] consistently depicts Tiberius as aiming at the revival of *Italian* man-power and passing his legislation on behalf of the Italian as well as of the Roman poor, and—correspondingly —as being supported by the Italians.[2] Cicero, however, makes the well-known statement:[3] 'Ti. Gracchus perseuerauit in ciuibus, sociorum . . . iura neglexit ac foedera.' This must mean that Tiberius confined his attempts to benefit people to Roman citizens—i.e. it flatly contradicts Appian. Unfortunately, what other evidence we have is also difficult to interpret. Plutarch (with apparent exceptions, which we shall notice) refers only to citizens; and an interesting piece of evidence he seems to give us dissolves on closer scrutiny. In *C. Gr.* 1, 3 he tells us of the first public appearance of Gaius, in defence of a Βέττιος. This name must be 'Vettius', and it was argued by Cichorius and accepted by Münzer[4] that this Vettius will have been one of the Vettii Sabini, a family that rises to public office in Rome a little later, and that he will have been one of the 'Italian supporters' of Ti. Gracchus, who was put on trial because of that support. The main argument seems plausible enough—especially as Plutarch's account strongly suggests a great political trial; but the word 'Italian' presents a dangerous ambiguity: the Vettii Sabini, it seems, were Roman citizens—not only because (we are told)[5] they rose to honours before the Social War, but because since 268 the Sabines had had the full citizenship. Thus the support of Vettius for Gracchus proves nothing to our point: Vettius may have been a Roman

---

[1] *Rom*, l.c., and pp. 76 f. (on the meaning of ''Ἰταλιῶται').

[2] But Göhler makes too much of the 'supporting evidence' of Velleius: the highly rhetorical passage ii. 3, 2, with its claim that Tiberius 'pollicitus toti Italiae ciuitatem' (which Göhler accepts, against the evidence of App. *b.c.* i. 34), cannot be used as evidence—any more than we can argue, from a similar passage about Gaius (ii. 6, 2), that Gaius wanted to give citizenship to the Transpadanes. Samonati believes in a 'promise', but no concrete proposals (*BMIR*, 1936, 29 f.)— an uneasy compromise.   [3] *rep.* iii. 41.

[4] *Unt. zu Luc.* 348 f. (by combination with Quint. i. 5, 56); *RE*, s.v. 'Sempronius', col. 1379; other scholars have not paid much attention to the matter.

[5] But in fact the moneyer or *q.* of *c.* 100 only calls himself P. Sabinus; and that *cognomen* is found in other *gentes* (e.g. the Titurii about the same time as the Vettii; the Calvisii and the Minatii a little later), while the *praenomen* is not found again in any of them. The identification of the moneyer is mere conjecture. If the Βέττιος of Plutarch is *not* a Sabinus, then he may well be a non-Roman (cf. P. Vettius Scato in the Social War).

citizen. Only on two occasions[1] does Plutarch seem to extend the interest of Tiberius to the whole of Italy; and even there he is ambiguous. Apart from this, nothing in Plutarch hints at any concern for the allies.[2]

The other evidence that bears on the matter is that of the *Lex Agraria* of 111. There, in l. 3 and probably in l. 15, we find references to land allotted by the Sempronian commission to Roman citizens only. Mommsen[3] took the references to be to colonial allotments, and in that case they would have no bearing on our point. But M. A. Levi[4] has shown that this is in fact very unlikely and that the assignments must be viritane assignments of *ager publicus* by lot.[5] It is very difficult, once this is recognized, to believe that land was indeed distributed to Italians under the Gracchan law, or that it was meant to be thus distributed.[6] When the Italians begin to object to the triumvirs' expropriations, there is no sign of any 'class war'[7] in the Italian cities on the subject. It seems, in fact, that Cicero's 'perseuerauit in ciuibus' must stand.

It is undeniably difficult to explain the divergent—and self-consistent—account of Appian. It has, on the whole, been the custom to rate Appian (in this part of his work) very highly and

---

[1] 9, 4–6: τοῖς ὑπὲρ τῆς Ἰταλίας μαχομένοις; but this is cancelled out by τῶν τοσούτων Ῥωμαίων a little farther on. The other possible instance is the journey through Etruria (8, 9). See below.

[2] Cf. the constant use of 'ὁ δῆμος' for his supporters (8, 7 *et al.*) and, in the closing scene, 'πολῖται' (17, 4); cf. also Plut. *Tib. Gr.* 9, 2; *C. Gr.* 1, 3; Taeger, op. cit. 72 f. Sallust (*Jug.* 31, 7) also mentions only the *plebs Romana*.

[3] *GS*, i. 98 f.

[4] *RFIC*, 1929, 237 f.—though not all his arguments are equally convincing.

[5] Larsen (*CP*, 1930, 279) shows that the use of the lot for such assignments was quite normal, at least in Cicero's day, where the allotments were not all of equal value.

[6] But Thomsen's argument (*Cl. et Med.* v. 35: based on the claim that only Roman citizens could hold *ager priuatus optimo iure*) is invalid. We do not know much about laws of land tenure before 90 B.C. and must not make such sweeping assertions. (Cf. Tibiletti, *Ath.* 1950, 217 and n. 1: long before 133 B.C. non-Romans could be given *ager publicus* together with citizens in cases where the latter received it as full private property—and we have no evidence as to the nature of their title.)

[7] Such as Drzerga seems to assume (*ap.* Göhler, *Rom*, 126). Thomsen (op. cit.), though not forced into it by his premises, lands himself in a similar conclusion. Göhler (l.c.) sees that the evidence does not justify this; but he has to postulate a large-scale change of attitude among the Italians between 133 and 129, without explaining why anyone should have changed his mind at all.

regard Plutarch, in particular, as a second-rate source.[1] Gelzer, in his review of Taeger's book, entered a judicious protest against this view,[2] and it is time that less reliance were placed on this one author to the exclusion of other sources. Though this is not the place for a detailed investigation, it must be stressed that Appian's account has obvious weaknesses[3] and that Plutarch, despite his dramatizing and moralizing temper, gives us much of value that we miss in Appian.[4] We need not, therefore, be *a priori* as ready as many have been to prefer Appian to Plutarch, where they offer incompatible but self-consistent accounts.

We have seen that Plutarch agrees with Cicero in confining Tiberius' aim, in his agrarian law, to Roman citizens. To this we found only one real exception:[5] the journey through Etruria, where there were (except for a small area north of the Tiber) only allied states.[6] Now it is interesting to observe the source of this one exception: it is C. Gracchus ἔν τινι βιβλίῳ.[7] Gaius, however, as we shall see, had good reason to seek to please the allies and, therefore, to stress his brother's interest in them. It is not always clearly recognized in fact (though often acknowledged in principle) that the 'Gracchan legend' owes many both of its general features and of its details to the publications of C. Gracchus. And here, perhaps, we have found the origin of Appian's 'pan-Italic' account. If Appian's narrative is directly based (as it seems to be) on the work of a Caesarian or (more probably) Augustan writer of Popular and perhaps Italian tendencies[8]—a writer who, therefore,

---

[1] Cf. Taeger, *Tib. Gr.*; Meyer, *Kl. Schr.* i. 384 f. (cf. Schwartz, *Gött. gel. Anz.* 1896, 800 f.).   [2] *Gnomon*, 1929, 299 f.—especially p. 303.

[3] See *Note Q*, p. 296.   [4] See Gelzer, l.c. (n. 2).

[5] See p. 171: 9, 4 f., we found, is clarified in the next clause as in fact restricted to Romans.

[6] Gelzer (l.c.) stresses the fact that there *was* this strip of *ager Romanus*. But it will hardly serve as the basis of this story, especially as Tiberius, on his way to and from Spain, will have twice traversed the whole region. But Gelzer is right in adding that observation of similar conditions on Roman and allied territory does not imply an attempt to remedy them on both at once.

[7] Plut. *Tib. Gr.* 8, 9. The 'booklet' has been taken to be a letter or treatise addressed to Pomponius (cf. *HRR*, i². 119; Taeger, op. cit. 8); but the portent recorded by Cicero (*div.* i. 36 and ii. 62) bears no obvious relation to the motives of the tribune Tiberius, and there is no reason to assign the two citations to the same work. The βιβλίον is very likely to be an *apologia pro fratre*—perhaps one of the speeches devoted to that *pium officium* and published (cf. Malcovati, *ORF²*, 197); more probably a written account of his brother's life or tribunate.

[8] Cf. Gelzer, op. cit. 299–300. This is nowhere refuted by Göhler, though he

would be most likely to avail himself of the material provided by C. Gracchus[1]—we need not regard his version as authentic. From an account by Gaius stressing—perhaps exaggerating—his brother's interest in the Italians (as in the Plutarch fragment) and their support for him[2]—though Gaius could speak of plans, but not, of course, misreport the actual legislation—an author writing a century later might well, in the light of Gaius' own programme and in ignorance of legal detail, spin the story we have in Appian.

We shall therefore agree with Gelzer that Tiberius sought and obtained the support of the City plebs and the rural proletariat, even though we reject the attempt to support this view by reference to Appian's account. It is clear to us that the acquisition of this support extending all over Italy was not the chief aim of Tiberius Gracchus, i.e. that he did not aim at tyranny, but at genuine reform.[3] But to contemporaries, it seems, this was not always obvious.[4] His unconstitutional behaviour towards his colleague M. Octavius made men wonder how far he would go.[5] In the atmosphere of suspicion and fear engendered by this and by his attempt at re-election, it was no wonder that his *clientelae* created more *inuidia* than those of an average noble; and in the end it was this that helped to precipitate his downfall. One of the highest points in the distinguished career of the elder Tiberius had been his tour of inspection of Eastern kingdoms—a tour during which he had, of course, established the usual personal relations with the kings concerned—especially through the

rightly rejects (*Rom*, 82–83) Gelzer's attempt to translate Appian's 'Ἰταλιῶται' as 'agrestes'. The tendency of Appian's source is obvious from the whole narrative. (Cf. Taeger, op. cit. 10 f.) Gabba's *Appiano e la storia delle guerre civili* appeared too late to be considered here; I have elsewhere (in my review in *CR*, N.S. viii, 1958) commented on some of his views.

[1] The absence of direct quotation is, of course, no argument against this: Appian does not name sources (cf. Taeger, l.c.).

[2] This, as we shall see, was politically very necessary: by 123 the anti-Gracchan party had created the picture of Tiberius as the violator and Scipio as the defender of treaties—a remarkable achievement in view of the facts of the Numantine affair! Cf. also the often-quoted Velleius passage on Tiberius' intention of enfranchising the allies (p. 170, n. 2). Though statements of unfulfilled intention are not evidence for history (as Syme has frequently reminded us), they are often good evidence for the trends of propaganda.

[3] This seems the unanimous view of modern scholars and need not be argued here.   [4] Cf. the Optimate source of Vell. ii. 3, 6.

[5] Cf. the remark of T. Annius Luscus and its sequel (Plut. *Tib. Gr.* 14 f.).

beneficium of his favourable report on them at a critical time.[1] When Attalus, the most important of the kings thus under obligation to the Gracchi, died in 134, it was natural that the envoy bearing his will should lodge at the residence of his Roman patrons, the Gracchi—and there, we are told, he was seen by Q. Pompeius offering a diadem and royal robe to Tiberius.[2] It is difficult to accept this story as *bona fide* evidence; but it is of interest as showing the connexion between Eudemus (the Pergamene envoy) and Tiberius.[3] It was through this connexion that Tiberius learnt of the will of Attalus, who had left his kingdom to Rome; and it was thus that he was able to anticipate action by the Senate and present to the People his bill proposing the use of the estate for his projects.[4] The incident is of interest in that it is the first important example of a client's support going to his personal patron —or, to be precise (and this is more ominous still), his patron's son—rather than what may be called the interests of the Roman State (as interpreted by the governing oligarchy). For the first time foreign *clientelae* had been used in the factional struggles in Rome. It is likely that Pompeius, even if he could not foresee the consequences of this precedent, had realized, when he made his accusation (so unconvincing in itself), that something new and dangerous had indeed happened.

Tiberius was murdered, and law and order triumphed. Even his noble allies, giving timid support while he lived, hastened to approve of the manner of his death.[5] But his work could not be stopped—for the moment, at least: it was appropriated and advertised throughout Italy as the 'Government's'.[6] That this did not deceive the People is stated by Plutarch and confirmed by all our evidence.[7] Soon, however, a new factor appeared that had been omitted from the calculations of both sides.

The return of Scipio and his army was an asset to the oligarchy.

---

[1] Sources in *MRR*, i. 438.　　　　　　　　[2] Plut. *Tib. Gr.* 14.

[3] Noticed—but not discussed—by Pareti, *Storia*, iii. 333.

[4] Plut., l.c. That he had Eudemus' assistance in this is amply shown by Pompeius' accusation.

[5] On the attitude of Scaevola, cf. Val. Max. iii. 2, 17; Plut. *Tib. Gr.* 9, 1; Cic. *dom.* 91; *Planc.* 88.

[6] Plut. *Tib. Gr.* 21; cf. *ILS*, 23. The inscription has now been reclaimed for T. Annius (successfully, it seems) by T. P. Wiseman, *PBSR*, 1964, 30 f.

[7] *Tib. Gr.* 21 (though the moralizing account of Nasica's mission and end is wrong). Cf. Münzer, *Röm. Ad.* 258 f.

His influence with the People was unquestioned: they had been his supporters in his rivalries with his *inimici*.[1] On his return he took good care, in the tense political atmosphere, not to throw away their support by rash condemnation of the dead tribune, to which Carbo wanted to tempt him: he could plead ignorance due to absence.[2] The result of his wise policy was apparent when his *auctoritas* sufficed to have Carbo's bill (supported by C. Gracchus) permitting iteration of the tribunate rejected.[3] Scipio, however, had been as noteworthy for his *clientelae* outside Rome, which had recently even furnished him with a private army, as for his influence with the Plebs.[4] It was therefore to Scipio that the Italian landowners—most prominently, no doubt, the *iuuenes* whom he had taken to Spain—turned for help when the Sempronian triumvirs began to interfere with their holdings.[5] We cannot go into the involved question as to the reason for Italian anxiety in 129, and in particular as to the kind of land, and the classes of Italians, affected.[6] But we must stress again the fact that this anxiety was widespread and—to the Senate—alarming, and that there is no evidence whatever for 'class differences' in the Italian communities on the matter.[7] It is clear that large sections of the Italian allies must have been involved.[8]

---

[1] Plut. *Paul.* 38; cf. App. i. 19, *fin.* (References to Appian are, unless otherwise indicated, to *b.c.*)

[2] Vell. ii. 4, 4 has preserved his cautious answer (there is no reason to think the addition an invention, as it serves no tendentious purpose); the rest of the (Optimate) tradition has turned it into a categorical condemnation no doubt more suited to *magnitudo animi* (cf. Livy, *per.* lix; Val. Max. vi. 2, 3). The date must be 132/131, soon after his return from Spain (despite Fraccaro, *Studi . . . Gracchi*, 440 and *MRR*, i. 502).   [3] Cic. *am.* 95; Livy, *per.* lix.

[4] See pp. 168–9 (with notes). Cf. p. 166 (with n. 5) on his early career; for his possible gifts of booty to Italian towns, see p. 151 (with n. 3).

[5] App. i. 19; Livy, *per.* lix; Cic. *rep.* i. 31.

[6] Despite numerous discussions, there is still little to add to Last's account in *CAH*, ix. Thomsen (*Cl. et Med.* v. 35 f.) tries to show that Italian individuals could not hold *ager publicus* and that the land concerned had been handed over to cities (like the African land of *Lex Agr.*, l. 81). But while there may well have been land of the latter type (not necessarily in *latifundia*), there is no valid reason to deny the allies' right of *possessio*. Appian (i. 18) suggests that they either had it or were permitted to assume it, and we know nothing to the contrary (cf. p. 171, n. 6).

[7] See p. 171 (with n. 7). Cf. Livy, *per.* lix; Cic. *rep.* i. 31.

[8] App. i. 18 makes it appear that it was mainly the holders of land once assigned *uiritim*, and that the trouble was started by the survey and not by confiscations. But his account is not very clear. Another class involved will have been the descendants

That the Italians had a good case has never been denied: they had never had any profit to expect from the Sempronian law; and now their holdings were to be used for needy Roman citizens, mostly strangers to the land.

Scipio did not miss his chance of obliging both his Italian clients and the large landowners in Rome: still using careful tact and diplomacy, to avoid offending his Roman clients, he succeeded, against the opposition of the triumvirs and particularly of Fulvius, in paralysing the work of the commission;[1] and his death soon after—probably natural—provided the anti-Gracchans with a convenient martyr.[2] Unfortunately our evidence now fails us all but completely and, except for the fact that unrest continued,[3] we know nothing about the immediate effect of Scipio's death.[4] But the picture of events that Optimate tradition was building up is quite clear: Tiberius Gracchus as the violator of the allies' treaties, Scipio as their defender martyred by Gracchus' anti-Italian followers; and the oligarchy responsible for what moderate reform could beneficially be undertaken.[5]

It was in these conditions that the triumvirs, led by M. Fulvius Flaccus, determined on a bold counter-stroke, aimed at capturing the sympathies of the Italians and combining them with the Roman following, which the commission probably had never lost, against the oligarchy. The scarcity of evidence makes it difficult to recapture the sequence of events with certainty; yet, as the matter is of some importance, an attempt must be made to interpret our information. We learn from Cicero and Festus[6] that in 126

of the old owners of land confiscated but never divided. With the shortage of population in the south (and the lack of enthusiasm for assignments there—see Tibiletti, *Ath.* 1950, 192 f.) these will have formed a comparatively numerous group, which might consider itself particularly unfairly treated if it were now made subject to laws *de modo agrorum*.

[1] App. i. 19; *et al.* For Fulvius, see Plut. *C. Gr.* 10. Cf. *CAH*, ix. 42 f.

[2] App. i. 20; *et al.* The imputation of murder, which was not (probably because it could not be) made at the time, had become 'orthodox' by 122, when inquiry was no longer possible (cf. Plut. *C. Gr.* 10). See Carcopino, *Gracques*, 83 f. On Laelius' funeral oration (*ORF*[2], 121 f.), see *JRS*, 1956, 220: it refers to natural death.

[3] Livy, *per.* lix; cf. Dio fr. 84, 2. The 'seditiones' must refer to Italian unrest (as immediately above).

[4] The census figures are not useful evidence. For 128/127 we know nothing except the names of a few magistrates; for 126/125 our knowledge is scrappy, but careful investigation will yield results (see below).   [5] See p. 173, n. 3 ; p. 174 (with n. 6).

[6] Sources in *ORF*[2], 179 f. Despite Festus' *conscripsit*, *Br.* 109 shows that Gracchus and Pennus opposed each other in person.

C. Gracchus as quaestor spoke against an act by the tribune M. Iunius Pennus which expelled all aliens from Rome.[1] Next we hear that in 125 M. Fulvius Flaccus, as consul, proposed the citizenship or (if they preferred it) *prouocatio* for the Italian allies in return for acquiescence in the treatment of their holdings of public land under the Sempronian law.[2] That these notices must refer to connected events is generally recognized; but the precise connexion (and its significance) may, in fact, be recovered. It is clear that Pennus' law was not (like similar acts in 187 and 177) one requested and welcomed by the allies—C. Gracchus' surviving words could not, in that case, have been used.[3] It was a coercive measure, offending allied sentiment. The reason for its passing, in the circumstances, appears obvious: it must be fear of allied support for the Gracchan party. This, after the events of 129, would be most surprising, were it not for our knowledge of Flaccus' proposal of 125, a proposal which we know the allies supported.[4] Thus this proposal will have been in the air in 126; but we can go farther than that. As C. Gracchus was quaestor in Sardinia for over two years,[5] his attack on Pennus' law must have been made before he left with Orestes, i.e. in the first few months of 126.[6] Thus Pennus' bill (and therefore Flaccus' proposal) must have been discussed in the first few months of 126. This shows that Flaccus did not merely evolve his scheme after he had been elected consul for 125, but on the contrary included his scheme in his 'platform' when canvassing for election. It is only now that we can see the full reason for Pennus' law: if Italians flocked to Rome to support Flaccus, they had to be removed for the consular elections to be held without risk of fraud or intimidation: an action often regarded as a wanton insult,[7] or at least a tactless

---

[1] Broughton's 'Roman towns' (*MRR*, i. 508) rests on a misunderstanding of Cic. *off*. iii. 47. Fortunately Cicero is explicit ('usu *urbis* prohibere'—l.c.). Bernardi says ('G.S.' 70) that Pennus' bill failed, and he cites Plut. *C. Gr.* 3, 1 and 12, 1 in support; I cannot agree with this.   [2] App. i. 21; Val. Max. ix. 5, 1.

[3] He refers, by implication, to Roman *stultitia* and *auaritia* (Malcovati, *ORF²*, 180).

[4] App. i. 21: ἐδέχοντο ἄσμενοι—as, apparently, in 122 (see below).

[5] See p. 179, n. 3.

[6] Or, theoretically, even in December 127 (cf. *MRR*, i. 509). Cic. *Br*. 109 certainly implies that the conflict was immediate; in any case, the provisions of Pennus' law were hardly meant to be permanent (there is no parallel for such a thing).

[7] Thus apparently by Cic. *off*. iii. 47: he will hardly have known or investigated

blunder, takes intelligible shape. Despite the law of Pennus, however, Flaccus was elected and, when he entered office, submitted his proposal, refusing to listen to Senatorial vituperation.[1] At this point, providentially, envoys from Massilia appeared to ask for Roman aid against a Salluvian attack: the Senate assigned this *prouincia* to the consul Flaccus, who had to abandon his proposal and go north.[2]

Modern scholars sometimes charge him with trading the fate of his proposal for a chance of glory;[3] it is difficult to see what course they would expect him to have followed—and the charge, never brought against him by the Ancient tradition (uniformly hostile as it is), is shown to be groundless by his actions after his return. His friend C. Gracchus was to remember the Senate's manœuvre and try to make it impossible for the future by his famous *lex de prouinciis consularibus*, which modern accounts hardly ever explain.[4] But in the meantime the Senate's tactics had succeeded: the decision was put off.

The issue, however, was now clear, and the claims of Senatorial propaganda had been ruthlessly exposed.[5] Within four years of the 'martyrdom' of Scipio in the cause of the allies, the allies were firmly behind the Gracchans and the oligarchy was fighting against them. Nor have we any warrant for believing—what, at least ever since Mommsen, scholars have usually affirmed or implied—that the People so vigorously opposed Flaccus' bill that it was either rejected or virtually certain of rejection. Appian's statement that the People supported Flaccus and regretted his departure is explicit enough; and, reasonable in any case on account of the agrarian question, it is borne out by the People's consistent support for him after his return and for his known friend C. Gracchus. Their selfish opposition to Italian enfranchisement was, as we shall see, not an early or spontaneous growth: they cared little about abstract principles. That attitude was sown and tended by Fannius and his aristocratic supporters.

---

the precise background. In 126 (unlike 95) there was no time for a *quaestio* such as he would approve of, nor was fraud the chief point. A similar situation arose in 122 (Plut. *C. Gr.* 12—see below).

[1] App. l.c.; Val. Max. ix. 5, 1.   [2] App. i. 34.

[3] e.g. Cary, *History*, 287; cf. *CAH*, ix. 47.   [4] But see Fraccaro, *Opuscula*, ii. 35.

[5] On C. Gracchus' campaign to vindicate his brother's memory, see p. 172, n. 7 (cf. Cic. *Br.* 126). At least part of it must belong to the years before his election.

The reasons for this stand on the part of the oligarchy are not difficult to find: Appian rightly speaks of their unwillingness to make their subjects their equals. Natural conservatism combined, no doubt, with fear that the Assemblies—and even the Senate itself in due course—might be swamped, and the control of leading families over Italy through their local clients lost in a general equalization.[1] The tribunate of Tiberius Gracchus had divided the State into two hostile parties:[2] the oligarchy, for the first time for many years, had lost control of the Plebs and, for the first time ever, did not seem to be securely re-establishing it. When the Gracchan faction temporarily succeeded in uniting the support of the Plebs and the Italian allies behind the leadership of such great nobles as M. Fulvius Flaccus and C. Sempronius Gracchus, the shadow of future events was cast upon the political battlefield.

For the moment the sky cleared; but not for long. In 124 C. Gracchus returned from his Sardinian proquaestorship after more than two years' absence from Rome, vindicated himself against vexatious charges, and at once stood for the tribunate.[3] He found the situation a little changed, with some of the Senate's authority recovered. An obscure and isolated incident, the revolt of Fregellae, had shaken the Fathers out of a merely negative attitude. Opimius, who took and destroyed the rebellious city, was not allowed to triumph: a triumph over Latins would have been too tactless.[4] It may also have been at this time that the magistrates of Latin cities were given *ex officio* Roman citizenship.[5] Henceforth there was to be an increasing section of the governing classes of Italy firmly loyal to Rome—a fact the importance of which was only recognized to its full extent in the

---

[1] See Cary, op. cit. 287; cf. Marsh–Scullard, 64.   [2] Cic. *rep.* i. 31.

[3] *MRR*, i. 512. Plutarch's τριετία merely means 'three campaigns' (126–124); but it does exclude putting his return in 125.

[4] The revolt and destruction of Fregellae may, as is usually thought, have followed the failure of Flaccus' project. The sources (see *MRR*, i. 510) tell us nothing before the closing scene of the siege: accounts like Pareti's (*Storia*, iii. 352) are not even reasonable conjecture. It is important to notice that, despite general dissatisfaction (Asc. 17), Fregellae seems to have stood alone (*vir. ill.* 65, 2—mentioning Asculum—is generally rejected): the city had probably long been unpopular with the other Latin states. (See *CR*, 1955, 22 f.) For Opimius, see Val. Max. ii. 8, 4. Cf. Samonati, *BMIR*, 1936, 39.

[5] Suggested by Tibiletti (*RIL*, 1953, 54 f.).

Social War.[1] At the same time this process of enfranchisement was to be so slow that there was no danger of emancipation from the influence of the great Roman families: control of these new citizens, tied to the Roman nobility and sharing with it a strong interest in the preservation of the principle of oligarchy, would be easy enough.

It was to this situation that C. Gracchus returned. His past boded ill for the *inimici* of his brother: he had supported Carbo in 131 and opposed Pennus in 126, and he had (it seems) defended one of his brother's adherents.[2] This sufficed for an imputation of complicity in the revolt of Fregellae.[3] His record in Sardinia, furthermore, had shown that he could call on all the weapons of his station in achieving his aim.

Few characters in Republican history have been as much discussed as that of C. Gracchus, and from the point of view of this study no purpose would be served by adding to the number of general discussions. The aspect of him with which we are mainly concerned is that of a Roman dynast—a member (however unusual) of the *nobilitas*; and if this aspect is accordingly stressed in the account that follows, that is not to be taken as denying the existence, and importance, of other aspects. The fact of his conscious pride in his station is known to us, by a stroke of good fortune singular for this period, through his own words;[4] and his friends and enemies never forgot it. It is a point of cardinal importance for any interpretation of his career that he stands rather in the line of Caesar than in that of Saturninus.

Of his career in Sardinia we have an interesting account in Plutarch.[5] It will be remembered that Sardinia was one of the many places in which his father had established connexions.[6] Gaius used these, as his brother had done in Spain, both in the best interests of the Roman People and in such a way as to make his own importance clear:[7] he personally persuaded the cities to

---

[1] Tibiletti, op. cit. See below.

[2] On Carbo, see p. 175; on Pennus, pp. 176–7; on Vettius, p. 170 (with n. 5).

[3] Plut. *C. Gr.* 3—not (it seems) a formal prosecution.

[4] *ap.* Gell. xi. 10: 'ego ipse,. . . peto a uobis non pecuniam, sed bonam existimationem et honorem.' Cf. Sen. *ben.* vi. 34, 2 (his division of *amici*); Plut. *C. Gr.* 6, 4.

[5] *C. Gr.* 2.

[6] See p. 166.

[7] Well brought out by Münzer, *RE*, s.v. 'Sempronius', no. 47.

send supplies to the Roman army, when his commander L. Aurelius Orestes (himself a *nobilis*) had been so conspicuously unsuccessful in doing so that the Senate actually exempted them on grounds of hardship. This (as Plutarch points out) was not reassuring to his Roman enemies; and they suffered a further shock, when Micipsa sent grain shipments to the Roman army in Sardinia, announcing that he was doing so χάριτι Γαΐου Γράγχου.[1]

For the tribunician elections of 124 such a crowd flocked to the city from the whole of Italy that there were not enough houses for them.[2] It would be interesting to know who they were —*agrestes*[3] or *socii*. The former would not all—though most of them would—come to support him: they were those who hoped for, or feared, the resumption of the land commissioners' activities. But it is not unreasonable to believe that the latter, too, formed an important part of that crowd. We have seen that Gracchus had been associated with M. Fulvius Flaccus not only on the land commission, but in his scheme for enfranchising the allies, and that he had even been accused of complicity in the revolt of Fregellae. It must have appeared certain that Fulvius' scheme would now be revived. Moreover, Plutarch tells us that, though the crowd (and by implication he refers to Gracchus' supporters) was so large that some had to sit on housetops, Gracchus (contrary to his expectation) was only fourth in the list of tribunes elected; in the circumstances we might hazard the guess that a large number of his supporters will have been Latins, who could only carry one tribe.[4] Had they all been citizens, his election in first place—at a time when he had the support of the City plebs—must have been assured.

Whether Gracchus at once published his plans for the enfranchisement of the Italian allies, we cannot tell: the actual discussion of the proposal, at any rate, was deferred till 122, and on the whole the year 123—what we can glimpse of it—produces the impression of a lull, with Gracchus preparing his principal

[1] Plut. *C. Gr.* 2, 3. We have no reason to doubt this: Micipsa was the son of Masinissa, whose attachment to the Scipionic house we have noticed (pp. 137 and 164); and C. Gracchus was the grandson of Scipio Africanus (cf. Münzer, l.c.).

[2] Plut. *C. Gr.* 3, 1.

[3] We shall use this term, arbitrarily but conveniently, for 'Roman citizens domiciled in Italy outside Rome'.

[4] Mommsen, *Str.* iii. 396–7.

blows, and his enemies, conscious of their impotence, putting up little resistance.

This is not due to any love of him: they had first to find a tribune or consul willing to take the risks involved—particularly after Gracchus had strengthened his position against attack by his measures (not due to mere *pietas*) against his brother's enemies.[1] His first tribunate is not by any means devoid of legislation; yet his delay in pressing the *lex de sociis* has puzzled some historians. Not only must we remember that major laws demand thought and care: the chance survival of laws like the *Lex Repetundarum* and the *Lex Agraria* should warn us of that. But some time had inevitably to be devoted to preparatory legislation. Gaius, more than most other Roman leaders, learnt the lessons of the past: the frumentary law rewarded popular support and promised further profit; *pietas* for a brother's memory paralysed opposition to the survivor; and the reform of glaring judiciary abuses[2] struck at the foundations of the Senate's power. There is no need to deny genuine reforming zeal or genuine affection for his brother: C. Gracchus had the rare genius that consists in combining integrity with political skill. With his re-election secured, there was no hurry: the following year would—he hoped—bring a friendly consul and, as a colleague in the tribunate, one of the greatest men in the state: M. Fulvius Flaccus, consular, fresh from his triumph, and clearly the senior member of the Gracchan *factio*, had taken the unprecedented step of seeking the tribunate.[3]

During 123, then, there is no sign of any move in favour of the Italians. Gracchus does, however, show his concern for provincials, and particularly (we shall not be surprised to notice)

---

[1] *MRR*, i. 513–14. The best discussion of the vexed question of chronology is still Last, *CAH*, ix. 49 f.; but see Appendix A (pp. 299 f.). On Rubrius and Acilius, see *AJP*, 1954, 374 f. The title *de legibus promulgatis* (Gell. x. 3) is no help: we do not know which *leges* were included nor when the speech was made. (Fraccaro, *Ath.* 1925, 161, plausibly suggests 122.) Marsh (*History*, 53) is rightly cautious. He is also right (against many other scholars) in noting that Gaius' *inimici* did not come to love him in 123.

[2] Identified by Tibiletti (*Ath.* 1953, 33 f.) with the epigraphical *Lex Repetundarum*—perhaps wrongly: Last's analysis, with its two laws on the subject, still seems acceptable. In any case *a* law must be put in 123: the other (if there was one) is not to our point here. (Cf. art. cit. (n. 1, above).)

[3] See *RE*, s.v. 'Fulvius', no. 58.

those in whom he had an interest of patronage. His *lex iudiciaria* was undoubtedly intended to protect mainly the provincials, whose need for such protection had recently been demonstrated;[1] and his law against corrupting jurors[2] added a necessary safeguard to existing legislation. It is clear from these laws what were his views on the right relations of Rome with her subject allies. But the only provinces on behalf of which he took particular action were two in which his family was intimately concerned: Spain and Asia. In Spain, a Q. Fabius, probably the later Allobrogicus,[3] had been over-zealous in his exactions of grain; and though there was no question of extortion for his personal benefit, Gracchus persuaded the Senate to censure Fabius and make restitution to the provincials. In this way his father's reputation for justice among the Spaniards, which had served his brother (and the Roman People) well, was kept up by him—perhaps as some compensation for the diminution it may have suffered through the repudiation of Tiberius' treaty.

The connexion of Asia with the Tiberii Gracchi (father and son) we have already seen.[4] Asia had recently suffered under the maladministration of Aquillius, who had pacified it after the revolt of Aristonicus[5] and had been acquitted *de repetundis* through open bribery.[6] That other senators were involved in discreditable activities in the province or in connexion with it is very likely,[7] though we have no names. What precisely were the arrangements made by Aquillius and his commission, we cannot tell. They were probably some adaptation of the system practised in Sicily, whereby taxes were farmed out on the spot under the supervision of the governor.[8] Whatever these *acta* were, they had to be ratified by the Assembly, and it seems that this was proposed by a tribune (?) named Aufeius, perhaps in 124.[9] Gracchus

---

[1] App. i. 22. That *repetundae* laws would also protect Italian allies can hardly be doubted; but their chief application was to the provinces (cf. Last's comments on Göhler, *JRS*, 1940, 82–83).   [2] Cic. *Cluent.* 151 f.

[3] Plut. *C. Gr.* 6, 2. See Münzer, *RE*, s.v. 'Fabius', no. 110: we cannot tell which of the two provinces.   [4] See pp. 173–4.

[5] Sources in *MRR*, i. 504 and 509.

[6] App. i. 22; *Mith.* 57.   [7] Cf. C. Gracchus *ap.* Gell. xi. 10.

[8] The statement that they remitted most of the taxes (App. v. 4) is rightly rejected by most scholars (cf. Hill, *R. Mid. Cl.* 67, with references).

[9] Gell. xi. 10. Cf. Hill, *CR*, 1948, 112 f. But his emendation 'Aquillia' for 'Aufeia' is palaeographically unlikely and historically unsound—thus Pompey did not propose

opposed this; and though Aufeius perhaps succeeded for the moment,[1] Gracchus soon passed his own proposal establishing a tithe and having it farmed in Rome by the censors.[2] There is no doubt that many motives must have combined in making him frame his law. It certainly gave him the support of a powerful class (the later *Equites*) at a critical time—and, we may add, the support of those larger sections of the Roman People who had some interest in the activities of the big companies[3] and whose existence is often ignored. It also secured a certain revenue for the treasury, with the soundness of which Gracchus was much concerned.[4] One other point is worth noting: it promised to bring relief to the provincials themselves. Corrupt governors— as Verres was to show in Sicily and as Aquillius and his friends had probably just shown in Asia—could, under a system of local farming, divert most of the revenue into their own pockets and cause untold hardship. It must have appeared to Gracchus that the solution was to separate the functions of governor and tax-collector even more completely: to ensure that the governor had no supervision over the farming of the taxes. A step like this might well help both the treasury and the provincials, who would be protected by the mutual check of governor and *publicani*. That the latter would become a worse scourge than the governors ever had been, and that this system of balances would break down because the scales were now too much weighted in favour of the *publicani* (who could soon persuade, or even force, the governor into partnership in crime)—all this C. Gracchus could not easily foresee; and we cannot blame him. In Spain, the most disturbed of the Roman provinces, and one about which he was particularly well informed through family connexions, we hear of no complaints against *publicani*: unrest had been due to a succession of grasping and treacherous governors. As late as the

the ratification of his own *acta*, and the bill that Gracchus opposed must have stood in the name of its proposer. The name Aufeius, though not attested again, has obvious parallels (cf. Saufeius; also the root of names like Alfius, Alfidius, Alfenus). The date may be 124: Aquillius was accused *repetundarum* after his triumph (November 126) and the bill probably followed his acquittal. C. Gracchus was not in Rome again until 124 (see p. 179, n. 3).

[1] The wording '*lex Aufeia*' *prima facie* suggests that the bill was passed.

[2] Cf. the standard works; especially Magie, *Roman Rule*, i. 164 f. (and notes in vol. ii), with ample references.

[3] Pol. vi. 17.   [4] Gell. xi. 10; Vell. ii. 6, 3; Cic. *Tusc. disp.* iii. 48.

end of the century non-senators were still regarded as potential accessories in extortion, rather than as potential principals.[1] It was nearly thirty years before the breakdown of the new system was fully revealed in the events that led to and followed the administration of Q. Scaevola the Pontifex.[2] We may blame C. Gracchus for proceeding, in the heat of the political struggle, to overweight the scales himself by transferring the jury courts to the tax-farming class; but that was to come later and was no part of his original plan.[3]

There can be little doubt that Gracchus' settlement of the Asian taxes marks a sincere attempt to combine the advantages of the Roman People with the protection of the provincials from the principal scourge they had so far had to suffer from—the Senatorial governors and their friends. Together with his other actions regarding provincials, it is thus a return to the views of men like Cato as to the proper relations of Rome and the conquered peoples: to rule, but not to oppress; to enjoy the fruits of victory, but not to exploit. In this, as in his relations with the People, C. Gracchus is first and foremost the Roman aristocrat. And we have seen how, in conformity with the best traditions of his class, his actions are calculated to benefit above all (with due regard to Roman interest) those towards whom he had inherited the obligations of patronage and to strike at the power of his enemies.

It is only in his second tribunate that we hear of the agitation for Italian enfranchisement and of Fannius' and Drusus' opposition.[4] For it was only now that his enemies saw their chance of detaching from him the solid support of the People, which had hitherto made all attempts at resistance futile and dangerous. The courage and skill of M. Livius Drusus—whether or not we approve of his cause—deserve more admiration than they usually receive: they were as unexpected by Gracchus as almost unhoped for by his enemies; and the defection of C. Fannius—for motives

---

[1] Livy, xlv. 18, 4 (reflections attributed to a Senatorial commission) may be ignored: it is pure *ex post facto* composition. If non-senators were not from the first liable *de repetundis*, it must have been because in 149 (when the *quaestio* was established) it was not considered necessary: for their political power was due chiefly to the Sempronian legislation. Even in Glaucia's day they had to submit to the important encroachment of the clause *quo ea pecunia peruenerit* (Cic. *Rab. Post.* 8).

[2] Cf. *Ath.* 1956, 104 f.   [3] See p. 182 (with notes).

[4] The main sources in Greenidge–Clay², 41 f.

inscrutable to us on what evidence we have—added executive power and no mean oratorical talent. C. Gracchus had by now accumulated so much personal support, both in Rome and abroad, that his position was becoming far more intolerable than that of his brother had been. Thus, when he published his proposal to give the full franchise to the Latins and Latin status to the rest of the Italians[1]—a proposal which, like so much of his earlier legislation, was probably conceived as a genuine attempt at compromise, since Fulvius' more extreme proposal had proved unacceptable—opposition to it was announced by the tribune Drusus, who now embarked on an ambitious plan to oust Gracchus from popular favour and restore the People to its rightful place of clientship to the Senate.

The proposal itself was neither new nor unconstitutional. Full citizenship had often been given to Latin states, both before 338 (the great example of it) and since; and though we do not know of any case subsequent to the Hannibalic War, there was, on a smaller scale, the precedent (perhaps recent) of the citizenship given to Latin magistrates. The giving of Latin status to non-Latins was also traditional, as in the case of the Hernici and, fairly recently, that of Carteia.[2] No one could regard Gracchus' bill as revolutionary. Opposition to it was due to reasons such as had prompted opposition to M. Fulvius Flaccus; but in Gracchus' case the weight of *inuidia* was increased by his greater power and popularity. Yet, as Drusus and his friends saw, the problem had now been drawn into the light of day, and mere delaying tactics (like those that had defeated Flaccus in 125) would no longer serve.

It seems to have been during the absence of Gracchus in Africa that Drusus, with the support of the consul Fannius, fully developed his programme.[3] Before Gracchus' departure he seems

---

[1] See Appendix A (pp. 299 f.).

[2] Hernici: Livy, xxxiv. 42, 5; Carteia: id., xliii. 3. Cf. *RC*, 91 f. On the settlement of 338, see Ch. I (above). On *ciuitas per magistratum*, see p. 179.

[3] App. i. 23 f.; Plut. *C. Gr.* 10, 2 f. Cf. Appendix. Carcopino's theory of rotation of office among the Sempronian triumvirs comes up against the initial difficulty that the triumvirs are never mentioned in this connexion and that in any case there is no reason why they should be concerned with the colony of Junonia (for Gracchus' office in 121 see, for example, Sall. *Jug.* 42, 1). Cf. *MRR*, i. 516, n. 7; and, in general, Last, *JRS*, 1928, 228 f.

to have mainly relied on the veto, backed merely by sufficient propaganda to protect himself; and perhaps Gracchus' departure —difficult to explain, at such a critical time, if he had indeed, as Appian says,[1] lost the favour of the People to Drusus—was motivated by the hope that during his absence Fulvius would rouse the People against the new Octavius to such an extent that Gracchus would be able to deal with him on his return (perhaps with the help of his friend C. Fannius). He no doubt also hoped that his solid achievement at Junonia would contrast with Drusus' empty promises.

We need not set out the proposals of Drusus in full or discuss those that concerned only the Roman poor: argument is possible —but not relevant here and perhaps altogether fruitless—as to whether they show genuine concern for the People (within the framework of oligarchic rule) or are merely the demagogic auctioneering, ὥσπερ ἐν κωμῳδίᾳ, that Plutarch finds in them. We are concerned only with the way in which the anti-Gracchan faction sought to meet the dangerous situation created by the attempt of Gracchus and Fulvius to combine προστασία τοῦ δήμου with a bid for the support of the Italian allies. This was done in two ways, variants of the policy that moderns call *diuide et impera*. First, the People had to be turned against the Italians; secondly, the Italians—still dangerous if sufficiently united—had to be divided among themselves. As for the first point, we have had occasion to remark[2] that hitherto the People had shown no objection to Italian enfranchisement; nor is this surprising: it was a question which did not seem to concern them much, as long as they got their own benefits. They had therefore shown unwavering loyalty to Fulvius and to Gracchus, whose Italian policy had been well known since 126. It was C. Fannius, who had gained the consulship with the help of Gracchus, who now persuaded the People that their own interests were opposed to those of the Italians.[3]

---

[1] i. 24, *init*. On the chronology, see Appendix A.

[2] See p. 178.

[3] On C. Fannius, see Münzer, *RE*, s.v. 'Fannius', no. 7; Malcovati, *ORF²*, 142 f. (with references); *MRR*, i. 519. His speech is called 'bona et nobilis' (Cic. *Br*. 99)—a literary, not a moral judgement. He was suspected of not having written it himself (l.c.); and, as I argue in the text, the programme it presented and the arguments it advanced (cf. the fragment surviving—*ORF²*, l.c.) are probably not *only* his own.

His main line of argument can be gathered from a fragment of his speech[1] recorded by Julius Victor, and it is one not unfamiliar (in a different context) in our own day: if benefits are extended to too wide a circle, it means less for each individual, i.e. a loss for those already receiving them. The argument is not entirely without merit: there *would* be less room for each citizen at the games and assemblies if there were more citizens. And though Fannius is too often judged by his excerptor, it cannot be doubted that it is only chance that has preserved to us such a trivial illustration of this point and that there were weightier illustrations that Fannius will have used: if land was to be distributed, according to the Sempronian law, to poor citizens, there would be far more applicants for a limited amount of land, and the accession of distributable land confiscated from the allied *possessores* after enfranchisement[2] might not balance the number of new applicants; moreover, the proposals of Drusus for the founding of twelve colonies for citizens[3] may have held out a new limited benefit to be shared. Finally, it might even be pointed out that, if the citizen population were suddenly increased, the State might not be able to afford the corn subsidy: for the price fixed by C. Gracchus was already regarded as involving a subsidy and therefore as wasteful of public resources.[4]

These arguments, presented by an able orator and accompanied by the positive benefits offered by Drusus, struck home. Henceforth, down to the Social War, there is no more certain way of forfeiting the support of the Roman People than by suggesting an extension of the franchise. It is ultimately Fannius and Drusus who may be said to have induced in the Roman People the attitude that led to the Social War.

In this way the enemies of Gracchus achieved their first object. Their second object—to divide the Italians among themselves—was not difficult to attain; for the instrument had, perhaps unconsciously, been forged already. We have seen how the magistrates of Latin cities had at some time—perhaps only recently,

---

[1] See last note.   [2] On this Gracchan aim, see above (p. 177).

[3] Plut. *C. Gr.* 9, 2.

[4] Cf. Diod. xxxv. 25; Cic. *off.* ii. 72; *Sest.* 103. Last (*CAH*, ix. 57–60) rightly insists that the *lex frumentaria* did not offer a 'corn dole'. But that it involved a subsidy and was therefore disliked in high and conservative quarters is clear enough (ibid. 95; the anecdote about Piso Frugi (Cic. *Tusc. disp.* iii. 48) is conclusive).

after the revolt of Fregellae—been given *ex officio* Roman citizenship;[1] and so there was a small, but slowly increasing, and *ipso facto* powerful nucleus of Italians who, having attained their own desires, could be relied upon to oppose mass enfranchisement with all the social and political dangers it presented. It might have been possible to extend this provision to all the Italian allies, and thus the Social War would undoubtedly have been averted. We may well ask why this step was not taken. The answer must be found along the lines we have followed: if the main reason for the oligarchy's opposition to mass enfranchisement was the fear of losing control, that same fear would prevent any excessive extension of Roman citizenship even among the governing class of Italy. The ties with Roman noble houses, though extending all over Italy, would not remain as strong and solid, if the governing class of Italy suddenly awoke to a realization of its own collective importance and power; nor could the Samnite magistrate—as was to become only too clear later—be trusted to follow the lead of his Roman patron as faithfully as the Latin would. It was no doubt for this reason—a direct development of the main motive for opposition to general enfranchisement of the Italians—that a different solution was preferred.

That solution was quite simple. The governing class in the Latin cities was already on Rome's side; yet in case of general ferment that might not be enough to guarantee—as it normally would—the loyalty of their fellow-citizens to the State and to their patrons. Moreover, the Latins had a position of peculiar importance among the allies: they could vote—though only in one tribe—in Roman assemblies; and some of them (e.g. Tiburtines and Praenestines) lived near enough to Rome to be able to come to the City for the exercise of their vote—and their fists.[2] It was therefore decided to secure the support of the Latins as a whole: if it were won, Rome and her Latin allies could keep unrest among the other Italians in check,[3] while the contented Latins would throw in their weight in Roman elections on the

---

[1] See p. 179 (with n. 5). Special privileges seem to have been added to the grant, at any rate by 122 (Tibiletti, *RIL*, 1953, 45–46).

[2] Cf. above (p. 181), on the first election of C. Gracchus.

[3] See Beloch, *Bevölk.*, chs. 8–9, for estimates of population figures; Roman citizens seem to have formed about 40 per cent. of the population of the Peninsula (pp. 368 f.—free population only).

right side. Nor was enfranchisement necessary to content them: the main aim of the lower classes in Italy was not 'the vote', but its concrete advantages; and the chief of these was a certain amount of protection against arbitrary acts of violence by Roman magistrates.[1] It was this that Drusus provided for the Latins by extending the *leges Porciae* to them even on military service.[2] It was a shrewd move, gaining the support of the Latins against the rest of the Italians at small cost; and the Gracchans did not improve their position by conspicuously inviting Italians to join in their new colonies.[3] They soon found out that Italian support was now a liability rather than an asset. Before the final vote on Gracchus' *lex de sociis* could be taken, the Senate asked the consul Fannius to remove the Italians from Rome by edict (thus avoiding public discussion and the difficulties with which Pennus had met in 126). Gracchus, though still tribune, did not dare to resist.[4] The new alinement of forces was demonstrated on this occasion: those Italians who could not vote and had come merely to overawe were expelled; but the Latins, who had a vote and therefore a right to come, do not seem to have been molested—a further demonstration of Roman willingness to draw a distinction between Latins and other Italians.[5]

Gracchus' proposal was lost and he was not re-elected. Then came the violent end, and the final episode shows the success of the anti-Gracchan diplomacy: the man who killed C. Gracchus

---

[1] This point is made clearly by Sherwin-White (*RC*, 126 f.). That *prouocatio* was not, in fact, worth as much as it ought to have been is clear, *inter alia*, from the *Verrines*. (Cf. Tibiletti, *RIL*, 1953, 58 f.) But nearer the city it was not meaningless (as a series of consuls from Popillius to Cicero discovered): a noble offender's *inimici* would see to that. Cf. also next note.

[2] Implied by Plut. *C. Gr.* 9, 3 (often taken as referring to *prouocatio*: the two are not necessarily identical, though we are not sure of their relation). The case of Turpilius (Sall. *Jug.* 69, 4) is best explicable on the hypothesis that the man *ought* to have been exempt from such punishment (the 'nam' being elliptical); cf. Last, *CAH*, ix. 72 and 124. He was, in any case, a Roman citizen of 'Equestrian' standing (see p. 196). Cf. Cic. *Att.* v. 11, 2 (Marcellus' atrocity). That the Latins were not given *prouocatio* seems clear from the Taranto fragment of a *Lex Repetundarum* (see *AÉ*, 1950, no. 80), where this is offered as a special privilege (l. 10).

[3] App. i. 24 (the most likely interpretation).

[4] App. i. 23; Plut. *C. Gr.* 12, 1–2.

[5] Plutarch (l.c.) states that all non-Romans were expelled; but Appian (l.c.) says all those not entitled to vote. As he knows, while Plutarch does not, about the special status of the Latins in this matter (see Appendix A), he must certainly be believed. (Cf., for example, Last, *CAH*, ix. 80.)

was L. Septumuleius of Anagnia,[1] who had once been a supporter of Gracchus, but was now a friend of Opimius.[2]

Thus ended the first attempts to exploit Italian support in Roman politics. The nobility had started the game in its struggle against the legislation passed by Tiberius Gracchus; M. Fulvius Flaccus and C. Gracchus had won the Italians from their opponents, but finally lost the support of the Roman People. The governing oligarchy, by its diplomacy, had succeeded in making the peaceful enfranchisement of Italy impossible; yet it had detached the Latins from the other Italians and assured their friendship; it had thus sown the seeds of the Social War, but also of Rome's victory in it. Above all, it had missed what chance it might have had of preventing newly enfranchised citizens from supporting its opponents and helping in its extinction. The Roman People was to pay dearly for its short-sightedness; but the oligarchy, which had inspired and exploited that short-sightedness for political advantage, ultimately paid with its life.

[1] Cic. *de or.* ii. 269.
[2] Sources in *RE*, s.v. 'Septumuleius': Münzer's conjecture is convincing. This man is not a Latin, but an 'agrestis': this class had joined the City plebs in deserting Gracchus.

IX

THE ITALIANS—POLITICS
AND REVOLUTION

WITH the defeat of C. Gracchus the Italian problem disappears from view; and when it reappears, it does so in a new form, demanding—and in the end enforcing—urgent solution. In the interval other struggles engage our attention, as extra-Italian *clientelae* begin to follow the example of Italian *clientelae* in becoming a factor in Roman politics.

The Numidian royal house had, as we have seen,[1] loyally kept up its Scipionic connexion; and when Scipio Aemilianus wrote a letter to Micipsa commending the services his brother's illegitimate son Jugurtha had done him in Spain, the King treated his patron's commendation practically as a command—as Scipio no doubt expected him to—and raised Jugurtha at least to the level of his legitimate sons in the inheritance of his kingdom. It looks, in fact, as though Jugurtha was to have suzerainty over his partners, such as after Masinissa's death Micipsa seems to have had over his brothers: Sallust clearly implies this without ever stating it—and he is far less likely to have made the implication through carelessness than to be suppressing (as far as he could) a fact that would speak in the Prince's favour.[2] After Micipsa's death, Hiempsal, one of the King's sons, apparently rejecting his father's disposition, turned against Jugurtha and was killed by him; and the other son, Adherbal, was defeated and fled to Rome.[3] Thus began the first foreign war to have serious repercussions in Roman internal affairs—providing, according to Sallust,[4] the occasion for the first successful attack on the *nobilitas*. The story of this war in its impact on Roman politics has often been told,

---

[1] See Ch. VII, especially p. 137.

[2] Sallust, *Jug.* 9 ff. (all references to Sallust in this chapter are to this work). On Jugurtha's Roman connexions, cf. the excellent study by Allen in *CP*, 1938, 90 f. On Micipsa, see pp. 137–8.

[3] Sall. 11–13.

[4] 5, 1.

and its detail is beyond our scope.[1] But we must notice how well Jugurtha's connexions served him throughout, though Sallust's account does not permit us to gather the details. Charges of bribery against prominent nobles—leading to the Mamilian convictions—could easily be substantiated from the presents which, according to custom, Jugurtha would not fail to send to his influential friends.[2] As we have seen,[3] *clientela* was a profitable business for the patron, and according to traditional Roman ideas Jugurtha's gold could not reasonably be regarded as the wages of treason. There was not even much interest taken in the whole affair for a long time: it was regarded as a dispute between clients, and the Senate proceeded to settle it accordingly. First, a Senatorial commission was sent out—a common practice, which we have been able to observe in Roman dealings with the East—and it divided the kingdom between the two claimants, apparently according to both the desires of the inhabitants and Roman advantage.[4] When war was renewed, the Senate sent another commission consisting, according to Sallust, of *tres adulescentes*. This, in Sallust's account, is implied to be disgraceful; unfortunately—and perhaps not by accident—we are not given the young men's names. It is, however, only reasonable to suppose that they were members of families connected by ties of patronage with the Numidian royal family (as, most prominently, were the Scipiones).[5] That was regular Roman practice in similar circumstances, and young members of the great houses had often been successfully used on diplomatic missions.[6] It was only when

---

[1] See especially De Sanctis, *Problemi*, 187–223: he exposes the weakness of Sallust's case and the dangers of following his judgements; but he overstresses the part played by the *'Equites'*, at least in the early stages.

[2] See Allen, op. cit.

[3] Ch. VII, pp. 161 f.

[4] Sall. 16, 5 with 13, 1; cf. De Sanctis, op. cit. 200 f.

[5] Sall. 21, 4. A conjecture about the identity of one of the *tres adulescentes* may be worth making, though proof is impossible. Cn. Scipio, son of Cn. Scipio Hispanus, would be of the right age (*RE*, s.v. 'Cornelius', no. 321, and *MRR*, i. 546 conjecture 109 for his praetorship). As praetor he was debarred from going to a province 'quod recte facere nesciret' (Val. Max. vi. 3, 3). Was he perhaps a member of this unfortunate mission and suspected of taking a bribe? A Scipio would certainly be sent, if one was available.

[6] e.g. Scipio Aemilianus in Africa (App. *Lib.* 72—not official); Cn. Scipio Hispanus (*RE*, s.v. 'Cornelius', no. 347); P. Scipio Nasica Serapio (ibid. 354). Both Hispanus and Serapio, of course, had inherited the African connexion; and at the

this embassy failed that a weighty embassy, headed by Scaurus himself, was sent out.[1]

The Mamilian commission, with its wide terms of reference,[2] finally stopped the attempts of Jugurtha's patrons to assist him. For the first time since Rome entered the Mediterranean concert of powers,[3] the principle was laid down that the Roman noble, when representing the Roman People in dealings with other states, must act only in the interests of the Roman People, without regard for private obligations or profit. The assertion of this principle is a prominent part of that programme of honest and efficient government, which a series of great tribunes from C. Gracchus to Saturninus laboured to impose on the governing oligarchy. With the defeat of Saturninus, the last of the great Popular leaders, it was swept away in the triumph of the oligarchy, and it was only the downfall of the oligarchy that was finally to permit its partial acceptance and enforcement. By then its rejection by the dynastic families had brought the Empire to the verge of disintegration. It is this principle that provides the chief interest, for our purpose, of the Numidian interlude.

We now enter the age of Marius, when the potentialities of extra-urban *clientelae* first began to be fully revealed in the career of that great leader himself. Unfortunately the composition of his faction is not always clear, nor can its chronology and changes be established quite accurately. We shall therefore, while in general proceeding chronologically (as is necessary in a detailed examination), have to add wider surveys at appropriate times; and in order to make the importance of one source of his power (which is our special concern) intelligible, we shall have to glance at other sources of it; though we need not examine them in such detail.[4]

C. Marius, the Knight's son from Arpinum (which had been Roman *optimo iure* for only two generations), owed his first advancement, in the recognized manner, to the patronage of estab-

---

time neither, probably, was yet a senator. Other such missions may be conjectured: e.g. *RE*, s.v. 'Cornelius', no. 347, offering another example.

[1] Sall. 25.　　　　　　　　　　　　　　　　　　　　[2] Ibid. 40.

[3] On the mission to Ptolemy, see Ch. II, *init.*

[4] All work on this subject must be based on Syme's researches and particularly his *Rom. Rev.* (cf. 19 f., 65 f., 93 f.). Indebtedness at every point will be sufficiently obvious not to be always acknowledged in detail.

lished senatorial families—chief among them the Metelli, always on the look-out for new talent.[1] His early career was a hard, and often unsuccessful, struggle for advancement, in which the young man already showed how little one could rely on his loyalty; and the Metelli soon had enough of him. But it was in this period that, like Scaurus—whose case, despite Patrician birth, was rather similar to his own, though conjectures that they were friends are unfounded and improbable—, he laid the solid foundations of his later success by amassing a fortune and forming connexions among the class of *negotiatores* (the *Equites*, as they were to be called), whom C. Gracchus had recently raised to a political eminence not inferior to their economic power.[2] It was no doubt to these connexions that he owed his acquittal, when he was charged with *ambitus* after his election to the praetorship.[3] Persistence—and success—had its reward: some time before 110[4] Marius married into the Patrician family of the Julii Caesares— not a family recently in the highest ranks, but one of undoubted antiquity and prestige, and just then represented by energetic young men determined to rehabilitate its fortunes. Nor were even the Metelli indifferent: their old client seemed worth cultivating; and when Q. Metellus left for Numidia in 109, Marius was among his legates and soon proved his usefulness, apparently gaining the chief place (for purposes of military responsibility) among his staff.[5]

It was probably not long after arriving in Numidia that Marius carefully began to extend his influence and connexions

[1] Sources in *RE*, S.-B. vi, coll. 1367 f. Scaurus, Sulla and Pompey all at some stage in their careers (and Scaurus throughout) received the support of the Metelli. Of *noui homines*, we may conjecture P. Rutilius Rufus (*cos.* 105) and T. Didius (*cos.* 98). See *Hist.* 1957, 324 f. Of other patrons of Marius we know the Herennii (thanks to a famous, but inexplicable, incident—Plut. *Mar.* 5), themselves of Oscan origin (Münzer, *RE*, s.v.); and we may conjecture the Scipiones, as Marius served his first campaign under Aemilianus (Plut. *Mar.* 3, 2 f.). Marius' Equestrian rank was established by Madvig (*Kl. Schr.* 525 f.).

[2] On Marius' early life, see Passerini, *Ath.* 1934, 10 f.

[3] Plut. *Mar.* 5; cf. Val. Max. vi. 9, 14. The hostility of the Metelli at this time is shown by the fate of Cassius Sabaco (Plut. *Mar.* 5, 4 f.): he was expelled from the Senate (when a Metellus was censor) for being an accomplice in a 'crime' of which the principal (Marius) had been acquitted in a court of law. On the events of 119, cf. *JRS*, 1956, 91 f.

[4] The probable date of birth of the younger Marius (see *AJP*, 1954, 382, n. 43).

[5] This appears from Sallust's account (perhaps tendentious).

with a view to further advancement.[1] Sallust has clearly summarized the combination of interests that Marius attached to himself for his *honestissuma suffragatio*: the army, under his immediate
command; *equites Romani*, both those serving in Equestrian posts
under Metellus and those engaged in business (especially at Utica);
a Numidian pretender, slighted by Metellus; finally the Plebs
Romana. The latter's support, as Sallust observes, was providential
rather than planned: it was the time of the nobles' disgrace and
of their enemies' triumph in the Mamilian commission; the great
tribunes had just succeeded in uniting Plebs and *Equites*, without,
as yet, finding a leader for the force they had thus created. 'Ita
Mario cuncta procedere.'[2] The other interests, however, were
carefully and deliberately welded together by Marius, who thus
took signal advantage of the opportunities offered by the situation
in Rome. We may add an element neglected by Sallust, perhaps
because he considered it comparatively unimportant, perhaps
because the facts were bedevilled with Optimate propaganda:
the Latins also seem to have been deliberately courted by Marius.
So much—whatever the truth of the affair—emerges clearly from
the way in which he made capital out of Metellus' treatment of
Turpilius.

T. Turpilius Silanus, a Latin who had gained the citizenship
and (as a client of the Metelli) had attained positions of great
responsibility,[3] was convicted of treason and illegally scourged
and executed on Metellus' orders. Marius' enemies later claimed
that, behind the closed doors of the *consilium*, Marius had pressed
for the death penalty. That was bound to be said; yet it may well
be true. What is certain is that he made great political capital out

[1] Sallust's account, dating his *ambitio* from Metellus' insult (or shortly before),
has been shown by Passerini (op. cit. 19 f.) to be impossible and purely tendentious.

[2] Sall. 64–65. The complicated history of Roman domestic affairs in these years
cannot be treated in detail here. An interpretation will have to be stated without
proper discussion. The alliance of Plebs and *Equites* emerges most clearly from the
Mamilian Commission, set up by the tribal Assembly and manned by *Equites* (Cic.
Br. 128), with such disastrous results for the nobility. Yet down to 108 the nobles
retain the consulate: there is no one to challenge them.

[3] The status of Turpilius has given rise to much discussion. But the natural
translation for 'ciuis ex Latio' is 'a Latin become Roman citizen'; and this is made
all but unimpeachable by the fact that he attained the rank of *praefectus fabrum*
(Plut. *Mar.* 8; cf. Appian, who calls him a Roman). He had probably obtained the
citizenship *per magistratum* and owed his advancement to the Metelli (cf. Greenidge,
CR, 1896, 227).

of Metellus' action. For not only were the most influential of the Latins affected by the precedent—the noble's ill-treatment of his client could be claimed to have wider implications fitting in well enough with Marius' claim that the *nobilitas* was degenerate and no longer able to live up to its traditions and responsibilities.[1] This skilful political move makes it quite credible that Marius did indeed suggest the action in the first place; for that would present a clever dilemma to Metellus. We may be sure that, if Turpilius had been allowed to survive, Marius would have made equally skilful use of the chance to claim that the personal influence of the *nobiles* protected traitors—a claim not unfamiliar to the Roman People in the years of the Jugurthine War.

Marius was duly elected, amid displays of enthusiasm not by any means limited to the City Plebs;[2] and, like Scipio Aemilianus before him, he used his far-flung connexions (in his case, of course, personally acquired—on military service, according to Sallust; we may add his business contacts in collecting an army).[3] But he went much farther: by abolishing the census qualification for military service he laid the foundations of the personally recruited professional army characteristic of the late Republic. In the light of Marius' appeal to the soldiers in his candidature it is hard to believe that he did not suspect—though he certainly could not fully realize—the significance of the revolutionary opportunities for personal power thus opened up to the military leader born without hereditary *clientelae*.[4]

Gabba has shown that Marius' reform was only the culmination of a long process of lowering the qualification, due to increasing shortage of man-power.[5] Yet that hardly detracts from

[1] On the implications of this, cf. Cicero's speech *pro Roscio Amerino* (discussed Ch. X, *ad fin.*). It fits in with—and therefore confirms—Sallust's general account of Marius' propaganda line. This is the more valuable, as Sallust fails to mention Marius in connexion with this incident—a fact which Passerini, by a particularly dangerous argument from silence, takes as disproving the connexion. The small fragment of Appian (*Num.* 3) cannot count as evidence.

[2] Cf. Sall. 73.

[3] Sall. 84, 2.

[4] That he did is clearly stated by Sallust (86, 3); cf. below (pp. 204, 237 f.).

[5] *Ath.* 1949. He denies that the allies followed the example. But why should they hesitate to do so? He also denies that mass enthusiasm for Marius and mass enrolments belong to 107 and are connected with the reform (op. cit. 205). But this view rests on a mere mistranslation of Sall. 86, 4: for the true meaning of 'aliquanto' see, for example, Cic. *fam.* ix. 26, 3—it means 'considerably'.

the importance of this final step. For its effects were not even (it seems) confined to Rome: the allies' man-power problem was at least as acute as that of the Romans, as Appian's account of Tiberius Gracchus makes clear enough. Even if Rome could not legally prescribe to them how to levy their contingents—not that law counted for much in these matters, as we saw in a previous chapter—, they would no doubt gladly avail themselves of her *auctoritas*. At any rate, we soon find that the interests and loyalties of the allied contingents are too closely bound up with those of the legions to suggest any difference in recruitment.

It did not take many years for the first political effects to appear: the tribunates of Saturninus mark the first attempt to exploit the organized support of the new army. On 1 January 104 Marius had auspiciously inaugurated his second consulship, only a few weeks after the disaster of Arausio, by a magnificent triumph over Jugurtha.[1] He was now faced with the question of whether to lead his veteran army against the Cimbri. Fortunately, the barbarians' excursion into Spain had given him time, and he decided not to use the African veterans, but to base his army on the levy that his predecessor P. Rutilius Rufus had begun to drill into legions. His motives in doing so may have been manifold; but obvious among them, though only indirectly attested, must have been the fact that the African army, after years of colonial warfare—many of the veterans had served under Metellus—, was unwilling to engage in another and even more terrible war and was hoping for its rewards.[2] If (as is hardly likely) Marius had never before considered the problem of providing for the army he had led and (in part) enlisted, it must now have been forced upon his attention—especially as the success of future recruitment could not fail to be affected by his solution of it;[3] both the

[1] Plut. *Mar.* 12, 3.

[2] [Front.] *strat.* iv. 2, 2. Rutilius' firm handling of the situation: Gran. Lic. 21 B; Val. Max. ii. 3, 2. [Frontinus]—the only source that mentions the matter at all—says that the discipline of the veterans was inferior. This may, of course, merely reflect crass anti-Marian propaganda; but it may simply mean that they were not eager to fight—which is likely enough.

[3] See Passerini (op. cit. 115). Unfortunately he assumes that the African veterans were fighting the Cimbri, ignoring [Front.], l.c.; thus he is led to deny that provision had urgently to be made for them. (Thus also Samonati, *BMIR*, 1937, 25 f.) Yet, as there is no evidence to the contrary, and as [Front.], l.c., fits into a coherent pattern of events built up from other sources, we are not justified in ignoring the passage.

outcome of the war and his own further success depended on the way in which he discharged the obligations of patronage which, by his words and actions in 107, he had undertaken. It was in these circumstances that Marius allied himself with a young man of good praetorian family who, as quaestor, had recently been slighted by the Senate and was hoping to have his revenge as tribune—L. Appuleius Saturninus.[1] During Marius' absence on his campaign in the north, Saturninus undertook to win the favour of the People for a great plan providing for the veterans; and having achieved popular support by means of a *lex frumentaria*, Saturninus had little difficulty in passing his law giving— if we are to believe our source—allotments of 100 *iugera* to each of the African veterans.[2] We have abundant evidence for the fact that this law was actually carried out, perhaps during the next few years. The evidence from the epithets of the Imperial colonies of Uchi Maius and Thibaris[3] has been confirmed by the discovery of an important inscription at Thuburnica, mentioning Marius as the founder of that settlement;[4] and C. Julius Caesar, brother-in-law of Marius, probably founded a colony of his veterans on the island of Cercina.[5] Nor is there any reason to suppose that only citizens were to benefit; but on this we have no evidence.[6]

[1] On Saturninus, see Cic. *har. resp.* 43; *Sest.* 39. Cf. *RE*, s.v. 'Appuleius', no. 29. We do not know whether he was related to the Atinate family, though the coincidence of the names makes it quite likely; that he did not belong to it in the direct line is made very probable by Cic. *Planc.* 19.

[2] *vir. ill.* 73, 1 (mentioning the People's support for him). On the chronology of Saturninus' measures, see *CAH*, ix. 165 f.; *MRR*, i. 563 and 565; cf. Gabba's articles cited in these notes.

[3] References in *MRR*, l.c.; cf. Merlin–Poinssot, *Uchi Maius*, 16 f. (17, n. 4: Marii at Uchi).

[4] Quoniam, *CRAI*, 1950, 332 f. As that article makes clear, these settlements cannot have been founded by Marius as colonies, but probably arose out of *conuentus c.R.* of Marian settlers. (Cf. also Merlin–Poinssot, op. cit. 18.) We may yet get similar evidence from other places in the same region.

[5] *Insc. It.* xiii. 3, no. 7. Cf. no. 6 for another Caesar who seems to have served on the agrarian commission. The colony may belong to 100, as our sources do not mention a colonial law in 103 (though this is far from decisive). If so, it will have organized veterans already settled on the island (cf. last note). Gabba thinks 100 impossible ('Ricerche', 1951, 15 f.).

[6] The fact that Saturninus did not lose his popularity in 103 may not be used to show that his laws of that year conferred no benefits on the allies: there was no question of the citizenship, and land in Africa (to judge by the size of the allotments) was plentiful; so the citizen body would not easily be persuaded that it had anything to lose.

Before the end of that eventful year Marius reaped his first reward: his fourth consulate, pressed upon him by a grateful People, among which, as we know, the veterans were well represented.[1]

It is in 100, after Marius' decisive victories over the Germans, that this phase of his career reaches its climax. The great wars were finished and domestic politics returned to the centre of the stage; and another army of Marian veterans, expecting its reward, was at hand to be used in the political struggles. Saturninus had laid his plans: building on the foundations laid in 103, he revived the grandiose final plan of C. Gracchus—the union of *Equites*, Plebs and Italians, with the support of a noble *factio*; but he proposed to use the army of Marius in order to give this combination that armed support which (as the fate of the Gracchi and his own experience[2] had shown) was essential, in the last resort, to anyone wishing to break the oligarchy.

At this stage it will be useful to muster what detailed evidence we can find for the composition of the faction by which Marius (and—at least for a while—his associate Saturninus) was supported at this time. We must not be misled by Cicero's roll-call of great names opposed to the adventurer Saturninus in the final conflict:[3] we shall see that, before his fate appeared sealed, this solidarity was lacking. The wife of M. Lepidus, the future *cos*. 78, was an Appuleia, often (with sufficient probability) thought to be related to Saturninus.[4] Lepidus' case was not unlike that of the Julii Caesares, whose collaboration with Marius (for over a decade now) and with Saturninus we have already noticed:[5] of ancient Patrician lineage, they were eager to restore the fallen fortunes of their families. Not dissimilar, perhaps, was the case of the Dolabellae, who had missed the consulship in the last generation;[6]

---

[1] Plut. *Mar*. 14, 11 f. For the presence of veterans in Rome in 103, see *vir. ill.* 73, 1: Marius must have brought at least part of his army home for the triumph.

[2] For the violence used by some young nobles in order to prevent the passing of the *lex frumentaria*, see *ad Her.* i. 21 (in tendentious presentation). Saturninus was not slow in learning the lesson: cf. *vir. ill.* (l.c.). If we accept (as most historians do) an early date for the *lex frumentaria*, it follows that he was not the first to use force.   [3] Cic. *Rab. perd.* 20 f.

[4] *RE*, s.v. 'Aemilius', no. 72; cf. Münzer, *Röm. Ad.* 308. That she was Saturninus' daughter is sometimes said, but is mere guesswork.

[5] See pp. 195 and 199.

[6] Cn. Cornelius Dolabella, *cos*. 159 (*RE*, s.v. 'Cornelius', no. 132), will be the grandfather of the young men of 100.

a L. Dolabella may have been praetor in 100: we hear nothing of him in Cicero's roll-call of nobles against Saturninus.[1] A Cn. Dolabella (of whose career we know nothing) remained with Saturninus to the end.[2] It is tempting to see in L. Giganius (another faithful adherent)[3] a descendant of the great Patrician Geganii; but there is no precise evidence.[4] This nucleus of aristocratic adventurers is given solidity by the Patrician Valerii Flacci, another family willing to support promising young men,[5] and for generations established in the consular *fasti*:[6] L. Valerius Flaccus, *cos.* 100, is called 'more Marius' servant than his colleague', and it is clear that in his canvass he was allied with Marius.[7] Other men, not of outstanding family, but of sufficiently high rank, may be added: M' Aquillius, Marius' trusted legate, was absent in Sicily;[8] but M. Antonius returned—with an army —in the course of the year; C. Flavius Fimbria was in Rome, at least at the critical time;[9] and the list might be extended by careful investigation and conjecture.[10]

To these men—Patrician adventurers and *noui homines*, with a discreet sprinkling of more respectable families—we may add an element more important for our purpose: *agrestes* and new citizens. From Picenum, reservoir of Roman man-power, came the Labieni,[11] of good Equestrian family: their attitude may well be

---

[1] But he may have been in Spain—see *MRR*, i. 577.

[2] Oros. v. 17 ('Saturnini frater': whatever the word means, it shows that Saturninus had high connexions). It is interesting to see representatives of these same Patrician families collaborating again fifty years later.   [3] Oros., l.c.

[4] We must always bear in mind the emergence of men like Sulla and Catiline— not to mention the Pinarii (cf. *RE*, s.v.). The *praenomen* is certainly used among the old Geganii, making identification more tempting; and the name is rare. The slight difference in spelling is immaterial.

[5] e.g. Cato and later the Perpernae (*RE*, s.v. 'Valerius', col. 2295).

[6] *Coss.* 261, 227, 195, 152, 131, 100.

[7] Plut. *Mar.* 28, 8, quoting Rutilius Rufus, φιλαλήθης ἀνήρ. We may take his word for the fact of the alliance. Flaccus was later, under the Cinnan régime, one of the most prominent 'collaborators'. See Ch. X (p. 242, below).

[8] On Aquillius and his connexion with Marius, see *RE*, s.v. 'Aquillius', no. 11. On him and on M. Antonius, see also *Hist.* 1957, 330 f.

[9] Cic. *Rab. perd.* 21. This *nouus homo*, after a difficult and slow career, was made consul with Marius after the disaster of Arausio (*RE*, s.v. 'Flavius', no. 87). His two sons (ibid. 86 and 88) are on the Marian side in the Civil War.

[10] Thus we may confidently add the senatorial Herennii.

[11] Cic. *Rab. perd.* 20 f. Though in the final scene we find the two brothers on opposite sides, this is sufficiently explained by the quarrel between Marius and Saturninus.

typical of many of their class,[1] whose names would not reach us except (as in the case of the Labieni) by accident. Two men represent the municipal aristocracy: C. Norbanus and C. Saufeius. C. Norbanus is perhaps a man from Norba—a city later prominent on the Marian side against Sulla—; in any case a new citizen, who had been tribune as Saturninus' colleague (and, it seems, collaborator) in 103 and then served under M. Antonius as quaestor;[2] his name, like that of the Perpernae (whose relations with Marius unfortunately cannot be traced as early as this), proclaims his foreign origin. C. Saufeius, who, as quaestor, shared the death of Saturninus, comes of a well-known Tusculan family, prominent as *negotiatores*.[3]

These men of Equestrian rank or family were no doubt joined in their support of Marius by the *Equites* as a class. We have seen Marius' early connexions with them, which he had deliberately developed in Africa and, no doubt, strengthened by his Numidian victory, which at last restored peaceful conditions for Roman and Italian *negotiatores*. There is no evidence for the view, often expressed, that the *Equites* were a permanent force in politics: we know well enough that they were, precisely, the unpolitical part of the upper class. But when they thought—or could be persuaded—that their interests were at stake, they could react violently and would naturally give their support to men they trusted. This support was now secured for his faction by C. Servilius Glaucia, who, in 101 or 100, restored to them the control of the courts, which Caepio had taken from them.[4] In addition, there were the Plebs and the veterans, expecting benefits similar to those of 103. The veterans, indeed, had been the decisive element in securing for their leader that sixth consulship, which alone could hold out to them the promise of a Senate at least prevented from actively interfering, and for Saturninus that tribunate

---

[1] Gabba (*Ath.* 1951, 185 f.) greatly exaggerates when he speaks, solely on the strength of Cicero's statement about the Labieni, of Picene mass support for Saturninus; he tries to connect this with a supposed 'military *clientela*' of Marius in Picenum, for which there is no evidence at all.

[2] On Norbanus, see Münzer, *RE*, s.v. 'Norbanus', no. 5, and *H*, 1932, 220 f. (not, however, to be fully accepted on his career). Cf. *MRR*, i. 565–6, and *Hist.* 1957, 334 f.

[3] App. i. 32. See *RE*, s.v. 'Saufeius'.

[4] Cic. *Br.* 224; *Scaur.* 2. For the date, see Balsdon, *PBSR*, 1938, 106 f.; Piganiol, *CRAI*, 62 f.

which he promised to use in their interests; and it was on them (most of them *agrestes*) that Saturninus mainly relied for voting power in the Assembly.[1]

Thus the alliance of Marius, Saturninus and Glaucia seemed to dispose of all the necessary forces for overcoming oligarchic opposition—the combination of forces, in fact, is not unlike that which later helped Caesar and Augustus to victory:[2] the instrument of despotic power had been forged. What was lacking still was a suitable leader willing and able to use it with sufficient ruthlessness: that was to be Sulla's and Cn. Pompeius Strabo's distinctive contribution to Roman politics. And for the moment, as we shall see, circumstances did not favour its use.

That Marius, at the height of his glory, wanted despotic power, has never been seriously maintained. There is no evidence that the thought occurred to him. The idea of a *regnum* was still in the realm of political invective rather than of practical politics.[3] The aims of Marius—like those of Pompey after him—were more limited: the saviour of his country wanted to be *princeps ciuitatis*, accepted by the nobility as an equal and surpassing them in *auctoritas*. His first action on his return from his victories had been one of conciliation: he contented himself with a single triumph and, with conspicuous moderation, shared it with Catulus.[4] The way in which (with the help of Saturninus) he now proceeded to satisfy the claims of his soldiers shows no unconstitutional intentions: Saturninus proposed a distribution of land conquered from the Germans in Transalpine Gaul[5] and colonies in various provinces, among them Sicily and Macedonia–Achaea.[6]

---

[1] Livy, *per.* lxix; Plut. *Mar.* 29, 1; App. i. 29, *fin.*

[2] Syme, *Rom. Rev.*, *passim.*

[3] On *regnum* and its implications, see Allen, *TAPA*, 1953, 227 f.

[4] Plut. *Mar.* 27, 10. He got little gratitude: see *Hist.* 1957, 323 f.

[5] App. i. 29. Though Appian's wording does not make it quite clear which Gaul he means (Gabba, *Ath.* 1955, 225 f.), Transalpina is far more likely: the Germans had found allies among the Gauls there (notably the Volcae Tectosages—Plut. *Sulla* 4, 2; cf. Dio, fr. 90), and their land would now be quite properly confiscated in part and used for settlement.

[6] The list is important, but not necessarily exhaustive: colonies in Africa are not impossible (see p. 199, n. 5), and Corsica (Pliny, *n.h.* iii. 80; Sen. *cons. ad Helv.* 9) is quite likely. The *aurum Tolosanum* (i.e., probably, the fine collected from Caepio, which was deemed to replace it) was to be used to acquire more land (*vir. ill.* 73, 5), just as Ti. Gracchus had used the estate of Attalus for his plans.

It has been incontrovertibly shown by Passerini[1] that this was genuine demobilization: these are not the proposals of a man who, as Sulla was to do, wished to hold Rome in the permanent grip of his legions. Men at such a distance would be of no use in the day-to-day intrigues of Roman politics and could not easily be united for pressure. As Scipio had seen and Pompey was to see, the patron of half the Empire could be helpless in the Senate. Marius wanted the support of his men (in Africa or Gaul) as a moral force: the prestige that far-flung hereditary *clientelae* conferred on the noble, he, the *nouus homo*, had had to acquire through his own efforts—and he intended to keep it and surpass them all. It is the attitude that appears so clearly from the great speech given to him by Sallust.[2]

It was no doubt mainly for the same reason that the proposals were unacceptable to the oligarchs: as we saw in the case of Scipio,[3] it seemed essential for the survival of the oligarchy that no one man should have *auctoritas* beyond measure and should alone be the acknowledged *princeps uir*. This, in the Roman assembly, was a weapon as powerful as force and less insecure in the long run: especially as Marius—unlike the Gracchi—was a man who could not, in the last resort, be suppressed by force. Meeting the oligarchy on its own ground, and secure against its violence, he threatened to overcome and eclipse it. It was in this sense that his *regnum* might become fact.

We must next, however, notice that Saturninus' proposals probably went well beyond providing for the soldiers of Marius.[4] It is not impossible that the veterans of the German war might have been interested in emigrating to Greece and Sicily; but it is rather unlikely. Moreover, there would probably have been no difficulty in finding land for them in Gaul, where (e.g.) the Tectosages

[1] *Ath.* 1934, 126 ('grandiosa smobilitazione'). But I cannot follow Passerini in his *tour de force* of attempting to prove that this provision for his veterans was positively repugnant to Marius: what else could he have wanted to do with them?

[2] *Jug.* 85. (Note especially s. 4: '. . . cognatorum et adfinium opes, multae clientelae, omnia haec praesidio adsunt.') As we have already had occasion to notice in passing, Marius' hopes and methods, as presented in this speech, are amply confirmed by everything we know: Sallust is here at his best.

[3] Ch. VII, p. 166.

[4] The books usually refer to colonies founded for the Marian veterans, at the most adding the City Plebs (e.g. *CAH*, ix. 168 f.; Carcopino, *Hist.* ii. 343)—incorrectly, it seems, as the Plebs is nowhere mentioned and seems to have disliked the proposals.

had an extensive territory.[1] But there is some significance in the mention of Sicily and Macedonia–Achaea, with which our source presents us: as it happens, they were the two Roman provinces in which major wars—that of Aquillius against the slaves and that of Didius against the Scordisci—had just ended or were on the point of ending.[2] Now, it had long been the custom for Roman commanders to settle some of the men who had fought under them abroad in the province in which they had fought: we have seen the example set by Scipio in Italica[3] and followed by other commanders (particularly in Spain). Quite recently there had probably been examples of this in the case of the Balearic foundations of Metellus Baliaricus and (perhaps) in that of Narbo Martius; and we have seen how Marius, forced by the nature of his new army to provide for far larger numbers of his men, had had recourse to this traditional practice on a larger scale and settled the African veterans in Africa. It is therefore highly probable that it was intended, in a similar way, to settle the veterans of the German war in Gaul (and perhaps Corsica), and that the colonies in Sicily and Macedonia–Achaea were meant for the soldiers who had just been victorious in those provinces, i.e. for the armies of Aquillius and Didius. It is this that gives the legislation of 100 its peculiar significance: for the settlement, in the case of these armies, was made, not by their generals, but by Saturninus, acting under the *auctoritas* of Marius. Having created an army closely linked to its commander and depending on him for provision after service, Marius—it might seem—was now attempting to monopolize the powers of patronage thus provided. Once we have realized this, we need not wonder at the violence of the oligarchs' opposition. In fact, however, Marius, as we shall see, will have been innocent of these far-flung plans.

[1] See p. 203, n. 5. If the colony in Corsica belongs to this legislation, it would be more intelligible: it was not far from the recent theatre of war in Gaul and it would provide a stronghold in a difficult province.

[2] See *MRR*, ii. 4. Both victories should probably be dated in 100 at the latest (Didius' may belong to 101, if the law on the pirates—*SEG*, iii. 378—is of that year). Aquillius' victory is clearly dated to 100 by Obs. 45 (= 105), not in the least contradicted by Livy, *per. lxix, fin.*, as Broughton (l.c.) thinks: the epitomator habitually groups by subject-matter, not strict chronology, and 'foreign affairs' are often put last (with or without the phrase 'praeterea . . . continet').

[3] See Ch. V, p. 119.

That Marius was supporting the proposals of Saturninus—or that Saturninus was at least claiming this support—is made clear by the provision that Marius was to be allowed to confer the citizenship on a certain number of people in each colony.[1] It has been suggested, not unplausibly, that the main purpose of this clause was to legalize various gifts of the franchise that Marius had made, in his own words, without 'hearing the voice of the laws',[2] and that had hitherto been of very questionable validity.[3] In any case, we know that in fact Marius availed himself of this power of enfranchisement even though the colonies were not founded.[4]

It seems that, in this grand legislative scheme, Saturninus had —for the moment, at least—overlooked the City Plebs:[5] he had perhaps thought that both voting strength and physical force could be adequately provided by the veterans whom it was intended to benefit; and he may have relied on their loyalty secured in 103. It was this tactical error—akin to, though not identical with, that of C. Gracchus[6]—that his opponents used in order to bring about his downfall.

Marius' army had—in the usual way—consisted of both legionaries and allied contingents; and it is clear that Marius, who valued the support of the allies and held liberal views towards

---

[1] Our text of Cic. *Balb.* 48 says 'ternos'—an absurdly small figure on any interpretation of the scheme. Ihne's emendation 'trecenos' must be on the right track (*History*, v. 163, n. 1); though his suggestion that each colony was to consist of 300 old and 300 new citizens is quite baseless and improbable: the colonists were probably to be far more numerous than that. Parker (*CR*, 1938, 8–9) believes that the colonies were to be Latin colonies, in each of which Marius was to appoint the three chief magistrates. But Latin colonies would normally contain Roman citizens, and why should they be excluded from the first magistracies? Cf. note 3 (below).

[2] Plut. *Mar.* 28.

[3] Samonati, *BMIR*, 1937, 33 f. Cf. Ihne, *History*, v. 156, n. 3: 'As consul he could no more enfranchise a single stranger than he could have declared a citizen to be a senator or a magistrate.' Last's suggestion (*CAH*, ix. 169) that the scheme marks a return to Latin colonization, enabling demobilized allies to attain citizenship *per magistratum*, cannot be supported by evidence. (On Parker's view see n. 1, above). It was perfectly permissible for allied citizens to join Roman colonies: earlier in the century this seems to have been a standard way of attaining citizenship (Smith, *JRS*, 1954, 18 f).

[4] Cic. *Balb.* 48; cf. below.　　　　　　　　　　　　　　　[5] Cf. p. 204, n. 4.

[6] Saturninus tried to avoid the mistake of appearing to be the champion of the allies against the citizens' interests; but he was manœuvred by his opponents into a position where the charge could finally be made and exploited.

them, was bound to provide for the latter as well as for the former. It appears that in Saturninus' legislation this was done: he certainly had the support of the citizen veterans' votes, which at one time were probably decisive;[1] while the fact that the allies were to benefit emerges no less clearly from what follows. For the cry was raised by his enemies that the allies were excessively favoured —not that this should have convinced the citizen veterans, whose own interests were bound up with those of the allies who were to benefit; but the City Plebs, unmindful of former favours and resentful of favour shown to others, did not take much persuading, and even among the veterans suspicion might be sown between citizens and allies. Unfortunately, we have not enough detail of this campaign (as we have of that against C. Gracchus) to be able to follow it with any precision down to its final success. The ancient sources are, on the whole, preoccupied with the fate of Q. Metellus Numidicus, and it is only Appian who gives us a glimpse of political agitation and opinion. His account, however, bears the usual marks of over-compression. The issues and antagonisms were obviously complicated and propagandists were not interested in simplifying them. Thus Appian's sketchy summarizing has caused inextricable confusion: we can recognize contradiction and *non sequitur*, but cannot extract the full truth.[2] What is clear is that the Plebs strongly opposed the legislation and that unusual violence was needed in order to carry it. This force was provided by men from the country—probably citizen and allied veterans joining in defence of their common hopes. Once prejudice had been aroused, it might well be expected to override reasonable interest: in the final battle, with Saturninus and his friends manœuvred into the position of revolutionaries and murderers,[3] we find them still supported by ἄγροικοι—but

---

[1] See p. 200 (with n. 1). Cf. App. i. 29 f.

[2] App., l.c. This has led some to the bold simplification of taking 'Ἰταλιῶται' as meaning 'agrestes'. But that the allies were somehow prominently involved has been clear to careful scholars even when they accept this view (notably Last, *CAH*, ix. 169)—and the view thus becomes unnecessary. In itself it is improbable on the facts of Appian's word usage (Göhler, *Rom*, 76 f.—cf. Ch. VIII, pp. 172–3); and confusion caused by excessive abbreviation is not to be remedied by an act of simplification.

[3] On the difficulties in the story of Memmius' death, see Passerini, op. cit. 281 f.: Memmius was killed in a riot (not, it seems, of set purpose), and Glaucia's candidature had by then been disallowed on legal grounds. The murder of Nonius (?)

that these are now mainly allies is made very probable by the fact that the *ager Picenus* (that chief reservoir of citizen manpower) was on the whole opposed to them.[1]

Thus Saturninus was eliminated by the weapons forged against C. Gracchus, by whose programme he was certainly inspired:[2] the slogan of excessive favour shown to the allies, at least based on fact in the case of C. Gracchus, turned into mere invective, but was nevertheless successful; and the 'S.C. ultimum' dealt the final blow, after legal means of obstruction had been used to the full.[3] Again the oligarchy had been able to divide and conquer —but only at the cost of adding fuel to passions, which the un-questioning loyalty of the allies in the recent wars might have been allowed to extinguish. In avoiding the risk of losing its control (based on its *clientelae*) over Italy, it was precipitating a situation in which *clientelae* could not overcome other loyalties and interests; and in avoiding the risk of one man's acquisition of overwhelming prestige, it was creating the conditions for mili-tary dictatorship. The colonies were not sent out,[4] and Marius' veterans, many of them (no doubt) with nothing to lose from adventure and nothing to hope for from peace, were to take grim vengeance.[5]

The question remains: why did C. Marius support his own enemies? For surely Saturninus might have anticipated a greater man on a greater occasion in claiming that he had made enemies on Marius' behalf and now Marius had joined them against him.[6] The sources divide on this question according to their bias: on the one hand, the plain military man, uncomfortable and out-manœuvred in politics, forced into a position fatal to his political ambitions; on the other, the *callidissimus homo*, riding the storm with his usual skill and unscrupulousness.[7] The first, as Passerini

in the previous year (whatever the facts, which Appian's account makes anything but clear (i. 28), while Florus (iii. 17) adds to the confusion) had, at the least, gone unpunished until it was found convenient to rake it up.

[1] App. i. 32; Cic. *Rab. perd.* 22 (at least based on fact). Cicero does not mention the *socii* in the grand roll-call of those faithful to the State—and omission, in such a context, is significant.

[2] Cf. *CAH*, ix. 164 f. (excessively hostile).

[3] Thus Metellus' refusal to take the oath, and the disallowing of Glaucia's candidature.   [4] Cic. *Balb.* 48.

[5] On this, see below (pp. 238 f.).   [6] Cf. Caes. *b.c.* i. 4.

[7] On these two groups of sources, cf. Passerini, *Ath.* 1934, *passim* (especially 297).

has demonstrated, belongs to the sphere of moralist biography. The second is somewhat nearer the truth; but his motives in this case are nowhere explained or even examined. There is no doubt that his abandonment of his allies was deliberate and in accordance with careful policy: it begins with his casting doubts on the validity of Saturninus' law and reserving his views on it;[1] when, alarmed at this, Saturninus and Glaucia decide on Glaucia's candidature for the consulship of 99, this is disallowed by the presiding magistrate, who must have been Marius or his friend L. Valerius Flaccus;[2] and in the final act Marius shows no hesitation in suppressing the sedition.[3]

Part of the explanation is, no doubt, to be found—as in the similar case of Pompey—in Marius' hankering after respectability and acceptance by the nobility:[4] for the sake of these aims he tried to acquire prestige and power, and their pursuit now threatened to put him in a position where hostility would become insuperable hatred and his aims unrealizable. His policy had proved self-defeating. But there was an even greater danger: though Saturninus' laws were allegedly passed on his behalf— as shown particularly by the right of enfranchisement conferred on him—, it was, after all, Saturninus who had passed them. Saturninus, with his friend Glaucia, had shown every sign of having political aims and ambitions of his own: he had attached the Plebs to himself, while Glaucia had tried to gain the *Equites* as well, and both were effective orators;[5] now it was Saturninus and Glaucia who were collecting men from the countryside and were, in fact, leading Marius' own veterans—citizens and allies— in the struggle for the veterans' rights—including those of other armies:[6] such servants were too dangerous for their alleged master. Therefore the conditional oath—a sword of Damocles to be suspended over their heads, and a reminder to the veterans that it was, after all, Marius with whom the final decision would rest; therefore, also, the more positive and unambiguous action in disallowing Glaucia's candidature: with Glaucia aiming at the supreme magistracy, the danger was now real and the breach

[1] App. i. 30–31; Plut. *Mar.* 29.
[2] Cic. *Br.* 224—see p. 207, n. 3. On Flaccus, cf. p. 201 (with n. 7).
[3] Cf. the credit he claims for it in his *elogium* (*Insc. It.* xiii. 3, no. 17).
[4] See p. 203, and cf. *Hist.* 1957, 342 f.
[5] Cic. *Br.* 224.
[6] See pp. 204–5.

beyond healing. Marius' policy towards Saturninus and Glaucia is consistent and rational.

With the suppression of the sedition, Marius was again the saviour of the State and again, for a while, his enemies had to proclaim their gratitude. The story of Marius' abyss of disgrace after his sixth consulship is part of the biographers' romance: the augurate conferred in absence is enough to disprove it as it stands.[1] That part of Saturninus' legislation that profited him was, on the whole, not repealed.[2] Yet, like Pompey a generation later, Marius soon found that gratitude was less lasting than *inuidia*, and that the support of foreign nations and of his own veterans, settled abroad or even in Italy, was powerless to overcome it. He saw himself compelled to impress his greatness upon the Roman Plebs.[3] In this he succeeded to some extent; but his noble friends inevitably drifted away from him.[4] Finally, with the help of the Equestrian order, Marius seized a chance of taking the offensive against his *inimici* and secured the conviction of P. Rutilius Rufus.[5]

This was only the culmination of a period of intense political excitement which, unfortunately, remains obscure. Except for the dying embers of the conflagration of 100,[6] we have practically no evidence on the political life of the nineties, so that the trial of P. Rutilius Rufus has often seemed a bolt from the blue.[7] Yet the prosecutions of Aquillius, Marcellus, Norbanus and the younger Caepio show that tension was continuous; and we have already noticed shadowy indications of Marius' political activity.

---

[1] Cic. *ad Br.* i. 5, 3; cf. Plut. *Mar.* 31. See Passerini, op. cit. 348 f. That it was conferred for an act of obscure religious piety (Broughton, *Hist.* 1953, 210 f.) is unlikely.

[2] At the most, he had to give up the claim to found colonies for other men's armies as well as for his own; though even in these cases he retained the privilege of conferring citizenship, which had been connected with the foundations (Cic. *Balb.* 48: cf. pp. 211–12).

[3] Plut. *Mar.* 32; for his building activity in the nineties, see Platner–Ashby, *Top. Dict.* 259 f., 541 f. That Marius and his associates had incurred the hatred of Saturninus' surviving friends is natural enough—and attested (cf. *JRS*, 1956, 91 f.).   [4] See *Hist.* 1957, 331 f.

[5] See *Ath.* 1956, 111 f.

[6] Cf. *MRR*, ii, for the years 99 and 98.

[7] Thus Last (*CAH*, ix. 173) says that 'for a time the State came near to the felicity of those who have no history'. On this view, see *Hist.*, art. cit.

It is, however, mainly the problem of the Italian allies that now interests us; and that this problem comes to a head during this obscure decade is shown conclusively by the outbreak of war at the end of it. We have seen how the question of citizenship for the Italian allies had first arisen incidentally in connexion with the Gracchan land programme; and how, after the failure of C. Gracchus, it had disappeared from view without (it seems) leading to serious allied discontent—particularly as the Senate had succeeded, by carefully graded concessions, in driving a wedge between the Latins and the remaining Italians.[1] With the formation of Marius' personal client-army the importance of the allies for Roman political purposes increased, and Marius and Saturninus, recognizing this, tried to establish by precedent the principle —later well known, and regularized in the Empire—that citizenship might be gained by distinguished military service. This was implicit in Marius' enfranchisements on the field of battle and in Saturninus' attempts to break the hopeless deadlock of the Italian question. The estrangement between the general and the tribune, leading to the latter's downfall, for the moment again shelved the problem. But the hopes of the Italians had been played with too often, and this time much had happened that could not be forgotten. Moreover, Marius, though he had opposed the pretensions of Saturninus and Glaucia, was by no means willing to give up his Italian *clientela*: indeed, when the citizenship of one of those who had received it from him under (or under cover of) the laws of Saturninus was later impugned, on the ground that the colony in which he had been enrolled had not been founded, Marius' *auctoritas* secured the man's retention in the citizen register and, it seems, thus put an end to the insecurity of others in the same position.[2] It is significant that this was in 95 (or later) and that the arbitrary actions of Marius with

---

[1] See last chapter. That this policy continued beyond 122 is shown by the *lex iudiciaria* of Q. Caepio, passed in 106 (see *CR*, 1954, 101 f.).

[2] Cic. *Balb.* 48. The case (of T. Matrinius of Spoletum) came before the *quaestio* established under the *lex Licinia Mucia*. (See below.) The grounds on which the charge was based show, incidentally, that the laws of Saturninus had not been repealed, but merely ignored. This was seen by Passerini (op. cit. 348 f.), who correctly interpreted the much-misused passage Cic. *leg.* ii. 14; unfortunately Gabba (*Ath.* 1951, 13 f.) rejected his explanation without meeting his arguments. On the trial, see also *Hist.*, art. cit.

regard to the citizenship had apparently not been attacked before. In fact, the years immediately following 100 seem to be a time of uneasy truce between Marius and his friends on the one hand and the Metelli and theirs on the other. We have seen that Marius (in 98, it seems)[1] had been given an augurate in absence but did not stand for the censorship in 97: it looks like a bargain. The censors elected were L. Flaccus and M. Antonius, two of his friends before 100,[2] which further supports such an interpretation. The Metelli conceded as much as they could, in order to prevent (what might have been expected) a censorship of Flaccus and Marius; and Marius, not quite strong enough,[3] had to agree.

During these years we hear no word of the Italians: perhaps they had been, not indeed forgotten, but at least neglected for the sake of *concordia*—such as it was. At any rate, there was no attempt to deprive of their citizenship those who had so questionably obtained it from Marius.[4] Marius, on the other hand, had dissociated himself from Saturninus and his Italian followers and did not press their claims any further; or rather, perhaps, his friends in his absence did not. On his return, however, it became clear that—quite apart from the merits of their case—the Italians, as a source of support, must not be neglected. The bargain of 98 had shown Marius that he was not as strong as he thought; his enemies could be trusted to yield no more than they were forced to.[5] It thus became important to strengthen the body of voters with reliable elements. That seems to have been what the censors of 97–96 set out to achieve.[6]

The retention of their citizenship by the recipients of Marius' doubtfully legal *beneficium* must have encouraged some of their fellow-countrymen to hope for similar favour. At any rate, it seems very likely that these years saw an influx of Italians into

[1] On the augurate, see p. 210 (with n. 1). The chronology is too difficult to discuss here in any detail. Unlike Broughton, I think that Marius must already have returned from Asia by the time of the trial of Aquillius (thus also Greenidge–Clay[2], 112 f. and 116—but cf. *MRR*, ii. 8–9).   [2] See pp. 200–1.

[3] See p. 210 (with n. 3).   [4] See above, and cf. p. 206.

[5] The attack on Aquillius (Cic. 2*Verr.* v. 3; *de or.* ii. 194 f.) should probably be dated about 95 (see *Hist.*, art. cit., 330 f.)

[6] See *Hist.*, art. cit. That the censors, like Marius himself, may have been genuinely desirous of solving the Italian problem (in the way most advantageous to themselves), there is no reason to deny. But our study must deal with the political aspect.

Rome, many of whom, with remarkable laxity, the censors seem to have accepted for their lists of Roman citizens.[1] These men were not the sort of rabble that we may imagine in Saturninus' following, hoping for land distributions: they were *principes Italicorum populorum*,[2] men of Marius' own class, who, when they became citizens, would at once be *equites Romani*. Their support would be substantial and valuable; and now it was to go to the friends of Marius. This method was flagrant and unwise. In the very next year the *lex Licinia Mucia* undid the work, setting up a severe *quaestio* on illegal arrogation of citizenship.[3] The names of the consuls—especially of the upright Mucius[4]—sufficiently show how honest moderate opinion had been antagonized. There could be little doubt (after the experience of Saturninus in 100) that popular opinion would support the consuls' action. As a result of this swing in their favour, Marius' opponents now became bolder and ventured to attack his supporters and his personal clients: perhaps even at the beginning of the year, Norbanus had been prosecuted for *maiestas* in connexion with the trial of the elder Caepio; now T. Matrinius, a Spoletine enfranchised by Marius under the *leges Appuleiae*, was called before the new *quaestio*.[5] Had the test case succeeded, the result would not only have been the disfranchisement of a large number of men in the same dubious position: we must believe that Marius' other acts of enfranchisement (e.g. that of the Camertines)[6] would next have been called in question. As it turned out, Marius' *auctoritas* was sufficient to protect his client: the attack had failed. Nor was the other prosecution more successful: Antonius saved his ex-quaestor.[7]

The *lex Licinia Mucia*, which on many interpretations of this period appears an arbitrary and uncalled-for insult to the Italians—or at best the unfortunate result of honest legal pedantry—, thus

---

[1] This is shown by the *lex Licinia Mucia*, passed by the very next consuls after the completion of the *lustrum*. It is a pity that no census figures have survived; but Gabba (*Ath.* 1953, 262–3) is more hesitant than one need be about this.

[2] Asc. 68; cf. Gabba, l.c.; also Ch. VI (above), *ad fin.*

[3] See *Note R*, p. 297.

[4] Both these consuls were soon to become *adfines* of Marius through the marriage of the latter's son to the younger Licinia. (See *Hist.* 1957, 329.)

[5] Cic. *Balb.* 48; cf. *Hist.*, art. cit.

[6] See Ch. IX, p. 206; Ch. XI, pp. 260 f.   [7] Cic. *de or.* ii. 197 f.

finds its natural place in the history of this troubled period. As an attack on Marius' interests, it follows upon the censorship of his friends in 97–96, and fits into a pattern with the prosecutions (among others) of Norbanus and of Matrinius, and—no doubt by way of counter-attack—that of the younger Caepio. With the failure of all these attempts to upset the balance of forces, stalemate—*concordia*—was re-established: the marriage alliance between Marius and Crassus was its consequence.[1]

It seemed that another episode in the internal conflicts of the oligarchy had come to its usual indecisive end. If outsiders were affected, it is doubtful whether anyone noticed. It is only Cicero, a generation later, who describes the *lex Licinia Mucia* (whose precise political context he was probably at the time too young to understand) as unwise and inopportune.[2] The Italians, however, were exasperated. They were accustomed to being the plaything of political factions in Rome; but never before had *principes uiri* from among them been so grossly disappointed and insulted. Marius does not seem to have lost their confidence, as we shall see before long. If he and his friends had not succeeded in retaining them on the citizen register, that was clearly due to the superior might of the combination of oligarchy and People. And his stand in favour of Matrinius had no doubt retained hundreds of names on the register. His whole career had shown his goodwill towards them, and thoughtful men among them seem to have turned towards his cause: perhaps the *rhetores Latini* (whether or not they were Latins), later expelled by Crassus, were among them.[3] But for the moment, with the ferment of revolt working beneath the surface, *concordia* led to superficial quiet. Meanwhile, the seeds of further trouble were being sown in Asia.

Modern historians are fairly evenly divided on the question of the date of Scaevola's administration of Asia: some put it in or

---

[1] See p. 213, n. 4. The *toga uirilis* could be assumed quite early, where political ambition suggested it (cf. the case of Caesar): see Daremberg–Saglio, s.v. 'toga', col. 352. The usual age, however, was 16 or near it; and the younger Marius was 16 (probably) in 94.

[2] Cic. *ap.* Asc. 67. Unfortunately Cicero in his writings hardly anywhere shows much understanding of political events preceding 91. But his judgement in this instance may be a mere barrister's point.

[3] Detailed discussion (going well beyond the evidence) in Gabba, *Ath.* 1953, 269 f.

after his praetorship (the date of which is unknown), some in or after his consulship of 95 B.C.[1] But there is not a scrap of evidence for the earlier date, and it seems in every way preferable to put Scaevola's governorship after his consulship, where it finds its historical place without difficulty. It seems, in fact, that he and Rutilius were sent there, probably on the motion of Scaurus himself, in order to reorganize the long-suffering province.[2] Scaevola, then, left for Asia, where he and his legate earned the gratitude of the provincials and the hatred of the Roman *Equites*—and of Marius, who had interests in Asia and was Rutilius' enemy.[3] The latter, soon after his return in 93 or 92, was accused *de repetundis* and condemned by an Equestrian jury: it was a pure act of vengeance and (so far as we know) the first one since the *lex Acilia*. The *Equites*, it was known, had the support of Marius, Rutilius' old enemy, who thus tried to turn the renewed tension to his advantage:[4] it is interesting to observe that Scaevola himself, the *adfinis* of Marius, was not accused.

Next, flushed with success, Marius and his friends sought to break Scaurus himself, who had probably been responsible for Scaevola's appointment.[5] The result of this political flare-up was surprising. A young man of high family, a nephew (it seems) of Rutilius, determined—with the support of his friends and elders, especially Scaurus himself—on a bold counter-stroke that should combine necessary reform with political advantage to its authors: the younger M. Livius Drusus entered upon his tribunate. We can attempt no general survey of the momentous year 91:[6] as in the case of the Gracchi, we must follow one particular thread in the complicated web, without suggesting that it is the only one that matters.

[1] For a survey, see Magie, *Roman Rule*, ii. 1064; Broughton (*MRR*, ii. 5 f.) adopts the earlier date, Magie the later.

[2] Cf. *Ath.* 1956, 104 f.

[3] Sources in *MRR*, ii. 7–8 (both for the governorship and for the trial). On all this, cf. *Ath.*, l.c.

[4] Dio, fr. 97, 3; cf. p. 195, n. 1.

[5] On the *adfinitas*, see p. 213, n. 4. Only Marius' protection can satisfactorily explain Scaevola's safety. Q. Scaevola the Augur later repaid the debt (Val. Max. iii. 8, 5). On Scaurus, see *Ath.*, l.c.

[6] Accounts of Drusus and his work are to be found in all the standard works. Thomsen (*Class. et Med.* 1942, 13 f.) and Gabba (*GS*, 3 f.) deserve special mention among more recent studies.

M. Livius Drusus was the son of the man who had defeated
C. Gracchus,[1] and his plans show the influence of both of them.
His father, in his day, had detached the Plebs and the Latins
from C. Gracchus, and the son now planned to detach them from
Marius and his friends: C. Gracchus, as we have seen, had tried
to unite *Equites*, Plebs, and Italians against the oligarchy, and
Drusus now seems to have attempted to unite them behind it.[2]
There can be no doubt that he and his sponsors saw the urgency,
in particular, of the Italian problem: preparations for rebellion
must already have been going on and could hardly altogether
escape notice. It was Drusus' brilliant solution to bring about the
inevitable reform in such a way that the political credit and profit
would go to the Roman oligarchy; and Livy, indeed, regards this
as the main aim of his tribunate. The support of the grateful
clients might then be used, in particular, to ensure the subordination of the Equestrian order,[3] which had for a long time been an
unstable element and had now proved itself to be dangerous.

The result of this attempted 'diplomatic revolution' was to
bring out into the open and kindle into conflagration all the
antagonisms between classes and sections that had been alter-
nately smouldering and flaring up since the time of the Gracchi.
Drusus found that nothing could be done without offending
some sectional interest; and as his programme, if it was to answer
its purpose, had to be accepted as a whole, those affected in each
instance, though agreed on nothing else, were ready to unite
against him.[4] Nevertheless (it seems), at first everything went as
well as could be expected: the agrarian and colonial laws were too

---

[1] Suet. *Tib.* 3, 2. Drusus—like Sulpicius, the enemy of Marius' friends—was
close to the Cottae, who were also related to P. Rutilius Rufus (p. 195, n. 1): this
helps to fill in the background. Rutilius and Scaurus are, of course, linked by the
Metelli, always cementing the opposition to Marius. See *Hist.*, art. cit., for the
faction of Marius and that of his enemies.

[2] Some oversimplification in this outline is, in part, corrected in what
follows.

[3] Livy, *per.* lxx and lxxi. It has often been pointed out that it would be in the
census of 92–91 (one of the censors being Crassus himself) that the full effects of
the *lex Licinia Mucia* were first to appear. But the discord between the censors,
who did not complete the *lustrum* (see *MRR*, ii. 17), again shelved the problem and
left many Italians in an insecure legal position, which made them willing supporters
of anyone promising to help them (cf. Diod. xxxvii. 13).

[4] This is Appian's point (i. 35–36).

popular with the Plebs to fail, and though there were ominous signs of discontent among Italians who would have to give up holdings of *ager publicus*, the promise of enfranchisement secured the support of the majority of them.[1] Similarly, the *lex iudiciaria* (whatever its precise contents) had sufficient support among the nobility to pass in spite of fierce opposition.[2] It was only the citizenship proposal that led to the failure of Drusus' schemes.

Appian's confused account unfortunately does not make it clear whether this proposal, like the others, was passed and then invalidated; but it seems that it was not even passed.[3] All the interests that Drusus had offended combined against him, led by Q. Servilius Caepio (who, after a personal quarrel with Drusus, had become the champion of the *Equites*) and the consul L. Philippus (who had hated them).[4] Against this, Drusus probably retained the support of influential Senators (perhaps the majority of the House), and there is no reason to believe that he lost that of the Plebs: he seems to have made it quite clear to them that their chances of further agrarian and colonial assignations depended on the confiscation of public land held by Italians and this again—whether legally or in terms of what was practicable—on their enfranchisement.[5] But the Italians, whose support (as Appian says) was the main aim of his activity, were found to be divided: the colonial and agrarian legislation had caused some

[1] App., l.c.; Livy, *per.*, l.c. The *lex frumentaria* (Livy, l.c.) is not further discussed in our sources: it was by now the stock instrument of demagogy.

[2] Livy (*per.*, l.c.), making it clear that these laws were actually passed, is confirmed by Cicero's numerous references to the later invalidation of the *leges Liviae* (Greenidge–Clay², 109 f.). Philippus, later Drusus' chief opponent, had himself (if we may trust Florus, ii. 5, 4. f.) been threatened with prosecution together with Scaurus in consequence of the events of 92; there is no reason to think that he opposed the reform of the courts. (Cf., for what it is worth, Cic. *Cluent.* 153: 'cum cuncta quae tum erat nobilitate'.)

[3] The meaning of "Ἰταλιῶται" has been interminably discussed; see especially Kontchalovsky, *RH*, 1926, whose general views are amply refuted by Göhler, *Rom*, 76 f. Gabba (*GS*, 11, n. 4) says: 'Appiano ... sa benissimo che Etruschi ed Umbri sono anche essi Ἰταλιῶται'; but that does not explain how Appian can say of them: 'ταὐτὰ δειμαίνοντες τοῖς Ἰταλιώταις'. Appian is in any case guilty of confusion—at least that of using "Ἰταλιῶται", without warning, to mean only those who later fought—and were no doubt even then preparing to fight—for *Italia*.

[4] Sources in *MRR*, ii. 20. On Philippus I accept the view of Thomsen (art. cit. (p. 215, n. 6, above) and Hill (*Rom. Mid. Cl.* 135 f.), especially in view of Florus' evidence (n. 2, above). On Caepio, see *Hist.*, art. cit.

[5] Appian mentions the continued support of the Plebs.

alarm among them, and now Philippus seems actually to have succeeded in drawing crowds from Etruria and Umbria to Rome in a noisy and violent counter-demonstration against Drusus.[1] As we have seen, Appian has thoroughly obscured the story in his account: he does not say unambiguously what was the precise purpose of the Etruscans and Umbrians in coming to Rome and, in particular, what was the νόμος about which they complained. It is often assumed that it was the proposal *de ciuitate*, and that their purpose was to make it fail.[2] While it cannot be categorically denied that this is what Appian found in his source, it is certainly not what he in fact seems to say. He says that, having been introduced into the City by the consuls, they τοῦ νόμου φανερῶς κατεβόων καὶ τὴν τῆς δοκιμασίας ἡμέραν ἀνέμενον. The νόμος most recently mentioned (earlier in the chapter) is that on colonies (νόμος τῆς ἀποικίας, as Appian calls it), the application of which the Etruscans and Umbrians—like the Ἰταλιῶται (whatever that means)—were said to fear, and it is the obvious interpretation of the passage that this was the law they now attacked—not the proposal *de ciuitate*, to which we have no reason whatever to think them opposed. Fanciful speculations have been founded on misinterpretation of Appian's statement: it has even been said[3] that the Etruscan and Umbrian aristocracies opposed and feared enfranchisement, which would 'democratize' their cities: to such an extent can a false premiss make scholars misunderstand fundamental Roman political and social conditions. In fact, the Etruscan squire was as eager for the *ciuitas* as his Samnite counterpart—and no less afraid of colonial and agrarian legislation.

Nor, though the law had already been passed, was this attack belated: we know that towards the end of the year[4] Philippus counter-attacked Drusus and (it seems) tried—and at first failed —to move the Senate to condemn his laws already passed; and, probably after Crassus' death (i.e. some time between 20 September and 9 December, the end of Drusus' tribunate),[5] he succeeded

---

[1] App. i. 36. On Marius' probable connexion with these events, see below and *Hist.*, art. cit.

[2] Thus most recently Gabba (see p. 217, n. 3, above).

[3] Piotrowicz (*Klio*, 1930, 334 f.), unfortunately followed by Gabba.

[4] Certainly by September (Cic. *de or.* iii. 2).

[5] Cf. Diod. xxxvii. 10.

in having the laws declared invalid as passed contrary to the provisions of the *lex Caecilia Didia*.[1] It is very probable that it was in support of his agitation for cancelling the laws already passed that the consul had called in Italian elements disgruntled at the colonial legislation for the usual purpose of moral and physical pressure.[2] In any case, Appian puts the whole affair not long before Drusus' death. Appian's word 'δοκιμασία'[3] must denote the Senatorial inquiry into the validity of Drusus' laws. Appian, unfortunately, in his usual sketchy excerpting of a good source, has omitted all specific mention of the struggle for the invalidation of the laws (known to us from Cicero) and has thereby misled many modern scholars.[4]

Philippus' success (followed as it was by Drusus' death) was decisive. The Italians, again disappointed, took up arms. The tried system of *clientelae*, by which the Roman oligarchy had for so long been able to control the Peninsula through personal ties with leading families, broke down under the strain of repeated insult and disappointment.[5] In Rome, the triumphant *Equites*, after a short outburst of vengeance, were finally appeased when

[1] Cic. *dom.* 41 (cf. Asc. 69). There is no evidence at all for the common view (contradicted by our sources on 91) that *all* the laws had been passed *per saturam*, or that the *lex Caecilia Didia* dealt only with this particular illegality (Thomsen, art. cit. 30 f.; and, not known to him, already Hardy, *CR*, 1913, 262).

[2] That the agitation was heatedly pursued in public is clear from Cicero's account (p. 218, n. 4, above).

[3] Though it can be used for the vote taken on a bill (e.g. *b.c.* i. 10; 29), it is perfectly natural, and indeed better in accord with the original constitutional meaning of the word, to use it of the examination by the Senate of the validity of a law. (As there are hardly any instances of such action by the Senate, the absence of parallels for this meaning is quite insignificant.) In this case we know with certainty that precisely such an examination did actually take place. (This is pointed out by Marcks, *Überlief.* 10–11.) We may perhaps note Cicero's word '*iudicauit (Senatus)*' (l.c., n. 1, above).

[4] Marcks (op. cit. 5 f.) shows the sketchiness of Appian's account and its self-contradictions; he rightly points out that Appian is interested in the events of 91 only as a prelude to the Social War, which itself is only a prelude to the Civil Wars proper. We may observe Appian's explicit statement (ch. 55, *init.*) and his allocation of space: two chapters on Drusus (35–36), preceded by one (34) of general introduction on the Italian problem; then one on the consequences in Rome (37), one on the consequences in Italy and the beginnings of the revolt (38), then *fifteen* (39–53) on the Social War itself.

[5] The *locus classicus* is Cicero's account of Cn. Pompeius Strabo's talks with P. Vettius Scato (*Phil.* xii. 27). On the motives, interests, and state of mind of the upper classes of *Italia*, see Gabba's suggestive analysis (*GS*, 15 f.).

the seriousness of the danger was realized: for the duration of the war *concordia* prevailed.[1]

The Social War, as we have seen, marks the end of thirty-five years of agitation, in which the Italians had been the plaything of political factions in Rome. At first courted by anti-oligarchic leaders, they had been skilfully neutralized by the oligarchy, which set the Roman Plebs decisively against them and, by showing a degree of favour to the Latins, divided them among themselves. The army reform of Marius and its effect in Italy seem to have created a certain unity (based on common interests) among Roman and Italian veterans, while at the same time the upper classes of Italy found their position as subjects of Rome more and more irksome and came overwhelmingly to desire equality with the upper classes of Rome.[2] For a time it seemed as though military service could be made the path to citizenship; but with the quarrel between Marius and Saturninus this avenue was closed and the allies again sacrificed to the immediate interests of Roman politicians; though not before many individuals had been admitted. Next, Marius and his friends tried to retain and increase their following by encouraging viritane admissions of doubtful legality; but their opponents (and shocked general opinion) had put an end to this by the *lex Licinia Mucia*. Finally, with their position (and indeed personal safety)[3] endangered by internal developments, leading men among the oligarchy had attempted to enfranchise the Italians and use their support in Rome; but this again had been defeated by a combination of interests, not least among them those of Italian holders of *ager publicus* unwilling to surrender it to the Plebs—or, no doubt, to their own lower classes—as the price of citizenship.[4]

We do not, however, at any time hear of any 'class war' in

[1] The Varian *quaestio*, though not (like the regular courts) suspended at the outbreak of war, was suspended in due course (Cic. *Br.* 304; Asc. 73–74). On the consuls for 91 and 90, and the distribution of *legati*, see *Hist.* 1957, 337 f.

[2] See Gabba, l.c. (p. 219, n. 5, above): the *principes uiri* of Southern and Central Italy provided the leaders of *Italia*.

[3] Cf. Cic. *ap.* Asc. 21.

[4] The chief reason for the difference in attitude within the ranks of the Italians is obvious; and it is stated with clarity and common sense by Marcks (op. cit. 9): 'Sicherlich teilten sich ihre Interessen, je nachdem der Gewinn des Bürgerrechtes oder der Verlust von Land für sie bedeutender war.' This simple truth is too often obscured by wild speculation.

Italy on the question of enfranchisement. It has been shown by Gabba[1] that it is not true to say that the Social War was a kind of class war, with the upper classes on the whole loyal to Rome. On the contrary, they stood to gain most by enfranchisement; and we may add that the Latin cities, whose upper classes were already gaining the Roman franchise and were therefore satisfied, remained signally loyal to Rome in the War.[2] What is interesting, and has often been commented on, is the (apparently) regional division into rebels and loyalists: the original Confederacy is confined to the centre (including southern Picenum) and south of the Peninsula.[3] This is rightly connected by many historians with the special prominence of Umbrians and Etruscans in opposing Livius Drusus. It is indeed unnecessary—and unreasonable—to say that these nations did not want Roman citizenship: in the course of the War it clearly appears that they did, and in the end they extorted it by force.[4] But it seems that the aristocracy of these regions, while not so prominent in foreign trade (which had helped to make the southern aristocracy more conscious of the Roman yoke at home),[5] were owners of large estates and probably holders of large stretches of *ager publicus*, which—on what evidence we have—had not been taken from them by the Gracchan triumvirs.[6] If these holdings were to be the price that Drusus—as M. Fulvius Flaccus once had—asked for the grant of citizenship, they were not willing to pay it:[7] they no doubt hoped, perhaps through Marius' influence, to get the benefit without payment.

But the question next arises: what of the lower classes? Why did they not flock to Rome to oppose their local squires and support

[1] *GS*, 15 f. Cf. Sherwin-White, *RC*, 127.

[2] With the sole exception of Venusia (App. i. 39). Nor do we find any indication that the Latin lower classes were dissatisfied with this.

[3] App. i. 39; Livy, *per*. lxxii (incomplete list).

[4] App. i. 49–50; Livy, *per*. lxxiv (cf. Oros. v. 18 and—with the name of Faesulae, which probably also comes from Livy—Flor. ii. 6, 11). Those who maintain that the Umbrians and Etruscans in 91 opposed Drusus' attempt to grant them citizenship now have to postulate widespread and completely unattested revolutions in those regions in 90 (thus Piotrowicz, op. cit.): one improbable hypothesis has to be supported by cataclysmic *ad hoc* theories.

[5] Gabba, l.c. (n. 1, above); cf. Hatzfeld, *Traf.*, *passim*.

[6] This important point is made by Bernardi, 'G.S.', 67–68.

[7] Cf. p. 220, n. 4. The racial factor is also worth considering: *Italia* was practically an all-Oscan affair. On Marius' influence, see below and cf. *Hist.*, art. cit.

the agrarian law? Part of the answer is that some, no doubt, did, but that they are not singled out by our sources under their nationality: they were no doubt among the *ingens totius Italiae coetus* that followed and supported Drusus[1]—an indiscriminate mob of have-nots. But that is not all; for the account in Appian certainly suggests that Umbrians and Etruscans *as a whole* were opposed to Drusus' law; and though this may be an over-simplification, it is certainly not permissible, on the strength of it, to postulate a large-scale class war in these regions, with the few big landowners (called by Appian simply 'Etruscans and Umbrians') fanatically opposing Drusus, and the landless masses (not mentioned by Appian) no less fanatically supporting him. Yet this view of the situation is implied in many modern accounts.[2]

Though we may accept the existence of a land-owning aristo-cracy, less interested in trading and financial ventures than their southern neighbours, there is, in fact, little evidence for the theory that they had completely ousted the small landowner. It seems to rest only on the opposition of these regions to the younger Drusus—which it fails to explain—and on Tiberius Gracchus' observation of *latifundia* in Etruria.[3] But though there is no reason to doubt the existence of such estates, cultivated by slaves, in Etruria and Umbria as in other parts of Italy, yet we know that there was a considerable free population in Etruria and at least some of it was on the land: when Marius, after his exile, landed at Telamon, it provided him with a strong force.[4] For Umbria there seems to be no specific evidence either way. It is, however, of considerable interest to notice that Umbria and Etruria happen to be the regions for which we can trace some connexion with Marius: we know some of his clients in Umbria,[5] and Etruria was the region that he successfully chose for a landing and that was to pay a heavy price for its continued loyalty to his

---

[1] Sen. *br. vit.* 6.   [2] Cf. p. 218 (with n. 3).

[3] Plut. *Tib. Gr.* 8, 9 (cf. Piotrowicz, op. cit.).

[4] Plut. *Mar.* 41, 4: 'τῶν αὐτόθι γεωργούντων καὶ νεμόντων ἐλευθέρων . . . συντρεχόντων . . ., ἐν ἡμέραις ὀλίγαις χεῖρα μεγάλην ἤθροισε.' Cf. App. i. 67 (6,000 Etruscans). Plutarch, in fact, adds that Marius could afford to pick only the best!

[5] Cf. Gabba, *Ath.* 1951, 185, n. 1; we may add M. Annius Appius of Iguvium (Cic. *Balb.* 46). Gabba's evidence for Marian connexions in Picenum is, however, quite valueless, resting largely on a distortion of Cic. *Rab. perd.* 22; in fact, only the Labieni are known. Cf. p. 202, n. 1.

cause.[1] Though we have no proof of it, it is not impossible that the *eques Romanus* C. Maecenas, who opposed Drusus,[2] owed his citizenship to Marius.

All this must be set out at length in order to show that the problem is much more complicated than some of the standard accounts indicate.[3] It is difficult to draw the threads together satisfactorily; but where there is little evidence, what there is must not be set aside. We may begin by recalling the falsity (especially where Italians are concerned) of the assumption that it was only large landowners who held *ager publicus* and would be afraid of Roman laws *de modo agrorum*. Quite often, in fact, it may have been the case that a small farmer had merely extended his boundaries a little or at least could not prove his title, or even that, after formal confiscation by Rome, the original owners had remained undisturbed for generations.[4] There was thus a variety of local interests opposed to any redistribution. If, as is quite likely,[5] there were some large stretches of *ager publicus* in Etruria (viz. in the south), which yet had few colonies, we are entitled to assume that all such interests would be largely represented; and it is quite likely that, if a sufficient number of people were personally concerned, they would secure support from large sections of men of the same class who did not happen to be personally interested in *ager publicus*. It is thus perfectly credible that (as is implied in Appian) opposition in Etruria to Drusus' agrarian and colonial laws was widespread.[6] Many of these small farmers, who would not be excessively prosperous, must have volunteered for

---

[1] See Piotrowicz, op. cit. 337—connected by him with his 'democratic revolution' there.

[2] Cic. *Cluent.* 153. His political activity does not prove his Roman birth (cf. the case of Norbanus): especially as he remained an *eques Romanus*.

[3] We may add the well-known (and, in this context, significant) fact that Drusus' personal connexions were mainly with the later rebels—cf. Münzer, *RE*, s.v. 'Livius', col. 877. Again detailed study of connexions helps to explain what is otherwise puzzling. The ὅρκος Φιλίππου of Diodorus may be ignored, as it does not even seem to be contemporary propaganda (cf. Rose, *Harvard Theol. Review*, xxx, 1937, 165–81).   [4] App. i. 18; cf. Tibiletti, *Ath.* 1948, 121.

[5] See Piotrowicz, op. cit.

[6] We have no information at all about Etruscan reactions to the foundation of the colonies of Saturnia and Graviscae (183 and 181 resp.), briefly mentioned by Livy (xxxix. 55, 9; xl. 29, 1). In Rome there was no objection to them, as they were founded for obvious strategic reasons (cf. Salmon, *JRS*, xxvi, 1936, 53) and the territory required was small (Livy, ll.cc.).

service in Marius' armies, and as the colonies proposed by Saturninus were not founded, those in the armies that defeated the
Germans—the African veterans had no doubt been, on the whole,
settled in Africa—will, in the main, have returned to their native
cities: it is significant, as we have seen, that of the whole Italian
coastline it is Etruria that Marius chooses for his landing in 87
and his recruitment of a private army—and that he meets with
such success. Men flocked together κατὰ δόξαν αὐτοῦ, and he
reminded them of his Cimbric victories.[1] His reception in Campania on his outward journey had been quite different. Nor is it
difficult, now that we have recognized this, to understand the
continued loyalty of Etruria to his cause.[2]

In 91 we do not hear anything about Marius' attitude; but if
this reconstruction of the events leading up to Drusus' tribunate
is even approximately correct, Marius—the friend of the *Equites*
and enemy of the Metelli and their circle (and of P. Rutilius
Rufus in particular)—will have been opposed to Drusus' plans,
which were intended to capture his own supporters. We may
conjecture, then, that Marius, although he is not mentioned in
our sources—but as a politician he always preferred to work in
the background—, will have played his part in organizing his
clients against those of Drusus and in working upon the natural
suspicions felt by his friends in Umbria and Etruria against a
renewal of Gracchan schemes for redistribution of land, when
they thought that they had been lucky enough to escape the
attention of the Gracchan commission.[3] There is, of course,
nothing in all this to suggest that these men were opposed to the
extension of the Roman citizenship to the Italians (i.e. themselves)—and, as we have seen, that is in agreement with what the
rest of the evidence would lead us to expect. On the contrary (we
may now say), Marius' known and tried liberality in this respect,
by which many of these men had in fact already profited, will
have helped to persuade them that the price Drusus wanted was
not worth paying and that they might safely oppose him without

---

[1] Plut. *Mar.* 41, 4; App. i. 67. See *Note S*, p. 297.

[2] See discussion in Ch. XI. Piotrowicz (op. cit.) is led by his peculiar theory into
describing the Marian following as 'democrats' and explaining Etruscan support
for Marius by a democratization of the Etruscan cities consequent on their gaining
Roman citizenship! One absurdity leads to another.

[3] See p. 221 (with n. 6). On Marius, cf. *Hist.*, art. cit.

fearing that they would thus destroy their only chance of attaining the citizenship. It was only when, in the course of 90, they saw that even their loyalty in the new war was unrewarded and that the question of giving them the citizenship was (as far as we know) not even being discussed—it was only then that, recognizing their mistake, Etruria and Umbria planned (and, in part, proceeded to) rebellion: there was now no longer any danger of agrarian legislation to obscure the issue for them.

X

THE ITALIANS—REVOLUTION AND INTEGRATION

THE Social War, as might be expected, does not mark the end of the Italian problem, but only the beginning of its solution. We have seen how fear of the political effects of a mass influx of new citizens had for a long time prevented the oligarchy from adopting a generous policy of enfranchisement, and how, when Drusus, at last recognizing the necessity of taking the decisive step, tried to steal their opponents' policy, he could not carry his own faction with him to the end. Before the end of 90, with the rebels moderately successful and Etruria and Umbria on the point of joining them, quick action had to be taken, and a law of the consul L. Julius Caesar gave the citizenship to all who wanted it. Despite some discussion in a few cities,[1] it seems to have been universally accepted among faithful allies and penitent rebels, and though the principal rebel states fought on for some time, it seems that by the beginning of 88 all except the Samnites and Lucanians had surrendered and been accepted as citizens, perhaps under the *lex Julia*.[2] Enfranchisement was a fact, and the only question remaining was how to cope with the new situation: the new citizens must be prevented from influencing the Assemblies, where Senatorial control was already, at times, none too secure. The answer was to confine the new citizens to special tribes, few in number, where they would be not only outvoted, but hardly ever called upon to vote at all.[3] The details of these arrangements are not clearly reported in the sources. In 90 (probably in connexion with the *lex Julia*) a L. Calpurnius Piso, tribune or praetor, carried a law establishing two new tribes—presumably for those to be immediately enrolled under the *lex Julia*.[4] This principle seems to have been extended

---

[1] Cic. *Balb.* 21.

[2] App. i. 53. The enfranchising laws present many puzzles: they need separate treatment elsewhere.

[3] Ibid. i. 49.   [4] *MRR*, ii. 33 f.; Syme, *Hist.* iv, 1955, 58.

as more allies were enrolled, though we cannot be certain whether new tribes were created or some of the old ones used.[1] Thus, though enfranchisement had been conceded, its political effects were to be minimized.

The year 89 saw the gradual recovery of Roman arms, due to wise policy in extending the citizenship and to the military skill, especially, of the consul Cn. Pompeius Strabo in the north and the legate L. Sulla in the south. Strabo was sole consul for the greater part of the year; but, of course, he was conducting operations, and at home government seems to have been carried on by the Senate.[2] The Social War, in fact, like the Hannibalic War long ago, provided the oligarchy with an opportunity of strengthening its control of the government. With the chief magistrates in the field most of the time, the People depending on expert leadership, and its members protected from attacks in the law-courts,[3] the Senate's control was unchallenged and (as the outcome proved) successful. It was in this atmosphere of *concordia* that, with the war almost won and the resumption of forensic activity imminent, the tribune Plautius passed his reform of the law courts in the Senate's favour.[4]

Meanwhile great individuals had faded into the background. Marius, in spite of his good record in the first year of fighting, had retired from active service amid hostile rumours, probably because his numerous enemies prevented him from gaining another consulship and supreme direction of the War:[5] it had been thought safer to elect an undistinguished noble allied with the Metelli[6] and an energetic leader of non-consular family, whose successes in Picenum (a district he will have known well)

[1] Vell. ii. 20; App. i. 49.

[2] On Cn. Pompeius Strabo, see Gelzer, *R. St.* ii. 64 f.

[3] See pp. 219–20 (with n. 1).

[4] Asc. 79. It is hard to dissociate this from a notorious crime of this year, the murder of the praetor Asellio by (presumably) *Equites*. (On this, see Livy, *per.* lxxiv; App. i. 54; Val. Max. ix. 7, 4.) Though the attack on him was made in the Forum in full daylight, the assassins were never found (App., l.c.): it looks as though *concordia* was carefully preserved.

[5] On his part in the war, see Passerini, *Ath.* 1934, 358 f.; his conclusions on Marius' retirement are, however, unsatisfactory. Kiene's explanation (adopted in the text) seems most plausible.

[6] L. Porcius Cato may be the man who, as *tr. pl.* 99, tried to recall Numidicus (thus *RE*, s.v. 'Porcius', no. 7). But see *Hist.* 1957, 341 f.

had been one of the few comforts provided by a disastrous year.[1]
From a military point of view this turned out well: though Cato
was killed early in the year, Cn. Pompeius Strabo crowned a year
of steady progress by the capture of Asculum, probably in November,[2] and on 25 December he celebrated the only triumph of the
War.[3] But politically it was a mistake. The War, now practically
at an end,[4] had not lasted long enough to secure the permanence
of the Senate's ascendancy; moreover, the 'professional army'
was beginning to develop, and inevitably it would turn into a
client army attached to its commanders.[5] Marius, who had
created this army, had to some extent (as we have seen) recognized its political importance; but he regarded it only as an
aggregate of clients giving moral and political support according
to the old pattern, and there is no evidence that even now he saw
any farther.[6] But far-sighted men could not fail, if they were
unscrupulous enough, to have new thoughts on the bases of
political power in Rome. The War had given at least two such
men their opportunity: L. Sulla and Cn. Pompeius; and it was
merely a matter of chance which of them first had occasion to
take it.[7] Pompeius must have had large family estates in Picenum:
not only was he sent to the district as a legate in 90 and allowed
to operate very independently,[8] but it seems that he largely

---

[1] Cf. Gelzer, l.c. (p. 227, n. 2, above) and ibid. 59 f.: the only consul of the *gens*
was Q. Pompeius in 141, of a branch not closely related. Whether the family was of
Picentine origin (thus Syme, *Rom. Rev.* 28), we cannot tell. It is sometimes denied
on account of their tribe (the Clustumina)—thus, e.g., Gelzer, l.c. But that is not
decisive. In any case most of the family estates will have gone back to before the war
and not be due to it. (On this, see below.)

[2] Gelzer, op. cit. 68: I accept the very reasonable argument that *ILS*, 8888 should
be dated 89 and represents part of the rewards and distinctions distributed after
victory.   [3] *Insc. It.* xiii. 1, 84–85 and 563.

[4] The evidence suggests that only the Samnites and Lucanians (and one or two
fortresses) were still in arms at the end of 89: the triumph of Strabo must mean
that his theatre was then clear of enemies. But for the Civil War that supervened,
even the Samnites could hardly have held out long.

[5] On the client army, see Drexler's interesting study (*H*, 1935, 225 f.), and
especially Gabba, 'Ricerche' (*Ath.* 1951), *passim*.

[6] See pp. 237–8.

[7] On Sulla, see below. Gelzer.is inclined to think Strabo the first to use a private
army for personal power; Wiehn (*Ill. Heer.* 61 f.) ascribes the precedent to Sulla.
The question of priority of execution is, at most, of academic interest, where
inspiration and intention are obviously contemporaneous; but the credit, such as
it is, should probably go to Sulla (see pp. 234 f., below)   [8] Gelzer, op. cit. 63.

recruited his own army on the spot and probably recruited it particularly from among his own tenants—a practice well known at a later date.[1] During the War he took good care to extend his connexions in the district[2] and to ensure the personal loyalty of his army,[3] and by the time of his triumph he was at the head of a devoted army and in firm control of a populous district. He also tried to extend his connexions outside the Peninsula: on his return to Rome, he carried a law that led to the conferment of Latin status on the Transpadana—a signal *beneficium* conferred on another populous region, which was to show its gratitude to his son.[4] Pompeius had thus reached a degree of power and prestige that was beyond the legitimate station of one not even of noble birth; and it was bound to cause alarm. When the Senate, with the law-courts safely reconstituted, revived the Varian *quaestio* as a political instrument now to be used in its favour, Cn. Pompeius was at once accused, probably as soon as his consulship had expired.[5] The charge, Cicero tells us, was *maiestas*, but the grounds of it are not at all clear—nor, perhaps, important.[6] It is generally thought that he was acquitted—but that is a mere guess.[7]

[1] Pompey later retired to his father's estates in Picenum; and when he collected a private army, it was largely made up of his father's veterans (*b.Afr.* 22, 2; Val. Max. v. 2, 9). As there can have been no assignation of land to Cn. Pompeius Strabo's veterans after service, they must have lived in Picenum before. Comparison with L. Domitius Ahenobarbus in 49 (Caes. *b.c.* i. 34, 3) suggests that many will have come from his own estates. His influence there will have been one good reason why he was elected and sent to the district. On the large number of Strabo's officers who seem to come from Picenum, see Cichorius, *R. St.* 157.

[2] Cf. the sources on young Pompey's retirement to Picenum (Vell. ii. 29, 1; Plut. *Pomp.* 6; and see last note). I am not sure how (as is sometimes asserted) he could have acquired his enormous estates as well.

[3] Cf. the grant of citizenship to some Spaniards (*ILS*, 8888). On his army's loyalty, see below.

[4] Asc. 3; Pliny, *n.h.* iii. 138. The precise way in which it was done is not clear. See Ewins, *PBSR*, 1955, 73 f. On Pompey and the Transpadana, see Ch. XI, p. 268 (with n. 4). On Spain, see last note.

[5] Cic. *ap.* Asc. 79. As the *lex Plotia* belongs to the previous year, this case (the first heard under its provisions) must belong to the very beginning of 88. Varius himself, incidentally, was now condemned (Cic. *Br.* 305; Val. Max. viii. 6, 4).

[6] For some possible grounds, see Gelzer, *Nob.* 78 (recanted and amended *R. St.* ii. 71 f. and notes); Wiehn, op. cit. 64 f.

[7] Val. Max. ix. 7, *ext.* 2, says that he held his command (later that same year) 'aliquamdiu inuita ciuitate'. It is a tempting hypothesis that he returned to his army without awaiting the outcome of the trial: who was to call him to account? His later behaviour makes this quite credible.

Better attested—but no more plausible—is the story that he wanted to be re-elected for 88:[1] as we shall see, there were other candidates, and our detailed tradition leaves no room for him. In any case, he returned to his army and watched the interesting events of the new year in Rome.

For meanwhile, just as the Social War was approaching its end, another important military command had begun to whet the appetites of Roman leaders, so long kept in due subjection to authority: the King of Pontus, after more than a decade of cautious policy (on both sides) and indecisive negotiations, had been provoked into war—probably in part through Marius' intrigues—and Roman control of Asia was now collapsing.[2] At the end of 89, the disasters were still in the future: for the present it seemed an opportunity for collecting booty and glory, free from the trammels of constant supervision from Rome. Our sources do not present a clear and unified picture of the rivalry and competition for the command. What we hear most about is the conflict between Marius and Sulla, which led to civil war. We happen to know—mainly from casual references—that there was also rivalry between Marius and C. Caesar Strabo, and one important source regards this as the chief cause of the civil war that followed. But nowhere in the ancient evidence are these two conflicts related to each other.[3] Fortunately, the general implication in the sources that the incident of C. Caesar's candidature was very early in Sulpicius' tribunate enables us to see the pattern of events.

The tribune P. Sulpicius Rufus, a friend of M. Livius Drusus, entered upon his office on 10 December 89. Like Drusus, he was a gifted young man with good connexions, and he intended to resume Drusus' plan of pressing reform into the service of

---

[1] He probably instructed the tribune C. Herennius (perhaps a Picentine friend of his) to defend his interests in his absence (cf. *H*, 1955, 199 f.).

[2] Sources in *MRR*, ii. 35–36. The Roman commission responsible for the war was led by M' Aquillius (*cos.* 101) and probably included T. Manlius Mancinus, the pro-Marian tribune of 107. Marius had met the Eastern kings (Plut. *Mar.* 31) and had Eastern interests, bound up with those of the *Equites*.

[3] Caesar's attempt: Asc. 25 ('causa belli ciuilis'); cf. Cic. *Br.* 226; *har. resp.* 43 (the reason for Sulpicius' turning demagogue); Quint. vi. 3, 75. On the conflict with Marius, see Diod. xxxvii. 2, 12. Münzer (*RE*, s.v. 'Sulpicius', col. 848—the only careful treatment in recent literature) puts the conflict after Sulla's departure, making the consulship that of 87. But the sources clearly put it at the very beginning of Sulpicius' tribunate.

the oligarchy.[1] Among other actions on behalf of the *boni*, he naturally opposed the illegal candidature of the aedilician Caesar for the consulship, and when Caesar collected armed gangs, he matched force with force. There can be little doubt, in view of his well-known political connexions at the time, that it was only by accident that he thus found himself co-operating with Marius and his supporters: for the old man, disgruntled at the desertion of his aristocratic friends and at his political eclipse during the Social War, was determined that this time it should be *his* task to save the State again, and he was staking his claim against his former friend Caesar. The nineties had, on the whole, seen the abandonment of Marius by his aristocratic friends, who had flocked to him, for their own advantage, in the days of his glory. Catulus, the Caesares, M. Antonius, P. Crassus—to mention only a few—had abandoned him by 91; and the cautious approaches of L. Crassus and probably Q. Scaevola, and even the full co-operation of the disgruntled Q. Caepio, had failed to balance the loss or erase the memory. But this story has been pieced together elsewhere.[2]

Sulpicius was probably (as a close friend of Q. Pompeius Rufus)[3] supporting the plans of the Metelli and their associates: they intended the consulship for Q. Pompeius and his *adfinis*, the brilliant Patrician 'self-made man' L. Sulla, who, on Scaurus' death, had been taken up by the Metelli and married to Scaurus' widow Metella—perhaps partly because of his known *inimicitiae* with Marius, recently raised to fever heat by their joint client Bocchus with the connivance of the *boni*.[4] Sulla and Pompeius, probably already *adfines*, were elected and Sulla was given the command in the East.[5] Provisionally, it seemed like the end of the matter, and

---

[1] Sources: *MRR*, ii. 41–42. Only what is directly relevant can be discussed here.

[2] Marius' hopes: Plut. *Mar.* 34 (tendentious); Diod., l.c. See *Historia*, 1957, 331 f.; 338 f.

[3] Cic. *am.* 2: 'quocum coniunctissime et amantissime uixerat.'

[4] Plut. *Sulla*, 6, *init*. The approval of the Senate was needed for a dedication by a foreign ally, and thus the affair takes on the appearance of a deliberate political act by the *boni*. On Sulla's marriage, see ibid. 18: it was connected with his election. Pompeius' son married Sulla's daughter; we do not know when, but their eldest son was *tr. pl.* 52 and was probably born well before 85 (see *RE*, s.v. 'Pompeius', col. 2252).

[5] Plut. *Sulla* 7; *et al.* The consular elections were bound to be late in 89: Asculum only fell in November and the surviving consul, it seems, was still in the

the victorious oligarchy, emboldened by its victory, proceeded to try to curb the ambition of Cn. Pompeius Strabo by a political prosecution.

Sulpicius for his part, however, proceeded to put his main schemes to the vote: he proposed the distribution of the new citizens (and freedmen) among the thirty-five tribes; if any new tribes had been created, they were to disappear, and the new citizens should in no way be distinguished from the old.[1] He soon found that he could get little support for his scheme—less even than Drusus, whose chief supporters Scaurus and Crassus were dead. Among the old citizens the oligarchy, afraid—as ever since the question of Italian suffrage was raised—of losing its influence, could work up powerful opposition to Sulpicius. But he, accustomed by the affair of C. Caesar Strabo to the idea of gang warfare, openly began to collect bands of Italians and freedmen and to arm them in his support.[2] At this point the consuls turned decisively against him, preventing the vote on his bill.[3]

It was probably now that Sulpicius joined forces with Marius. His sudden change of front can only thus be explained at all satisfactorily.[4] It appears from Appian's account—if we look at the facts and ignore tendentious interpretation—that the bill on the redistribution of citizens was proposed first, i.e. by itself, and that the transfer of the Eastern command to Marius came later, only after Sulla had left the City. It was bound to be said that it had all been concerted from the beginning; but we know too much about Sulpicius' character and personal and political background to believe it. It was only now that Marius and Sulpicius had common interests of a positive kind. Both of them had been rebuffed by the oligarchy, Sulpicius thus insulted by his personal friend the consul; and, unlike M. Drusus,[5] he would not submit to indignity. Once more the *boni* had unwisely injured the

field on the 17th (*ILS*, 8888—cf. p. 228, n. 2); he triumphed on 25 December (ibid. n. 3) and may well not have been able to hold the *comitia* before.

[1] *MRR*, l.c. (p. 231, n. 1).

[2] That much of Plutarch's account may be believed (though the charge is a commonplace): it provides an explanation for the odd story (*Sulla*, 8) that Sulpicius was seen counting out money on a table in the Forum.

[3] Plut. *Sulla*, 8; App. i. 55, *fin.* Plutarch's account (also *Mar.* 34 f.) is probably based on Sulla's Memoirs and in any case clearly tendentious.

[4] This is substantially the view of Last (*CAH*, ix. 203).

[5] Diod. xxxvii. 10, 3.

dignitas of a proud young aristocrat. There was room for a bargain profitable to both men, and they had already, no doubt, established some kind of friendly relations in their joint opposition to C. Caesar. The point of the bargain is clear. Marius had the support of the *ordo equester*, which had been shocked and embittered by the recent disasters in the East, coming as they did at a time when the Senate had strengthened its control over the government at home.[1] Marius was undoubtedly the man whom the *Equites* would trust in such a crisis.[2] On the other hand, they might well be suspicious of a friend of the hated M. Livius Drusus, especially if he proceeded to mob violence. Nor could they be expected to have much sympathy with a policy of complete equalization towards the allies. The fate of C. Gracchus, of Saturninus and Glaucia, and of Drusus himself, was a clear warning. Although the business interests of *Equites Romani* and the allied banking and commercial classes were identical and their contacts close and friendly, the political power of the *Equites* in the Assemblies and law-courts was too great to be lightly shared with their business associates; and the large number of newly-enfranchised potential *Equites*, confined to a few tribes, could not press for complete equality without creating more antagonism. On the other hand, once equality were conferred, the numerous wealthy traders and bankers would be an element whose support in the Assemblies was well worth having; and Marius, who (as we have seen) had always maintained his Italian interests, though hitherto mainly in the north, would eagerly seize this chance of conferring a signal *beneficium* on the upper classes of the south.[3] It was this, in addition to the Eastern command, that Sulpicius now offered to Marius, in return for the support of the *Equites*: support for Sulpicius' law about the new citizens was the price they were to pay for the transfer of the Asian command. Thus Sulpicius would obtain his vengeance on his faithless friends and, of course, the support of an important body of voters for his further advancement.

---

[1] See above. We may well compare the effect of the massacre of Cirta (Sall. *Jug.* 26–27).   [2] Cf. Hill, *R. Mid. Cl.* 140 f.; Gabba, *GS*, 38 f.

[3] Gabba (op. cit. 59 and *passim*; cf. 'Ricerche', *Ath.* 1951, 256 f.) claims that they already had firm connexions with Marius and that Campania in particular was a centre of Marian influence. This cannot be supported (see *Hist.* 1957, 344 f.). We may usefully compare Marius' experiences in Campania on his flight from Rome with those in Etruria on his return; see below.

The immediate success of the bargain must have satisfied both parties: Sulpicius could now rely on the support of the *Equites* by their votes, fists and money, and after serious rioting the consuls had to flee and his laws were carried. Marius at once sent his friend and fellow-townsman Gratidius to take over Sulla's legions.[1]

Sulla, however, now made his significant contribution to Roman politics: with his loyal army, in spite of the scruples of nearly all his officers, he marched on Rome.[2] Ever since 133, when the 'Optimates'[3] had saved the Republic by killing a sacrosanct tribune, it had been clear that force was to be the decisive element in political life. Saturninus, after some personal experience of this, had tried to apply the lesson on the 'Popular' side, using Marius' veterans for intimidation and riots. The attempt had failed for political reasons. M. Livius Drusus, relying, with high support, on the Plebs and his Italian friends, had been defeated by his own weapons. Then came the Social War and with it new possibilities for the use of decisive force. For two years or more, commanders led their armies (largely recruited, according to the new pattern, among the classes[4] that had nothing to lose and hoped to gain everything) against men who were, on the whole, of the same culture and often the same language, and who were bound to their 'enemies' by many bonds.[5] Thus soldiers became accustomed to civil war on Italian soil and to fighting, not on behalf of their country against a foreign enemy whom they knew as such, but at their commanders' behest against old comrades in arms: patriotism could hardly be aroused by the devastation of Italy. Nor was there a lack of astute and unscrupulous leaders to foresee the consequences: Cn. Pompeius Strabo and Sulla deliberately aimed at attaching their armies to their personal leadership.[6] Marius—

---

[1] For the complete legislation, see *MRR*, ii. 41–42; for the tribune's Equestrian support, see Plut. *Sulla*, 8 and *Mar.* 35. The story of his ἀντισύγκλητος (what is the Latin for it?) of 600 members, at a time when the Senate only had about 300, fortunately refutes itself. For Gratidius, see Val. Max. ix. 7, *ext.* 1.

[2] App. i. 57. On the significance of this, see p. 228 (with references, n. 7).

[3] Velleius, ii. 3, 2.

[4] Even freedmen were used (Livy, *per.* lxxiv; cf. App. i. 49, *init.*).

[5] Cf. especially the purple patch in Diod. xxxvii. 15; also Florus, ii. 6, *init.* Appian (l.c.) sees the decisive importance of the Social War in the downfall of the Republic.

[6] On Pompeius, see p. 229; of. below. On Sulla, see Plut. *Sulla*, 6, 16–17.

perhaps too old to learn, perhaps (as a Knight from Arpinum) brought up in too scrupulous reverence of Rome—did not see this new development.[1] He and Sulpicius were taken completely by surprise; they clearly had no chance of organizing resistance to the legions and relied only on some last-minute scruple among the enemy that might prevent the sacrilege of seizing the City by armed force: when no such scruple could be evoked, nothing remained but precipitate flight.[2] Marius, Sulpicius and their supporters were declared enemies (and any that could be caught executed) and, among other measures of political reorganization,[3] the Sulpician laws were repealed: Sulla, sacrificing the support of the Italians (who were already indebted to the other side for the chief *beneficium*), hoped thereby to gain that of the City and in particular that of the *boni*, some of whom were a little restive at his methods.[4] One man might still beat Sulla at his own game: Cn. Pompeius Strabo, watching Rome from his camp in Picenum. Sulla could therefore combine a favour to the aristocracy, which hated Strabo, with considerations of personal safety in proposing a bill depriving him of his command and transferring it to his own colleague and *adfinis* Q. Pompeius Rufus. This extraordinary measure was probably taken because of Strabo's contumacious disregard of earlier orders to return, perhaps in connexion with his trial. It seems that it was vetoed by Strabo's ally, the tribune C. Herennius, and that Rufus therefore had only a *Senatus consultum* to base his claim on;[5] but be that as it may, soon after he appeared in Strabo's camp, the latter's army showed the personal loyalty with which he had imbued it by murdering the consul.[6] Sulla, alarmed at seeing his equal, left Rome to attend to his

[1] See p. 228 (above). Cf. pp. 237–8.
[2] App. i. 57 f. Cf. Passerini, *Ath.* 1934, 369–70.
[3] The details of Sulla's actions in his first consulship are inextricably entwined in the sources with those of his dictatorship. We need not consider them.
[4] *MRR*, ii. 40–42: Appian and Plutarch are the chief sources. For the suspicious attitude of some of the *boni*, see Plut. *Sulla*, 10, 4: τὴν σύγκλητον ἀδήλως ἡνίασεν (also the δυσμένεια of the Plebs). Q. Scaevola (Val. Max. iii. 8, 5) probably felt sure of some support. In any case, it is clear that Sulla had to remove his army and permit fairly free elections. His desertion by his officers in his march on Rome (see above) shows the scruples of the upper classes; and they deserve credit for them.
[5] I have argued this (with the caution necessitated by the evidence) in *H*, 1955, 107 f. Cf. pp. 229–30 (with n. 1).
[6] App. i. 63; Vell. ii. 20, 1; Livy, *per.* lxxvii; Val. Max. ix. 7, *ext.* 2.

Eastern war, and Strabo remained in Picenum, watchful and enigmatic, surrounded by his army (now the best left in Italy) and his clients.

With the departure of Sulla and his army, his new constitution was bound to be attacked at its most vulnerable point: the consul Cinna rallied the dissatisfied Italians round himself by proposing the renewal of the *leges Sulpiciae*.[1] It is not surprising that they should quickly have found a champion: the unquestioned success of Marius and Sulpicius had demonstrated the power of the alliance of interests represented by the *leges Sulpiciae*. It had been crushed by an army; but now that this army was removed—and no other army was in sight to take its place—, the alliance (it must seem) was bound to be successful, and the question was merely who first chose to revive it and profit by its success.

Cinna was helped by the attitude of the oligarchy and especially of his colleague Cn. Octavius. The latter, exploiting the anti-Italian feeling still found in the City and seeing a chance of personal domination, drove Cinna out of Rome, and had him deposed and the *flamen Dialis* L. Cornelius Merula made consul—the only man in the commonwealth who, on account of the taboos with which his office was hedged round and the piety with which he observed them, could be relied upon to take no active part in the events that Octavius knew must be imminent.[2] Cinna thus became a martyr in the cause of the Italians—within a short time he had enrolled a large army from among enthusiastic new citizens.[3] What was perhaps more surprising: he was favourably received by the remnants of Sulla's army left behind in Campania, which thus for the first time demonstrated the converse of the attitude of mind that we have noticed as characteristic of the personal 'client army': abandoned by its leader—feeling, perhaps, betrayed in being cheated of the opportunity for Eastern spoils—, it was prepared to acclaim whoever offered better terms.[4] Cinna, joined

---

[1] Sources (very numerous) in *MRR*, ii. 46. They agree that the status of the Italians was the main issue. [2] *CAH*, ix. 262.

[3] Thirty legions, if we may believe our text of Velleius (ii. 20, 4)—as we surely may not: cf. Appian's statement that the forces of Octavius were superior (i. 69—likely from the course of events). Whether Cinna promised freedom to slaves (App. i. 65; *et al.*) or whether that is merely a stock charge, we have no means of telling.

[4] Cf. Drexler's illuminating discussion (*H*, 1935, 225 f.) of this attitude in another case.

by many disaffected Romans, now marched on Rome with a large and heterogeneous army.[1] Before long news reached him that Marius, whom he had perhaps invited to return, had landed in Italy.

Marius, on being forced to leave Rome, had at first gone to Campania, where he had a villa and no doubt some friends, and whence (at the worst) escape beyond the seas would be possible. The reception he got, however, was anything but friendly, and he was glad to escape with his life.[2] Leaving Italy, he finally, after more adventures (perhaps involving a landing in Sicily),[3] reached Africa, where his son and others had earlier taken refuge. Africa was indeed the natural choice; for, apart from Italy and Gaul (too near Italy to be safe), it was the region chiefly connected with his fame. It was in Africa that he had won the war against Jugurtha, and he could therefore hope for loyalty from the natives and the local princes, who owed their power to his *beneficium*.[4] Perhaps as important a consideration, however, was the string of settlements of his veterans who had been assigned land and (in some cases) perhaps even organized in colonies by the legislation of 103 and 100.[5] It was to these settlements that Marius turned when the governor of Africa proved hostile and the King of Numidia treacherous; and it was in the most sheltered and inaccessible of them, the island of Cercina, that he found safe refuge and a military base.[6] Marius, as we have seen, had had no intention of providing himself with a series of strongpoints for purposes of political intimidation or even personal safety. Yet this turned out to be their importance to him, and the lesson was obvious for anyone who would see: within a few years Sulla had drawn the conclusion.[7] The military colony, ever since Scipio's foundation of Italica[8] a recognized means of recompense for soldiers who

---

[1] Sources in *MRR*, ii. 46. The chief source is Appian (i. 65 f.).

[2] His villa: Plut. *Mar.* 34, 3. For a survey of his 'Campanian connexions', see *Hist.*, 1957, 344 f. The accounts of his flight are submitted to detailed scrutiny by Passerini (*Ath.* 1934, 371 f.).

[3] Passerini, op. cit. 373 f.

[4] This aspect will be discussed in the next chapter.

[5] See Ch. IX, p. 199 (with notes). There is no reason to doubt that these settlements included Italians.

[6] Plut. *Mar.* 40, 14; *Insc. It.* xiii. 3, no. 7 (Cercina).

[7] See below (pp. 245 f.).   [8] Ch. V, p. 119.

would not return to their homes, had by Marius' army reform been turned into a necessary gratuity for whole armies; and the opposition of the oligarchy to the provision for Marius' veterans had only strengthened the natural tendency towards regarding this gratuity as the *beneficium* of the commander: where the government would not assume responsibility, the leader necessarily became the champion of his men, thus reinforcing their allegiance to him even after their discharge.[1] It is ironical that Marius, the man who had done more than anyone else to bring about this state of affairs, had done so on antiquated premisses, intending merely to beat his enemies at their own political game;[2] and that finally his very inability to see the uses of the weapon that he had created (leading to his expulsion from Rome by a man who saw them) forced him into a position where he accidentally discovered and, by the example of his experience, ultimately taught his great enemy the complementary lesson: the use of the veteran colony to give permanence to the political power of the private army.

On hearing of Cinna's first successes, Marius, with a small force, set sail for Italy, landing at Telamon in Etruria. It is worth stressing again how his reception there differed from his previous experiences in Campania, where—naturally enough—he did not try to land now. We have already seen[3] how quickly he collected an army among those who had known him in his glory—his Cimbric veterans, who had returned to their over-populated land when the attempt to provide for them was finally defeated, but who (if they ever did blame Marius for this failure) would not desert their *imperator* in his hour of misfortune.[4] When Marius with his forces joined Cinna and brought the mind of an expert strategist to bear on the problem of besieging the City, the Senate

---

[1] On all this, see Gabba's brilliant discussion of 'il veteranesimo' in *Ath.* 1951, 211 f., treating the problem in all its aspects. It will be clear (without detailed discussion) that I do not always share his views on Roman political matters.

[2] Cf. Ch. IX, p. 203. [3] Ch. IX, p. 222 (with n. 4).

[4] The *colonia Mariana* in Corsica (Plin. *n.h.* iii. 80; Sen. *cons. ad Helv.* 7, 9; Sol. 3, 3), probably a settlement of Cimbric veterans (despite Gabba, *Ath.* 1951, 18 f.), perhaps influenced his choice of a landing-place. (Thus Wiehn, *Ill. Heer.* 59 f.) But we do not hear of his actually getting any support from there. That the settlement (whether originally a colony or not—cf. the African ones) was founded by Marius himself is repeatedly affirmed in the sources and undoubtedly true. Hill calls Marius' following 'a motley gang of freed slaves and desperadoes' (op. cit. 143)—thus surpassing the ancient tradition, uniformly hostile as it is.

at last realized the futility of its attitude to the Italians and took some steps to attract them to the defence of the Republic. What these steps were is not clear, as our sources have different and (in part) conflicting accounts, without giving enough evidence to enable us to judge with certainty. What is certain is that negotiations were begun with the Samnites fighting Metellus; that the terms they demanded were not immediately accepted (whether by the Senate or by Metellus himself); and that, despite some gesture by the Senate, the Samnites joined Marius, and the other Italians showed little enthusiasm for the Republic that considered treating them fairly only when it desperately needed them.[1]

The decision now seemed to rest with Cn. Pompeius. His was the only veteran army of any size in Italy,[2] and it had shown that it was devoted to him. He was firmly entrenched in Picenum and had connexions in the Cisalpina and as far away as Spain. But Pompeius was playing his own game, and he had no reason to love the nobility that hated him and had already tried to break his power.[3] The consular elections for 86 were at hand, and it was clear whom the dominant faction wanted to take charge of the State: they had already recalled Q. Metellus Pius (*pr.* 89 and just eligible for election) to save them.[4] There was little doubt what would follow: the consul would be asked (as another consul had been in 88) to take over Cn. Pompeius' army, and he, if the loyalty of his men did not extend to the murder of another consul (and this time a Metellus), could face a trial and certain exile. Like Caesar in 50, Cn. Pompeius could be safe only if he relied on his army in order to get a consulship.[5] He thus carefully used his army merely in order to raise his price, and he seems to have privately negotiated with Cinna without the knowledge of their associates—probably planning a consulship of Cinna and Pompeius for 86.[6] If the Italians, by suitable legislation, were attached

---

[1] See *Note T*, p. 297.

[2] Marius' veterans from Etruria were only a few thousand men (one legion, we are told), Cinna's only the remains of Sulla's army from Nola; and it does not look as if Metellus had a large force.   [3] Cic. *ap.* Asc. 79; cf. above.

[4] Gran. Lic. 29 B, on whom every account must be based.

[5] This is clear in Granius: 'ut eum magistratum ipse inuaderet qui timebatur.' These events have been elucidated and brilliantly discussed by Gelzer (*R. St.* ii. 77 f. and notes).

[6] That Pompeius had contacts on Cinna's side is clear from the help later given to his son (Cic. *Br.* 230; Val. Max. vi. 2, 8). The 'conspiracy' against Pompeius

to the new consuls, the latter, with Pompeius' private army and connexions, could defy not only the oligarchy, but even Marius, whose support was not as solidly based. There is little doubt that Pompeius—from what we have seen of his policy—would welcome the chance of taking his share of the credit for giving the Italians equality: he was the last man not to appreciate the weight of their support for Cinna, and he could use them to prepare for the inevitable reckoning with his enemy Sulla, who (fortunately) had made the great mistake of neglecting and offending them. Though it is not often profitable to speculate on plans that were not executed, the secret negotiations of Pompeius and Cinna, combined with what we know of the actual achievement of Pompeius, imply an ambitious plan for the use of a private army, backed by *tota Italia*, against the domination of a faction led by a proconsul in the East—a plan that might have at least speeded up the 'Roman Revolution'.

Owing to intervention by the enraged gods,[1] the plan was not executed. There followed, instead, the capture of Rome and *Cinnae dominatio*. It is an obscure period, blackened (like the reign of Domitian) by the zeal of those who, in a happier age succeeding, had to justify their survival and advancement by dwelling upon their constant perils. In fact, after the first days of massacre (and especially after Marius' death), the new rulers of Rome settled down to a policy of peace and conciliation—the only policy, as they well knew, that might avoid civil war with the veteran legions of the East, or, if it did not, would at least give the régime a moral advantage that might be sufficient for victory.

Unfortunately it is not easy to tell how the new régime acted towards those Italian allies who had swept it into power. That the Samnites got what they had been promised[2] is certain: they were strong enough to enforce their demands. For the rest (i.e. on the question of distribution among the tribes), the evidence is

among his own army need not be taken very seriously: all the evidence shows that he had his men well in hand and used them as he liked. The sources inflate it to extol young Pompey.

[1] On the death of Cn. Pompeius, see *CAH*, ix. 264 (with n. 1).

[2] See p. 239 and *Note T* (p. 297). The Lucanians (of whom we do not hear any more) may have been in the same position. Judging by the part they took in fighting Sulla (cf. Livy, *per.* lxxxviii), we may suspect that the Samnites, during these years, were left in a semi-independent state.

conflicting. We are told that Sulla's laws were repealed[1] and, this ought strictly to imply the revalidation of those of Sulpicius; and indeed, we know that Marius technically assumed his Asian command.[2] On the other hand, we find in the *Periocha* of Livy the statement that 'nouis ciuibus S.C. suffragium datum est' under what seems to be the year 84; and a little farther on it is followed by the statement that freedmen were distributed among the thirty-five tribes.[3] Though the former phrase is vague, it can only refer to that redistribution which would make their votes effective.[4] It is difficult to believe that the Epitomator's statement does not come from Livy; and, supported as it is by the quite independent reference to freedmen, it must be accepted as implying that this important part of Sulpicius' legislation was not immediately revalidated: unless further evidence is found contradicting this, we must believe that, having attained his object, Cinna denied the promised reward to those who had followed him and refused to repeat the step he himself had taken at the beginning of his first consulship.[5] The explanation is that once again the Italians were to be sacrificed to *concordia*. The new rulers set out to attract their opponents by studied moderation: anyone who wished was allowed to leave and join Sulla (even his wife and children were not stopped) without being declared a public enemy. Sulla himself had been thus outlawed in the first days of the terror; yet this was quietly ignored—if not repealed—and negotiations with him continued for years: the Government desired nothing more earnestly than to persuade him to come to terms acknowledging its authority.[6] It is clear that this moderation

---

[1] App. i. 73, *ad fin.*, in very general terms.

[2] Flaccus was his successor (App. i. 75). Cinna, by regarding him as proconsul in 87 (Plut. *Mar.* 41, 6), implied that he ignored Sulla's repeal of Sulpicius' law.

[3] *Per.* lxxxiv—it may even be early 83.

[4] No one at any stage mentions the old *ciuitas sine suffragio*.

[5] Appian's passing and general reference to the repeal of Sulla's laws (see n. 1, above) cannot be regarded as evidence really contradicting this; the Epitomator's statement is also accepted (unfortunately without discussion) in *CAH*, ix. 264.

[6] Metella and her children: Plut. *Sulla*, 22, 1 f. (in hostile presentation: Κίννα δὲ καὶ Κάρβωνος (i.e. as late as 85/84!) ἐν Ῥώμῃ τοῖς ἐπιφανεστάτοις ἀνδράσι χρωμένων παρανόμως καὶ βιαίως—but we know of no actual names). Negotiations with Sulla are reported in all the sources. Cf. also the sending of Flaccus to Asia with instructions to Sulla to co-operate (*FGrHist*, iii B, Memn. fr. 24 (p. 353); cf. Plut. *Sulla*, 20, no doubt from Sulla's Memoirs and distorted by an attributed discreditable motive—unfortunately reproduced in *CAH*, ix). Sulla outlawed: App. i. 73; but

was, up to a point, very successful: despite the distortions of later tradition, we know of many noble families whose members 'collaborated' and held office under the *dominatio*, some of them even opposing Sulla right up to the end as the rebel he was.[1] It is against this background that we must see Cinna's behaviour towards the Italians: it was not that he wanted to drop the project of their redistribution and thus completely break faith—had his action appeared in this light, we should have expected the Italians to take immediate strong measures. But he did not want to pass it by force, against the will of the Senate, and he might well point out to the Italians that it would not give them sufficient security if he did so: for the sake of his policy and for their own, it might be better to wait until the Senate could be persuaded. Meanwhile the censors of 86/85 enrolled all the Italians they could find and—as important—performed a very useful *lectio Senatus*.[2] But, whatever may have been the intentions and explanations of the rulers, the Italians in fact had once more to wait until the Republic needed them.

By the end of 84 *concordia* was beginning to wear thin: in the East Sulla had overcome Fimbria; in Italy Cinna had been murdered by his army, and Carbo's desire to retain the sole consulship had brought him a stern rebuke from the tribunician college.[3] Moreover, the Italians were once again showing that it was a mistake to trifle with them: having been cheated of their reward for the sake of *concordia*, they were no longer so eager to support the régime: Rome's factional quarrels—a point Roman politicians never remembered—did not, as such, concern them. Thus Cinna, trying to embark his newly-levied men for Greece,

---

those who joined him were not declared *hostes* until after the invasion of Italy (App. i. 86), when it was inevitable.

[1] Detailed discussion is impossible here; but we may note the Valerii Flacci (*cos.* 86 and *princ. sen.*); Scipiones (*cos.* 83 and his son); Pisones (*q.* 83); Philippus and Perperna (censors 86—cf. Perperna's son, *pr.* 82?); Bruti (*tr. pl.* 83; *pr.* 82); P. Cethegus (in Africa); C. Caesar (nominated *fl. Dial.*); C. Fimbria (in Asia); C. Censorinus (who killed Octavius); Cn. Ahenobarbus (killed by Pompey).

[2] The figure given is 463,000 (Jer. *chr.*, p. 151 H)—which, with Italy unsettled, a large army absent in the East, and the greater part of the Eastern provinces inaccessible to the home government, is a creditable effort on the part of the censors. It is absurd to argue from this figure (as is sometimes done) that the Italians were not enrolled. For the *lectio Senatus*, cf. Cic. *dom.* 84, which incidentally informs us of the *praeteritio* of Ap. Claudius.   [3] App. i. 78.

was murdered by them,[1] and Carbo, when trying to raise levies in Italy, did not find things at all to his liking: he had to proceed to the extreme step of demanding hostages from the cities, and this caused such ill-feeling[2] that the Senate ordered him to abandon it.[3] It was perhaps now that, relying on the consul's unpopularity, young Cn. Pompeius, the son of Strabo, began to use his position as his father's heir in order to impede the consul's levies in Picenum. In this enterprise he succeeded so well that, after Sulla's landing in Italy, he felt enough confidence in his own popularity and the cities' dislike for the Government to imitate on a larger scale and on Italian soil the action that some distinguished Romans had taken in provinces where they had personal influence: to enrol a private army (chiefly from among his father's veterans) to fight in Sulla's cause.[4] Thus the faction that had owed its success to Cinna's recognition of the value of Italian support made the mistake of its enemies (and many predecessors and even successors) in over-estimating the political importance of the City of Rome, with its Plebs and its cliques, with the result that it failed to interest Italy in its survival. Confronted with this alarming development and with the failure of his coercive measures, Carbo at last persuaded the Senate to pass a resolution supporting the redistribution of the new citizens; some time later, a similar promise to the freedmen was also at last redeemed.[5] But now it was too late: Sulla was about to land in Italy.

Faced by the trained legions, skilful propaganda and Eastern resources of Sulla, the régime revealed its instability. Carbo, long unwilling even to share the consulship, had suddenly surrendered it to C. Norbanus and to a Scipio clearly not chosen for personal ability: *nobilis* and new citizen were to symbolize *concordia*.[6] Yet again and again the Italian levies showed no desire to face massacre and abandoned their leaders,[7] and Italian cities opened their

---

[1] Sources in *MRR*, ii. 60.

[2] Cf. the story of the heroic M. Castricius of Placentia (Val. Max. vi. 2, 10).

[3] Livy, *per.* lxxxiv.

[4] Cf. pp. 228–9 (above) and discussion in Ch. XI, pp. 266–9 (below): the rise of Pompey is traced there as a whole.

[5] Livy, *per.* lxxxiv; cf. p. 241 (with n. 3).

[6] *MRR*, ii. 62. On Norbanus, see Ch. IX, p. 202 (with n. 2).

[7] Livy, *per.* lxxxv; App. i. 87–88; Plut. *Sulla*, 28; *Pomp.* 7, *fin.* Cf. Gelzer, *R. St.* ii. 85.

gates to the usurper.[1] Moreover, the consuls, chosen for advertisement, proved unequal to their task, and their subordinates would not co-operate.[2] Carbo, therefore, who had probably shown himself throughout the real leader of his party, resumed the consulship for 82 and for his colleague chose the young son of Marius,[3] in spite of his youth and inexperience. Carbo, clearly, was to have supreme command; but it is the other consul who deserves comment. With Italy proving uninterested and unreliable, it was decided, as a last resort, to appeal to the old magic of Marius' name. It is interesting that it was Marius' son that was chosen— not, for example, M. Marius Gratidianus, his nephew, who combined with the name extreme popularity in Rome and the legal qualifications and practical experience for the consulship.[4] Apparently a nephew (both by birth and by adoption) was not enough, and even experience was not taken into account—for legal niceties clearly no longer mattered: the important thing was to entrust the last desperate levy and command to a homonymous son of the great leader whom the Italians had trusted.[5] Nor was this plan unsuccessful: Sulla had at last to go out of his way to woo Italian support. With characteristic boldness and ability to appreciate situations, he formally bound himself not to reverse the law giving the Italians full equality:[6] at least they should be assured that there was no material advantage for them in joining his enemies. Yet, in spite of this, the name of C. Marius aroused enthusiasm such as the Government had hitherto conspicuously failed to evoke: while during the first few months we hear of little resistance to Sulla and numerous desertions,[7] the year 82 (and perhaps the end of 83—we cannot be sure of exact chronology), on

[1] Starting with Brundisium—much to its profit (App. i. 79).

[2] Cf. Plut. *Pomp.* 7, 4.

[3] App. i. 87; Vell. ii. 26, 1; *vir. ill.* 68, 1. Cf. *RE*, s.v. 'Papirius', no. 38, coll. 1027–8.

[4] *RE*, s.v. 'Marius', no. 42. For his popularity, see Cic. *off.* iii. 80 f.: he wanted to become consul, but was only given a second praetorship (Asc. 84), we do not know when.

[5] Cf. App. i. 67: πιστὸς εἶναι δοκῶν. This cult of the dead leader, used to compensate for the shortcomings of his survivors, has obvious modern parallels.

[6] Livy, *per.* lxxxvi: 'foedus percussit.' Not having Livy, we cannot be sure precisely what Sulla did; but it must at least involve *iusiurandum*. It is worth noting that this step is taken so late (that does not usually emerge from modern accounts) and not straight after the landing: it was not a part of his original policy.

[7] Cf. *CAH*, ix. 272 f.

the contrary, is a record of desperate loyalty to the losing cause.[1]
Everywhere north of Campania—except for Picenum, dominated
by young Pompey—there was fierce fighting, and, as might be
expected, the Etruscan cities particularly distinguished themselves by loyalty to the name of Marius: Sulla's vengeance bears
sufficient witness to that.[2]

Sulla, perhaps more than any other Roman before Augustus,
compels admiration by his ability to learn, especially from his
enemies, and to recognize—and thereby anticipate—the trend
of events.[3] We have seen how he realized the importance of a
private client army long before C. Marius, to whom it owed its
existence; after his victory he showed that he had learnt another
important lesson: how to perpetuate the influence of that army.
Marius had discovered by accident the importance of his veteran
colonies (and especially of a cluster of them) as military bases for
his personal use, and he and young Pompey had begun the use
of veterans for the recruiting of armies against their private
enemies and the lawful government of Rome. Sulla now applied
these lessons and set out to surround Rome with a ring of colonies
that should both ensure his personal safety on his retirement
(which he may already have been planning)[4] and enable his constitution (the inauguration of which he naturally expected to
survive by some time) to continue, under his private surveillance,
with sufficient force at its disposal to discourage attempts to upset
it. That this was his purpose was probably recognized at the time.[5]
The colonies were planted, on the whole, close to Rome[6] and on

---

[1] Cf. Diod. xxxviii. 12.

[2] On the fighting, see *CAH*, l.c. Sulla's colonies and assignations: Gabba, *Ath.*
1951, 270 f. (cf. *Hist.* 1957, 346). See also Piotrowicz, *Klio*, 1930, 337. It is worth
noting that non-Latin *nomina* of magistrates under the Cinnan régime are nearly
all Etruscan, though the men are not always new citizens: thus M. Perperna and
his son; Burrienus; C. Carrinas; and C. Verres (*q.* 84)—see Schulze, *Lat. Eig.* 287.
On the names of P. Albinovanus and C. Norbanus, see Syme, *Rom. Rev.* 93. (On
Norbanus, see also p. 202, n. 2, with references—not that the matter is certain.)

[3] The secret of his *felicitas*, in politics and strategy, was adaptability and 'le tact
des choses possibles'. His error of political judgement in 88 (see above) is the
exception that proves the rule: he cut his losses and took his present chance, and
he never repeated the error.

[4] This rejects Carcopino's view (*Sylla, passim*) that Sulla's retirement was forced.
Most of his arguments have been refuted by various scholars.

[5] e.g. App. i. 96.

[6] Cf. n. 2 (above) and, on the whole question, Gabba, *Ath.* 1951, 229 f.

R

territory confiscated from cities that had supported Marius. But strategic usefulness was the overriding consideration, and neither were all the vast territories confiscated throughout Italy[1] given over to veterans,[2] nor did Sulla neglect the possibility of using some existing *ager publicus* or ownerless land for his settlements.[3] In Campania, where the land was good and the veterans would be close to Rome, there were nevertheless few settlements— further evidence (as we might expect from the comparative lack of fighting there) that Sulla on the whole found that region quite co-operative;[4] as for the *ager publicus* there, the Treasury was too dependent on it to permit its distribution.[5] Most of the settlements were in the north, especially in Etruria; and a colony was even sent to Corsica to watch the Marian settlement there as well as the Etruscan coastline.[6]

Sulla kept his word, and, except for the punishment of particularly obstinate opponents, did nothing to alter the status of the newly-enfranchised Italians. This problem now 'ceased to be a living issue'.[7] Naturally, it would take some time for the new citizens to find their level in the body politic. The Civil War, following upon the Social War, had cut across Italy, creating sharp divisions within each region and city and leading to violent changes in standing and property. Thus in Arpinum the Marii and Gratidii had followed the losing cause; the third of the great local families, the Tullii Cicerones, had probably been on the winning side and earned the reward of prudence: young M. Cicero, backed by a powerful ring of *nobiles*, was chosen to represent the interests of the nobility in a *cause célèbre*[8] and in due course became quaestor *suo anno*, though the family had not previously been prominent.[9] Statius, the Samnite, a leader of his people in the Social War, deserted them in time to be honoured

---

[1] Cf. App. i. 96; Flor. ii. 9; there is no evidence for Sullan colonies at Spoletum and Florentia; for the latter, on the whole, the evidence points the other way.

[2] Florus (l.c.) says 'sub hasta uenierunt'; and we know of the vast estates acquired by Sulla's followers.

[3] This was probably done in some of the cases marked as 'incerte' by Gabba (p. 272).

[4] See Gabba's list (cited p. 245, n. 2).   [5] Cf. Cic. *leg. agr.* ii. 81.

[6] Cf. *Hist.* 1957, 346.   [7] *CAH*, ix. 272.

[8] See below. The case of Roscius of Ameria was the making of Cicero's career.

[9] *RE*, s.v. 'Tullius', no. 28, coll. 824 f. Cicero's father seems to have acquired a town house! On young Cicero's own part in the Civil War, see *Rosc. Am.* 136.

by Sulla with citizenship and elevation to the Senate.[1] At Ameria, the leading family of the Roscii was divided against itself, with the senior Roscius apparently cautiously neutral and his more daring relatives eager in support of Sulla.[2] A Campanian called Gutta was an officer in the Marian armies;[3] yet a man called Ti. Gutta (and the name is very rare) appears almost certainly as one of Sulla's new senators.[4] In Picenum, fortunately, the interest aroused by young Pompey permits us more than glimpses of local conflict.[5] There might be honourable reasons for joining one party rather than the other; but the victor took no notice and punished *fides* as a crime.[6] As often in times of civil war, there might be less honourable reasons: criminals might seek safety in the enemy's ranks; but if they chose the right side, they returned to honour and affluence.[7] Although it is obviously true that some regions, owing to personal bonds or political considerations,[8] showed a decided preference one way or the other, the common 'regional' view of Italian allegiance,[9] whether or not combined with a 'class' view,[10] is a misleading over-simplification. The greater part of Italy, disillusioned by deceit and indifference, had not greatly cared for either party by 83: as far as Campania, Sulla met with little resistance, and we have seen that only the name of C. Marius finally aroused short-lived enthusiasm for Sulla's enemies. (For Sulla himself there was never much.) That is why

---

[1] App. iv. 25. On the interpretation, see Syme, *PBSR*, 1938, 23, n. 116 ('88 B.C.'); Gabba, *Ath.* 1951, 264 ('86 B.C.'). The most plausible view is perhaps that he made up for his rebel past by supporting the right side in the *bellum Sullanum*. Unless he did the latter, it is, in any case, hard to understand how he survived in honour and wealth. The year of his enrolment in the Senate cannot be deduced from Appian's text. Young Pompey provides a perfect parallel for a man who made up for a tainted past by prudence and energy of this sort.   [2] Cic. *Rosc. Am.*, *passim*.

[3] App. i. 90: he probably fought for *Italia* in the Social War (*Hist.* 1957, 345).
[4] Gabba, l.c. (no. 82).
[5] Plut. *Pomp.* 5–6, refuting the *ex parte* generalization of Cic. *Phil.* v. 44. Diod. xxxviii. 13 suggests similar scenes all over Italy.   [6] App. i. 96.
[7] We happen to have a good example in the case of Statius Albius Oppianicus of Larinum (Cic. *Cluent.* 24 f.).
[8] For the former: Etruria and Picenum, which we have examined; for the latter: Samnium, as appears from our accounts of the battle of the Colline Gate.
[9] e.g. Gabba, op. cit.
[10] As, to some extent, by Gabba. We know very little about the lower classes of Italy and have no right to generalize about their attitude; but it looks as though, on the whole, they saw no 'class interest' in supporting either party, but acted as occasion appeared to demand.

Sulla's victory, in spite of many local and individual changes, finally—except for Etruria—produced little political and economic change over Italy as a whole:[1] men might be proscribed and estates change hands; but the community, normally, was not much affected.

With Sulla's opponents everywhere punished and his supporters firmly in power, the question at once arose how this new Italy, centred in one man, would behave when that man disappeared from the scene and normal government was resumed. We have seen how the oligarchy had always feared the full enfranchisement of the Italians and the sudden increase in the number of voters. Now it was a fact and the future had to be considered in terms of it. Put more concretely, the question was: who would be the heirs of Sulla's monarchic power? The great families had, of course, taken care to keep up their connexions: the Roman franchise could no longer be conferred on Italians, as it could on men from outside the Peninsula;[2] but a noble's personal protection might still secure a man great advantages even in his home town.[3] However, the intricate pattern of personal relationships that had enabled the oligarchy to rule Italy—at least down to the Social War—and that might seem to hold out the only chance of absorbing the new voters into the *res publica* without violent changes—that pattern had broken down in the Social War, and years of civil war had prevented its restoration. Now military monarchy had temporarily captured the State, inevitably undermining still further the power and standing of the great families that had helped to bring it about and now had to bow to it. Once that monarchy was removed, the nobles might find their control over Italy gone and the new citizens acting without any respect for their guidance. Moreover, there must have been some fear of Sulla himself. Whenever a noble, from Tiberius Gracchus to the younger M. Drusus, had attained excessive power—even where, as in the case of Drusus, he fully intended to use it on behalf of the *boni*—the result had been to make them suspicious and turn them against him with the catch-cry of *regnum*.[4] Sulla, of course, had power

[1] Thus rightly Gabba (*Ath.* 1951, 229 f.), dissecting and in part refuting the modern tradition. Yet these facts are difficult to explain on his premiss.

[2] Cf. next chapter.

[3] e.g. Oppianicus (p. 247, n. 7, above); cf. also the case of Sex. Roscius (treated below).   [4] On this, see Allen, *TAPA*, 1953, 227 f.

such as no one in Rome had ever dreamt of, and he used it with flagrant arbitrariness and disregard of constitutional form. However close his connexion with the Metelli, some suspicion of his intentions and jealousy of his position must have reinforced the fears naturally felt about his *pessimum exemplum* and its consequences. It is possible that the Metelli decided to insure themselves by an alliance with Pompey, the young man who had just successfully defied the Dictator:[1] not to secure Sulla's overthrow,[2] which—with his work not yet complete—would not have profited them, but with the multiple purpose of attaching to themselves a young man of promise, resource and power;[3] of having the backing of his army and his skill after Sulla's retirement; and—this much we may concede—of delicately providing a counterweight to the Dictator's excessive power: it was an adaptation of the old game of politics to the new conditions. This, no doubt, is the real explanation for Servilius' change of heart about Pompey;[4] and we may connect it with Pompey's marriage to Mucia,[5] though we cannot date this important event precisely.[6]

That Sulla had no intention of making his *regnum* permanent is sufficiently clear from his constitutional settlement, framed so as to secure the rule of the Senate. Perhaps in order to disarm the suspicions of his associates, he himself took the consulship of 80, sharing it with the head of the house of the Metelli. Whether he abdicated his dictatorship is not known.[7] It is in this consulship that the *cause célèbre* of Sex. Roscius of Ameria was tried.[8] It was indeed an important case: Sex. Roscius, protected by some of the

[1] See Ch. XI, pp. 273-5.

[2] Thus Carcopino, *Sylla*, 186 f.—misdating all the crucial events (cf. below), but right in stressing the importance of the coalition.

[3] On his *clientelae*, see Ch. XI.

[4] Plut. *Pomp.* 14, 8; [Front.] *strat.* iv. 5, 1. The man is almost certainly P. Servilius Vatia Isauricus (*cos.* 79), a grandson of Metellus Macedonicus.

[5] Cf. Carcopino, l.c.

[6] Certainly between the death of his second wife Aemilia (early 81; cf. Plut. *Pomp.* 9, 4) and early 79, the year in which Mucia's eldest child appears to have been born (Carcopino's calculations on this point seem reliable). Within these limits we cannot specify. Carcopino arbitrarily chooses a late date, to suit his misdating of Pompey's triumph to 79 (on this, see *H*, 1955, 107 f.).

[7] Cf. App. i. 103, where the pretence of δημοκρατικὴ ἀρχή is stressed. His actual use of the dictatorship is not attested after 81, though Appian (l.c.) seems to imply that he formally retained it in 80. We cannot tell how far Appian may be trusted on this point.   [8] See *Note U*, p. 297.

greatest noble families, was being persecuted by Chrysogonus, a freedman of Sulla. The nobles could take no open action: Roscius could not be defended without an attack on Chrysogonus, and any such attack made by a prominent man might be regarded as a veiled attack on Sulla.[1] The defence was therefore entrusted to a young man of obscure family, but known to have great oratorical gifts and to have been on the right side in the late Civil War.[2] Cicero's speech *pro Roscio Amerino* quite clearly expounds the difficult position of the *nobiles* supporting his client[3] and the extreme importance of the case for the whole *nobilitas*: the bad Roscii, his opponents, 'cum multos ueteres . . . patronos hospitesque haberent, omnis eos colere atque obseruare destiterunt ac se in Chrysogoni fidem et clientelam contulerunt'.[4] The point at issue was nothing less than whether the *nobiles* could maintain their influence in the Italian countryside, or whether the Italians —the new voters and legionaries—should be encouraged to follow any upstart—even a freedman—who acquired sufficient *potentia*.[5] On the answer the future of the *res publica* depended, and Cicero was briefed to put the issue clearly and take a firm stand: it was thought that, if it were done with sufficient care, he, the unknown youth, could do it with impunity.[6] Yet it took courage to assail Sulla's henchman, and Cicero was later to be justifiably proud of his early speech.[7] He had the difficult task of convincingly dissociating Sulla from the deeds of Chrysogonus—for this was not only good policy and indeed the only hope of personal safety, but was in fact genuinely demanded by the situation: Sulla must be brought to see the inevitable result, if he continued to protect Chrysogonus and expose the real weakness of the *nobiles*—a result that (they might confidently expect) he was the last person to want. Moreover, the speech (probably published at once) was a proclamation to the peoples of Italy: with lashing irony Cicero contrasts the *fides* of a freedman,[8] a lawless, insatiable and

---

[1] Cic. *Rosc. Am.* 1 f.; cf. 124 f.

[2] Ibid. 136; 142. (Cf. p. 246, with n. 9.)

[3] See n. 1 (above): they are present but do not speak.

[4] *Rosc. Am.* 106. (Numbers in the rest of the notes on this chapter refer, unless otherwise indicated, to sections of this speech.)

[5] 'adulescens uel·potentissimus hoc tempore [the phrase is significant] nostrae ciuitatis' (6); cf. 133 f.   [6] Cf. n. 1 (above) and text.

[7] *off.* ii. 51.   [8] See n. 4 (above).

predatory creature,[1] involving his agents in perfidy[2] and crime,[3] in return for the cession of a share in the spoils,[4] with the sacred relationship between an Italian family and its hereditary protectors;[5] and he dwells on the way in which, in spite of the dangers involved, the *nobiles* have stood by their client Sex. Roscius, giving him due help and protection.[6] This is skilfully combined with sorrow over the miserable state of affairs in which danger to their lives prevents them from speaking in court, 'quem ad modum consuerunt', to defend the interests of their client.[7] The appeal is not only explicitly to the jury, but by implication to Sulla: if he wants the *res publica* to work, he must support the *nobiles* and not let his favourite exploit their weakness.[8]

It was true; and as Sulla was serious about the success of his *res publica*, it was bound to succeed: Roscius was acquitted.[9] Cicero had made his name and could hope for powerful support in the public career he was contemplating.[10] The *nobiles*, in a striking example, had vindicated their *fides* and their power to protect their clients. The case of Sex. Roscius was the *coup de théâtre* that alone could restore their prestige and influence in Italy after the shocks of Social War, Civil War and military dictatorship.[11] Now Sulla could retire, and the *boni*, protected by his veteran settlements and strengthened administratively by his reforms and morally by the case of Roscius, could resume the direction of the enlarged Republic according to the old pattern.[12]

---

[1] 6–8 ('nullo iure', 'quibus satis nihil est', 'praedam', 'scelere', &c.)—notice how he is thrown together with his accomplices, the 'bad' Roscii.

[2] 109 f.; cf. 23 ('procurator Chrysogoni'—with a social sneer).

[3] See n. 1 (above), and *passim*.

[4] 108: 'has manubias . . . concessisse'.   [5] 106.

[6] 1; 27 (Metella's help); 119; 144; 147 f.

[7] *Init.*, especially 5; cf. 148 f.   [8] Cf. 136 f.

[9] Plut. *Cic.* 3, 5–6 (embroidered).   [10] 3.

[11] It may be suggested (but must not be overstressed) that the speech also tactfully hints that the *nobilitas* and the Senatorial order are the champions of order and decency against the lawlessness of the present régime. There is perhaps just enough to cause such an impression without dangerous frankness (e.g. 139 f.); but, of course, in this respect the speech may have been retouched later.

[12] Gabba (*Ath.*, N.S. xxxiv, 1956, 137) has made the attractive suggestion that, if during the next decade they prevented the election of censors—for there is no reason to think that Sulla abolished the censorship—, it was in order to retard the complete enrolment of the Italians.

XI

EXTRA-ITALIAN *CLIENTELAE*—THE RISE OF POMPEY

IN the last two chapters our chief concern was with Italian *clientelae*—both civilian and military—and, by extension, with colonies of veterans both in Italy and abroad; and it was only incidentally that we referred to the non-Italian following of the great leaders and families. But now it is time for the latter to engage our chief attention. The Italian problem, for the moment, was settled, and settled (it seemed) much more satisfactorily for the ruling families than the opponents of Italian enfranchisement a generation earlier must have feared. There had been local upheavals, of course, as civil war split the local *nobiles* no less than the Roman nobility.[1] But the pattern had remained the same: with the defeat of Chrysogonus the fabric of the nobles' power in the Peninsula had been restored and, interwoven with the political ascendancy restored to them by Sulla and reinforced by his colonies of veterans, it seemed likely to resist any strain it might have to bear. The establishment of a local family as war-lords in Picenum; the growth of military *clientelae*, drawing men off into new and dangerous allegiances; finally, the creation, in the Cispadana, of a strong body of citizen manpower subject to provincial governors—these and similar flaws were to become more and more apparent as time passed. But the firmness of the oligarchy's belief in the solidity of the fabric is fully demonstrated by the pained astonishment that attended the discovery, in 49, of the fact that beneath the solid surface the fabric had rotted away.

Meanwhile, just as the explosion of the Gracchan reformism had drawn the Italians into the whirlpool of Roman politics, the more terrible explosion of civil war engulfed the extra-Italian nations. But before following these events in detail, we must first fill in the necessary background of this inquiry. We have seen

---

[1] Ch. X, pp. 246 f.: the cases of Arpinum, of Ameria and of Larinum, of Statius the Samnite, and a few others: we see that there is no essential difference between old *municipia c.R.* and newly-enfranchised cities.

how the extension of Roman power had led to a corresponding extension in the personal influence of the Roman oligarchy, the conquerors and administrators of the Mediterranean area; and how, since this personal influence necessarily depended on personality, it could—but need not—lead to dynastic spheres of influence like that of the Cornelii Scipiones or that of the Sempronii Gracchi. Hitherto we have considered this phenomenon in general terms, noting its general significance, and the rare occasions[1] when it assumes direct importance in Roman political affairs. We must now discuss an instrument we shall have to use extensively for the tracing of these connexions in detail: the study of names.

It is fortunate for the historian that this instrument is available —and, despite pitfalls,[2] may be used with some confidence—for a period in which these spheres of influence suddenly assume such great importance. This is entirely due to the historical accident of the importance of the name in Rome in expressing certain types of *clientela*. When a non-citizen became a citizen, the chief mark of the change was the acquisition of a Roman name, complete with *praenomen*, *nomen*, tribe and *cognomen*. The *cognomen* was often a convenient use of the old non-Latin name for distinguishing purposes; and it seems to have been generally used among new citizens much earlier than among the old.[3] In the case of a slave, the choice of a name presented no difficulty: from time immemorial it had been customary for him to adopt the *praenomen* and *nomen* of his master who, as *patronus*, henceforth took for him the place of that father (*pater*) whom in law he could not have:[4] the process of manumission was his civil birth. This, of

---

[1] e.g. some of the activities of the Gracchi (Ch. VIII) and perhaps the downfall of Scipio Africanus (Ch. VII).

[2] The obvious one of the haphazard nature and distribution of our evidence need only be mentioned—it cannot be avoided, but must be minimized by care in checking with other evidence. (An attempt—in an arbitrarily limited, but significant, field—is made in Appendix B.) More dangerous snares of interpretation are discussed below.

[3] These remarks on names do not claim to be more than an indispensable summary introduction to what follows.

[4] On this, cf. Introduction (on the *patria potestas* of the patron). The visible symbol appears in the 'filiation' in the name: compare 'M. Tullius *M.f.* Cicero' with 'M. Tullius *M.l.* Tiro'. This parallelism comes out clearly in the Greek usage —cf. Mommsen, *GS* viii. 547 f.

course, was by far the most common way in which new citizens were created. The other way was by naturalization of free aliens. Here also there was originally little difficulty: for in the early days of Rome, these would be of Latin or Italic stock, bearing names that either could be used in Rome just as they stood or required only slight phonetic Latinization to pass without excessive comment.[1] Right down to the enfranchisement of Italy, this practice continues: bearers of Italian names do not adopt new ones on naturalization; and this fact has been of great advantage to the social historian.[2] In fact, as Rome extends her influence so far that things Italian become familiar by contrast, even the process of Latinization ceases:[3] this is a mark of the extension of the Roman horizon.[4]

In due course the censors had to face the problem of naming new citizens whose original nomenclature—Greek or barbarian—bore no relation to that of Italy. This may first have arisen at a late stage of Roman history: the first recorded cases appear in the middle of the Hannibalic War,[5] and we have no reason to believe

---

[1] To take the most famous example: 'Attus Clausus' becomes 'Appius Claudius' (Livy, ii. 16, 4). Etruscan names, though more remote from Latin, were also thus Latinized: 'Cneve Tarchunies' becomes 'Cn. Tarquinius' (cf. Schulze, *Lat. Eig.*, *passim*). Whether these instances are historical (as, in outline, they probably are) or merely reflect the tradition and practice of (say) the fourth century B.C., does not matter for our purpose.

[2] Attested instances in the late Republic, just before the general enfranchisement: M. Annius Appius; P. Caesius; T. Coponius; L. Cossinius. (For details, see Appendix B.) Our masters in the use of this evidence are Münzer and Syme. In the provinces this practice does not seem to be uniformly continued; thus among the Oscan Mamertines we find M. Cassius (probably named after a Roman) and the Pompei (Percennii): see Appendix B. (The case of the Ovii is uncertain, as Cicero, in the context, gives only names borne before enfranchisement. Perhaps Messana was influenced by its Greek surroundings.)

[3] As early as 456 (if tradition is to be believed) we get a *nomen* in *-ienus*, and from the late second century *nomina* in *-anus*, *-a(s)*, *-es*, &c., become increasingly common, penetrating to the highest dignities with M. Perperna (*cos.* 130) and his son (*cos.* 92, *cens.* 86). Gardthausen (*RhM* 1917–18) plausibly argues that the name of a new citizen depended on the censor who enrolled him and that the increasing number of *nomina* reflects the censors' increasing difficulty in coping with the expanding register. We may add increasing familiarity with what had once been strange. Where the citizenship was given by *priuilegium*, the name may, of course, have been laid down by the People. But this does not affect our general argument.

[4] For this, see Klingner, 'Italien' (cited in Bibliography).

[5] Sosis the Syracusan and Moericus the Iberian in 211 (Livy, xxvi. 21, 11); Muttunes the Carthaginian in 210 (Livy, xxvii. 5, 7—see below).

THE RISE OF POMPEY

that it had been done much earlier than this emergency. A method
was readily found for dealing with these cases. Helped, no doubt,
by the fact that the names were of a type with which Rome was
chiefly familiar in the case of slaves, and considering the fact that
the *beneficium* of citizenship would establish links of *clientela*, the
Romans decided that the new citizen should, like the slave, bear
the names of his benefactor, with his old name as *cognomen*. Thus
Muttunes the Carthaginian, sponsored by the consul M. Valerius
Laevinus, became M. Valerius Muttunes.[1] The only difference
was that this was *clientela* in the wider sense, not giving *patria
potestas* or other legal and ritual rights to the patrons, and that
the new citizen in this case, therefore, has no substitute for
filiation.[2]

Thus the precedent was set, and there is no reason to believe
that under the Republic, while instances of the enfranchisement
of non-Italians remained few, it was ever substantially departed
from.[3] Even so, the name of the new citizen was not mechanically
fixed. As even in the case of slaves—hedged round with ancient
ritual—the usual practice could be modified and a name other
than that of the patron given (with the latter's consent) in order
to mark some special obligation or connexion,[4] it is not surprising
that the name of the naturalized alien need not always be that of
the man immediately responsible for his enfranchisement; for
such responsibility might well be formal rather than real. Even
the plebiscite giving the citizenship to Muttunes was carried by

[1] Livy, l.c.; Ditt. *Syll.* 585, 32 f. (giving the correct form of the name). The later
signum (see *RE*, s.v.) almost certainly goes back to these 'retained' *cognomina*.

[2] This, of course, has proved valuable in tracing foreign descent from names as
given in inscriptions. It does not, however, seem to have been fully investigated
how far the absence of filiation applies to Latins and other Italians, as it certainly
seems to apply to non-Italians. In their own names and languages most Italian
tribes express filiation (*RE*, s.v. 'Namenwesen', 1657); if their families had *conubium*
with Rome, there is no *a priori* reason why they should not continue to do so on
naturalization: this ought to be investigated as a matter of fact.

[3] Under the Empire, of course, hosts of new 'provincial' *nomina* appear, especially in the West (cf. Schulze, op. cit. 48 f.). Under the Republic there seems to be
only one known instance of this, against many of the older practice (see Appendix
B (i)): it is that of the Cyprian slave(s) brought home by Cato, and it is mentioned
as a special case. Varro, *l.L.* viii. 81 may indicate the existence of other such names;
but the passage is corrupt and too difficult for useful discussion.

[4] The best-known case is that of M. Pomponius Dionysius (Cic. *Att.* iv. 15, 1).
This development is probably late.

a tribune;[1] but—justly enough—he took his name from Laevinus.
What we see in this first known instance is confirmed by several
cases we know in the late Republic: thus the poet Archias received
the citizenship through the incorporation of the community of
Heraclea, and he took the *nomen* of the family of his Roman
friends, the Luculli;[2] P. Cornelius Megas (?), enfranchised by
Caesar at Cicero's request, was named after Dolabella who had
conveyed that request; C. Avianius Philoxenus, in a somewhat
similar position, took the name of a friend of Cicero's who was no
doubt his particular protector.[3]

It is clear from this that, while the appearance of the *nomen* of
one of the great Roman *gentes* in the provinces *prima facie* shows
(except where it is too common or can most reasonably be
ascribed to later incidents) a connexion between the provincials
and the *gens* concerned—a connexion that can often be even more
clearly traced by additional attention to *praenomina* and (where
it is known) the tribe[4]—it must not be held that the enfranchisement was directly due to a member of that *gens*. To this must be
added another caution: towards the end of the Republic, at least,
it had become fairly common for provincials to adopt Roman
names as evidence of Romanization, no doubt to impress both
their less enterprising fellow-citizens and Italian residents. It
does not seem that there could be any legal exception taken, provided they were careful enough not to claim Roman citizenship
(i.e. membership of a tribe)—in which case, at least after 95, they
could be attacked under the *lex Licinia Mucia*, though perhaps
they had a good chance of escaping prosecution.[5] In the East this
practice of adopting Roman names later becomes quite common,
and instances occur in the late Republic;[6] and we have the

---

[1] Livy, xxvii. 5, 7.

[2] Cic. *Arch.*, *passim*. His *praenomen* (Aulus) is obscure.

[3] Cic. *fam.* xiii. 36 and 35.   [4] On all this, cf. Appendix B.

[5] On the *lex Licinia Mucia*, see Ch. IX, pp. 213 f. There is nothing to suggest
that its application was limited to the city of Rome; however, we have no evidence
that anyone got into trouble over it in the provinces, and Cicero's comments on
Cornelius Artemidorus and Cornelius Tlepolemus (see Appendix B) imply that one
could hope to get away with false claims. On the adoption of Roman-sounding
names without arrogation of *ciuitas*, see below. Münzer (*RE*, s.v. 'Diokles', no. 39)
thinks that it 'allerdings strafbar war, aber in der Praxis öfter vorkam'; but he gives
no evidence for the first part of his statement.

[6] Cf. Hatzfeld, *Trafiquants*, 10 f. (quoting Plut. *Pomp.* 24, 5—hardly relevant—

attested case of a Sicilian Greek.[1] But that it was not merely
the invention of some clever Greeks, but done throughout the
Empire, is made clear by the evidence we have for its occurring
in Spain. Cicero reports that some Fabii of Saguntum were
enfranchised by Q. Metellus Pius and Pompey,[2] and this in a
context where the names given seem all to be those borne before
enfranchisement; and this is decisively confirmed by the men
from Ilerda in the *turma Salluitana*, who are certainly using
Roman names before enfranchisement—even on this official document.[3] Again the names chosen—unless they are common ones
like 'Cornelius', no doubt chosen for its very inconspicuousness
—must indicate some connexion with the Roman *gens* concerned;[4] but again we must not at once ascribe the enfranchisement to a member of that *gens*. The upshot of all this is that,
while we may use the appearance of a *nomen* (provided it is distinctive) in the provinces as a mark of the influence of the Roman
gens concerned, we must not assume that the bearer of such a
name is necessarily a Roman citizen[5] or, if he is, that he was
enfranchised by a member of that *gens* or even through the influence of such a member: for he may, on enfranchisement,
simply have retained a name he was already using, or adopted
that of an old patron of his family.

This preliminary study enables us to use our evidence with
greater precision than has sometimes been done and makes it
more (and not less) valuable for our purpose. To illustrate the
influence of the great Roman families in the provinces with precise data, I have collected the evidence of names for the Iberian
Peninsula and for Narbonensis (which is the old Transalpina, for
purposes of this study) and used a conveniently accessible work
of reference as the basis for analysing a test sample of the African

as evidence for its rarity in the time of the Republic). The Roman name adopted
was often incomplete: it looks as if this had been done on purpose, to avoid the
appearance of illegal arrogation of citizenship.

[1] Diocles 'Popilius cognomine'—see Appendix B, under *Incerti*; cf. p. 256, n. 5.
The connexion of this practice with the *signum* is obvious (cf. p. 255, n. 1).

[2] *Balb.* 50 f.

[3] *ILS*, 8888. Other suggestions have been advanced to explain this; but in view
of the facts here set out no other explanation is needed.

[4] On the Fabii in Spain, see Appendix B. Cf. ibid. for other examples.

[5] Our evidence, such as it is, perhaps entitles us to assume it unless we have
proof to the contrary; but the point is not usually of any great importance.

province. The results are set out in Appendix B.[1] To show the significance of the analysis, a list of representatives of the *gentes* analysed who are known to have served in those provinces under the Republic has been added, with brief comments and (where this was thought useful) references to later connexions. Though the figures do not always turn out precisely as one might expect on the strength of this list, correspondence is sufficiently marked to be very significant[2] and to show that its absence is probably due to special causes—particularly the hazard of survival in the evidence and our ignorance of large portions of the provincial *fasti* under the Republic. Thus the most common *nomina*[3] in the Spanish provinces, if we omit some irrelevant ones, are (in this order) Fabius, Aemilius, Licinius, Sempronius, Caecilius, Pompeius, Junius and Antonius.[4] Except perhaps for the last, none of these names is unexpected. The primacy of the Fabii—known also, as we have seen, from the literary sources— is borne out by their long record of service, and the appearance of the Sempronii in this prominent position also confirms the literary records; nor does either of these *gentes* gain such a place in our other two provinces.[5] In Narbonese Gaul, Pompeii, Licinii, Domitii and Caecilii appear among the first five: all of them *gentes* whose representatives we know from other evidence as having not only served in the province, but actually taken a political interest in it;[6] and the Pompeii—as we should expect—vastly predominate. In our slice of Africa, Caecilii and Calpurnii (among the first three in the list) may take us right back to the Jugurthine War. And throughout, many detailed observations underline the significance of the analysis.[7]

[1] pp. 309 f. [2] Striking instances are noted in the Appendix.

[3] Counting *certi* and *incerti* and including all the names with more than 100 representatives. (For a warning on the figures, which cannot claim to be precise, see Appendix.)

[4] Cornelii and Valerii have not been included, as they are ubiquitous and give no scope for fruitful analysis. *Nomina* borne by emperors have also been omitted, except for Sulpicii.

[5] For more detailed analysis and comment, see Appendix B.

[6] See below. The *nomen* 'Aemilius', holding second place in Gaul, is another of the ubiquitous ones. It was, however, thought worth including because, despite its promiscuous extension, it never succeeds in wresting first place from more lawful claimants.

[7] Particularly revealing is the occasional significance of *praenomina*: see Appendix B under Aemilii, Caecilii, Domitii, &c. For the tribe, see Memmii.

It will be seen at once that a large number of these connexions go back to the second century. This is obvious where the *gens* concerned later declined: Fabii, Fulvii and Sempronii show no consul during the period covered by the analysis, yet are prominent in the tables. Thus it is clear that, even where later connexions exist and are known, those going back to the second century must be given their full weight—particularly in Spain, known for personal loyalty.[1] These connexions have sometimes been ascribed, over-schematically, to enfranchisement by various commanders in the middle of the second century.[2] This implies belief in large-scale extensions of the Roman franchise in the provinces in the second century—a belief untenable in view of what evidence we have.[3] We have already seen that no such theory is needed to explain the connexions, and the error is due both to failure to notice this and to the misleading analogy of the custom, traceable only from the very end of the second century, which permitted commanders in the field to bestow the franchise for merit. As we have seen in the case of Muttunes and others, the idea of the franchise as a reward for outstanding service to Rome in war was not new,[4] any more than (as we saw in the last chapter) was the idea of settling veterans in the provinces in which they had fought. Yet at the end of the second century these two ideas are given new and revolutionary extensions; and in both cases this seems to be due to Marius. We have already noticed this in the case of the veteran colonies.[5] In the case of the franchise, Cicero in his speech in defence of Balbus (who owed his citizenship to such a grant) mentions grants of citizenship by commanders—apparently without reference to Senate and People—as quite a common practice. It seems to have become the

---

[1] Cf. Premerstein, *Werden*, 54 (with n. 1).

[2] Thus, unfortunately, Münzer; e.g. *RE*, s.v. 'Fabius', no. 100; 'Iunius', no. 31.

[3] Especially (in a general way) the long Italian struggle for the franchise. The illegitimate offspring of Roman soldiers in 171 were only given Latin status (Livy, xliii. 3, 1 f.—even that was a great innovation); and apart from the special case of the priestesses of Ceres (Cic. *Balb*. 55) we know of no instance of enfranchisement between that date and the age of Marius (see below). Isolated cases will have escaped our notice; but mass enfranchisement cannot be postulated, where the evidence can be more satisfactorily explained in another way. (Cf. Hatzfeld, op. cit. 9.)

[4] See p. 254, n. 5. The Praenestines could have had it in the Hannibalic War, but refused (Livy, xxiii. 20, 2)—no doubt to the regret of their descendants.

[5] Ch. X, pp. 237–8.

custom for the People no longer (as, for example, in the case of Muttunes) to insist on individual scrutiny of such cases, but to pass an enabling law under which commanders could, *de consilii sententia*, make such grants themselves. We happen to know of a few such enabling laws and, as our knowledge of them is in each case purely fortuitous (i.e. they are not recorded for their own sake as political events), there were probably many more;[1] though this right did not (at least during our period) become an automatic adjunct of *imperium*.[2] We are not specifically told when it was first conferred on a holder of *imperium*: the first example we know of—the *lex Julia*—may well be the first case of it, passed (as has been suggested)[3] to enable loyalty to be signally and immediately rewarded at a most critical time. In any case, Cicero's list of such grants of citizenship[4] does not, except for those made by Marius, go back beyond the Social War.

The case of Marius, however, is the exception that proves our rule. For we know of only two instances of enfranchisement by Marius that certainly go back to the time before the Social War: that of T. Matrinius of Spoletum and that of two Camertine cohorts.[5] The former can hardly have been isolated, though, of course, after the test case had been decided, the others were not brought into court. In fact, as we have seen,[6] the relevant legislation of Saturninus was probably passed (in part, at least) with the purpose of legalizing the position of such men, to whom Marius had given the citizenship. This implies that he had not been entitled to do so,[7] and that this was so is shown by the case

---

[1] The *lex Julia* of 90 B.C. (*ILS*, 8888—giving us the formal conditions); the *lex Gellia Cornelia* of 72 B.C. (Cic. *Balb.* 19 and *passim*); the *lex Munatia Aemilia* of 42 B.C. (*FIRA*, 55, l. 10). Cf. Mommsen, *Str.* iii. 135. Perhaps we should add the *lex Calpurnia* (Sisenna, fr. 120 P).

[2] This is clear from the case of the *lex Gellia Cornelia*, passed only after the end of the Sertorian War.   [3] *RC*, 131.

[4] *Balb.* 46 f. (see Appendix B). The case of Alexas of Heraclea, enfranchised by P. Crassus (*cos.* 97), is a possible exception; but his birthplace suggests that his services also were rendered in the Social War, in which Crassus was a legate. The enfranchisement may have been completed (despite Cic. *Arch.* 11) in 89, when Crassus was censor and would thus have an excellent opportunity.

[5] Cic. *Balb.* 46 f. The case of M. Annius Appius of Iguvium, coupled by Cicero with that of the Camertines, may belong to the same time; but we know neither that nor anything else about it. It is not unlikely (if one may speculate) that it was similar to that of Matrinius; and perhaps there were others (see text). Cf. *Balb.* 48, *init.*

[6] Ch. IX. p. 206 (with n. 3).   [7] Cf. Ihne's comment (quoted p. 206, n. 3).

of the Camertine cohorts, whom he enfranchised after the battle with the Cimbri, excusing himself later with the famous aphorism that he had been unable to hear the voice of the law for the din of battle.[1] The fact that none of these grants was later challenged, even under the *lex Licinia Mucia*,[2] merely proves the *auctoritas* of Marius, as confirmed in the case of Matrinius. It does not prove that he had acted lawfully.

We have now seen that there is no proved case of what we may call 'imperatorial enfranchisement' before Marius;[3] that Marius seems to be the first commander to exercise such a right, and that even in his case it was recognized to be illegal, though nothing could be done about it; and we may add that, as far as we know, Marius thus enfranchised only Italians, whose interests throughout he had much at heart. It was probably only in the new situation confronting Rome in the Social War that such a right was actually conferred on commanders; and after this it may indeed have been common, but was not by any means taken for granted.[4] It is therefore not until the Social War, which brought the citizenship to the whole of Italy south of the Po, that the enfranchisement of non-Italians begins to become at all common. With the citizen body suddenly doubled, the addition of a few (or even a few hundred) provincials at a time no longer appeared heinous or formidable.

Thus we may take it that there was no mass enfranchisement by commanders in Spain and elsewhere in the second century— nothing more than the establishment of personal connexions. This, however, leads to an important conclusion: it was (as far as

---

[1] Plut. *Mar.* 28, 2; *apophth. Mar.* 5; Cic. *Balb.* 46; Val. Max. v. 2, 8. Valerius asserts that Marius' action was 'aduersus condicionem foederis', which would mean that the treaty with Camerinum contained a clause like that with the Iapudes and those with some Gallic tribes (Cic. *Balb.* 32). But Cicero says (s. 47) that it had no such clause. Valerius (or the excerptor on whom he drew) seems to have merely misunderstood Cicero's meaning in s. 46, taking him to imply that Marius broke the treaty. His later phrase 'uerba iuris *ciuilis*' shows that we must not expect accuracy.

[2] Cic. *Balb.* 48, discussed in Ch. IX.

[3] C. Marcius, ἀνὴρ Ἴβηρ ἐκ πόλεως Ἰταλικῆς (App. *Iber.* 66), an officer in 143 B.C. (not in *MRR*), was probably *Hispaniensis*, not *Hispanus* (notice his birthplace and cf. L. Marcius (pp. 117 f., above) in the Hannibalic War).

[4] Cn. Pompeius Strabo's application of the law to non-Italians may have given offence (cf. Gelzer, *Nob.*, 78—though he withdraws it in *R. St.* ii. 72). When the Senate, in 78, signally honours Asclepiades and two others for outstanding services, it does not give them the citizenship (*FIRA*, 35). That was still carefully guarded.

we can see) not until about the end of the century that provincials began to use Latin names,[1] and even after this such a name was *usually* adopted only on enfranchisement; we may therefore notice the tenacious loyalty with which individual provincials remain attached to the families of their benefactors, even where these families disappear from the limelight—a loyalty which is exhibited, often after several generations, in the choice of their Latin names. This observation is the complement of the more obvious one of the endurance of public and communal connexions, and it gives content to the latter. The basis of Roman control over the provinces was, in an important sense, not political, but personal—as that of Roman control over Italy had been. The method, ingrained in the Roman character and the oligarchic *Weltanschauung*, had not changed over the centuries. Rome had imposed her pattern on her world, and the latter—especially the tribal societies of the West—easily adapted itself to it. As we shall have occasion to see in detail (and as a study of the period after 70 B.C. reveals more clearly), it was precisely in the last struggles of the Republic that opportunities for extending personal connexions in the provinces were increased and eagerly created. And provincial society, brought into the pattern generations earlier, welcomed and used these increased opportunities. The mystery of the cohesion of the Empire through successive civil wars, and despite manifest misgovernment, now becomes more intelligible. The Empire was based on the personal loyalty of leading men throughout the provinces[2] to leading families at Rome, and this attachment proved to be independent of political vicissitudes and, as we have seen, on the whole unaffected even by the fortunes of those families.[3] It was the foundation on which the emperors were to build.[4]

---

[1] The men from Ilerda in the *turma Salluitana* have fathers with unpronounceable barbarian names; I have not found a second-century example from the East either.

[2] That it was, on the whole, the leading men with whom such connexions were formed is clear from the outlook of the Roman nobility and by comparison with conditions in Italy. We can also often see it in the cases of enfranchisement known to us (cf. Appendix B).

[3] This, of course, is only generally true and needs qualifying.

[4] Cf., e.g., Ramsay, *Social Basis of Roman Power in Asia Minor*, Aberdeen, 1941. Unfortunately, Ramsay does not consider the Republican period, which might have yielded some interesting information.

We must now turn to tracing the increasing importance of extra-Italian *clientelae* in Roman internal politics. We have seen the first signs of it in the age of the Gracchi—the private army of Scipio Aemilianus, recruited abroad as well as in Italy; the importance of the hereditary Asian connexion for both Tiberius and Gaius Gracchus; these and minor signs have been noticed as they arose.[1] For the next generation, however, interest centres on the Italians: extra-Italian connexions merely retain, on the surface, the position they had previously held.[2]

There is, however, a new spirit abroad: the sudden importance of the Italians must, to some clear-sighted men, have pointed forward to the coming importance of the provinces. It is perhaps in connexion with Transalpine Gaul—that new field, on the threshold of Italy, now laid open to Roman penetration—that we may notice the first signs of this. Three men are particularly associated with the conquest of the Transalpina: C. Sextius Calvinus, Cn. Domitius Ahenobarbus and Q. Fabius Maximus (the son of Q. Fabius Maximus Aemilianus).[3] The first of these left no important descendants,[4] and his efforts to establish his interests there were ultimately in vain. Only the *castellum* called after him bears witness to them.[5] The other two, however, established a lasting connexion. As we have seen, 'Domitius' is one of the most common names in the province, and we shall soon see that this is correlated with an active and maintained political interest. Fabius also left no prominent descendants: after his glorious career and that of his cousin, the son of Servilianus, the family goes into a decline, from which it is only rescued by the successful adherent of Caesar.[6] Yet the rise of the latter shows that the family was not extinct, and we have seen how it maintained its connexions with Spain. In the Transalpina, too, the name is reasonably common,[7] and through an odd accident—of

---

[1] See Ch. VIII. Cf. Ch. IX, *init.*, for Jugurtha's connexions.

[2] See Ch. VII, where, in illustrating the ordinary working of *clientela*, we could choose our examples indiscriminately from the whole period studied.

[3] They were consuls in 124, 122 and 121 respectively. (See *MRR*, i, for these and the following years.)

[4] The sickly orator (Cic. *Br.* 130; *de or.* ii. 246), who must be his son, did not get beyond the praetorship (*MRR*, ii. 18).

[5] On Aquae Sextiae, see especially Strabo, iv. 1, 5 (getting its status right).

[6] *RE*, s.v. 'Fabius', no. 108 (the *cos.* 45).

[7] Fifty examples (see Appendix B), giving it a place a quarter of the way down the

great historical importance—we happen to know of the persistence of the link through the generations of obscurity: when the Allobrogan envoys in 63 were considering betraying the Catilinarian conspirators, they turned in the first place to the obscure Senator Q. Fabius Sanga, the most active of their patrons.[1] Unfortunately we know nothing about this man;[2] but it is clear that he was the senior Fabius alive at the time, and it must be this (as is generally observed) that was the cause of the connexion.

So far we have noted nothing but the ordinary examples of provincial *clientela*, where it was cultivated. It is in the case of the Domitii Ahenobarbi that we may for the first time perhaps observe something more. The consul of 122 had had more to do with arrangements in the newly-conquered territory than any other man: he had stayed there for several years, thoroughly pacifying it, building the great highway that bore his name, and fortifying it with an armed post on the strategic site of Narbo, an old Gallic settlement.[3] Perhaps before he had finished his work, powerful agitation in Rome led to the establishment of a citizen colony at Narbo. This agitation was led by a pushing young demagogue, L. Licinius Crassus (the orator), who took the chief part in founding the colony.[4] The opposition of the Senate was fierce, and to some extent this may have been due to the influence of Domitius, who disliked such interference. In any case, it seems that his son was in the end also put on the board for the founding

list of names investigated. But we must remember that Caesar's adherent (see last note) will have had something to do with that. Fabius Maximus, the philosopher from Narbo, is worth mentioning (see Appendix). [1] Sall. *Cat.* 41, 4.

[2] Münzer (*RE*, s.v. 'Fabius', no. 143) denies that he can be descended from Allobrogicus and suggests descent from a freedman of the family. We should need to have some parallels to such an odd case of a client's inheriting his patron's *clientelae* (with the family not even extinct), before we could accept this view. Speculation seems unprofitable. (On C. Fabius, Caesar's legate in 49, see *Note V*, p. 298.)

[3] Sources in *MRR*, i. 516; 522; 524. Broughton accepts (p. 524) the *communis opinio* that Domitius 'organized the province' (of Transalpina); but there is no evidence for any such organized province before the Cimbric War, which first showed the need for permanent supervision. Even after this we often find proconsuls of Cisalpina (or perhaps Citerior) in charge—e.g. C. Flaccus in 85 and 83; Lepidus in 77 (see below); Pompey in 77 and after (see below); L. Licinius Murena (?—see Allen, *CP*, 1953, 176 f.). On the duration of Domitius' command, see Appendix B (ii), s.v. 'Domitius'. [4] Sources in *MRR*, i. 528.

of the colony.[1] We have already dealt with the importance of the colony (such as it is) to our inquiry.[2] But we must here notice the fact that—as Domitius had perhaps feared—Crassus seems to have taken an interest in the newly-conquered territory and tried to establish his influence there: the Licinii take fourth place in our list of *nomina* (greatly outnumbering the Domitii), and this remarkable position can only in part be due to the Murenae. When Crassus went to a province in 95 in his consulship (retaining it in 94), it was that of Gaul—probably including the Transalpina.[3] It is no doubt to this beginning in 119 and its sequel that we may ascribe the notorious enmity between the orator and the son of the conqueror of Gaul, who himself took a serious interest in the province: thus we know that he prosecuted M. Junius Silanus for injuring a Gallic *paternus hospes*.[4] This enmity between the two who had perhaps jointly founded Narbo came to a head in their censorship in 92, when Domitius launched a personal attack on his colleague, which, after an undignified scene, led to their abdication.[5] In the long run, the Domitii won: the loyalty of Massilia in the Civil War of 49 is the climax of their sustained interest in this region.

If the Domitii took their provincial connexions seriously enough to be led into grave *inimicitiae* on their account, it was probably because Cn. Ahenobarbus could read the signs of the age of Marius. But it is not until the Civil War that began in 88 that we find the military and political importance of the provinces decisively demonstrated.[6] We have seen how Marius and his friends sought refuge in the province of Africa and finally found it in his veteran colony of Cercina, which became the springboard

[1] Accepting the most common interpretation of the coins of Crassus and Domitius (*MRR*, ii. 644).

[2] See Ch. VII, p. 163.

[3] Broughton (*MRR*, ii. 11 and 13) thinks it was 'probably Cisalpine Gaul', where there certainly seems to have been some fighting (Cic. *inv.* ii. 111—not to be rejected without further evidence). But cf. p. 264, n. 3, on the status of Transalpina: it is quite likely that Crassus simply had 'Gallia' as his province.

[4] Cic. *div. in Caec.* 67.

[5] Cic. *Br.* 164 *et al.*; cf. *Fasti Antiates*. We cannot tell, of course, whether Ahenobarbus was more concerned with Narbo Martius or with the natives—as for the former, the importance of colonies was soon fully to emerge in the case of Marius. Our evidence, such as it is (see above), shows interest in both.

[6] On another far-sighted man, Cn. Pompeius Strabo, see below.

for his victorious return.[1] The praetor M. Brutus escaped to Spain, where his family was influential.[2] With the victory of Marius and Cinna, it was their enemies' turn to flee, and at least two of them imitated the idea of Marius and M. Brutus and sought refuge in provinces with which they were connected, both of them by hereditary and personal links: Q. Metellus Pius fled to Africa and M. Crassus to Further Spain.[3] Metellus could not only count on the effect of his father's name, but had himself served under his father in the Jugurthine War and established personal contacts.[4] Crassus, similarly, had served in Ulterior under his father, the consul of 97.[5] For some time both of them probably remained quiet, being content to have saved their lives. But when the home government began to totter, these ambitious nobles embarked on the plan of collecting private armies from among their clients to fight against the lawful government. This decision is a milestone in the history of the decline of the Roman Republic. Sulla's march on Rome[6] had shown how the new 'military *clientela*' had burst the bonds of the oligarchic Republic; Metellus and Crassus, taking the next step, showed how the Roman noble's ordinary connexions—even those outside Italy— could be converted into this new and dangerous form of *clientela* —a possibility that may have been glimpsed before, but was now tested and henceforth recognized and established. In Metellus' case there was at least some legal cloak for his actions: he was still proconsul of the Roman People (a dignity which could perhaps —despite the precedent of the elder Q. Caepio—not be legally revoked)[7] and might therefore claim the right to enrol an army— though hardly against the wishes of, and in obvious hostility to, Senate and People.[8] But when Crassus, probably encouraged by

---

[1] See Ch. X, p. 237.

[2] Gran. Lic. 23 B. Cf. Appendix B for Iunii in Spain.

[3] Plut. *Cr.* 6, 2; 4, 1 f. On what follows, see Wiehn, *Ill. Heer.* 29 f.

[4] Sall. *Jug.* 64, 4. A. R. Burn (*CR*, lxiii, 1949, 52–3) has drawn attention to the achievements and fame of Q. Metellus Pius.

[5] Plut. *Cr.* 4, 1. On his host Paciaecus, probably *Hispaniensis*, see Appendix B, 'Incerti', s.v. 'Vibius'.   [6] See Ch. X, p. 234. Cf. Wiehn, op. cit. 61 f.

[7] As Appian points out (i. 80); this, at any rate, was later to be Sertorius' claim.

[8] Metellus and his force will have had something to do with the rising against the lawful governor of Africa, C. Fabius Hadrianus (cf. Wiehn, op. cit. 30). If so, however, he cannot (as Wiehn says, rejecting Linden's excellent emendation Λιβυστίδι in App. i. 80) have been in Liguria at the time.

the success of Metellus in the neighbouring province, followed
his example, it was pure usurpation, such as was to be only too
common before very long.

The example of Metellus and Crassus was to have grave consequences for the Republic; but at the time Metellus was proconsul, thereby masking—as we have seen—the enormity of his
action,[1] while Crassus' army was not large enough to attract
much attention.[2] Public imagination was chiefly struck by
another young man, Cn. Pompeius, the son of Strabo. His father
had left him, both literally and in the political sense, a *damnosa
hereditas*, and it was only some powerful support—probably also
due to his father—that protected him from serious harm after the
victory of Marius and Cinna. Having safeguarded his life and
fortune, he seems to have stayed in Rome, and early in 84 we find
him in Cinna's army preparing to embark for Greece.[3] But when
he saw the bad morale of the army and their leader's lack of
authority, he withdrew to his estates in Picenum, alleging that his
life was in danger.[4] Secure among his father's adherents, he seems
to have lived quietly until Sulla's landing in Italy.[5] We may take
it—though our sources, concentrating on the praise of Pompey,
do not say so—that he soon heard how Sulla had been joined,
among other great men who flocked to his camp,[6] by Crassus and
Metellus with their armed forces. Not content now with obstruct-
ing the levy of the proconsul Carbo, he decided to imitate their
example and raise a private army. For this he was particularly
well placed. For his father had (as we have seen) considerable
private estates in Picenum and many of his veterans lived there.
These and his private clients now flocked to the standard of
Pompey who, exercising almost royal power, soon collected a
whole legion and in due course (we are told) two more.[7] This

---

[1] We do not hear of much comment, though he had collected στρατιὰν οὐκ
εὐκαταφρόνητον (Plut. *Cr.* 6, 2). See Burn (cited p. 266, n. 4).

[2] 2,500 in Spain, according to Plutarch (*Cr.* 6, 1). But not all will have accompanied
him to Africa, Greece and Italy.   [3] See Gelzer, *R. St.* ii. 81f.; *Pompeius²*, 31 f.

[4] Plut. *Pomp.* 5, 1. There seems to be no support in the sources for Chilver's
view (*OCD*, s.v. 'Pompeius') that he had been there all the time.

[5] This is Gelzer's view, and it accords with Plutarch's account and Livy, *per.* lxxxv.

[6] Plut. *Pomp.* 6, 1. Metellus before Pompey: App. i. 80. Crassus joined Sulla in
Greece (Plut. *Cr.* 6, 2).

[7] On his exercise of power, see Plut. *Pomp.* 6, 3. (Cf. Dio, fr. 107.) Three legions:
ibid., s. 4; at first one: App. i. 80.

force was far larger than those of Crassus and (probably) even Metellus, and it soon acquired cohesion and prestige by some victories over the Government's levies.[1] Clearly, the young adventurer had to be taken seriously, and Sulla, forgiving his father's ambitious intrigues and his own past connexions with the Cinnans, took him very seriously indeed, going to extremes of flattery.[2] Moreover, Sulla seems to have grasped the basis of Pompey's power and decided to continue, for the sake of his own victory, the young man's policy of building on his father's connexions. Strabo, as consul in 89, had passed the famous law giving Latin status to the Transpadanes—an important and populous region whose support was worth having—and this established a relation of clientship.[3] Sulla now took advantage of this by sending Pompey (after he had completed his task in Picenum and adjacent districts) to Cisalpine Gaul, under the supervision of the experienced Q. Metellus Pius, and the result was very much to his satisfaction—as well as to Pompey's.[4] After Sulla's victory, the young man—too dangerous to be ignored, and too powerful in his own right to be dispatched, as a minor war-lord could be[5]—had to be captured for the oligarchy: he was married to Aemilia, daughter of Sulla's wife Metella by her first marriage (with Scaurus, the *Princeps Senatus*).[6] This was the reward of audacity and good fortune: by the unscrupulous use of his *Hausmacht* he had forced his way into the inner ring of those about to restore the oligarchic constitution. Despite Sulla's own serious intention, his settlement, imposed by an aristocratic adventurer and his client army upon a conquered country, with the help of minor dynasts and their private armies—this return to an 'ancestral constitution', wanted only by a small faction, was a farce and an abortion. The

---

[1] Plut. *Pomp.* 7.

[2] App. i. 80; Plut. *Pomp.* 8.

[3] *Lex Pompeia*: Asc. 3. Cf. Ch. X, p. 229. For the persistence of the connexion, see Cic. *Att.* v. 11, 2.

[4] Plut. *Pomp.* 8, 4 f., exaggerating Pompey's merits. Appian's narrative may serve as a corrective. For an account of the campaigns, see Gelzer, *R. St.* ii. 92 f. That the Cisalpina favoured the Marian government is only to be expected; as it happens, it is explicitly stated (App. i. 86, *ad fin.*). It is very likely that the presence of Pompey was at least partly responsible for the revulsion of feeling there (App. i. 92, *init.*).

[5] The *nouus homo* Q. Lucretius Ofella (Plut. *Sulla* 33; *et al.*).

[6] Plut. *Pomp.* 9. On the persons concerned, see *RE*, s.vv.

example of Sulla and of his helpers—Q. Metellus Pius, M. Crassus and Pompey—bore more fruit than his settlement.[1]

The immediate result was to scatter the remaining Marian leaders; and, as is to be expected, several went to provinces in which they could count on personal connexions—some, indeed, with official commissions from the Government. C. Norbanus may not have wanted more than a refuge in Rhodes; for the East, recently organized by Sulla, could hardly be tampered with. In any case, he seems to have lived there quietly for some time, before committing suicide to avoid extradition.[2] Two leaders were more enterprising: M. Perperna and Q. Sertorius. Perperna seems to have left Italy at an early stage in the fighting—we do not hear of him in connexion with it—and went to Sicily, to defend this important corn-growing province.[3] His grandfather had fought (and won an ovation) there in the first Sicilian slave war.[4] Sertorius, praetor in 83, was certainly assigned the province of Citerior and went there after the fall of Suessa (probably in 82).[5] The assignment was due to his familiarity with the province, where he had served under T. Didius.[6] His success in combining the leadership of the natives with the position of a Roman commander is too well known to need renewed discussion and documentation.[7] The remaining Marian leaders went to Africa,

---

[1] Cf. Syme, *Rom. Rev.* 17. That even the *nobilitas* was united in favouring Sulla and opposing the Mario-Cinnan régime is a palpable untruth, produced and fostered by the survivors after Sulla's victory. Before 83 Sulla had very few avowed partisans. (Cf. Ch. X, pp. 240 f.) On the feelings of the Equestrian order and the Italians there is less doubt, as no one proceeded to falsify the records.

[2] Livy, *per.* xcv; App. i. 91 (note 'ὕστερον'); Oros. v. 20 f. On his connexions in the East (he had served as quaestor under M. Antonius), see Münzer, *RE*, s.v. 'Norbanus', no. 5. His suicide was a public reproach to the Rhodians (App., l.c.).

[3] Broughton (*MRR*, ii. 67) makes him 'Marian governor of Sicily' as *pr.* 82. This, however, goes beyond our information: the date of his praetorship is unknown (Diod. xxxviii. 14 cannot be pressed). It is possible that he was sent to Sicily, as Sertorius was to Spain, because of his connexions there; this would explain the lack of references to his presence in Italy at any stage.

[4] *MRR*, i. 492 and 498–9 (rightly accepting the notice in Florus). That our Perperna (*RE*, s.v. 'Perperna', no. 6) was a grandson of this man can hardly be doubted (though Broughton does not give his filiation).

[5] Sources in *MRR*, ii. 63.

[6] Plut. *Sert.* 3 f. Cf. Wiehn, *Ill. Heer.* 39.

[7] See especially Schulten's *Sertorius* (Leipzig, 1926) and Treves in *Ath.* 1932; Gabba, *GS*, 77 f., unsuccessfully tries to depict Sertorius as the champion of *Italici* in Spain—there is no basis for that.

not (as far as we can see) on account of any personal connexions, but because there was good hope that the influence of Marius' name would help the *epigoni* of his cause.

To deal with the chief remaining threat to the new régime—the forces in Sicily and Africa—Pompey was sent to Sicily with propraetorian *imperium* and six legions,[1] probably already with the intention that, if successful, he should cross to Africa. He was now, as we have seen, in the inner ring of the new oligarchy, and this—and his successes in Italy—partly explains why it was he who was given this mission of responsibility and confidence. Q. Metellus Pius, who might have appeared a more suitable person, stayed in Rome to hold a consulship in 80. Perhaps Pompey's very youth and lack of standing was an advantage in the eyes of the Dictator who, even if intending from the start to re-establish the oligarchy, would hesitate to give a prominent member of it such independent power as this commission would have conferred.[2]

Sicily was seized almost without a blow and some leaders of the opposing party lost their lives.[3] Pompey was blamed for cruelty,[4] but the favourable sources insist that he punished only those whom he could not help punishing and even aided others in saving their lives.[5] In fact he probably showed neither excessive bloodthirstiness nor excessive clemency—he was neither a Sulla nor a Caesar. Throughout, he was clearly eager to extend his personal influence among the chief citizens, and a middle course was therefore indicated. In this effort he was highly successful: his *hospites* and his enfranchised clients among local notables are freely attested. The interest he thus acquired in Sicily was to

[1] Sources for (and discussion of) his official position in Gelzer, *R. St.* ii. 88 f. The number of his legions is known for the African war (Plut. *Pomp.* 11, 2): if he left some garrison forces in Sicily, he may have had more there. It seems clear from the size of these forces that a crossing to Africa was envisaged from the start.

[2] Cf. Dio's comment on Sulla's distrust of well-known men (fr. 108), which, though perhaps influenced by the experience of Imperial Rome, may be based on tradition.

[3] Plut. *Pomp.* 10, 2 f.; cf. Cic. *leg. Man.* 30 ('non terrore belli, sed consili celeritate'); Münzer, *RE*, s.v. 'Perperna', no. 6. For the death roll, see Livy, *per.* lxxxix; *et al.* The fate of Perperna is not clear: he is said to have joined Sertorius in Spain both on this occasion and after the defeat of Lepidus in 77. See *RE*, l.c., and (oddly giving both, without discussion) *MRR*, ii. 67 f. and 91.

[4] Plut. *Pomp.* 10; Val. Max. vi. 2, 8; *et al.*

[5] Plut., l.c.; cf. Cic. *leg. Man.* 61: 'singulari innocentia, grauitate, uirtute.'

have important consequences.[1] In the meantime, however, he had to think of the immediate future. He had seen—none better—the importance of a solid basis for power, and, when Sulla next ordered him to proceed to Africa to deal with the Marians there, he left his brother-in-law Memmius in charge of Sicily to secure his position against whatever might come.[2]

In Africa the Kingdom of Numidia was torn between two loyalties—to Sulla and the house of the Metelli, and to the memory of Marius. In 88–87, when Marius had tried to find refuge there, the governor of Africa had been hostile, and King Hiempsal, after some cautious tergiversation, finally decided to follow his lead and back what he no doubt thought the winning cause.[3] There can be little doubt that this determined his position in the years following; for the restored Marians would not forget his actions. In any case we may safely assume that it was Hiempsal who sheltered Q. Metellus Pius and assisted him in collecting his large army against a Marian governor of Africa.[4] When, in 82, the defeated Marian leaders flocked to Africa, they had the support of a Numidian pretender Hiarbas, who seems to have driven out Hiempsal. Pompey defeated the Marians (led by the young Cn. Ahenobarbus) and the forces of Hiarbas and restored Hiempsal to his throne.[5] Again a portentous precedent had been set: the forces of a client kingdom, normally and traditionally used by the Roman State against its enemies,[6] had for the first time been employed to decide a Roman civil war. With the Roman State divided against itself, personal attachment must take precedence

[1] On Sthenius and the Verres trial, see below. For enfranchised clients, see Appendix B.

[2] Plut. *Pomp.* 11, 2—'ein Stück charakteristischer Familienpolitik' (Gelzer, *R. St.* ii. 94). Pompey obviously could not hope that Memmius would stay in charge of Sicily for long and (trusting to his own *celeritas*, on which we have so many admiring comments) no doubt hoped to have finished in Africa before Memmius could be superseded. On the vexed question of the stemma of the Memmii, see references in the Appendix.

[3] Cf. Ch. X, p. 237; Plut. *Mar.* 40, 3 f.; App. i. 62.

[4] See above (pp. 266 f.).

[5] Gelzer, *R. St.* ii. 94–95 (with sources). That Bogud, King of Mauretania, assisted Pompey (Oros. v. 21, 14—i.e. Livy) is, in the circumstances, natural enough. Hiempsal's son Juba was to be Pompey's friend and Caesar's enemy in the Civil War of 49: Pompey knew how to cultivate his connexions. (Cf. Dio, xli. 42, 7 and Caes. *b.c.* ii. 25: Curio had tried to annex Juba's kingdom in 50.)

[6] See Part I, *passim.* Cf. Sands, *Cl. Pr.* 103 f. and Appendix A.

of loyalty to the State as a whole, and the client king becomes the arbiter of Rome's destiny, while nominally the vassal of a Roman noble. From Hiempsal and Hiarbas the road leads straight to Deiotarus, Juba and Cleopatra.

The Civil War that may be said to have lasted from 88 to 81 thus marks a turning-point in our inquiry. We may sum up the new situation by saying that all types of foreign connexions—in Italy, among Italians overseas, in the provinces, and even with kings beyond the provinces—suddenly acquire a new importance as reservoirs of military power that could be used by ambitious individuals against the Roman State. Hitherto (even, as we saw, in the case of Marius before 88) only sources of wealth and prestige or more recently—in the case of the Italians—means of exercising political pressure, they have now been absorbed into the new 'military *clientela*' that developed as the combined consequence of Marius' army reform and the Social War. This development cannot be ascribed to any one man—Pompey or another.[1] Far-sighted men had for some time been assiduously and even jealously cultivating foreign connexions, whose increasing importance first began to appear in the age of the Gracchi. When the Social War re-created, for a time, the conditions of the Hannibalic War, in the new circumstances brought about by Marius' professionalization of the army, military *clientela* naturally emerged as a decisive weapon in internal power politics.[2] With the Civil War immediately supervening, the new weapon was bound to be used at once without limitations of patriotism or geography. Sulla may be regarded as the connecting link: the man who first led an army of citizens against Rome and who later combined with a foreign enemy against the Roman Government.[3] But the cases of Q. Metellus Pius, Crassus and Pompey show how natural and inevitable the development was.

It is, however, undoubtedly true that it was Pompey who most

---

[1] As Wiehn (Sulla and Pompey) and to some extent even Gelzer (Cn. Pompeius Strabo) tend to do.   [2] On this see Chapter X.

[3] The 'stab in Sulla's back' (thus *CAH*, ix) by the Cinnan government is a creation of apologists (ancient and modern) and probably ultimately derived from Sulla's Memoirs. (See Ch. X, p. 241, with n. 6.) In fact it was Fimbria who defeated Mithridates, and the latter was snatched from certain destruction by Sulla, who allied himself with the King against the common enemy—the Roman government (cf. p. 281, with n. 2, below).

clearly recognized the potentialities of the new weapon, and who showed the least hesitation and the greatest skill in at once playing the game of politics according to what he saw to be the new rules. We have seen the success this brought him in Italy and the way in which he seized the chance of extending his personal power in Sicily. It was after his African victory, used to the same effect,[1] that the first test of his new power came—a test that, as his Sicilian dispositions show, was not unexpected. For Sulla at once ordered him to dismiss five of his six legions, hand over the remaining one to a successor and return to Rome as a *priuatus*:[2] having won the war for Sulla, he was to return to the station befitting his age, without visible reward; and it is clear that his previous marriage to Aemilia (who was by then dead)[3] would not have saved the young adventurer from being discarded, once he was no longer useful and had been robbed of his unlawful power. It was against this that Pompey had wanted to provide, and with his usual political skill he took the next step in his game.

There was naturally dissatisfaction among the soldiers at their unceremonious dismissal, and Pompey thereupon wrote to Sulla that he was 'forced' by the army to disobey his order—rather as his father had once been 'forced' to retain his command against the successor sent by the Senate.[4] This was to become Pompey's favourite method: to mask his desire for personal power and advantage by pretending unwillingness and manœuvring until he was 'forced' to accept:[5] he had already shown a similar technique in refusing to join Metellus in Gaul until Metellus invited him.[6]

Sulla was at first astounded: as we have seen, it may well be that he had chosen Pompey for his particular task precisely because he expected no danger from this young man; and now he was faced with insubordination. At first he thought of attempting a punitive expedition;[7] but wiser counsels prevailed: on a truer

---

[1] See p. 271 (with notes). For Pompei in Africa, see Appendix B: they are a fair proportion.

[2] Plut. *Pomp.* 13, 1.   [3] Ibid. 9, 3.

[4] App. i. 63; Livy, *per.* lxxvii. The similarity is pointed out by Gelzer (*R. St.* ii. 95 f.). Pompey's reluctance is vividly painted by Plutarch (*Pomp.* 13, 1 f.).

[5] Most notably in 66 (Plut. *Pomp.* 30, 5 f.); cf. Caelius' immortal characterization (Cic. *fam.* viii. 1, 3); also Sallust's 'oris probi, animo inuerecundo' (*hist.* ii. 16).

[6] Plut. *Pomp.* 8, 4 f. Cf. Drumann in Drumann–Groebe, s.v. 'Pompeius', p. 336: 'Man mußte ihm danken, daß er sich fügte, und der Schein war gerettet.'

[7] Plut. *Pomp.* 13, 3—the famous παίδων ἀγῶνες.

appreciation of the position he had to admit defeat.[1] Not that
Pompey had used threats—he was too shrewd for that. But the
situation was clear at once to a man like Sulla. Pompey had six
legions in Africa, and they had hailed him *imperator* and ap-
plauded his imitation of Alexander the Great;[2] nor could there
be any doubt that they would follow him loyally in a war waged
—allegedly—on their behalf as much as on his own. Sicily, full
of Pompey's clients in leading positions, was under Pompey's
brother-in-law Memmius (we do not know with what forces, but
there must have been some); and he also had a fair-sized fleet,
collected for the African War,[3] and could count—at least while
things went reasonably well—on the assistance of the Kings of
Numidia and Mauretania. Thus he would be unassailable in
Africa and strongly entrenched in Sicily—both important corn
provinces—with good chances for an offensive against Italy. In
Italy, however, Sulla's régime was not by any means secure:
confiscations and proscriptions had established the conditions
for revolt—as Lepidus was to see—and a renewal of war, against
a brilliant young commander with a solid block of personal power
in Picenum in the heart of the Peninsula, good connexions in
Cisalpine Gaul and enthusiastic support from among the popu-
lace, could not be lightly faced. Moreover, in the West there was
Sertorius, ready to fan the embers of rebellion.

This has been set out at length, as the true nature of this crisis
—of the conflict between Sulla and Pompey and the sources of
Pompey's strength—is obscured by Plutarch's idealizing account
(though he gives us all the relevant facts) and has not found satisfactory treatment in modern works.[4] Yet it is of great significance,
not only for our study, but as a turning-point in the history of
the Roman Republic. Pompey's coolly unscrupulous approach to
power politics—his exploitation of personal power and the private army—was seen to be justified by success. The triumph

---

[1] Plut. *Pomp.* 13, 3: 'πυθόμενος τἀληθῆ'—not only in Plutarch's trivial sense.
Plutarch comments on the popular enthusiasm for Pompey.

[2] Ibid. 12, 3; 13, 5 (the name 'Magnus'); 2, 1–2 (cf. Sall. *hist.* iii. 88). To the
number of the legions (and any auxiliaries he may have had) we must add the
deserters from Domitius' army—at least 7,000 (Plut. *Pomp.* 11, 2).

[3] Plut. *Pomp.* 11, 2: 120 *naues longae* and 800 transports.

[4] Even Gelzer's masterly study is here insufficient. I have briefly surveyed the
situation in *H*, 1955, 115, n. 6.

which, once his legions were encamped outside Rome, he extorted from a resentful Sulla and an unwilling Senate[1] may be taken as the symbol of his victory, not only over Hiarbas, but over *mos maiorum* and the traditional Republic which Sulla was at this very time trying to restore;[2] but the triumph was only the flourish underlining the message of his successful defiance of the law and the ruler. The lesson of the last decade had been learnt more quickly and thoroughly than might have been expected. Having shown his worth, Pompey had again to be secured by a marriage alliance—with Mucia Tertia, connected with the Metelli.[3]

It was M. Aemilius Lepidus, the Patrician consul of 78 and friend of Pompey,[4] who first tried to apply his lesson. He appealed to the old *Mariani* (especially the dispossessed Etruscans) for aid in overthrowing Sulla's settlement.[5] What we must note, however, is that this was not his only political weapon. Indeed, it seems that he had laid careful long-term plans during his consulship and that it was only his rash march on Rome, perhaps due to excessive confidence in his immediate strength, that led to his quick collapse; though credit must be given to L. Philippus, who secured timely and vigorous action by the Senate,[6] and to Pompey and Catulus, who brought about the rebel's military defeat.[7] In 78 Lepidus had secured for himself the province of Gaul, probably both Transalpina and Cisalpina.[8] This not only gave him a recruiting ground in the peculiar 'citizen province', but a footing in the province beyond the Alps (whose importance, as we have seen, had been recognized before) and a direct land connexion, from his base at Faesulae, with Sertorius in Spain,

---

[1] Plut. *Pomp.* 14. Sulla's suppressed resentment was shown when he ignored Pompey in his will (ibid. 15, 2 f.). The exact importance of the by-play with the soldiers' dissatisfaction (ibid. 14, 5; [Front.] *strat.* iv. 5, 1) is uncertain: it was probably meant to appeal to the *boni*—as it did ('einen ausgezeichneten Eindruck' —Gelzer, *Pomp.*², 40)—and to impress upon the soldiers the fact that Pompey was their master. For the tribune Herennius, see Ch. X, p. 235.

[2] Cf. Gelzer, *R. St.* ii. 97 f.

[3] Cf. Carcopino, *Sylla*, 188 f. (independent of his main thesis).

[4] Plut. *Pomp.* 15, 1; *Sulla*, 34; though Sulla's opposition to him is probably exaggerated.

[5] Sources in *MRR*, ii. 85 f. Note especially Plut. *Pomp.* 16: ἤδη πολλὰ τῆς Ἰταλίας κεκινηκότα.

[6] Sall. *hist.* i. 77.   [7] Plut. *Pomp.* 16; *et al.* See below.

[8] Transalpina: App. i. 107; that he legally held the Cisalpina is clear from what follows. (Cf. p. 264, with n. 3; p. 265, n. 3.)

who seemed to be in process of completing the conquest of the Iberian Peninsula.[1] As Lepidus was fomenting unrest—and probably planning revolt—even in his consulship in 78,[2] this choice of province cannot be accidental. We know that he held the Cisalpina with a strong army under M. Brutus—the husband of Servilia and father of the tyrannicide—and that he established his own headquarters in Etruria—probably near Faesulae, a centre of discontent, where he would be in close touch with him.[3] There can be no doubt that Lepidus had important connexions in the Cisalpina: his great-grandfather, the great *Princeps Senatus*, had been there in his consulship in 187 and built the Via Aemilia that bore his name,[4] and Reggio (Regium Lepidi) and the modern Italian province of Emilia still symbolize the survival of his memory. As *iiiuir* in 183 he had helped to found the colonies of Mutina and Parma and in 177 that of Luna, and in 173 he had been on a commission to distribute land in the Cisalpina;[5] and the connexions thus formed and maintained no doubt profited his descendant. M. Brutus, his legate, had his base at Mutina,[6] where he was shut in by Pompey; and when, after his surrender, Pompey granted him his life, he fled to Regium Lepidi—probably the place most likely to be stirred to enthusiasm for a Lepidus even at that stage—and had to be killed on Pompey's orders, no doubt for continued subversive activities on Lepidus' behalf.[7]

---

[1] Cf. *MRR*, ii. 90.

[2] App. i. 105; Sall. *hist*. i. 55. On the chronology, see Holmes, *Rom. Rep.* i. 363 f.

[3] Plut. *Pomp*. 16, 2 f.; *Brut*. 4, 1 f.; Sall. *hist*. i. 79.

[4] Livy, xxxix. 2, 10; Strabo, v. 1, 11 *fin*.

[5] *MRR*, i. 380; 399; 409–10. He had also visited Transalpine Gaul as an envoy (ibid. 421); but there is no evidence of permanent connexions (the number of Aemilii cannot be regarded as significant). On his activities in the Cisalpina, see Ewins, *PBSR*, 1952, 54 f.—an excellent survey, but unfortunately without any political discussion. That the *Princeps Senatus* is the great-grandfather of the revolutionary (not his grandfather) seems likely in view of the time that separates them. We cannot tell whether Cic. *Phil*. xiii. 15 is accurate.

[6] Plut. *Pomp*. 16, 3; *et al.*

[7] Cf. Gelzer. *Pomp*.², 44 f., with sources. Brutus himself may have inherited connexions in the Cisalpina, where he may have gone into hiding after Sulla's final victory (he had been active against Sulla in 83—see *RE*, s.v. 'Iunius', no. 52—and would hardly have been pardoned in the first terror): a M. Brutus had fought there as *cos*. 178; moreover, his own wife was the granddaughter of the inglorious Q. Servilius Caepio (*cos*. 106). M. Brutus in 81, then, may perhaps be added to the lengthy list of prominent Romans who found refuge in times of trouble with their provincial friends.

Pompey himself, when asked by the Senate to collect an army at short notice, will have called on his obvious and conveniently placed reservoir of Picenum.[1] We may add that he will also have brought into play his Cisalpine connexions, inherited from his father and confirmed by himself, which had served him well under Sulla.[2] In any case, his success was quick and decisive, cutting Lepidus' carefully established connexion with the Transalpina (and Spain) and converting his defeat into complete disaster.[3] Lepidus fled to Sardinia, where he died ingloriously. A large part of his forces, under Perperna, escaped and joined Sertorius.[4]

The first attempt to exploit the resources of the Gallic provinces—in particular, the citizen manpower of the Cispadana—in support of a military *coup* against the State had failed. It was not, as it has sometimes seemed to moderns, a negligible incident: an Aemilius Lepidus at the head of a large army, backed by both the Gauls and a large part of Italy, and supported by a considerable faction in the Senate, was a very real danger. His strong support in high places, mentioned by Sallust, is confirmed by the fact that elections for the consulship could not be held in 78.[5] The names of the consuls finally elected—a Lepidus and a Brutus, related to M. Lepidus and his chief lieutenant—are revealing: double coincidence is unthinkable. It is clear that the *Sullani* had to pay a high price to buy off the proconsul's supporters; and the bargain was probably fully described by Sallust.[6] It was mainly his own rashness that led to his defeat; and even so, the very means used to overthrow him may be regarded as ominous: the proconsul of Gaul was defeated by the Sullan veterans under Catulus and young Pompey's private power in Picenum and the Cisalpina. The former were naturally a wasting asset, while the latter, at present used on behalf of the State, boded it no good

[1] Gelzer, l.c. (last note).

[2] See p. 268 (with n. 4).

[3] See p. 268, n. 4. Cf. Gelzer, l.c., for a good reconstruction of the campaign.

[4] Plut. *Pomp.* 16; Livy, *per.* xc; App. i. 107, *fin.*; *et al.* We do not know of any Sardinian connexions of Lepidus or Perperna; it was in any case the only escape.

[5] Sall. *hist.* i. 77—*oratio Philippi*—, especially ss. 5, 6, 22.

[6] Mam. Lepidus Livianus had not been aedile and was disliked by the People: before being elected in the very year of his kinsman's disgrace, he had already suffered a *repulsa* (Cic. *off.* ii. 58). Cf. Sall. *hist.* i. 86. The consuls later refused to fight against Sertorius (Cic. *Phil.* xi. 18), no doubt not through mere cowardice.

for the future. Young Caesar, though he would have nothing to do with Lepidus, whose character he knew,[1] undoubtedly learnt from his plans and their failure.

Meanwhile Pompey, at the age of twenty-eight, was in a dominating position; and when he suggested—informally—that he might be sent to join Q. Metellus Pius in the war against Sertorius, the suggestion, welcomed by the enemies of the Metelli (notably L. Philippus, Pompey's old protector), obviously could not safely be rejected: in spite of Catulus' scruples he was sent out *pro consule*, and Italy, for a time, could breathe freely.[2]

During the next few years Pompey pacified Gaul and (with the help of Metellus) Spain. With the military details we are not concerned. What interests us is the extension of his personal influence over the remaining Western provinces—except for Sardinia, relatively unimportant—: after the Cisalpina, Sicily and Africa, he now extends his power over the Transalpina and the Iberian Peninsula. This is not accidental: we have seen that Pompey's experiences and actions reveal the deliberate acquisition and use of personal power. In Spain, moreover, he had inherited connexions from his father,[3] and Pompey, having learnt his lesson in Picenum and the Cisalpina, was not the man to neglect them. We have the evidence in the names of men enfranchised by him and the numbers of their descendants,[4] and above all—though circumstances were to rob him of the fruit of his labours in Gaul—in the continued loyalty of Spain: when, in 65, Cn. Calpurnius Piso was sent to govern Citerior in the course of machinations by Pompey's enemies in the Senate against

[1] Suet. *Jul.* 3.

[2] Sources in *MRR*, ii. 90. Philippus had been an enemy of Scaurus (head of the 'Metellan' faction) in 91, and later (it seems) had supported the Cinnan régime against Sulla (the protégé of the Metelli). He had defended Pompey after Cn. Pompeius Strabo's death (Cic. *Br.* 230). Echoes of a 'whispering campaign' against Metellus, obviously contrary to the facts, survive in Plut. *Pomp.* 17–18.

[3] Cf. the decree on the *turma Salluitana* (*ILS*, 8888). It is scarcely possible to accuse Strabo of aiming at personal power in Spain (cf. Stevenson, *JRS*, 1919, 95 f.): this, in 89, would hardly be thought of. Wiehn (op. cit. 61) describes this act of his as 'mehr ein Mögen als ein Können'; we may perhaps think it a long-term investment.

[4] See Appendix B: especially the Balbi in Spain and the family of Pompeius Trogus in Gaul; note that in Gaul the Pompei are second and in Spain seventh on our list—the latter rather remarkable in a province where so many families already had vested interests.

his interests, he was soon murdered.[1] The Spaniards, known for fanatical loyalty,[2] were worth winning; and Pompey, new to a field in which generations of Roman nobles had staked their claims, used all the arts of diplomacy to substitute for their network of peaceful private connexions his own conception—learnt in civil war—of political allegiance.[3]

In Rome, needless to say, the prospect of Pompey's further aggrandizement was viewed with alarm by some members of the oligarchy—foremost among them no doubt the Metelli, who could not easily forgive his behaviour towards the leader of their house.[4] It seems that his enemies succeeded in preventing him from receiving adequate supplies, in the hope (we may suppose) that this would enable Metellus to win the chief victories and eclipse Pompey's fame. This, at any rate, is what actually happened: for a long time Metellus was far more successful than Pompey. But Pompey was not the man to submit to such behaviour. At the beginning of 74 the Senate received a letter from him that was to have a dominating influence on Roman politics during the next few years:[5] he announced quite plainly that, if he were not better supported, he would return to Italy with his army—followed (he hinted) by Sertorius. That would be disastrous; and Pompey could be trusted, in this case, to mean what he said. Moreover, in the East war had just broken out again, and the consul L. Lucullus hoped for the chief command; therefore Pompey must be kept away and busy.[6] Thus the consul, cousin of Q. Metellus Pius and enemy of Pompey, suddenly became active in collecting supplies on his behalf. But that was only for the

---

[1] *ILS*, 875; Sall. *Cat.* 19, 1 f.; Asc. 92: 'occisus . . ., ut quidam credebant, a Cn. Pompei clientibus, Pompeio non inuito.' There is no serious reason to suspect Pompey himself.

[2] See *Note V*, p. 298.

[3] See last note. Cf. Cic. *leg. Man.* 13; *Balb.* 9 (stressing his integrity). The method used—severe punishment for irreconcilables and generosity towards those who could be won over—seems to have been the same as in Sicily in 82.

[4] See above. Pompey, who could hardly afford to make new enemies, tried to atone for this once he had got what he wanted (Plut. *Pomp.* 19, 5); but Metellus, on the whole, would not go near him (ibid.), except where military necessity demanded it.

[5] Sallust's version (*hist.* ii. 98) seems to be substantially accurate; cf. Plut. *Pomp.* 20, 1; *Luc.* 5, 2; *Sert.* 21, 5.

[6] Plut., ll.cc. On the chronology of the Mithridatic War, see *MRR*, ii. 106 f.: we have no serious reason for rejecting Plutarch's account of events at Rome.

moment: meanwhile long-range plans could be made to defeat this young adventurer, now clearly a public danger.

The nature of these plans is worth detailed investigation, for the evidence, fragmentary as it is, permits us to some extent to reconstruct them. Briefly, the intention was to make Pompey unpopular in Rome, while using the time of his absence in Spain in order to build up an overwhelming power in the Eastern provinces to support the Republic against him. The former aim was pursued by means of a propaganda campaign throwing the blame for the oligarchy's refusal to reform the Sullan constitution on Pompey; he was now made out to be the chief of the Sullan dynasts. The oligarchs in 73 are found proclaiming their inability to take decisive action before Pompey's return.[1] In the meantime more concrete measures were taken to prepare against intimidation. The year 74, in which Pompey's letter was received, marks the creation of two great *imperia* in the East: that of Lucullus against Mithridates and that of the praetor M. Antonius against the pirates—the former involving cumulation of provinces and the latter quite unheard-of powers.[2] Both these appointments were engineered by the same faction: an alliance of enemies of Pompey, embracing perhaps both Optimates and *Sertoriani*. Plutarch's tale of intrigue is borne out, in more refined tones, by a chance remark of Cicero's.[3] The centre and backbone of the faction were the Cottae, with two successive consuls in 75 and 74

[1] Sall. *hist.* iii. 48 (Macer's speech), 21 f.: 'differunt uos in aduentum Cn. Pompei, quem ipsum ubi pertimuere sublatum in ceruices suas mox dempto metu lacerant. neque eos pudet, uindices uti se ferunt libertatis, tot uiros sine uno aut remittere iniuriam non audere aut ius non posse defendere.' Modern treatment of this speech (even Gelzer's in *APAW*, 1943, Heft I) is unsatisfactory.

[2] Lucullus probably received Asia as well as Cilicia in 74 (*MRR*, ii. 107 f.) and, as events show, the right to act in Bithynia as well; for his large army, see sources in *MRR*, ii. 101. His command is certainly an example of the 'special *imperia*' of the late Republic. On M. Antonius' *infinitum imperium* (Cic. 2*Verr.* ii. 8; iii. 213), which has caused much trouble to constitutional historians, see Béranger, 'A propos d'un *imperium infinitum*' (*Mél. Marouzeau*, 19–27).

[3] Plut. *Luc.* 6; Cic. *par.* v. 40 (Cethegus). This Cethegus—a Marian who joined Sulla before it was too late (App. i. 80)—was a friend of Lepidus (probably, as we have seen, in good company) and enemy of Philippus: in the *oratio Philippi* (Sall. *hist.* i. 77, 20) he is the only man attacked by name, and his career is clearly stigmatized (s. 7—that cap may have fitted others!). Thus he was also an enemy of Philippus' protégé Pompey and was no doubt one of those who corresponded with Sertorius (Plut. *Pomp.* 20, 4). That he secured Antonius' command—not only Lucullus'—is reported by ps.-Asc. *in Verr.* 206 Or.

and a programme of moderate concessions to win the support of the People.[1] It was no doubt hoped that the Mithridatic War would be glorious and relatively short: Lucullus had known Mithridates at a time of great weakness and only his own high treason (in pursuit of Sulla's policy) had saved the King's life.[2] Antonius, with command of the sea and (it could be hoped) control of its islands, would be a powerful aide—both against Mithridates and, if need be, against threats by Pompey, when Lucullus, with a large and victorious army and the resources and loyal following of the East,[3] could turn his attention to dealing with the presumptuous adventurer whom he hated.[4] It is one of the supreme examples of the irony of history that, owing to incompetence and ill fortune, this grandiose attempt to defeat Pompey with his own weapons not only miscarried, but paved the way for the two commands (against the pirates and against Mithridates) by which Pompey, finishing off the wars thus begun, was to reach the summit of his power and glory.

Prudent men, meanwhile, thought it safer to keep on good terms with Pompey, especially when—with the new supplies voted in 74—he was obviously bringing his war to a speedy conclusion. Thus the consuls of 72, L. Gellius Publicola and Cn. Cornelius Lentulus Clodianus, passed the famous law that permitted him to bestow the citizenship on worthy foreigners.[5] He had no doubt done so under Sulla, and he used the power, now again granted, very liberally, taking his chance of confirming old loyalties as well as of creating new ones.[6] Metellus seems to have

[1] On the famous 'ex factione media consul' (Sall. *hist.* ii. 48, 8), see Henderson in *JRS*, 1951, 115. It will be seen that our investigation, as far as it permits conclusions, supports her view of the meaning of the Latin. The Cottae were associates of the arch-intriguer Cethegus (ps.-Asc., l.c.)—which no doubt helps to account for the family's conspicuous success. M. Cotta, Lucullus' colleague and a man of no mean ability, got an important naval command. On the earlier history of the family, see *Hist.* 1957, 320 f.: they are closely associated with the Metelli.

[2] Plut. *Luc.* 3.

[3] His attempt to gain the favour of the provincials in Asia (which ultimately led to his own undoing) is well known (Plut. *Luc.* 23; App. *Mith.* 83).

[4] Plut. *Pomp.* 20, 1; *Luc.* 5, 4 f.

[5] Cic. *Balb.* 19—see p. 260 (with nn. 1 and 2). Cf. Syme, *Rom. Rev.* 44 and 66 (their collaboration with Pompey).

[6] In general, see Appendix B. Sex. Pompeius Chlorus, at least, must have got the citizenship in Sullan days (2*Verr.* ii. 23: 'ciuis R. uirtutis causa [note the official phrase—cf. *ILS*, 8888] iam diu'). By contrast the Percennii of Messana are only

received a similar power, and he also was generous in its use:[1] for he, better than most men, knew the value of such connexions by personal experience. But it was Pompey again who captured the popular imagination, assisting it by means of his spectacular Pyrenean trophy.[2] His agents in Rome were no doubt easily successful in persuading the People (full of resentment against the oligarchy) that it was Pompey who had saved an incompetent noble commander and turned defeat into victory.[3]

Meanwhile political intrigue was further complicated by the activities of C. Verres. There is little doubt that it started merely as an unusual instance of rapacity in an unknown provincial governor: for most of his misdemeanours (as carefully listed by Cicero) there can be no political reason. But before long—still in 72—he was unwise or unfortunate enough to choose as one of his victims Sthenius of Himera,[4] a conspicuous example of Pompey's *clementia* in Sullan days and one of Pompey's most important Sicilian clients.[5] Sthenius fled to Rome and succeeded in mobilizing the consuls Gellius and Lentulus—both, as we have seen, friends of Pompey—in his support. They secured a resolution of the Senate in his favour; but no further action was taken, no doubt owing to the influence of Pompey's enemies. At the end of the year, Sthenius, giving up hope of help from the Senate, went to one of the new tribunes, M. Lollius Palicanus, a mob orator from Picenum[6] devoted to Pompey's cause. Palicanus at once gave him his support and spoke out strongly against Verres, who had also injured other clients of Pompey.[7] He linked this with a demand that the juries should not remain a monopoly of senators and that the powers of the tribunes should be fully restored.[8] Whether he at that time had instructions from Pompey (then on his way back from Spain), or whether he was playing his

'nunc Pompei' (ibid iv. 25)—i.e., no doubt, under the *lex Gellia Cornelia*. Pompey, as we shall soon see, had his eye on Sicily.

[1] Cic. *Balb.* 50 f.; *Arch.* 26: 'qui ciuitate multos donauit.'

[2] Pliny *n.h.* iii. 3, 18; vii. 26, 96; Sall. *hist.* iii. 89. Cf. p. 284.

[3] Cf. Plut. *Pomp.* 21, 2.

[4] On all this, see Cic. 2*Verr.* ii. 83 f.   [5] Plut. *Pomp.* 10, 6.

[6] 'humili loco Picens, loquax magis quam facundus' (Sall. *hist.* iv. 43). The date of his tribunate should not be doubted (rightly *MRR*, ii. 126, citing Niccolini).

[7] See below.

[8] Sources: *MRR*, ii. 122. The ascription to him (by Schol. Gron.) of the details of the later law of L. Cotta may be doubted; but his general views are clear.

own hand, hoping—rightly, as it turned out—to gain Pompey's approval in the end, we cannot tell; and it does not matter much.[1] At any rate we find Pompey, after his election to the consulate, subscribing to Palicanus' programme, with an oblique attack on Verres: the injuries to his Sicilian clients—whom he was still cultivating[2]—had to be avenged, if his influence was to be maintained; and, as we see from Cicero's speech, it was very doubtful whether a jury of senators would convict Verres. Thus Pompey, whether or not he had in fact had previous plans along these lines, was compelled, in defence of those interests which he had laboured so hard to consolidate, to ally himself with the 'Popular' leaders and embrace the anti-oligarchic programme.

The case of Verres had thus acquired a quite fortuitous political importance. With Pompey and his friends opposed to Verres, it is not surprising that the Metelli rose in his support. Indeed, we know from Cicero that three of them—the consul and the praetor of 69 and the governor of Sicily, Verres' successor—supported the accused and used their influence both in Rome and in Sicily on his behalf: Cicero found difficulties placed in his way in collecting evidence and had to tread warily to avoid giving excessive offence; and Verres' chief advocate was the other consul of 69, the orator Hortensius, *adfinis* of Pompey's enemy Catulus.[3] Cicero, on the other hand, freely used the evidence of Sicilians enfranchised by Pompey and aggrieved by Verres and had their help as his *hospites* in Sicily.[4] It thus becomes clear that the Verres case, besides exerting at least some influence on Pompey's political attitude in the critical years 72–70, ended by being a trial of strength between the faction of Pompey—whom Cicero had known in Cn. Pompeius Strabo's camp, whose support against Verres he both obtained and paraded, and whom (in general) he was probably beginning to court even then as a likely patron for a *nouus homo* seeking political advancement—and the faction of the Metelli, whom Pompey had deeply offended. The exile of Verres, coinciding as it did with the overthrow of the Sullan constitution,

[1] Pompey's burning of the correspondence of Sertorius (Plut. *Pomp.* 20, *fin.*) shows that he was then already thinking of an understanding with the enemies of the ruling *factio*.

[2] On the Percennii, see p. 281, n. 6.

[3] See *Note W*, p. 298.

[4] For examples, cf. the names given (with references) in Appendix B (i).

marks the end of that great family's last serious bid to retain its political supremacy. In the provinces—and this is what chiefly concerns us here—Pompey's vindication of his ability to look after his clients could not fail to have a profound effect. This, perhaps, as much as any other reason is responsible for Pompey's firm grip on newly-organized Spain, where, as we have seen, so many other families had earlier connexions and Q. Metellus Pius, in particular, had tried to extend those of his house in the Sertorian War.[1]

With his victory secure, Pompey could afford to wait. In and after his consulship he refused to accept an ordinary provincial command:[2] Cn. Pompeius Magnus could not be expected to govern an ordinary province, like any consular who had risen through the normal *cursus*. Once in Rome, he found his political influence less than he had expected—less, perhaps, than it had been in his absence—, especially as his colleague and enemy M. Crassus was (by natural ability, inherited connexions and practice) vastly superior to him in Senatorial intrigue;[3] yet time was working in his favour. The pirates, not shaken by the incompetence of M. Antonius,[4] were more of a menace than ever;[5] and Lucullus had not finished the great war in the East and was incurring unpopularity in Rome.[6] With the West firmly attached to him, Pompey waited, with an eye on Eastern events. His Spanish veterans, disappointed in their hopes of reward despite the passing of the *lex Plotia*,[7] were standing by for further use and further adventure. For a year or two our sources fail us; but by 67 Pompey moves openly for the conquest of the East.

[1] For this, see p. 282 (with n. 1).   [2] Vell. ii. 31, 1.

[3] Plut. *Pomp.* 23, 3–4; cf. 22, 3.

[4] Livy, *per.* xcvii; Sall. *hist.* iii. 16.

[5] Cic. 2*Verr.* v, *passim*; Oros. vi. 3, 5; *et al.*

[6] His reorganization of Asia (see p. 281, n. 3) may probably be dated in this year. In 69 the province was taken from him, no doubt at the instance of the *publicani* whom he had offended. (Sources in *MRR*, ii. 133; cf. 108. Cf. also Hill, *R. Mid. Cl.* 187.)

[7] For this law, see Cic. *Att.* i. 18, 6; Plut. *Luc.* 34, 3; Dio, xxxviii. 5, 1 f. (showing that it was not, in fact, carried out). I should like to thank Professor R. E. Smith for these references. (Cf. now his article in *CQ*, 1957, 82 f.)

EPILOGUE

WE have come to the end of the second part of our inquiry and may now conclude with a brief summing up and a glance at the future.[1]

In the international sphere, the idea of *clientela*, ingrained in Roman private life, was bound to be analogously applied to inter-state relations as soon as Rome had grown beyond equality with her friends and partners: this pattern of *mos maiorum* could not but be reproduced when Roman statesmen, moving in—and owing their position to—this intricate network of relationships, came to deal, on behalf of their city, with her inferiors abroad. We find traces of it even during the conquest of Italy; it emerges clearly as soon as Roman power spreads beyond the seas; and in the Greek East it finally becomes obtrusive and flamboyant, receiving its imprint, in part, from the colourful personality of T. Quinctius Flamininus. Modified by Greek and Eastern conceptions, it yet remains essentially Roman and therefore often strange and unintelligible to those cast in the role of clients, until the knot is cut by the sword in 146 B.C. We also observe some remodelling of Roman ideas. Roman hesitancy in weighing up rights and duties had been responsible for many of the mis-understandings. The original intention seems to have been to leave the 'free' client a fair amount of freedom: he was either a specially honoured friend (as in Sicily) or intended to act as a shock-absorber on the boundaries of Roman interests (as in Illyria and, probably, at first in Greece), and therefore of little direct concern to Rome, unless he grew too powerful in his own right or intrigued with the potential enemy on the other side. This applied, of course, both to kings and to cities—there was no essential difference between them and, as Scipio rightly pointed out, Rome held no brief for republicanism. Gradually, interest and intervention increase—particularly in Greece and, after 167, in the farther East—and after 146 the new pattern stands out

---

[1] In view of the ample documentation of the preceding chapters, the conclusions of which are here to a large extent summarized and brought into focus, notes on this chapter have been deliberately cut down to a bare minimum.

clearly: there is no longer any question of freedom and independence, and Mommsen's view of these states as 'reichsangehörig', though technically still inaccurate, is factually correct. There is still no essential difference between kings and cities: the Senate legislates for both classes and both are expected to obey. There is only the accidental difference that, after 133, on the whole, the cities are small enclaves in territory directly administered, while the kings, with larger territories, serve the old purpose of shock-absorbers on the outskirts, so that they often in fact preserve a certain freedom of action. This, however, is ultimately illusory and more than counterbalanced by the natural instability of these dynasties, which the Senate (as we saw) both formally and informally exploited with great skill. And though a Roman recommendation on a small point can be ignored and clever diplomacy can play on Roman unwillingness to take direct punitive action, a peremptory demand, presented with the full weight of the Senate's *auctoritas*, must be obeyed at once, whatever its claims to justice.[1] As for the 'free' cities, the case of Utica, finally seat of the governor of Africa, is a good example of their status, and our detailed information on the restrictions imposed upon the *ciuitates liberae* of Sicily provides us with a commentary. And, as has often been noted,[2] the idea of clientship and the concrete example of these cities had adversely affected even those with formal—or informal 'Senatorial'—treaties: as we have seen (and as is clear, especially, in the case of Italy), the treaty was soon regarded as providing only the basis for the moral superstructure of *clientela*. Thus diversity of privilege was merged in uniformity of subjection.

It is not surprising that Rome, with the political organization of an already overgrown city state, preferred clientship to annexation. It has been said[3] that after 133 B.C. foreign policy must be viewed 'against a background of civil contention'. It would be truer to say that, just as before 133 there are no 'party' differences on foreign policy, so after 133, when the word 'party' may be interpreted somewhat differently, there are still no essential

---

[1] The story of Nicomedes and Mithridates (before his first war with Rome) is illuminating: see Magie, *Rom. Rule*, i. 204 f.

[2] e.g. Sherwin-White, *RC*, 157 f., and Horn (there cited). Sherwin-White rightly stresses the fact that the presence (and the kind) of *foedera* by now made little difference.

[3] Frank, *Rom. Imp.* 263; though Frank's treatment is not consistent.

'party' differences on such matters. C. Gracchus' attack on the settlement of Aquillius[1] is the act of a genuine patriot and an honest man; his arrangement for the Asian taxes, though (as it turned out) unwise, was meant as an improvement for the provincials as well as for the Treasury and shows no desire to oppress them for the benefit of a Roman class—an attitude that would be unthinkable in such a man and such a patron. Saturninus' insult to the envoys of Mithridates[2]—undoubtedly intended and generally understood as an affront to the King's Roman patrons, who (it was to be publicly demonstrated) were powerless to protect their client—has no major significance beyond this quite conventional one: the schemes read into it by many moderns are refuted by the remarkable absence of any interest by Saturninus, at the height of his power, in the King or his affairs.[3] It is the Senate that, in 96, calls the fractious client to order; and though the actual war that broke out in 88 seems to have been precipitated by the intrigues of Marius and his friends, there is no evidence that his enemies were in principle opposed to it: Sulla was eager enough for the command. The question was when and how the war was to be started—and who, in Rome, was to profit by it; and Marius chose his time.

The Jugurthine War is the exception that proves the rule: it is used by the 'Popular' leaders as a weapon against their enemies; but they have no positive policy to propound and, once Marius is in charge, they settle down to acquiescence in whatever happens. Nor does it occur to anyone to make victory a ground for annexation. In fact, except for Asia, we have no evidence of any new province between 146 and the Sullan settlement (unless perhaps Cisalpina was organized after the Social War); though Transalpina was probably of necessity given some sort of permanent supervision—not necessarily provincial organization—after

---

[1] See *MRR*, i, under 123 B.C. (discussed in Ch. VIII).

[2] Diod. xxxvi. 15: the account suggests that the interpretation here adopted was also that of Diodorus' source.

[3] The law on the suppression of piracy (*FIRA*, no. 9), often ascribed—for no very good reason—to Saturninus and his followers, and then assumed (without any evidence) to have been necessarily displeasing to the *boni*, appears to be merely a piece of non-controversial routine legislation—as is indeed suggested by the fact that our relatively ample accounts of Saturninus' schemes contain no reference to it or to the ideas which some moderns read into it. In any case, it has no direct relevance to Mithridates.

the defeat of the German hordes. Asia, with its complex history so strangely interwoven with internal events in Rome (and, during the period that concerns us, still so little known), stands alone and provides no pretext for generalization. Cyrene—also left to Rome, but with no Aristonicus to force annexation upon a reluctant Senate—is more typical: no one in Rome thought of annexation or even reasonable assumption of responsibility; for patronate (as we saw) by now imposed few categorical duties.

Thus, except for the 'Italian question' and (for a short time and in a limited way) the Jugurthine War, foreign policy is not a matter of 'party' controversy in Rome down to 70 B.C. Nor can we trace any further development in Roman thought about Rome's relations with other states. It therefore seemed advisable to end the first part of our survey in 146 B.C. or 133 B.C. (as was appropriate to each field surveyed), as there is no profit—for our purpose—to be derived from further detailed study of Rome's foreign relations. The few exceptions to this statement duly appear in Part II of this study.

It is only after the Sullan settlement, and towards the very end of the period of this study, that a distinct change in policy might be noticed: Sulla's disgraceful peace with Mithridates was never ratified by the Senate and, when Nicomedes died and left Bithynia to Rome, the country was proclaimed a province; and so was Cyrene at last (74 B.C.).[1] There is, of course, no sign in all this of a 'Popular' expansionist policy—these things happened at the height of the Senate's power. But does it mean that the Senate had changed its mind and given up the idea of a system of client states for a policy of annexation and direct administration? Such a change might perhaps be explained as the consequence of the First Mithridatic War and the proof it had furnished of the unreliability of Rome's 'free' allies in the East; and it might be correlated with increased Roman activity, during these years, in the ill-defined province of Cilicia, itself probably a creation of Sulla.[2] On the face of it, the creation of these three provinces looks like a landmark; but it is easy to exaggerate its importance.

---

[1] App. *Mithr.* 67 f.; Livy, *per.* xciii. On Cyrene, see p. 140.

[2] Syme, 'Cilicia' (*Buckler Studies*), *init.* The *prouincia* of the elder M. Antonius had not been a 'province' in the territorial sense, and Sulla's command in 92 was probably a revival of this. Cf. also my brief discussion in *Ath.* 1956.

Cyrene is a special case: as we have seen, its affairs had lapsed into disorder, and the assumption of direct responsibility by Rome was probably a favour it owed to its patron L. Lucullus, the consul of 74 B.C. Cilicia is a counsel of despair: Asia, ever since its inception, had not been primarily a military province —with one exception (and that the special case of Q. Mucius Scaevola Pontifex) we know of no consular governors[1]—and was always a strategic liability; and 'Cilicia' had to reinforce and defend it, particularly (but not only) against pirates and hill tribesmen. The need for 'Cilicia' had been amply proved, even to those who would not see, by the First Mithridatic War and its immediate consequences. As for Mithridates, it is clear that his power had deliberately been left unbroken by Sulla and was again increasing rapidly: it is not surprising that the Senate was suspicious and, besides using its traditional diplomatic weapon of leaving his legal status ambiguous, would not hand over Bithynia to a pretender sponsored by him or even leave it 'free' as a fertile field for his intrigues. The annexation of Bithynia turns out to be a forced move in the traditional Roman game of weakening a suspect client. Perhaps, under the impact of a series of disasters, there is a clearer recognition of the needs of the Eastern situation; but there is no evidence for a radical change of policy: Lucullus made no move to add a province to the Roman Empire.

By now, however, policy has become the plaything of private and factional ambition: we have seen how large Pompey bulks behind the events of 74, and he was to do so much more before very long. Thus, at the end of the period of our survey, the first of its two aspects—*clientela* in public policy—merges into the second—the *clientela* of individuals—and for the next generation no such distinction would be necessary or even appropriate. The foreign *clientelae* of Roman individuals and families, for long a source of profit and prestige to the patron and an instrument of empire more solid than the legions, become instruments of domestic discord, as tension increases after 133. The Italians, readily roused to present lawful complaints, become the plaything of internal politics and in the end are driven to revolt on behalf of a claim that at first was not their own. That revolt, pitting kinsmen and comrades in arms against one another and

[1] Cf. *Ath.*, art. cit. (last note).

subjecting Italy to ravage by her own sons, breaks the traditional loyalty to *mos maiorum* and piety towards Rome; and the client army—the instrument that a *nouus homo* and great Roman politician of the old school had created as a prop to dignity and *auctoritas*—becomes for the moment, in the hands of a brilliant and unscrupulous Patrician, the tool of naked military domination. Meanwhile overseas *clientelae* are thrown into the struggle for Rome, and Pompey first combines the client army and a network of *clientelae* spanning the Roman world into the bases of personal predominance.

So it might have appeared in 70, where we leave this survey. In the end, after many vicissitudes, things were to turn out differently. Pompey, the son of a *nouus homo*, was like Marius in respecting *mos maiorum* at heart and lacking the will to establish a revolutionary domination without thought of the future. It was another Patrician, of even older lineage than Sulla and even more brilliant and unscrupulous, who brought matters to their logical conclusion. But the discussion of Caesar's triumph and failure is far beyond the scope of this volume, which has merely tried to investigate the foundations on which he built. Perhaps another volume will some day continue the inquiry through a period of more abundant evidence.

NOTES

NOTE A, p. 2. In Classical Law there are particularly the immunity from *actiones famosae* and some other legal constraints (the *interdictum unde ui*, the *iusiurandum de calumnia*, &c.); see *dig.* xxxvii. 15, 5 f. *et al.* The prohibition against unfavourable testimony between patron and freedman, found in various forms in a large number of laws (the *Lex Ursonensis*, the *lex Iulia de ui*, &c.), as far as it benefits the patron, should also be assigned to this class. Kaser (*ZRG*, 1938, 112 f.) is right in stressing the non-legal implications of these words, which may well stand for the ideas originally embracing the whole of the freedman's position as regards his patron—their converse being the *fides* of the latter towards the former. Here as elsewhere codification became necessary in a more advanced society.

NOTE B, p. 7. Premerstein also cites the following passages: Dion. ii. 9, 2 and 11, 1; Ter. *Eun.* 885 f. and 1039 f.; and Gell. v. 13, 2. For the patron's presumed acceptance of the offer, he refers to Gell. xx. 1, 40 ('clientem in fidem susceptum'), which tells us nothing beyond what is obvious (i.e. that the patron did accept the client). Nor are the other passages more instructive: those from Terence (see p. 8, n. 5) are not intended—and must not be thought—to give us any legal information. Gellius (v. 13, 2) does say: 'qui sese . . . in fidem patrociniumque nostrum dediderunt'; but (*a*) the last word need not be taken as having a formal meaning (i.e. *applicatio* is not necessarily included under *deditio in fidem*); (*b*) Gellius may well be wrong on a *ius* that was *obscurum et ignotum* in the second century B.C.: no one maintains that in his day *clientela* of the voluntary sort still retained its old obligations. Of the two Dionysius passages, the former is taken from an account of Romulus' social organization and is thus of no value beyond showing later theories, while the second refers to *patrocinium* over communities (not individuals) and is beside the point here. *De or.* i. 177 is discussed in the text.

NOTE C, p. 21. Gelzer (*RE*, s.v. 'Latium', coll. 954 f.) discusses its authenticity and refers to various views. Steinwenter (*RE*, s.v. 'ius Latii', col. 1265) persuasively argues for a fourth-century date. But see *RC* (pp. 19 f.) for a convincing defence of the traditional date: there was certainly a coalition against the Volsci and the Aequi and 'under cover of this treaty the Romans established a *de facto* supremacy' (ibid., p. 22); but we should perhaps be a little less confident in accepting the traditional terms. The treaty seen by Cicero (*Balb.* 53) must have been a fourth-century document (cf. Steinwenter, l.c.), and a *foedus aequum* between Rome on the one hand and the Latins on the other is more than we need believe for the early fifth century. The treaty with the Hernici has probably been similarly retouched to Rome's advantage. But again, whatever the details, all that we require (and may confidently accept) is the recognition of a widespread hegemony. Sherwin-White acutely traces the rise of Rome's influence to her co-ordinating position between the Latins and the Hernici.

NOTE D, p. 24. Lavinium is the only Latin city that may have been *foederata* —and, as we have seen, it was probably a *municipium*. But there is unimpeachable evidence that the *foedus Cassianum* continued to be regarded as, in some form, valid and as the basis of the relationship between Rome and the Latins. Cicero, in a famous passage (*Balb.* 54), calls the Latins *foederati*. Sherwin-White dismisses this as 'rhetorical malpractice' (*RC*, 92); and so, no doubt, it is. Yet the text of the treaty, as we learn, was preserved in a public place even in Cicero's lifetime, and the practice of equally dividing war booty seems, with necessary adaptations, to have been generally continued (cf. *RC*, 101). Once we abandon (as this study aims at doing) an ultra-legalistic view foreign to Roman tradition, we must accept the persistence, in some form, of the Cassian treaty, though its spirit had long since departed. As for the *leges* of Latin colonies, it is not known when the system of formal charters was begun (it can hardly be primitive). Perhaps Ariminum was the first city to receive one (Rosenberg, *H*, 1920, 356–7 —never, to my knowledge, refuted). But the differing institutions of these colonies (cf. *RC*, 110–11.) suggest that the *lex*, where there was one, was not always the same. Yet the concept of Latinity embraced them all—and not only them, but the remaining states in Latium.

NOTE E, p. 30. *The Italiots and naval service.* I have tried to show that we need not assume that the Italiots contributed to the army of the Confederacy (p. 29, n. 7). With the negative evidence of Pol. ii. 24, we may follow Mommsen against Horn. (Passages like Minnio's speech in 193—Livy, xxxv. 16, 3—can hardly be pressed.) But Horn's argument that other cities contributed *both* ships *and* military units is not securely based either. He badly misinterprets the case of the *coloni maritimi* (Livy, xxxvi. 3, 5): as Mommsen saw, the passage clearly shows the *first* attempt to draft them into naval service; its success meant that henceforth they were liable. (Thus also now Salmon, *Phoenix*, 1955, 70.) Before 191, no one had thought of drafting them. In Livy, xlii. 48, 7, 'Uria' must be wrong (though it is accepted by the Teubner editors). That small township could never have mustered such a formidable contingent. (Cf. p. 36, n. 6: Thurii?) There remains only Paestum, admittedly an odd case. This Latin colony, Livy says (xxvi. 39, 5), owed ships *ex foedere*. This doubly unique statement cannot be simply accepted without reservation as the sole support of an extensive theory like Horn's. Otherwise we might also find ourselves committed to arguing from it that all Latin colonies had *foedera*. It is easier to assume either that Paestum was indeed in some respects a special (and perhaps unique) case, or that Livy is mistaken and the ships were voluntarily supplied, or specially imposed, in view of the state of emergency in Italy.

That naval service did, as Mommsen thought, remain inferior to land service in dignity emerges from Horn's own account: he admits that, except for the *coloni maritimi* [after 191], free-born Roman citizens were not normally drafted into it. But by the time our main stream of evidence begins to flow, old conceptions were changing, and only the odd and clearly anachronistic phrase 'socii nauales' remained. For the facts (and some conjectures, indicated as such) see Thiel, *History*, especially 32 f.: what facts there are support Mommsen.

NOTE F, pp. 48 f. Täubler's date (*Vorgesch.* 44—'generally accepted', according to Kramer) is based on a mistranslation of Polybius' phrase about the first Saguntine appeal to Rome ([Καρχηδονίων]... τὰ κατὰ τὴν Ἰβηρίαν ἤδη πραττόντων

(iii. 30, 2)) as 'die Frühzeit der kolonialen Tätigkeit der K. in Spanien'. Hamilcar's conquests in Spain began in 237 (cf. Meltzer, *Gesch. d. Karth.* ii. 396): can one reasonably call 231 their 'Frühzeit', even compared with (say) 225? What Polybius is in fact saying is clearly that the Carthaginians were by then already [and the Romans not yet—cf. p. 48] actively interested in Spain. Täubler's 'Verträge mit kleinen Staaten am Gegengestade im Osten', which Rome is said to have entered into about the same time, are equally unsupported by evidence.

NOTE G, pp. 49 f. How the Ebro treaty ever got involved in the negotiations that preceded the War (as we must believe that it did) is almost beyond conjecture. That it contained no reference to Spain apart from the Ebro clause is stated by Polybius (ii. 13, 7); and this can hardly be circumvented. (For attempts, see De Sanctis, 'Annibale', in *Problemi*; Täubler, op. cit. 49 f.; Meyer, *Kl. Schr.* ii. 345 f.; Hoffmann, *Livius*, 20 f.) Polybius believed, at one time, that Saguntum lay north of the Ebro (iii. 30, 3): none of the numerous attempts to explain this away is convincing. It is possible that not only Roman annalists after the event, but also Roman senators before it, believed this, especially as Massilia, their chief informant at the time, was interested in not making her information too precise. Roman knowledge of geography, in the case of countries with which the Romans were not yet familiar, was not always good: compare the treaty with Antiochus III, which baffles all commentators.

NOTE H, p. 51. The existence of a formal treaty with Saguntum is usually assumed without discussion. The only sustained attempt to establish it by argument appears to be that of Täubler (*Vorgesch.* 42 f.); but his argument is as faulty as it is characteristically unpleasant in tone. 'Die Aufeinanderfolge von *deditio* und *foedus* ist nicht belegt und nicht möglich', he asserts, referring to his *Imp. Rom.*, where this point is also posited *a priori*; the evidence to the contrary, of which every page of many books of Livy is full, is all rejected as apocryphal. This kind of reasoning is not to be taken seriously. It is quite possible that Saguntum received a treaty at some time between 219 and Cicero's age (*Balb.* 50 f. does imply that it had one): Utica may be a parallel case (Cic., ibid., compared with *Lex Agr.* 80), unless Cicero has made a slip—as, of course, he equally well may have in the case of Saguntum. Cicero's evidence, far from 'entscheidend', is therefore useless. As for the fact that Polybius calls the Saguntines σύμμαχοι of Rome, Täubler asserts that 'συμμαχία zur Bezeichnung des Deditionsverhältnisses [i.e. 'Treuverhältnisses'] bei ihm nicht vorkommt'; but compare Pol. i. 40, 1: the Panhormitans are called σύμμαχοι—and Panhormus was a *ciuitas libera* (Cic. 2*Verr.* iii. 13). Similar violence is done to Polybius' use of 'παρασπονδεῖν', which Täubler insists on translating 'breach of treaty'; in fact it means 'breach of faith'—cf., e.g., iii. 7, 5. Täubler believes that Hannibal, in iii. 15, 7, is claiming that Saguntum is no longer entitled to Roman protection, as the Romans had broken their own treaty with the city. It is by such logic and mistranslation that Täubler's view that Rome had a treaty with Saguntum must be supported; and this is worth pointing out, as Täubler's is the only serious attempt to establish the existence of a treaty. I have tried to show that the alternative view is the simplest interpretation of our evidence.

NOTE I, p. 57. Täubler (*Imp. Rom.* i. 210 f., 430 f.) believes that the treaty follows Greek and not Roman tradition; but he arbitrarily limits Roman tradition to the perpetual *foedus* (in fact, to that of the second century B.C. and after). The point is precisely that Rome in this case did *not* want to be permanently involved and made a *temporary* alliance (cf. Heuss, *Völkerr. Grundl.* 37 f.). Possibly the clause dividing the command was put in by the Aetolians. That the clause on the fate of conquered territory was not 'Greek international law' is clear from the reaction of Greek opinion (Pol. xi. 5, 8; and especially ix. 39, 3: ἅπερ εἰκός ἐστι πάσχειν τοῖς ὑπὸ τὰς τῶν ἀλλοφύλων πεσοῦσιν ἐξουσίας; cf. x. 15, 5). Täubler has to dig up a Greek precedent in 493—which is much farther back than we need go to find a good Roman one: such a clause occurs in the 'second Carthaginian treaty' (Pol. iii. 24, 5), which, as we have seen, is probably an alliance in the face of a threatened Latin War. Täubler, in his usual way, makes it, in that case, *Carthaginian* practice. Admittedly our evidence is poor and we cannot be certain that the Romans were in fact following that precedent: there may well have been intervening examples. But we must not distort what evidence we have. We now have the language of the fragment of the Aetolian treaty to show that Roman ideas were dominant (Klaffenbach, *Röm.-ätol. Bund*, 20).

NOTE J, p. 75. Livy, xxxiv. 48, 3 f.: 'haec uelut parentis uoces' (50, 1) strikes the keynote; and the 'pium officium' (s. 4) of the Achaeans confirms the relationship as (from the Roman point of view) one of *clientela*. There is no reason to doubt that Livy found this point of view in Polybius (cf. the latter's comments on Demetrius of Pharus—p. 47, n. 1). Jones (*Greek City*, 113) is typical of many scholars in claiming that Rome 'from the first took up the attitude of a suzerain' towards the cities she freed. But the Romans would have been as shocked to hear the matter put in such definite legal terms as the Greeks. (See p. 79, with n. 1.) Holleaux, in a very careful discussion (*CAH*, viii. 194 f.), posits alliances where none are attested and cannot be safely followed in his legal theory, but does give a fair and acute political analysis. For the detailed history of the war with Nabis, see Aymard, *Prem. Rapp.*, ch. iii.

NOTE K, pp. 100, 104 f. Sources: Pol. xxx. 30, 1 f.; xxxi. 1, 2 f., *et al.*; the tribunal at Sardis: xxxi. 6, 1 f. The status of the Gauls is obscure. Manlius seems to have left them free, provided they kept the peace; if so, this was reasserted by the Senate in 166 (Pol. xxx. 28; Livy, xxxviii. 40, 2 might be a free translation of this). But we must remember that 'autonomy' did not mean full freedom (we have seen that autonomous cities had paid tribute to Antiochus and to Eumenes): they seem in fact to have been under Eumenes' supervision until their revolt in the war with Perseus. Manlius had consulted Eumenes over his settlement (Pol. xxi. 41, 7); and the Gauls are certainly in his sphere of influence by the time of the war with Pharnaces (Pol. xxiv. 14, 1 f.; xxv. 2, 4—the former passage seems to show that he had not gained his influence in Galatia *as a result* of that war). We cannot be certain what precisely the Senate meant to achieve in 166: perhaps to prevent their complete subjugation by Eumenes, perhaps to sow the seeds of conflict by (as it must by then have known) a deliberately vague decision. In any case, this was the result: Prusias and his friends went on to complain that Eumenes had not left the Gauls *wholly* free, but was supporting Pergamene parties in Galatia, and the Senate from time to time reaffirmed the 'autonomy' of the Gauls and (it appears) extended it (Pol. xxx. 30). The conflict, however, went on down to Eumenes' death (see beginning of this note, and text). We have epigraphic evidence for Eumenes' support of Pergamene parties and Attalus' prudent refusal to continue it (Welles, *Royal Corr.* 241 f.).

NOTE L, p. 111. Heraclea Pontica (Memnon, fr. 26, 4—Magie (*Buckler Stud.* 178) thinks it 'untrustworthy'); Cibyra (*OGIS*, 762)—usually dated soon after 188, on the strength of Pol. xxi. 34, 13, which, but for the finding of the inscription, would never have suggested the existence of a treaty. Magie puts it 'in any case earlier than 167', because of the city's action against Polyaratus (Pol. xxx. 9, 13 f.); but this is merely the action of a small and therefore faithful client, with or without a treaty. Until some clear evidence for the existence of such treaties at such an early date is found (and especially of 'Senatorial' treaties—see Accame, *Dom. Rom.* 79 f., and cf. text), we are not entitled to put our provisional date before Pydna; in view of precedent (see p. 86, on the Achaean treaty), soon after Pydna, as a reward for the signal loyalty shown in the case of Polyaratus, would be a reasonable guess—but no more. The statue of Roma at Cibyra (*OGIS*, 762, 15) is not likely to have not merely existed, but become the centre of civic life, 'soon after 188'; or at least, the onus of proof is surely on those who maintain that it did. Alabanda built a temple to Urbs Roma (Livy, xliii. 6, 5) only, it seems, after the defeat of Perseus (Magie, op. cit. 174, n. 2).

NOTE M, pp. 106, 125. Livy, xxx. 15, 11 is a tailpiece to the romance of Sophonisba; the details cannot be relied on (17, 8 f. is not confirmation). On the other hand, the status of Masinissa (a rebel and an adventurer) was so uncertain that Roman recognition of him as 'king' would be worth a good deal—especially with a victorious Roman army on the spot. If this does mark the origin of *appellatio*, it is an isolated example, not (as far as we can see) repeated for generations (Ch. IV, p. 106, with n. 3). A scrap of support is Livy's mention of the gift of a *scipio eburneus*: the punning device was in fact used as the ensign of the Scipiones (cf. *BCH*, 1904, 271 f. and plate xii). But the detail is not beyond the invention of an annalist. Again, we have no parallel to the gift of the *scipio* until much later (Livy, xlii. 14, 10: Eumenes). Thus, if the story *is* genuine (which cannot be ascertained), it does not mark an event of immediate importance.

NOTE N, pp. 127, 129. Livy, xxxiv. 62, *fin.*; cf. Zon. ix. 18. According to Kahrstedt (*Gesch.* iii, 582 f.), Livy confuses this dispute with that about the *Emporia* (c. 30 years later). Gsell (*HAAN*, iii. 316 f.) points out that such a confusion is difficult to account for, particularly as it is, of course, impossible to move the Scipionic mission down to the later date. The Livian passage may ultimately go back to a good Carthaginian history—it links the dispute with Carthaginian internal politics and it is anti-Roman in tone. The simplest solution is perhaps to suppose that the dispute of 193 gave Masinissa Lepcis and the coast as far as some point east of the Lesser Syrtis, while that of the sixties concerned the territory round the Gulf. The confusion in Livy would then be due to the fact that the name 'Emporia' was normally (it seems) used for the latter district only, but could be applied to a larger area (cf. Haywood, *CP*, 1941, 251 f.); and it would consist in the contamination of an (annalistic?) account, ultimately based on a Carthaginian source, related under 193, with the Polybian version (which we have) of the events of 161: each purporting to deal with a dispute over the 'Emporia', but not using the word in the same sense. Saumagne ('Prétextes') tries to make out that both Polybius and Livy go back to one pro-Roman source, which presented the disputes in the form of lawsuits arising out of a possessory interdict. This strained interpretation leads to some odd blunders. It is true that Livy (or his immediate source) has used a few ill-digested bits of legal jargon; but that does not amount to a 'theory' or justify the rewriting of history (even legal history—e.g. p. 205).

NOTE O, pp. 156, 160. C. Claudius Pulcher (*cos.* 92) was patron of Messana by 99 (Cic. 2*Verr.* iv. 6); Münzer (*RE*, s.v. 'Claudius', no. 102, col. 2694) plausibly traces the relationship back to Ap. Claudius Caudex (*cos.* 264). He was also asked to give Halaesa a constitution in 95 (Cic. 2*Verr.* ii. 122). It is possible (Münzer, *RE*, s.v. 'Caecilius', no. 72, col. 1204) that the patronate of the Metelli over Sicily in the time of Verres (ps.-Asc. ad *div. in Caec.* 100 Or.) went back to L. Metellus (*cos.* 251); but so little is known about the careers of later Metelli that this is far from certain. (Numidicus may well have been praetor in Sicily: cf. Cic. 2*Verr.* iii. 209.) Münzer suggests a similar connexion for the Lutatii Catuli, where it need not be assumed (*RE*, s.v. 'Lutatius', no. 8, *init.*): Q. Catulus (*cos.* 102) had probably governed Sicily (Cic., l.c.). Nothing is known—or has been satisfactorily conjectured—about the 'Claudius Drusus' of Suet. *Tib.* 1, 2.

NOTE P, p. 163. Gelzer (*Nob.* 81 f.) quotes Cic. *Q. fr.* i. 1, 31: 'tuas uirtutes consecratas et in deorum numero conlocatas uides.' Deification (whatever it might imply) was literally possible by the end of the Republic: even Theophanes of Mytilene received it (Ditt. *Syll.* 753). Much earlier, Flamininus at Chalcis had already come very near it (Plut. *Tit.* 16, 4): it would be interesting to know whether the action of the Chalcidians was immediate or a tribute by a later generation. Games founded in a man's honour are worth mentioning as related to this; best known are the Σωτήρια καὶ Μουκίεια in Asia (*IGRR*, 188), and the Marcellia at Syracuse (Cic. 2*Verr.* iv. 151 *et al.*), celebrated on the anniversary of the capture of Syracuse by M. Marcellus. (Gelzer, l.c., by an odd slip ascribes them to the honour of C. Marcellus, governor of Sicily in 79!) Verres tried to substitute 'Verria' for them (Cic., l.c.)—hardly through any dislike for the Marcelli, but because he knew that the Syracusans could not afford another festival of this sort. Even the quaestor M. Annius had an ἀγὼν ἱππικός in his honour (Ditt. *Syll.* 700, 38 f.)!

NOTE Q, p. 172. See, e.g., ch. 8, placed out of its context (cf. Gelzer, l.c. (p. 172, n. 2)) and containing a strange motive for the law (in fact probably only of Caesarian date—see Gelzer) fixing a minimum number of free labourers; the story of the flocking to Rome of Allied *possessores* (ch. 10), for which the evidence points to 129 and which the course of events makes suspect in 133; the strange breach of continuity in ch. 12, which has forced some editors to assume a gap in the text after the first adjournment—a solution too kind to an author who next proceeds to keep the Assembly waiting while Tiberius dashes backward and forward between it and the Senate (where he cheerfully hopes for support and is indignant at not getting it). At the end of that chapter the name of Octavius' successor is probably wrong—see Münzer, *RE*, s.v. 'Mucius', no. 1. Things do not improve with the incoherent account of the elections (ch. 14) and the electoral (?) Assembly on the Capitol, if not in the Temple itself (ch. 15).

NOTE R, p. 213. On the scope of the *lex Licinia Mucia*, see Husband, *CP*, 1916, 321 f., improved by Gabba (*Ath.* 1953). It is usually wrongly called an expulsion act (thus recently Scullard in Marsh–Scullard, 416–17; Broughton in *MRR*, ii. 11). This is based solely on Schol. Bob. 296 Or., where the purport of the law is given as 'ut redire socii et Latini in ciuitates suas iuberentur'. It is not hard to see how the scholiast arrived at this palpable blunder: for Asconius (p. 68 Cl.) gives the law as 'ut in suae quisque ciuitatis ius redigerentur'. (The law may have been called 'de ciuibus (?) redigundis'—Cic. *ap.* Asc. 67.) The misunderstanding is easy, but should not be copied: Cicero (*off.* iii. 47) makes the matter clear beyond doubt when he *contrasts* this law with expulsion acts.

NOTE S, p. 224. This analysis of the situation in Etruria leads us to the reasonable inference that of the veterans who supported Saturninus many will have come precisely from Etruria, which was not far from Rome. Etruria, in certain areas, probably suffered from overpopulation (contrary to what is often maintained in modern discussions). Plutarch's account certainly suggests this, and it is not contradicted, but rather supported, by what we hear of the emptiness of the land and the *latifundia* worked by slave labour (Plut. *Ti. Gr.* 8, 9): extension of this state of affairs was bound to lead to overcrowding in the rest of the country. For Umbria, unfortunately, there is no evidence, and it cannot be profitably discussed. On Marius' Umbrian connexions see p. 222 (with n. 5).

NOTE T, pp. 239 f. See Gran. Lic. 23 f.; Livy, *per.* lxxx; App. i. 67 f. The *Periocha* says, after Marius' capture of Ostia (end of lxxix): 'Italicis populis a senatu ciuitas data est. Samnites, qui soli arma recipiebant, Cinnae et Mario se coniunxerunt.' Appian, according to whom all but the Samnites and the Lucanians were already citizens (i. 53), says that the Senate instructed Metellus to come to terms with the Samnites; that he refused to accept their terms; and that Marius then granted them all they asked. Granius, who has the fullest account, says that the Senate refused the Samnites' terms 'dignitatem antiquam p.R. tuentibus patribus', but that Cinna sent Fimbria to announce that *he* accepted them; a few lines later we find: 'dediticiis omnibus ciuitas data.' These accounts cannot be reconciled by compromise; but Granius', circumstantial and usually reliable, is probably the best. App. i. 53 may anticipate: perhaps a large number of the ex-rebels were only now admitted to the benefits of the *lex Julia*. Compare the discussions in *CAH*, ix. 264 and (by Scullard) in Marsh–Scullard, 419.

NOTE U, p. 249. Gell. xv. 28. Though there is some confusion, Gellius has started from the following *facts* he knows: (i) that the *pro Quinctio* was delivered in 81; (ii) that the *pro Sex. Roscio* was delivered in the following year (i.e. certainly 80). It is quite possible that Gellius even had a life of Cicero with a table of consular dates (the passage rather suggests it). Asconius (cited by Gellius) probably also had 80 (though, not having him directly, we cannot be sure); and so—more likely than not—did Fenestella, whom Asconius either misunderstood or took to task for a misleading looseness of expression common enough in our sources (cf. *H*, 1955, 117, n. 3, with references). For the facts of the case, see Carcopino, *Sylla*, 156 f.

NOTE V, pp. 264, 279. Cf. Caes. *b.c.* i. 29, 3; 61, 3; *et al.* Cf. also Premerstein, *Werden*, 17. Caesar has to admit the *beneficia* that Pompey has conferred on Citerior. Fortunately, the case of the Balbi proves that they were not confined to that province (in which Pompey was chiefly active). Caesar, having himself served in Ulterior, may be unwilling to admit his enemy's claims on it. However, we must not forget the influence of the other noble houses that were Pompey's allies in the Civil War (e.g. Junii Bruti and Caecilii Metelli). On the other hand, what we know of the pre-eminent position of the Fabii in the Peninsula links up with the fact that in 49 Caesar chose a C. Fabius (though perhaps not a member of the Patrician house) to lead the invasion of Spain.

NOTE W, p. 283. Q. Metellus (Creticus), *cos.* 69, later notoriously kept up the feud with Pompey in the latter's war against the pirates (Plut. *Pomp.* 29). On him and his brother L. Metellus, Verres' successor in Sicily and *cos.* 68, see *RE*, s.v. 'Caecilius', nos. 74 and 87. Cf. Cic. *Verr.*, *passim.*; e.g. 1*Verr.* 26 f.: 'arcessit alter consul designatus Siculos: ueniunt nonnulli, propterea quod L. Metellus esset praetor in Sicilia. cum iis ita loquitur: se consulem esse, fratrem suum alterum Siciliam prouinciam obtinere, alterum [M. Metellus, of whom little is known—cf. *RE*, l.c., no. 78] esse quaesiturum de pecuniis repetundis; Verri ne noceri possit, multis rationibus esse prouisum.' It is worth noting that the collusive would-be prosecutor whom Cicero flays in the *diuinatio* is a Q. Caecilius, almost certainly owing his citizenship to the Metelli (see Appendix B (i): 'Q. Caecilius Niger'). Another supporter of Verres was P. Cornelius Scipio, father of the man we know best as Metellus Scipio. This aspect of the Verres trial deserves more comment than it often gets.

APPENDIX A

Note on the Chronology of 122 B.C.

ANY discussion of the events of 122 B.C. presupposes some views on the order of events in that year; and the views here presupposed must be explained, if the text is to become intelligible. For the limited purposes of this study we may, however, concentrate on the measures that concern the Italian allies, deliberately ignoring other problems (e.g. that of the judiciary legislation, on which see *AJP*, 1954, 374 f.) no less worthy of study. No complete chronology of C. Gracchus' tribunates (or even of his second year of office) is here attempted. (See Fraccaro's masterly discussion, now accessible in vol. ii of his *Opuscula*.)

(a) The Legislation on the Allies

Appian (*b.c.* i) and Plutarch (*C. Gr.*) are the only sources that matter: Vell. ii. 6 is too rhetorical to be taken seriously. As is known, they seem to contradict each other. Last (*CAH*, ix. 49 f.—based on Warde Fowler) dissects the law, claiming to follow Plutarch; but Plutarch, if we are to take him as mentioning two bills at all, gives *first* one on the Italians and *then* one on the Latins (see below)—which cannot make sense on any theory. Thus Last is finally forced into arbitrarily reversing this order and abandoning the source altogether. Fortunately, there is no need to think that Plutarch is trying to record two bills. (That no one else does is admitted.) Appian (23) is coherent, consistent and credible: he knows the constitutional anomaly of the 'Latin' vote in the Roman Assembly, and he says that Gaius now offered the Latins full citizenship (πάντα τὰ 'Ρωμαίων) on account of their συγγένεια, while offering the vote—no doubt, as is usually thought, the 'Latin' vote—to the rest of the Italians. Plutarch shows no knowledge of the 'Latin' vote; yet there are traces of its being mentioned in his source. In 5, 1 he depicts Gaius as ἰσοψήφους ποιῶν τοῖς πολίταις τοὺς Ἰταλιώτας— odd, if hitherto they had had no ψῆφος at all. That this is a misunderstanding of his source is suggested by 9, 3 (τοῖς Λατίνοις ἰσοψηφίαν διδούς—8, 3, less explicit, suggests the same source and meaning): in the case of the Latins the word makes sense—and it makes the same sense as Appian's account, as far as the Latins are concerned. That Plutarch's source also mentioned the Italians is clear from 5, 1: Plutarch can hardly have inserted them without any authority, however muddled his facts. That Plutarch failed to understand his source is not surprising: he is neither familiar with, nor interested in, the details of the Republican constitution. Thus it is very likely that Plutarch's source—reporting the grant of ἰσοψηφία to the Latins and mentioning the Italians—in fact gave the same proposals that Appian records more accurately. We must also cite Cicero: with welcome clarity he informs us (*Br.* 99) that the measure opposed by Fannius dealt with both *socii* and *Latini*—indeed, as is argued in the text, the attempt to sow division between them is the work, not of Gaius, but of his enemies. We may thus take it that there was only one measure on the allies (Latins and Italians) and that it belongs—as is clear from the opposition of Drusus and Fannius—to the second tribunate.

(b) *Junonia and the Order of Events*

The foundation of Junonia, as everyone should now admit, was voted by Rubrius in 123 (see *AJP*, 1954, 374 f.) and carried out by C. Gracchus in 122. But reconstruction of the events of 122 is made difficult by the fact that Appian and Plutarch have contradictory accounts of Gaius' absence from Rome, so that at least one of them must be wrong. The cardinal fact, which we have no right to reject in any scheme, is the seventy days' duration of Gaius' absence (Plut. 11). This is our only precise datum. Appian's account is very compressed: the story of the final riot follows almost at once upon Gaius' return to Rome, without any mention of the tribunician and the consular elections or even of the beginning of Opimius' consulate. A great deal must have happened in this time: the omissions, as we can see from Plutarch's fuller story, are serious and the gap must be due—as so many errors in Appian are—to over-compression. The story of Junonia appears at first sight to be placed at the end of Gaius' tribunates; but on closer inspection we can see that in fact Appian has simply omitted to mention it (like so many other things) and has to tell it later in order to make the final riot (caused ultimately by the report of the 'wolves' at Junonia) intelligible. His account of Junonia is therefore of no relevance to chronology. Plutarch has a much fuller story about the events of the year; it is marred, as we have seen, by his ignorance of constitutional matters and (for the historian) by his habit of grouping by subject-matter rather than chronology. But where he makes an explicit chronological statement, the quality of his source is clearly such that it should be accepted. One such statement (see above) is that about the seventy days. Another puts the expulsion of the Italians from Rome, caused by the promulgation of some bills and the flocking of crowds to Rome, *after* Gaius' return from Africa (12, 1: ἐπανελθών); and the tribunician and consular elections seem to follow it. Plutarch does not mention the *lex de sociis* explicitly in this connexion: his method leads him to treat it elsewhere (see (*a*), above). But it is an obvious inference that this was the bill that caused the flocking of Italians to Rome; and Appian (23) explicitly asserts the connexion. Thus the whole climax of this agitation may be put after the return from Junonia.

If Gaius' absence of seventy days precedes the struggle over the Italian bill and the elections—and Plutarch (12, *init.*) in fact suggests a fairly long interval—, it must come early in the year: we have already noted that Appian is not to be taken as contradicting this. Our *terminus ante quem non* is the beginning of the tribunician year (10 Dec. 123), and some time may be allowed for the development of the initial conflict with Drusus. At the other end, late April seems the latest reasonable date for Gaius' return (although here we cannot be precise). Thus we may say with fair probability that the seventy days must come somewhere between the middle of January and the end of April.

That Fulvius accompanied Gaius is asserted by Appian and denied by Plutarch. There can be no doubt about our choice. Appian assigns no individual activity to Fulvius in Africa (he only couples him with Gaius), while Plutarch has a great deal to say about his activities in Rome in Gaius' absence; and we recall that the story of Junonia in Appian is merely an explanatory flashback. Thus we must unhesitatingly follow Plutarch. *A priori* it is, of course, unlikely that Fulvius should temporarily abandon the cause for which he had, as a triumphal consular, assumed the tribunate, and should leave it, without a prominent defender, at the mercy of vigorous opponents. (Cf. also pp. 186-7.)

That Drusus first expounded his full programme in Gaius' absence is not stated explicitly: as we have seen, neither of our main sources can be relied on for the precise order of events. But Appian (23, *fin.*) tells us that he proceeded in two distinct stages—a point that Plutarch again misses owing to lack of interest and competence in constitutional matters: Appian says that Drusus first interposed a simple veto and then developed his counter-bid. Moreover, it is clear from Plutarch's detailed account that Drusus' success in Gaius' absence was utterly unexpected by the latter. This suggests the view that it was during that absence that Drusus' full programme was first propounded. The following schedule sets out the views here reached and presupposed in the text:

(i) Gaius proposes his *lex de sociis*; Drusus vetoes it (Dec.–Jan.);
(ii) Gaius leaves for Africa; Drusus expounds his programme and makes headway against Fulvius (between Jan. and April);
(iii) Gaius returns and promulgates the bill;
(iv) the Italians flock to Rome and are expelled;
(v) the bill is defeated (Fannius' great speech probably here or in (iv));
(vi) Gaius is defeated in the elections.

APPENDIX B

(i) *Singillatim ciuitate donati*

GOODFELLOW (*Rom. Cit.* 32 f.) discusses the granting of citizenship to individuals in rather a perfunctory manner. This list aims at including all those who, during the last few generations of the Republic, are attested as having received the Roman citizenship otherwise than through the incorporation of their communities. The following classes are not included:

1. freed slaves;
2. the *turma Salluitana*, which has been sufficiently published and discussed (best in Cichorius, *R. St.* 130 f.);
3. those enfranchised by Caesar (or after his death),* as they are outside the scope of this work; this division has been found more convenient than a strict time limit.

In general, the Roman name is given, where it is known or can reasonably be conjectured. For descendants of men whose enfranchisement is not directly attested, see below.

Name	Native city (*&c.*)	Enfranchised by	Evidence	Notes
Alexas	Heraclea (in Lucania)	P. Licinius Crassus (*cos.* 97)	Cic. *Balb.* 50	Perhaps for service rendered when Crassus was a legate in the Social War (cf. p. 260, n. 4).
M. Annius Appius	Iguvium	C. Marius	,, ,, 46	
Aristo	Massilia	L. Cornelius Sulla Felix	,, ,, 50	
Q. Caecilius Dio	Halaesa	Q. Metellus (Pius or Creticus?)	,, 2*Verr.* ii. 20 f.	A very well connected man (l.c.).
Q. Caecilius Niger	Sicily	a Q. Metellus?	,, *div. in Caec., passim*	Plut. (*Cic.* 7, 5) calls him ἀπελευθερικός—which is most improbable, as

* *Note*: for treatment of these, cf. Goodfellow, *Rom. Cit.* 90 f.

Name	Place	Enfranchised by	Source	Notes
M. Caecilius (his brother)	Sicily	a Q. Metellus?	Cic. *div. in Caec.* 29	Cicero, in his careful denigration of the man, never mentions it.
P. Caesius	Ravenna	Cn. Pompeius Strabo	,, *Balb.* 50	
Calliphana	Velia	the People, *de s.s.*, on the motion of C. Valerius Flaccus (*pr.* 96?)	Val. Max. i. 1, 1; Cic. *Balb.* 55	
M. Cassius	Messana	?	Cic. *Balb.* 52	No senator called M. Cassius is known, except for the praetorian (?) of *FIRA*, 36 (=Ditt. *Syll.* 747).
A. Claudius (Clodius) Apollonius	Drepana	?	,, *2Verr.* ii. 140; iv. 17	For Clodii in Sicily, see under *Incerti*, below. For the praenomen Aulus, cf. A. Clodii in Delos (*BCH*, xxxvi. 26–27).
T. Coponius	Tibur		,, *Balb.* 53	A successful prosecutor.
Cornelius Artemidorus	Perge	?	,, *2Verr.* iii. 28 *et al.*	Münzer (*RE*, s.v. 'Cornelius' 64) suggests he was enfranchised by Cn. Cornelius Dolabella (*pr.* 81). But Cicero's language (iii. 69) suggests a sudden enfranchisement (hinting at irregularities) by Verres in Sicily. In that case 'Cornelius' may merely have been chosen as a common name.
L. Cornelius Balbus	Gades	Cn. Pompeius Magnus	,, *Balb., passim*	His *praenomen* and *nomen* derive either from L. Gellius Publicola and Cn. Cornelius Lentulus (*coss.* 72), or from L. Lentulus Crus, who may have served in Spain under Pompey (cf. Münzer, *RE*, iv. 1261 and 1382).
L. Cornelius L.f. Balbus (his son, *cos.* 40)	,,	,,	,, ,, ,,	
L. Cornelius P.f. Balbus (the *triumphator*)	,,	,,	Sources in *RE*, iv. 1268 f.	
P. Cornelius Balbus	,,	,,	*Fasti tr.* for 19 B.C.	Known only from filiation; the brother of L. (*cos.* 40).

Name	Native city (&c.)	Enfranchised by	Evidence	Notes
Cornelius Tlepolemus	Cibyra	?	Cic. 2Verr. iii. 69 et al.	Cicero (l.c.) questions his citizenship and Münzer believes him (*RE*, s.v. 'Cornelius' 397). But Cicero offers no evidence and he (like Artemidorus, above) was probably enfranchised by Verres in Sicily.
L. Cossinius	Tibur		,, *Balb.* 53	A successful prosecutor. He may have become praetor in 73 (Plut. *Crass.* 9, 6); but his son was not a senator (Cic., l.c.).
(M.?) Cyprius Nicias Porcianus	Cyprus	probably the People, *de s.s.*	Plut. *Cat. Min.* 39, 2 (cf. Dio xxxix. 23, 2)	Treasurer to Ptolemy of Cyprus: although in status a slave, he merits inclusion here.
Cn. Domitius Sincaicus	Sardinia	Cn. Pompeius Magnus	Cic. *Scaur.* 43	Possibly during Pompey's *cura annonae.*
Q. Fabius	Saguntum	Q. Metellus Pius	,, *Balb.* 50	Other Fabii of Saguntum (enfranchised by Pompey), ibid.
Hasdrubal	Gades	Cn. Pompeius Magnus	,, ,, 51	
Q. Lutatius Diodorus	Lilybaeum	L. Sulla Felix	,, *2Verr.* iv. 37	At the request of Q. Catulus (*cos.* 78).
Minatus Magius	Aeclanum	'Populus Romanus'	Vell. Pat. ii. 16	With two sons, in the Social War.
T. Matrinius	Spoletum	C. Marius	Cic. *Balb.* 48	
Ovii	Messana	Cn. Pompeius Magnus	,, ,, 51	We do not know their name after enfranchisement.
Cn. Pompeius Basiliscus	Messana	,,	,, *2Verr.* iv. 25	
Sex. Pompeius Chlorus	Sicily (Halaesa?)	,,	,, ,, ii. 102	citizen 'iam diu' in 70 (ibid. 23).
Pompei Percennii (?)	Messana	,,	,, ,, iv. 25	'nunc Pompei': i.e. not long before 70. They may have dropped the Oscan name on assuming that of Pompei.
Cn. Pompeius Philo	Tyndaris	,,	,, ,, iv. 48	
Cn. Pompeius Theodorus	Sicily	,,	,, ,, ii. 102	
Cn. Pompeius Theophanes	Mytilene	,,	Ditt. *Syll.* 755 et al.	

Name	Place	Ref.	Notes
Cn. Pompeius Trogus	Vocontii	Just. xliii. 5, 11 f.	
Cn. Pompeius } (his sons) Pompeius Trogus }	"	" "	
Valerius	Sardinia	Cic. *Scaur.* 29	
C. Valerius Caburrus	Helvii	Caes. *b.G.* i. 47, 4	Flaccus was proconsul in Transalpine Gaul and 'Celtiberia', 85–81 (?).
C. Valerius C.f. Donnotaurus } (his sons) C. Valerius C.f. Troucillus }	"	" " vii. 65, 2	

Incerti (in time or status)*

Name	Place		Ref.	Notes
T. Caecilius: see Eutychides (Calpurnius) Piso	Aquitani	?	Caes. *b.G.* iv. 12, 4	Grandson of a chieftain connected with Pisones (? L. Piso, *cos.* 112, who fell in Gaul).
Cassius Dionysius	Utica	?	Varro, *r.r.* i. 1, 1	Date unknown, but certainly by 44 (Cic. *Phil.*).
Sex. Clodius (the rhetor)	Sicily	?	Suet. *gramm.* 29	
M. Clodius Archagathus	Halaesa	?	Cic. *fam.* xiii. 32	Letter written 46 B.C.
Clodius Philetaerus	?	?	" " xiv. 4, 6	Usually regarded as a freedman; but in view of Cicero's contact with Sicily and the many Sicilian Clodii (see esp. immediately above) he may well be a Sicilian.
C. Clodius Philo	Halaesa	?	" " xiii. 32	Letter written 46 B.C. All these Clodii may be beneficiaries of Caesar. The name may be derived from both the Pulchri and the Marcelli: both houses had Sicilian connexions. (See esp., for Halaesa, Cic. 2*Verr.* ii. 122.)

* N.B. This list does not claim to be exhaustive.

Name	Native city (&c.)	Enfranchised by	Evidence	Notes
Cornelius Alexander	Miletus	L. Sulla Felix?	Cf. Goodfellow, 35	He was probably a slave (see Goodfellow).
(Cornelius?) Hiero	Cibyra	?	Cic. 2*Verr*. iv. 30 *et al.*	Brother of Cornelius Tlepolemus; Cicero does not mention his enfranchisement.
Curtius Nicias	Cos	Cn. Pompeius Magnus?	Suet. *gramm.* 11	Herzog (*Hist. Z.* 1922) has shown that he is identical with the tyrant of Cos; but he may still be a slave by birth (note τοῦ Δάμου υἱός, on the tyrant's inscriptions, instead of a father's name). Equestrian Curtii are active in the East at the time; the careers of senatorial Curtii are obscure.
T. Didius T.f. Cor.	Carthago Nova	T. Didius	*CIL*, ii. 3462	May be (with his father) enfranchised by T. Didius (*cos.* 94); but may be only a descendant of a man enfranchised by—or named after—him. Hübner (*CIL*, l.c.) cannot date the inscription.
Eutychides	Corcyra?	?	Cic. *Att.* iv. 15, 1 *et al.*	Enfranchised by Atticus or through his efforts. May be a slave, or (thus Münzer, *RE*, s.v.) an important Corcyraean. Cicero's tone (l.c. and *Att.* v. 9, 1) supports the latter view.
Fabius Maximus	Narbo(nensis?)	?	Porph. ad Hor. *Sat.* i. 1, 23	Münzer believes him to be descended from a family enfranchised by Allobrogicus. But cf. the Q. Fabius who we know was enfranchised by Q. Metellus Pius (above). Maximus, an adherent of Pompey (Porph., l.c.), probably owed him the franchise.

Name	Place		Reference	Notes
M. Folvi(os) Garos [sic]	?	?	CIL, i². 2268 = ii. 3302	On an Iberian inscription. No Fulvius is known to have served in Spain after 167 (see below).
Vaalus Ga[b]inius [sic]	Avennio?	?	CIL, i². 2280 = xii. 1038	'Vaalus' is probably a Gallic cognomen (see Mommsen, CIL, xii, cit,). For Gabinii connected with Gaul, cf. P. Gabinius Capito ('Cimber Gabinius' —Cic. Cat. iii. 6) who treated with the Allobroges in 63.
Q. Junius	?	?	Caes. b.G. v. 26 f.	A man in Caesar's army who may be Spanish. Münzer (RE, s.v. 31) thinks the family was enfranchised by Callaicus; but that is most unlikely. (On Junii in Spain, see below.)
C. Norbanus Sorex	?	?	See RE, l.c.	An actor and friend of Sulla. May be a freedman of the Norbani or an alien enfranchised by one of them (thus Münzer, RE, s.v.) and deserting them in time.
Diocles 'Popilius cognomine'	Lilybaeum	?	Cic. 2Verr. iv. 35	Münzer (RE, s.v. 'Diokles', 39) thinks he had taken a Roman name without being a citizen, 'was allerdings strafbar war [no evidence is quoted for this], aber in der Praxis öfter vorkam'. See Ch. XI, p. 256.
L. Sulpicius Q.f. Q.n. Col.	Carthago Nova?	?	CIL, i². 2274 = ii. 3504 (not dated)	The tribe seems to sho.. that he is not of free Spanish descent: it is most suited for one of freedman descent. He may be descended from a freedman of the Patrician house. (For the praenomen 'Quintus', see RE, s.v. 'Sulpicius', 69 (a Galus) and 94–95 (Rufi)—the first of them connected with Spain. The praenomen 'Lucius' is rare.)
P. Terentius Varro Atacinus	Narbo	?	Jer. Chr. (ad 82)	See Syme, CQ, 1938, 43 f.

Name	Native city (&c.)	Enfranchised by	Evidence	Notes
Vibius Paciaecus	?	?	See *RE*, s.v. 'Paciaecus'	Despite Schulze, *Lat. Eig.* 28 (accepted by Münzer, *RE*), the stem of the *cognomen* seems as good Oscan as the *nomen*. (On 'Paccius' and 'Vibius' as *praenomina*, see Münzer, *RE*, s.v. 'Paccius'.) Thus the man and his family must be of Italic descent. The ending '-aecus' is difficult (Iberian according to Schulze) and shows foreign influence. If the family was among the early immigrants (e.g. the settlers at Italica), it may not have used *cognomina* until it had been settled in Spain for generations.

We may add here that general reference to the enfranchisement of unnamed persons is often made (e.g. Cic. *Balb.* 50: a man from Avennio, among very few enfranchised by M. Crassus, and 'erosnouem [*sic*] Gaditanos', enfranchised by Sulla). Q. Metellus Pius is said to have been particularly generous in this respect (Cic. *Arch.* 26).

(ii) (a) *Names of leading Republican* gentes *in Spain, Gaul and Africa*

The following table shows the distribution of the names of various important Republican *gentes* in Spain, Narbonensis (= Transalpina, for our purposes) and Africa (Proconsularis)—provinces in which such analysis is feasible and fruitful. It is compiled from the indexes of the following works: (a) Spain: *CIL*, ii (Suppl.) and *Eph. Ep.* viii–ix; (b) Gaul: *CIL*, xii and Espérandieu, *Inscr. Lat.*; (c) Africa: Gsell, *Inscr. lat. de l'Alg.* i (these seem sufficient for a test collection). For technical reasons entire consistency has been impossible and figures (especially where large) are only approximate. The *gentes* chosen are all those which provided consuls between 100 and 49 B.C. (except for the Aurelii, Claudii and Julii—unsuitable for our purpose, as they are the *nomina* of emperors) and a few other important and interesting ones. (These latter are marked †.) The Cornelii and Valerii (see *RE*, s.vv.) are omitted on account of the excessive diffusion of their names in the late Republic.

Name	Spain	Gaul	Africa
Acilii	34	11+2*	1
Aemilii	183+2*	107+6*	77
Afranii	4	5	..
Antonii	120+7*	61+1*	42
Aufidii	18+1*	8	12+1*
Caecilii	142+5*	61+3*	103
Calpurnii	69+3*	19	52
Cassii	57+3*	71	11
Coelii	18+2*	55+1*	1
Didii	13+3*	7+1*	7
Domitii	67+4*	80+1*	46+2*
Fabii†	303+9*	50	35+1*
Fulvii†	60+4*	25	2
Gabinii	1	1	20
Gellii	10+1*	15+1*	21
Herennii	45+2*	10+1*	17+2*
Hortensii	..	14+2*	10
Junii	129+5*	47+4*	46
Licinii	165+18*	102+1*	25
Livii	5+1*	11+1*	4
Lutatii	4+1*	7	2+2*
Manlii	45+1*	8+4*	1
Marcii	62+2*	27	8
Marii	64+4*	54+2*	30
Memmii†	23+3*	12	14+1*
Mucii	1	1	3+1*
Norbani	21+1*	2	

* = *incerti.*

X

Name	Spain	Gaul	Africa
Octavii.	42+3*	42	14+1*
Papirii .	8	5+1*	3
Perpernae	3	..	..
Pompei	132+9*	223+2*	39+2*
Porcii .	72+3*	23	4
Postumii	43+2*	2	41
Pupii .	1	..	..
Rutilii .	13	17+5*	4
Scribonii	12+1*	4	13
Semproniï† .	146+8*	24	9
Sertoriï†	12	..	..
Servilii.	19	23	21
Sulpicii	70+3*	19	3
Terentii	93+3*	51+3*	9
Tullii .	7	9+4*	16
Volcacii	..	1	..

(ii) (*b*) *Members of the Roman* gentes *concerned who are known to have served in Spain, Gaul and Africa*

The following is a list of members of the Roman *gentes* considered in (ii) (*a*) (omitting Herennii, Octavii and Tullii, whose names—far more common in Italy than prominent in the *Fasti*—seem most likely to have been carried to the provinces by emigration), who are known to have served in Spain, Gaul and Africa. In general, the list aims at being exhaustive only for the years 200–44 B.C.; other names have been added where it seemed specially useful. An evaluation of the evidence is attempted in the text of Ch. XI.

The sources are not usually given, where they present no important problems and may be found without difficulty in *MRR* under the appropriate year. Citations of *RE* followed by a numeral refer to the number of the entry under the *nomen* concerned. 'Gaul', unless otherwise defined, throughout means the province of *Gallia Transalpina*, 'Spain' either (or any) of the Iberian provinces. Dates (unless marked 'A.D.') are B.C.

ACILII

No known connexion, except for a L. Acilius, legate in Citerior 181.

AEMILII

Spain: M. Lepidus Porcina, *procos.* in Citerior 136;

M. Lepidus (the Triumvir), *procos.* in Citerior 48–47 and 44–43;

L. Paullus, *pr.* in Ulterior 191 and *procos.* 190–189; *patronus* of the province in the scandal of 171.

Gaul: M. Lepidus (*cos.* 78) was assigned this province; see Ch. X, p. 275
   (with n. 8);
   M. Lepidus (the Triumvir), *procos.* 44–43;
   M. Scaurus (the *Princ. Sen.*): see *vir. ill.* 72, 3.

Africa: M. Lepidus (the Triumvir) governed Africa 40–36;
   M. Scaurus (the *Princ. Sen.*), envoy to Jugurtha 112, legate 111.

We may add the careers of the sons of L. Aemilius Paullus, Scipio
Aemilianus and Fabius Aemilianus (see below, under their adoptive
gentes). The connexion with Spain was kept up in the early Empire: cf. the
cos. A.D. 6. Nearly half the *praenomina* in Spain are accounted for by 'Lucius'
(cf. also the L. Aemilius Paulus, *CIL*, ii. 4189), half the remainder by
'Marcus'.

AFRANII

L. Afranius (*cos.* 60) is the only important member. He was in Spain
under Pompey in the Sertorian War, when the army also spent some time
in Gaul, and again as Pompey's and his successors' legate for most of the
period 55–46. After his praetorship he governed either Gaul or a Spanish
province (*MRR*, ii. 130–1). Whether he governed a Gallic province after
his consulship cannot be established. (Cf. Momigliano, *JRS*, 1940, 77.)
There is a dedication to him by the colony of Valentia (*ILS*, 878), considered to be the Spanish Valencia; but why not Valence? This city first
becomes important in 61–60, in the Allobrogan revolt (Dio, xxxvii. 47);
the colony there (date unknown—but it is not called 'Iulia') might very
suitably be due to the *cos.* 60. The name of Afranius Burrus attests the
connexion of L. Afranius with the province.

ANTONII

No Republican connexions are known except for an obscure adherent
of Sertorius (to whom moderns usually assign the *praenomen* 'Marcus'):
Sall. *hist.* iii. 83; Plut. *Sert.* 26 f. The Triumvir served in Gaul under
Caesar and later held Narbonensis as a special province (43–40); his
brother Lucius governed Spain in 40.

AUFIDII

Little is known about the careers of the few senatorial Aufidii; there is
no clear reference to the overseas service of Orestes (*cos.* 71), but he may
have held a Gallic province in 76 (*MRR*, ii. 96). An adherent of Sertorius
conspired against his commander and escaped to Africa (Plut. *Sert.* 26 f.).
The name is widespread in Italy (e.g. families at Pisaurum and Amiternum:
ILS, 1129; Varro, *r.r.* ii. 9, 6; cf. Hor. *sat.* i. 5, 34: Fundi) and perhaps no
conclusions should be attempted.

CAECILII

Spain: Q. Metellus Macedonicus, *procos.* in Citerior 142, legate there 136;
Q. Metellus Baliaricus, *procos.* in Spain and the Balearic islands 122–121;
Q. Metellus Pius, *procos.* in Ulterior 79–71;
Q. Metellus Nepos, *procos.* in Citerior 56–55.

Africa: Q. Metellus Numidicus, *cos.* 109 and *procos.* 108–106;
Q. Metellus Pius Scipio Nasica (*cos.* 52), *procos.* 48–46.

It is worth noting that in Africa the Caecilii surpass all the other *gentes* we have listed: they are, in fact, even 1⅓ times as numerous as the ubiquitous Aemilii. In Spain the Balearic Islands are particularly associated with them: Baliaricus (see above) founded Palma and Pollentia. At Palma Caecilii (particularly with the *praenomen* 'Quintus', which is rare enough in general to be worth special notice when it does appear) are numerous: e.g. *CIL*, ii. 3676 (= i². 2247: a Republican instance) f.; there is even a Quinta Caecilia. At Pollentia there is a Q. Caecilius Q.f. (*CIL*, ii. 3696). At Mago (Minorca) we also find Caecilii, including a Quintus (ibid. 3714 f.). This is worth setting out in detail because of the paucity of Balearic inscriptions. In Spain and in Gaul, 'Quintus' accounts for over a third of known *praenomina*, in Africa for over a quarter—both well above the count of a random sample of *CIL*.

CALPURNII

Spain: Calpurnius Lanarius, officer in 81 (see Syme, *Hist.* 1955, 58);
C. Piso (*cos.* 180), *pr.* 186 and *procos.* (?) 185–184 in Ulterior;
L. Piso Caesoninus, *pr.* in Ulterior 154;
Q. Piso, *cos.* 135 in Citerior;
L. Piso Frugi, *pr.* in Ulterior 112 (?—see *MRR*, i. 538–9);
Cn. Piso, *q. pro pr.* 65–64;
Cn. Piso (*cos.* 23), *pro q.* under Pompey (49?—see *MRR*, ii. 100).

Gaul: C. Piso (*cos.* 67), *procos.* 66–65;
L. Piso Caesoninus (*cos.* 112): legate 107 (for his connexions there, see Münzer, *RE*, 88; cf. the Piso in our list of *Incerti*, above).

Africa: L. Bestia, *cos.* 111; earlier *iiiuir* (*a.d.a.*)—see *ILS*, 28;
L. Piso Caesoninus, *cos.* 148;
Cn. Piso (*cos.* 23) fought against Caesar in 46.

Calpurnii serve in Spain and Africa in the early Empire—the *coss.* 7 and A.D. 27; also the *cos. suff.* A.D. 21 or 22 (see Degrassi, *Fasti Cons.*, p. 8).

Cassii

Spain: Q. Longinus, quaestor for Pompey in Ulterior 52, *propr.* for Caesar 49–47.

Gaul: C. Longinus (*cos.* 124) may have fought there in his consulship (Eutr. iv. 22);

L. Longinus, *cos.* 107, defeated by the Tigurini.

A L. Longinus (*pr.* 66) negotiated with the Allobroges on Catiline's behalf in 63 (*RE*, 64).

Africa: L. Longinus (*cos.* 107) was sent there in his praetorship to summon Jugurtha to Rome. The account in Sallust (*Jug.* 32) suggests previous relations.

Coelii

Again a common Latin name. But note that C. Caldus (*cos.* 94) seems to have governed Citerior in 98 (?—see *MRR*, ii. 3). A Caldus served under P. Quinctilius Varus in A.D. 9 (Vell. ii. 120).

Didii

Spain: T. Didius (*cos.* 98) governed Citerior 98–93;

C. Didius was a legate of Caesar.

Appropriately, the name is found mainly in Spain (on T. Didius T.f. at Carthago Nova, cf. our list above).

Africa: The Didii there may go back to A. Gallus (*ILS*, 970—this suggests the restoration '[Africa]e' for his province).

Domitii

Spain: M. Calvinus, *procos.* in Citerior 79;

Cn. Calvinus (his son), *procos.* 39–36.

Gaul: Cn. Ahenobarbus, *cos.* 122 and *procos.* 121–119 (?)—the milestone reported in *CRAI*, 1951, despite Broughton (*MRR*, ii. 644), does not imply that he stayed in Gaul until 118 or later;

Cn. Ahenobarbus, his son (*cos.* 96), *iiiuir col. ded.* at Narbo (?—see *MRR*, ii. 644);

L. Ahenobarbus, son of the *cos.* 96, was assigned the province for 49 and commanded at Massilia against Caesar.

Gaul is the main sphere of influence of the Ahenobarbi.

Africa: Cn. Ahenobarbus, *propr.* (?) for the Marian government, 82–81. Cf. also the *cos.* 16.

The very rare *praenomen* 'Gnaeus' is found throughout.

FABII

Spain: C. Fabius, legate 49. (See *Note V*, p. 298.)

    Q. Buteo, *pr.* in Ulterior 196;

    Q. Buteo, quaestor in Ulterior 188–186 (?—possibly a Maximus; see *MRR*);

    N. Buteo, *pr.* in Citerior 173 (died at Massilia);

    L. Hispaniensis, quaestor under Annius 81, then an officer under Sertorius (on the *cognomen*, see Gabba, *GS*, 91);

    Q. Labeo, *pr.* and *procos.* in Citerior, late second century (*MRR*, i. 544; ii. 464);

    Q. Maximus—see Buteo (above);

    Q. Maximus Aemilianus, *cos.* 145 and *procos.* 144–143 in Ulterior, legate of Scipio at Numantia;

    Q. Maximus Servilianus, *procos.* in Ulterior 141–140;

    Q. Maximus Allobrogicus (son of Aemilianus), probably under Scipio at Numantia (*MRR*, i. 491), *propr.* 123;

    Q. Maximus, legate of Caesar 46–45.

This agrees with the evidence of our lists that the connexions of this *gens* were chiefly with Spain. Cf. Cic. *Balb.* 50–51, and see further at the end of this entry.

Gaul: Q. Maximus Allobrogicus, *cos.* 121 and *procos.* 120–119 (?). On Q. Sanga, patron of the Allobroges in 63, see p. 264.

Africa: C. Hadrianus, *pr.* 84 and *propr.* 83–82.

'Fabius', as we have seen, is the most common name on our list in Spain (and not nearly as common elsewhere—there was no indiscriminate extension), despite the long eclipse of the family between the end of the second century and the time of Caesar. We may note that the *praenomen* 'Quintus', characteristic of the family, is very common: one quarter in Spain (where the wide diffusion of the *nomen* would work against its survival), over a third in Africa, and about one-fifth in Gaul—all well above a random distribution. This is worth studying as showing the influence of a great Patrician family where it is not directly attested. The connexion is kept up under the Empire (cf. the *cos.* 11). The African Fabii may in part go back to the *cos.* 10.

FULVII

Spain: Cn. Fulvius, *pr.* in Citerior 167;

    Q. Flaccus, *pr.* in Citerior 182 and *procos.* 181–180;

    M. Flaccus, legate in Citerior 181 (?—see *MRR*, i. 391);

    M. Nobilior, *pr.* 193 and *procos.* 192–191 in Ulterior;

M. Nobilior, *tr. mil.* in Ulterior 180 (?—see *MRR*, i. 391);

Q. Nobilior, *cos.* 153 in Citerior.

For L. Fulvianus, see under Manlii.

Gaul: M. Flaccus, *cos.* 125 and *procos.* 124–123.

Again the main connexion is with Spain, and again it is maintained despite the later eclipse of the *gens*. The *praenomen* 'Quintus' accounts for one quarter of the known *praenomina* in Spain and does not occur with this *nomen* elsewhere—a useful check.

GABINII

On Valus Gabinius and P. Gabinius, the Catilinarian, see p. 307. We do not hear of any senatorial Gabinii serving in the West. Was A. Gabinius (the *cos.* 58) perhaps a legate or quaestor of Pompey in the Sertorian War? (For his origin and connexions, see Syme, *Rom. Rev.* 31; and compare T. Labienus.)

GELLII

No connexion is known.

HORTENSII

'Lucius' is by far the most common *praenomen* in the lists, and this suggests a connexion with the noble family. The only one we can trace is the speech of the orator in his youth on behalf of Africa (Cic. *de or.* iii. 229).

JUNII

Spain: P. Brutus, *procos.* (?) in Ulterior 189–188;

D. Brutus Callaicus, *cos.* 138 and *procos.* 137–136 in Ulterior (*MRR*, i. 488);

M. Pennus, *pr.* in Citerior 172 and *propr.* (?) 171;

M. Silanus, *propr.* 210–206: the first propraetor there (with Scipio Africanus);

M. Silanus, *pr.* 113 (?).

Note that M. Brutus (*pr.* 88) fled to Spain after Sulla's march on Rome.

Gaul: D. Brutus Albinus, after serving under Caesar, governed the province 48–46;

M. Silanus, *cos.* 109 (and *procos.* 108?).

A M. Silanus (the later *cos.* 25) was in Narbonensis under Lepidus in 43.

Africa: see under Licinii.

One Junius (*cos.* A.D. 28) governs Spain and two (*cos. suff.* A.D. 10 and *cos.* A.D. 19) Africa in the early Empire.

Licinii

Spain: P. Crassus (*pr.* 176) may be mentioned as refusing to go there;
P. Crassus, *cos.* 97 and *procos.* 96–93 in Ulterior;
L. Lucullus, *cos.* 151 and *procos.* 150 in Citerior;
C. Nerva, *pr.* in Ulterior 167;
A. Nerva, *pr.* in Citerior (?) 166.

On M. Crassus (later *cos.* 70) in Spain, see pp. 266 f.

Gaul: L. Crassus (*cos.* 95), *iiiuir col. ded.* for Narbo 118; perhaps governed
the province 94;
L. Murena, *procos.* of both Gauls 64–63;
C. Murena (his brother), his legate.

Africa: P. Crassus Dives Junianus, legate 46;
L. Lucullus (*cos.* 74), *propr.* 77–76 (?—see *MRR*).

In the early Empire, note *CIL*, vi. 1442 (Spain).

Livii

Few are found in our provinces. This agrees with the small number found epigraphically and with the eclipse of the *gens* in the late Republic. On the Ocellae, probably descended from the Salinatores, see Cichorius, *R. St.* 253 f. (Cf. *MRR*, ii. 384; 476.) On M. Drusus (*tr. pl.* 91) and Africa, see *RE*, 18, col. 871.

Lutatii

No wide connexions. Q. Catulus (*cos.* 102) may have reached Gaul. Among two recorded *praenomina*, 'Quintus' is found once (also once in a filiation), and this suggests a direct connexion with the noble family.

Manlii

Spain: L. Acidinus, one of the first pair of proconsuls, 206–199;
L. Acidinus Fulvianus (his son), *pr.* 188 and *procos.* 187–185 in Citerior;
A. (?) Torquatus, legate of Pompey in the Pirate War: based on the Balearic Islands (cf. Drumann–Groebe, iv. 422—wrongly identified; *MRR*, ii. 151); there is a family of Manlii among the handful of inscriptions from Pollentia (*CIL*, ii. 3698);
P. Vulso (?): see *RE*, 31; governed Citerior 195–194 and Ulterior 182–180; the *saltus Manlianus* and [Castra] Manliana may be named after him (*RE*, 31).

There is a (doubtful) Manlius among the Sertorians (*RE*, 5). Cf. also Gaul, below.

Gaul: L. Manlius, *propr.* 78; he crossed to Spain;
Manlius Lentinus, legate of Pomptinus (62–60?).

Africa: L. Manlius, as quaestor, received Masinissa's son in 168 (an Acidinus?);

A. Manlius is reported as a legate of Marius 107–105 (as so often, he may be a Manilius);

A. Torquatus (see Spain, above) governed Africa (69?).

It will be seen that connexions are mainly with Spain.

MARCII

Apart from L. Censorinus (*cos.* 149 in Africa), no senatorial Marcii are recorded in our provinces before the Civil War. On Marcii in the Civil War, see *RE*, 32 and 52. The diffusion of the name in Spain is no doubt chiefly due to L. Philippus (*cos. suff.* 38, *triumphator* 33); in Africa there is the *cos. suff.* A.D. 34. On L. Septimus and C. Marcius from Italica, see p. 261, n. 3.

MARII

C. Marius, as is well known, is connected with all these provinces. His brother M. Marius governed Ulterior (?) in or about 102, founding a city there (App. *Iber.* 100). A M. Marius was quaestor under Sertorius *c.* 76—perhaps not related to the noble family. In Gaul a L. Marius (almost certainly unrelated) was a legate under Pomptinus (62–60?). In Spain the *praenomen* 'Gaius' accounts for about one-third, 'Marcus' for about another third of recorded cases—which seems significant despite the relative frequency of these *praenomina* in general. In Gaul 'Gaius' accounts for nearly half, while 'Marcus' is not abnormally prominent; in Africa (where the Marian settlement is particularly easy to trace—see text of Ch. XI) 'Gaius' is the only *praenomen* recorded. This distribution of *praenomina* is useful evidence for the value of the method.

MEMMII

On the vexed question of the Memmii serving in Spain under Pompey, see Münzer in *RE*, 6, 7, 14 (some corrections Biedl, *WS*, 1932, 107 f.). The *tr. pl.* 111 had also served in Spain, in the Numantine War (see *RE*, 5).

In Africa there is unfortunately no record of Republican Memmii. Groag (*RE*, 28) conjectures that the spread of the name there is due to an African proconsulate of the *cos.* A.D. 63 (C. Regulus). The tribe of the Reguli is unknown; but the *Galeria* found in Africa among important Memmii (see *RE*, 20) is known to be that of senatorial Memmii in the Republic (ibid. 14). However, the link is probably to be sought in Gaul: P. Regulus, *cos. suff.* A.D. 31, honoured in an inscription from Ruscino, is probably (despite Groag, *RE*, 29) of noble Narbonese origin and descended from a man enfranchised (by Pompey during his stay in Gaul?) through the good offices of a Memmius. As the *Fasti Ostienses* have shown us D. Valerius Asiaticus as *cos. suff.* A.D. 35, a Gallic consul four years earlier need not surprise us.

Mucii

No service in our provinces is known, as the lists lead us to expect.

Norbani

No service in our provinces. The diffusion of the name in Spain will undoubtedly be due to C. Flaccus (*cos.* 38, *triumphator* 34).

Papirii

C. Carbo (*cos.* 120) served as *iiiuir a.d.a.* in Africa (*ILS*, 28). His son C. Carbo served on L. Crassus' *consilium* in Gaul (see above, under Licinii). In Spain we do not hear of any senatorial Papirii; yet there, as it happens, the connexion is demonstrated by the name of a L. Papirius Carbo from Emporiae (*Eph. Ep.* ix, no. 406—first century A.D.).

Perpernae

Appropriately enough, the name is confined to Spain, the only one of these provinces where we know of a senatorial Perperna (the ally and assassin of Sertorius).

Pompei

Cn. Magnus, of course, is connected with all three provinces. Q. Pompeius (first consul of the *gens*) spent most of his official career in Spain, as commander 143–139 (see *MRR*) and legate 136. On Cn. Strabo, see pp. 229, 278.

A Q. Rufus is *procos.* of Africa 62–59. Other Pompei appear in Spain and Africa during the Civil War as leaders of the Pompeian cause.

Porcii

Mainly connected with Spain ever since Cato the Censor (*cos.* 195 and *procos.* 194 there; *patronus* of Citerior in the scandal of 171). C. Cato (*cos.* 114), going into exile, chose Tarraco (Cic. *Balb.* 28) in preference to the usual, more civilized, resorts; this confirms our statistical evidence and shows the continuance of the connexion.

Gaul: M. Cato (*MRR*, ii. 22).

Africa: M. Cato (*cos.* 118) died on a mission there (Gell. xiii. 20, 10); M. Cato Uticensis, *propr.* 47–46.

Postumii

Spain: L. Albinus, *pr.* 180 and *procos.* 179–178 in Ulterior.

Africa: Sp. Albinus, *cos.* 110 and *procos.* 109 in the Jugurthine War;
      A. Albinus (his brother), his legate.

Pupii

    M. Piso (*cos.* 61) was *procos.* in Spain 71 (?)–69. The only Pupius in our list (M. Puupius M.l., heading a list of *magistri* at Carthago Nova (*CIL*, i². 2271 = ii. [*Suppl.*] 5927)) must be a freedman of his.

Rutilii

Spain: P. Calvus, *pr.* in Ulterior 166 (?);
      P. Rufus (*cos.* 105), *tr. mil.* at Numantia.

Africa: P. Rufus (*cos.* 105), legate in Numidia 109–107.

Scribonii

    None before 49, except for C. Scribonius, *praef. soc.* 181 in Citerior. In the Civil Wars we have C. Curio, the Caesarian commander in Africa, and later L. Libo (the *cos.* 34?) as *pro q. pro pr.* (date unknown) in Ulterior.

Sempronii

Spain: Asellio, the historian, *tr. mil.* at Numantia 134–132;
      Ti. Gracchus, *pr.* 180 and *procos.* (?) 179–8 in Citerior; he pacified
      the Celtiberi and founded Graccurris;
      Ti. Gracchus (his son), quaestor at Numantia 137;
      C. Gracchus (brother of preceding), *tr. mil.* (?) at Numantia 134–
      133;
      P. Longus, *pr.* in Ulterior 184, *procos.* 183–182;
      C. Tuditanus, *pr.* 197 and *procos.* 196 in Citerior.

Gaul: M. Rutilus, legate of Caesar, seems the only instance.

Africa: Ti. Gracchus, *tr. mil.* (?) 147–146, under Scipio.

    The Sempronii in Africa probably go back to L. Atratinus (*cos. suff.* 34), the *triumphator* of 21.

    Our figures confirm the historical records in showing the special influence of the *gens* in Spain—an influence remarkable in view of the decline of the *gens* in the late Republic (no consul between 129 and 34).

Sertorii

    The connexion with the only great member of the *gens* is confirmed by the fact that in all but one of the recorded cases the *praenomen* is 'Quintus'.

How exactly the connexion worked (i.e. whether grants of citizenship made by Sertorius were recognized by Pompey—this is not by any means inconceivable in view of his complicated political game, which we have tried to follow in Ch. XI—or whether old friends of Sertorius, on receiving the citizenship later (perhaps from Caesar), were allowed to take his name), we unfortunately cannot tell. Sertorius had been *tr. mil.* under T. Didius (97–93 ?); but enfranchisement at that time is unlikely. On Sertorii at Valentia (a Sertorian stronghold in the War), see Schulten, *RE*, s.v. 'Valentia', no. 4.

SERVILII

Spain: Cn. Caepio, *pr.* 174 and *propr.* 173 in Ulterior;

    Q. Caepio (his son), *cos.* 140 in Spain and *procos.* 139 in Ulterior —he founded Castra Servilia (Pliny, *n.h.* iv. 117) and built the *monumentum Caepionis* (Mela, iii. 1, 4);

    Q. Caepio (his son, *pr.* 109 and *procos.* 108–107 in Ulterior (on him, cf. *RE*, 49);

    P. Vatia Isauricus (*cos.* 79) may have governed a Spanish province after his praetorship. (But he triumphed *pro pr.*—*MRR*, ii. 30—, which makes it rather unlikely.)

Gaul: Q. Caepio, *cos.* 106 and *procos.* 105.

On Q. Fabius Maximus Servilianus, see under Fabii.

The total in our list is surprisingly small in view of the clear connexion, in particular, with Spain. But we have a Cn. Servilius, probably of native extraction (his tribe is the *Galeria*), in Baetica (*CIL*, ii. 1608) and a family of Cn. Servilii at Nemausus (*CIL*, xii. 3908–9), although they perhaps come from Narbo; their rare *praenomen* points unmistakably to the noble family of the Caepiones.

Africa: The Servilii here probably go back to M. Nonianus, *cos.* A.D. 35.

SULPICII

Spain: Ser. Galba (the orator), *pr.* 151 and *procos.* 150 in Ulterior;

    Ser. Galba (his son), *pr.* 111 and *procos.* 110 in Ulterior (*MRR*, i. 539 f.);

    C. Galus, *patronus* of Ulterior in 171; therefore probably an officer there under L. Aemilius Paullus, 191.

P. Sulpicius Rufus (*cens.* 42) appears in Spain and also in Gaul as a legate of Caesar.

Gaul: Ser. Galba, legate of Pomptinus (62–60), then of Caesar.

    Cf. also Spain.

Africa: C. Galba, *iiiuir a.d.a.* (*ILS*, 28)—probably the *sacerdos* condemned
in 109, who may have been a legate in 110 (*MRR*, i. 544).

A Ser. Sulpicius is one of the senators with Juba in 49.

Note that Ser. Galba, the later Emperor, served in Aquitania and
governed Africa as well as Citerior.

TERENTII

A very common name. Yet some connexion with the senatorial Terentii
is very probable: it is in Spain that the name is most common, and it is
there that many of them served.

Spain: L. Massiliota, *tr. mil.* in Citerior 182–180;

A. Varro, *pr.* 184 and *procos.* 183–182 in Citerior;

? Varro (his son?), killed as *q.* by the Lusitani 154;

M. Varro (the scholar), legate of Pompey in the Sertorian War and
again (*pro pr.*) 50–49 in Ulterior (see *MRR*, ii. 100).

Gaul: Q. (?) Culleo, officer under Lepidus 43.

Though we know of no earlier connexion of the Varrones with Gaul,
the name of Varro Atacinus (see Syme, *CQ*, 1938, 43 f.) attests its existence.
Did he owe his name to the scholar, then (at the time of the Sertorian War)
in Pompey's army, which spent some time in Gaul?

VOLCACII

The name is exceedingly rare. A C. Tullus served under Caesar in Gaul,
at least in and after 53 (*MRR*, ii. 232 f.). Cf. Syme, *JRS*, xxxix, 1949, 18.

BIBLIOGRAPHY

(i) ANCIENT AUTHORS

IT has not seemed necessary to list editions of texts: where a difference in reading is important for purposes of this study, it has been discussed. On the whole, Oxford and Teubner texts have been used. A few authors have been cited only according to accepted editions (e.g. Dio according to Boissevain, Asconius according to the pages of the Oxford text). Where any doubt might arise, an indication has been added. In citations of Appian the chapter numbers only (not those of Viereck's sections) are given, in citations of Cicero the section numbers only (not those of chapters). This is in accordance with common practice in this country.

(ii) MODERN WORKS

This Bibliography collects all the works cited—in an abbreviated form—in the Notes and Appendixes, except for

(*a*) standard works of reference (e.g. *CAH* and *RE*) and individual contributions to them;

(*b*) works cited only once or twice.

Works in class (*a*) may be assumed to be familiar to readers; works in class (*b*) have been cited, where they appear, with full bibliographical details.

ACCAME, S. *Il dominio romano in Grecia dalla guerra acaica ad Augusto*. Roma, 1946.
ADCOCK, (SIR) F. E. '*Delenda est Carthago*', *CHJ*, viii, 1946, 117 f.
AFZELIUS, A. *Die römische Eroberung Italiens (340–264 v. Chr.)*. København, 1942.
——— *Die römische Kriegsmacht während der Auseinandersetzung mit den hellenistischen Großmächten*. København, 1944.
ALLEN, W. (JR.) 'The Source of Jugurtha's Influence in the Roman Senate', *CP*, xxxiii, 1938, 90 f.
——— 'Caesar's *Regnum*', *TAPA*, lxxxiv, 1953, 227 f.
——— 'The Acting Governor of Cisalpine Gaul in 63 B.C.', *CP*, xlviii, 1953, 176 f.
AYMARD, A. *Les Premiers Rapports de Rome et de la confédération achaienne*. Bordeaux, 1938.
——— 'L'Organisation de la Macédoine en 167 et le régime représentatif dans le monde grec', *CP*, xlv, 1950, 96 f.
BADIAN, E. 'Notes on Roman policy in Illyria (230–201 B.C.)', *PBSR*, xx, 1952, 72 f. [Now *Studies in Greek and Roman History*, 1.]
——— 'The Treaty between Rome and the Achaean League', *JRS*, xlii, 1952, 76 f.
——— '*Lex Acilia Repetundarum*', *AJP*, lxxv, 1954, 374 f.

—— 'Lex Seruilia', CR, N.S., iv, 1954, 101 f.

—— 'The Prefect at Gades', CP, xlix, 1954, 250 f.

—— 'L. Papirius Fregellanus', CR, N.S., v, 1955, 22 f.

—— 'The Date of Pompey's First Triumph', H, lxxxiii, 1955, 107 f.

—— 'Q. Mucius Scaevola and the Province of Asia', Ath., N.S., xxxiv, 1956, 104 f.

—— 'P. Decius P.f. Subulo', JRS, xlvi, 1956, 91 f.

—— 'Caepio and Norbanus', Hist., vi, 1957, 318 f. [Now Studies, 34.]

BALSDON, J. P. V. D. 'Q. Mucius Scaevola the Pontifex and ornatio provinciae' CR, li, 1937, 8 f.

—— 'Some Questions about Historical Writing in the Second Century B.C.', CQ, N.S., iii, 1953, 158 f.

—— 'Rome and Macedon, 205–200 B.C.', JRS, xliv, 1954, 30 f.

BELOCH, K. J. Der italische Bund unter Roms Hegemonie. Leipzig, 1880.

—— Die Bevölkerung der griechisch-römischen Welt. Leipzig, 1886.

—— Griechische Geschichte, 4 vols. in 8. Berlin–Leipzig², 1912–27.

—— Römische Geschichte bis zum Beginn der punischen Kriege. Berlin, 1926.

BENGTSON, H. 'Randbemerkungen zu den koischen Asylieurkunden', Hist. iii, 1954/5, 456 f.

BERNARDI, A. 'I "cives sine suffragio"', Ath., N.S., xvi, 1938, 239 f.

—— 'Roma e Capua', Ath., N.S., xx, 1942, 86 f.; xxi, 1943, 21 f.

—— 'La guerra sociale e le lotte dei partiti in Roma', NRS, xxviii/xxix, 1944–5, 60 f. [Cited 'G.S.']

—— 'Ius Ariminensium', Studia Ghisleriana, i (Studi Ciapessoni), 1948, 235 f.

BICKERMANN, E. (= BIKERMAN). 'Les Préliminaires de la deuxième guerre de Macédoine', RPh, lxi, 1935, 59 f.; 161 f.

BIEDL, A. 'Nochmals zur Familiengeschichte der Memmier', WS, xlix, 1932, 107 f.

BROUGHTON, T. R. S. The Magistrates of the Roman Republic. 2 vols. New York, 1951–2. [Cited MRR.]

—— 'Notes on Roman Magistrates', Hist. ii, 1953/4, 209 f.

CARCOPINO, J. La Loi de Hiéron et les Romains. Paris, 1914.

—— Autour des Gracques. Paris, 1928.

—— Points de vue sur l'impérialisme romain. Paris, 1934.

—— Sylla, ou la monarchie manquée. Paris⁴, 1947.

—— Des Gracques à Sulla. Histoire romaine, ii. 2, in Histoire générale, ed. G. Glotz. [Bloch, joint editor of the volume, did not write the historical section here cited.] Paris, 1954. [Cited Hist. rom.]

CARY, M. A History of the Greek World from 323 to 146 B.C. London², 1951.

—— A History of Rome down to the Reign of Constantine. London², 1954.

CICHORIUS, C. Untersuchungen zu Lucilius. Berlin, 1908.

—— Römische Studien. Leipzig–Berlin, 1922.

DE FRANCISCI, P. 'La Revocatio in servitutem del liberto ingrato', Mélanges . . . Georges Cornil. Vol. i. Ghent–Paris, 1926, 295 f.

DE SANCTIS, G. Storia dei Romani. Vols. i–iv, 2. Torino, &c., 1907–53.

DE SANCTIS, G. Problemi di storia antica. Bari, 1932.

324   BIBLIOGRAPHY

DREXLER, H. 'Parerga Caesariana', *H*, lxx, 1935, 203 f.

DRUMANN, W., edited GROEBE, P. *Geschichte Roms in seinem Übergange von der republikanischen zur monarchischen Verfassung*. 6 vols. Leipzig, 1899–1929.

DUVAL, P.-M. 'A Propos d'un milliaire de Cneus Domitius Ahenobarbus Imperator', *CRAI*, 1951, 161 f.

EDSON, C. F. (JR.) 'Perseus and Demetrius', *HSCP*, xlvi, 1935, 191 f.

EWINS, U. 'The Early Colonisation of Cisalpine Gaul', *PBSR*, xx, 1952, 54 f.

—— 'The Enfranchisement of Cisalpine Gaul', *PBSR*, xxiii, 1955, 73 f.

FINE, J. VAN A. 'The Problem of Macedonian Holdings in Epirus and Thessaly in 221 B.C.', *TAPA*, lxiii, 1932, 126 f.

FORNI, G. 'Manio Curio Dentato uomo democratico', *Ath.*, N.S., xxxi, 1953, 170 f.

FRACCARO, P. 'Studi sull' età dei Gracchi', *Studi storici per l'antichità classica*, v, 1912, 317 f.

—— 'Ricerche su Caio Gracco', *Ath.*, N.S., iii, 1925, 76 f.; 156 f. [Now *Opuscula*, ii, 19.]

—— 'L'organizzazione politica dell' Italia romana', *Atti del Congresso internazionale di diritto romano*, Pavia–Roma, 1934, i. 195 f. [Now *Opuscula*, i. 103.]

FRAENKEL, E. 'Zur Geschichte des Wortes *fides*', *RhM*, N.F., lxxi, 1916, 187 f.

FRANK, T. *Roman Imperialism*. New York, 1914.

—— ' "Dominium in solo provinciali" and "ager publicus" ', *JRS*, xvii, 1927, 141 f.

GABBA, E. 'Le origini dell' esercito professionale in Roma: i proletarî e la riforma di Mario', *Ath.*, N.S., xxvii, 1949, 173 f.

—— 'Ricerche su alcuni punti di storia mariana', *Ath.*, N.S., xxix, 1951, 12 f.

—— 'Ricerche sull' esercito professionale romano da Mario ad Augusto', *Ath.*, N.S., xxix, 1951, 171 f.

—— 'Politica e cultura in Roma agli inizî del I secolo a. C.', *Ath.*, N.S., xxxi, 1953, 259 f.

—— 'Le origini della guerra sociale e la vita politica romana dopo l'89 a. C.', *Ath.*, N.S., xxxii, 1954. [Cited throughout (as *GS*) in the pagination of the separate offprint, which alone was constantly available to me.]

GARDTHAUSEN, V. 'Namen und Zensus der Römer', *RhM*, lxxii, 1917–18, 353 f.

GELZER, M. *Die Nobilität der römischen Republik*. Leipzig, 1912. [Now *Kl. Schr.*, i. 17.]

—— Review of Taeger, *Tib. Gr.* (q.v.), *Gnomon*, v, 1929, 296 f. [Now *Kl. Schr.*, ii. 73.]

—— Review of Göhler, *Rom und Italien* (q.v.), *Gnomon*, xvii, 1941, 145 f. [Now *Kl. Schr.* ii. 86.]

—— 'Das erste Konsulat des Pompeius und die Übertragung der großen Imperien', *APAW*, 1943, no. 1. [Now *Kl. Schr.*, ii. 146.]

—— *Römische Studien*. 2 vols. Leipzig, 1943.

—— *Pompeius*. Second edition. München, 1959.

GÖHLER, J. *Rom und Italien*. Breslau, 1939.

GOETZFRIED, K. T. *Annalen der römischen Provinzen beider Spanien . . . 218–154*. Erlangen, 1907.

GOODFELLOW, C. E. *Roman Citizenship*. Bryn Mawr, 1935.

GREENIDGE, A. H. J. 'The "provocatio militiae" and Provincial Jurisdiction', *CR*, x, 1896, 225 f.

—— and CLAY, A. M. *Sources for Roman History, 133–70 B.C.* Second edition, revised by E. W. Gray, Oxford, 1960.

GRIFFITH, G. T. 'An Early Motive of Roman Imperialism (201 B.C.)', *CHJ*, v, 1935, 1 f.

GSELL, S. *Histoire ancienne de l'Afrique du Nord.* Vol. ii, 1921; vol. iii, 1921. Paris². [Cited *HAAN*.]

HARDY, E. G. 'Three Questions as to Livius Drusus', *CR*, xxvii, 1913, 261 f.

HATZFELD, J. *Les Trafiquants italiens dans l'Orient hellénique.* Paris, 1919.

HAYWOOD, R. M. 'The Oil of Leptis', *CP*, xxxvi, 1941, 246 f.

HEAD, B. V. *Historia numorum.* Oxford², 1911.

HEINZE, R. '*Fides*', *H*, lxiv, 1929, 140 f.

HENZE, E. W. *De civitatibus liberis quae fuerunt in provinciis populi Romani.* Berlin, 1892.

HERZOG, R. 'Nikias und Xenophon von Kos', *Hist. Z.* cxxv, 1922, 189 f.

HEUSS, A. *Die völkerrechtlichen Grundlagen der römischen Außenpolitik in republikanischer Zeit. Klio*, Beiheft 31. Leipzig, 1933.

—— *Stadt und Herrscher des Hellenismus in ihren staats- und völkerrechtlichen Beziehungen. Klio*, Beiheft 39. Leipzig, 1937.

HILL, H. 'The So-called Lex Aufeia', *CR*, lxii, 1948, 112 f.

—— *The Roman Middle Class in the Republican Period.* Oxford, 1952.

HOFFMANN, W. *Rom und die griechische Welt im vierten Jahrhundert. Philologus*, Suppl. xxvii, 1. Leipzig, 1934.

—— *Livius und der zweite punische Krieg. H*, Einzelschriften, viii. Berlin, 1942.

HOLLEAUX, M. *Rome, la Grèce et les monarchies hellénistiques au IIIe siècle avant J.-C. (273–205).* Paris, 1921.

—— 'Les Conférences de Lokride et la politique de T. Quinctius Flamininus (198 av. J.-C.)', *RÉG*, xxxvi, 1923, 115 f.

—— 'Fragment de sénatus-consulte trouvé à Corfou', *BCH*, xlviii, 1924, 381 f.

—— 'La lettera degli Scipioni agli abitanti di Colofone a Mare', *RFIC*, N.S., ii, 1924, 29 f.

—— 'La Politique romaine en Grèce et dans l'Orient hellénistique au IIIe siècle (Réponse à M. Th. Walek)', *RPh*, l, 1926, 46 f.; 194 f.

—— 'Le Consul M. Fulvius et le siège de Samé', *BCH*, liv, 1930, 1 f.

HORN, H. *Foederati.* Frankfurt, 1930.

IHNE, W. *The History of Rome.* 5 vols. (Engl. ed.) London, 1871–82.

JONES, A. H. M. 'Civitates liberae et immunes in the East', *Anatolian Studies presented to W. H. Buckler.* Manchester, 1939, 103 f.

—— *The Greek City from Alexander to Justinian.* Oxford, 1940.

KAHRSTEDT, U. *See* MELTZER, O.

KASER, M. 'Der Inhalt der patria potestas', *ZRG*, lviii, 1938, 62 f.

—— 'Die Geschichte der Patronatsgewalt über Freigelassene', *ZRG*, lviii, 1938, 88 f.

KIENAST, D. *Cato der Zensor.* Heidelberg, 1954.

KIENE, A. *Der römische Bundesgenossenkrieg.* Leipzig, 1845.

KLAFFENBACH, G. 'Der römisch-ätolische Bündnisvertrag vom Jahre 212 v. Chr.', *SDAW*, 1954, no. 1.

KLINGNER, F. *Römische Geisteswelt*. München³, 1956. [Citation is confined to the essay 'Italien. Name, Begriff und Idee im Altertum'.]

KONOPKA, Z. ZMIGRYDER. 'Les Relations politiques entre Rome et la Campanie', *Eos*, xxxii, 1929, 587 f.

KONTCHALOVSKY, D. 'Recherches sur l'histoire du mouvement agraire des Gracques', *RH*, cliii, 1926, 161 f.

KRAMER, F. R. 'Massiliot Diplomacy before the Second Punic War', *AJP*, lxix, 1948, 1 f.

LARSEN, J. A. O. '*Sortito* and *sorti* in *CIL*, I, 200', *CP*, xxv, 1930, 279.

—— 'Was Greece Free between 196 and 146?', *CP*, xxx, 1935, 193 f.

—— 'The Peace of Phoenice and the Outbreak of the Second Macedonian War', *CP*, xxxii, 1937, 15 f.

—— Review of Petzold, *Eröffnung* (*q.v.*), *CP*, xxxviii, 1943, 58 f.

—— '*Consilium* in Livy xlv. 18. 6–7 and the Macedonian *synedria*', *CP*, xliv, 1949, 73 f.

LAST, H. M. Review of Carcopino, *Autour des Gracques* (*q.v.*), *JRS*, xviii, 1928, 228 f.

—— Review of Göhler, *Rom und Italien* (*q.v.*), *JRS*, xxx, 1940, 81 f.

LEVI, M. A. 'Intorno alla legge agraria del III a. C.', *RFIC*, N.S., vii, 1929, 231 f.

MCDONALD, A. H. 'Scipio Africanus and Roman Politics in the Second Century B.C.', *JRS*, xxviii, 1938, 153 f.

—— 'The History of Rome and Italy in the Second Century B.C.', *CHJ*, vi, 1939, 124 f.

—— 'Rome and the Italian Confederation (200–186 B.C.)', *JRS*, xxxiv, 1944, 11 f.

—— Review of Klaffenbach (*q.v.*), *JRS*, xlvi, 1956, 153 f.

—— and WALBANK, F. W. 'The Origins of the Second Macedonian War', *JRS*, xxvii, 1937, 180 f.

MADVIG, J. N. *Kleine philologische Schriften*. Leipzig, 1875.

MAGIE, D. 'The "Agreement" between Philip V and Antiochus III for the Partition of the Egyptian Empire', *JRS*, xxix, 1939, 32 f.

—— 'Rome and the City-States of Western Asia Minor from 200 to 133 B.C.', *Anatolian Studies presented to W. H. Buckler*. Manchester, 1939, 161 f.

—— *Roman Rule in Asia Minor*. 2 vols. Princeton, 1950.

MALTEN, L. 'Aineias', *ARW*, xxix, 1931, 33 f.

MANNI, E. *Per la storia dei municipii fino alla guerra sociale*. Roma, 1947.

MARCKS, E. *Die Überlieferung des Bundesgenossenkrieges, 91–89 v. Chr.* Marburg, 1884.

MARSH, F. B. *A History of the Roman World from 146 to 30 B.C.* (ed. Scullard, H. H.). London², 1953.

MATTHAEI, L. E. 'On the Classification of Roman Allies', *CQ*, i, 1907, 182 f.

—— 'The Place of Arbitration and Mediation in Ancient Systems of International Ethics', *CQ*, ii, 1908, 241 f.

MELTZER, O. *Geschichte der Karthager*. Vols. i–ii. Berlin, 1879–96. Vol. iii (by Kahrstedt). Berlin, 1913.

MERLIN, A., and POINSSOT, L. *Les Inscriptions d'Uchi Maius d'après les recherches du capitaine Gondouin*. Paris, 1908.

MEYER, EDUARD. *Kleine Schriften*. 2 vols. Halle a.S., 1924.

MEYER, ERNST. *Römischer Staat und Staatsgedanke*. Zürich, 1948.

MOMIGLIANO, A. Review of Syme, *Rom. Rev.* (*q.v.*), *JRS*, xxx, 1940, 75 f.

MOMMSEN, T. *Römische Forschungen*. 2 vols. Berlin, 1864–79.

—— *The History of Rome*. 4 vols. (Engl. ed.) London, 1880–1.

—— *Römisches Staatsrecht*. 3 vols. Leipzig, 1887–8. [Cited *Str*.]

—— *Gesammelte Schriften*. 8 vols. Berlin, 1905–13. [Cited *GS*.]

MÜNZER, F. *Römische Adelsparteien und Adelsfamilien*. Stuttgart, 1920.

—— 'Norbanus', *H*, lxvii, 1932, 220 f.

NICCOLINI, G. *I fasti dei tribuni della plebe*. Milano, 1934.

—— 'Le leggi *de civitate Romana* durante la guerra sociale', *RAL*, s. 8, i, 1946, 110 f.

NISSEN, H. *Kritische Untersuchungen über die Quellen der vierten und fünften Dekade des Livius*. Berlin, 1863.

OOST, S. I. *Roman Policy in Epirus and Acarnania in the Age of the Roman Conquest of Greece*. Dallas, 1954.

OTTO, W. 'Zur Geschichte der Zeit des 6. Ptolemäers', *ABAW*, N.F., Heft 11, 1934.

PARETI, L. *Storia di Roma e del mondo romano*. iii: *Dai prodromi della III guerra macedonica al "primo triumvirato"*. Torino, 1953.

PARKER, H. M. D. 'On Cicero, *Pro Balbo* 21, 48', *CR*, lii, 1938, 8 f.

PASSERINI, A. 'Caio Mario come uomo politico', *Ath.*, N.S., xii, 1934, 10 f.; 109 f.; 257 f.; 348 f.

PETZOLD, K.-E. *Die Eröffnung des zweiten römisch-makedonischen Krieges*. Berlin, 1940.

PICARD, C. 'Un Groupe archaïque étrusque: Énée portant Anchise', *RA*, s. 6, xxi, 1944, 154 f.

PIGANIOL, A. 'Venire in fidem', *RIDA*, v, 1950, 339 f.

—— 'Sur la nouvelle table de bronze de Tarante', *CRAI*, 1951, 58 f.

PINSENT, J. 'The Original Meaning of *municeps*', *CQ*, N.S., iv, 1954, 158 f.

PIOTROWICZ, L. 'Quelques remarques sur l'attitude de l'Étrurie pendant les troubles civils à la fin de la république romaine', *Klio*, N.F., v, 1930, 334 f.

PLATNER, S. B., and ASHBY, T. *A Topographical Dictionary of Ancient Rome*. London, 1929.

PREMERSTEIN, A. v. 'Vom Werden und Wesen des Prinzipats', *ABAW*, N.F., Heft 15, 1937.

QUONIAM, P. 'A propos d'une inscription de *Thuburnica* (Tunisie)', *CRAI*, 1950, 332 f.

REINACH, T. *Mithridate Eupator, roi de Pont*. Paris, 1890.

ROSENBERG, A. 'Die Entstehung des sogenannten Foedus Cassianum und des lateinischen Rechts', *H*, lv, 1920, 337 f.

SALMON, E. T. 'Roman Colonisation from the Second Punic War to the Gracchi', *JRS*, xxvi, 1936, 47 f.

—— 'Roman Expansion and Roman Colonization in Italy', *Phoenix*, ix, 1955, 63 f.

SAMONATI, G. 'Osservazioni sui rapporti tra Roma e i federati dal 133 al 124 a. C.', *BMIR*, vii, 1936, 29 f.

—— 'Lucio Apuleio Saturnino e i federati', *BMIR*, viii, 1937, 25 f.

SANDS, P. C. *The Client Princes of the Roman Empire under the Republic*. Cambridge, 1908.

328 BIBLIOGRAPHY

SAUMAGNE, C. 'Les Prétextes juridiques de la troisième guerre punique', *RH*, clxvii, 1931, 225 f.; clxviii, 1931, 1 f.

SCHULTEN, A. *Numantia*. 4 vols. [Vol. i only used.] München, 1914.

—— *Geschichte von Numantia*. München, 1933.

SCHULZE, W. *Zur Geschichte lateinischer Eigennamen*. *Abh. Ges. d. Wiss. zu Göttingen, Phil.-hist. Kl.*, N.F., v, no. 5. Berlin, 1933.

SCULLARD, H. H. *Scipio Africanus in the Second Punic War*. Cambridge, 1930.

—— 'Charops and Roman Policy in Epirus', *JRS*, xxxv, 1945, 58 f.

—— *A History of the Roman World from 753 to 146 B.C.* London³, 1961.

—— *Roman Politics, 220–150 B.C.* Oxford, 1951.

And see MARSH, F. B.

SHERWIN-WHITE, A. N. *The Roman Citizenship*. Oxford, 1939. [Cited *RC*.]

STEVENSON, G. H. 'Cn. Pompeius Strabo and the Franchise Question', *JRS*, ix, 1919, 95 f.

SUTHERLAND, C. H. V. *The Romans in Spain*. London, 1939.

SYME, R. 'The Origin of Cornelius Gallus', *CQ*, xxxii, 1938, 39 f.

—— 'The Allegiance of Labienus', *JRS*, xxviii, 1938, 113 f.

—— 'Caesar, the Senate and Italy', *PBSR*, xiv, 1938, 1 f.

—— 'Observations on the Province of Cilicia', *Anatolian Studies presented to W. H. Buckler*. Manchester, 1939, 299 f.

—— *The Roman Revolution*. Oxford, 1939.

TAEGER, F. *Tiberius Gracchus*. Stuttgart, 1928.

TÄUBLER, E. *Imperium Romanum*. Vol. i [all publ.]. Leipzig, 1913.

—— *Die Vorgeschichte des zweiten punischen Kriegs*. Berlin, 1921.

TARN, W. W. *Alexander the Great*. 2 vols. Cambridge, 1948.

THIEL, J. H. *A History of Roman Sea-power before the Second Punic War*. Amsterdam, 1954.

THOMSEN, R. 'Das Jahr 91 v. Chr. und seine Voraussetzungen', *Cl. et Med.* v, 1942, 13 f.

TIBILETTI, G. 'Ricerche di storia agraria romana', *Ath.*, N.S., xxviii, 1950, 183 f.

—— 'Le leggi "de iudiciis repetundarum" fino alla guerra sociale', *Ath.*, N.S., xxxi, 1953, 5 f.

—— 'La politica delle colonie e città latine nella guerra sociale', *RIL*, lxxxvi, 1953, 45 f.

WAGENVOORT, H. *Roman Dynamism*. Oxford, 1947.

WALBANK, F. W. 'Φίλιππος τραγῳδούμενος', *JHS*, lviii, 1938, 55 f.

—— *Philip V of Macedon*. Cambridge, 1940.

And see MCDONALD, A. H.

WELLES, C. B. *Royal Correspondence in the Hellenistic Period*. New Haven, 1934.

WENGER, L. 'Hausgewalt und Staatsgewalt im römischen Altertum', *Miscellanea Francesco Ehrle*, ii [= *Studi e Testi*, xxxviii]. Roma, 1924, 1 f.

WIEHN, A. K. E. *Die illegalen Heereskommanden in Rom bis auf Caesar*. Marburg, 1926.

WISSOWA, G. *Religion und Kultus der Römer*. München², 1912.

ZIPPEL, G. *Die römische Herrschaft in Illyrien bis auf Augustus*. Leipzig, 1877.

INDEX

THIS Index aims above all at collecting all references to persons and places and providing sufficient information to identify them: in this it supplements the text, where such identification could not always be conveniently made explicit. Roman names will normally be found under the *nomen*; cross-references are provided under the most important *cognomina*. The names of Roman Emperors, however, are given in their most familiar form. In the case of consulars the date of the *first* consulship has been given, in other cases (wherever possible) the date of the highest magistracy or other office attained. As it would have been impracticable to distinguish between references to countries (or cities) and to their inhabitants, all such references will be found under the name of the country (or city) concerned—e.g. 'Latins' is included under 'Latium', 'Panhormitani' under 'Panhormus'; but the name of the people only has been listed where that of the region is not in ordinary use—e.g. 'Salluvii'. There are cross-references in all difficult cases. The following are not included in this Index: (i) names occurring only in Appendix B; (ii) the items 'Rome' and '*clientela*', which would have called for analysis of the whole book.

* This (not 'Septimius', despite *MRR*) is probably the form that Livy wrote. I should like to thank Dr. A. H. McDonald for valuable advice on this point.